INTERNATIONAL COUNSELING
Case Studies Handbook

EDITED BY

Roy Moodley
Marguerite Lengyell
Rosa Wu
Uwe P. Gielen

AMERICAN COUNSELING
ASSOCIATION
6101 Stevenson Avenue, Suite 600 • Alexandria, VA 22304
www.counseling.org

INTERNATIONAL COUNSELING
Case Studies Handbook

10 9 8 7 6 5 4 3 2 1

AMERICAN COUNSELING ASSOCIATION
6101 Stevenson Avenue, Suite 600 • Alexandria, VA 22304

ASSOCIATE PUBLISHER
Carolyn C. Baker

DIGITAL AND PRINT DEVELOPMENT EDITOR
Nancy Driver

PRODUCTION MANGER
Bonny E. Gaston

COPY EDITOR
Kimberly W. Kinne

Cover and text design by Bonny E. Gaston.

LIBRARY OF CONGRESS CATALOGING-IN-PUBLICATION DATA

International counseling case studies handbook/edited by Roy Moodley, Marguerite Lengyell, Rosa Wu, and Uwe P. Gielen.
    pages cm
    Includes bibliographical references and index.
    ISBN 978-1-55620-335-0 (pbk.: alk. paper)
1. Counseling.   2. Psychotherapy.   I. Moodley, Roy, editor.   II. American Counseling Association.
BF636.6.I5795 2015
    309—dc23

2014046605

Contents

Preface   VII
About the Editors and Contributors   XIII
Acknowledgments   XXI

PART ONE
WORKING WITH CASE STUDIES

CHAPTER 1
How to Critically Use Globally Discerned Case Studies
in Local Contexts   3
Eunjung Lee

PART TWO
COUNSELING AND PSYCHOTHERAPY IN AFRICA

CHAPTER 2
Counseling and Psychotherapy in Egypt: Omar's Story   15
Mona M. Amer

CHAPTER 3
Counseling and Psychotherapy in West Africa: Mazabalo's Story   23
Lonzozou Kpanake

CHAPTER 4
Counseling and Psychotherapy in Nigeria: Dayo's Story   31
Olaniyi Bojuwoye

CHAPTER 5
Counseling and Psychotherapy in Morocco: T.M.'s Story   39
Nadia Kadri and Dounia Belghazi

CHAPTER 6
Counseling and Psychotherapy in South Africa: Mr. Dlamini's Story   47
Lionel J. Nicholas and Maria Damianova

CHAPTER 7
Counseling and Psychotherapy in Sub-Saharan Africa:
Karimi's Story   55
Gladys K. Mwiti and Naomi James

PART THREE
COUNSELING AND PSYCHOTHERAPY IN AUSTRALIA AND ASIA

CHAPTER 8
Counseling and Psychotherapy in Australia: Cynthia's Story   65
Nadine Pelling

CHAPTER 9
Counseling and Psychotherapy in China: Yang's Story   73
Shi Qijia, Yu Ping, Doris F. Chang, and Wolfgang Senf

CHAPTER 10
Counseling and Psychotherapy in India: Radha's Story   79
Priya Pothan and Tony Sam George

CHAPTER 11
Counseling and Psychotherapy in Japan: Masako's Story   87
Shigeru Iwakabe and Carol Zerbe Enns

CHAPTER 12
Counseling and Psychotherapy in Malaysia: Aaron's Story   95
See Ching Mey

CHAPTER 13
Counseling and Psychotherapy in Pakistan: Zohra's Story   103
Humair Yusuf

CHAPTER 14
Counseling and Psychotherapy in the Philippines: Jojo's Story   111
Maria Isabel E. Melgar and Roberto E. Javier

CHAPTER 15
Counseling and Psychotherapy in South Korea: Misun's Story   117
Eunsun Joo

PART FOUR
COUNSELING AND PSYCHOTHERAPY IN CENTRAL, NORTH,
AND SOUTH AMERICA

CHAPTER 16
Counseling and Psychotherapy in Argentina: Michael's Story   125
Diego Benegas Loyo

CHAPTER 17
Counseling and Psychotherapy in Brazil: Sr. K's Story   133
*William B. Gomes, Vânia Maria Domingues, and
Maria Adélia Minghelli Pieta*

CHAPTER 18
Counseling and Psychotherapy in Canada: Kamalpreet's Story   141
Robinder P. Bedi and José F. Domene

CHAPTER 19
Counseling and Psychotherapy in the
Caribbean (Trinidad and Tobago): Olivia's Story   149
Gerard Hutchinson

CHAPTER 20
Counseling and Psychotherapy in Mexico: Mrs. Fabiola's Story   157
*María Fregoso-Vera, Samuel Jurado Cárdenas, and
Angélica Riveros Rosas*

CHAPTER 21
Counseling and Psychotherapy in the United States:
Rolando's Story   165
Gargi Roysircar and Vincent Pignatiello

PART FIVE
COUNSELING AND PSYCHOTHERAPY IN EUROPE

CHAPTER 22
Counseling and Psychotherapy in Denmark: Marianne's Story   175
Nanja H. Hansen and Andrea L. Dixon

CHAPTER 23
Counseling and Psychotherapy in France: Alice's Story   183
Jacques Pouyaud and Nicole Baudouin

CHAPTER 24
Counseling and Psychotherapy in Germany: David's Story   189
Karen Krause and Silvia Schneider

CHAPTER 25
Counseling and Psychotherapy in Italy: Miriam's Story   195
Thierry Bonfanti

CHAPTER 26
Counseling and Psychotherapy in the Netherlands: Tom's Story   203
*Giel Hutschemaekers, Caroline Vossen, Wubbo Scholte,
and Wiede Vissers*

CHAPTER 27
Counseling and Psychotherapy in Spain: Andres's Story 211
Carolina Marín-Martín and José M. Prieto

CHAPTER 28
Counseling and Psychotherapy in Russia: Client A's Story 219
Alla Kholmogorova and Svetlana Volikova

CHAPTER 29
Counseling and Psychotherapy in the United Kingdom:
Winston's Story 227
Del Loewenthal

PART SIX
COUNSELING AND PSYCHOTHERAPY IN THE MIDDLE EAST

CHAPTER 30
Counseling and Psychotherapy in Iran: Javad's Story 237
Behrooz Birashk

CHAPTER 31
Counseling and Psychotherapy in Israel: Lee's Story 243
Sharon Ziv Beiman

CHAPTER 32
Counseling and Psychotherapy in Lebanon: Zeina's Story 251
Brigitte Khoury and Yasmine I. Fayad

CHAPTER 33
Counseling and Psychotherapy in Palestine: Shaden's Story 259
Shafiq Masalha and Rana G. Nashashibi

CHAPTER 34
Counseling and Psychotherapy in Turkey: Ceren's Story 267
Senel Poyrazli and Murat Balkis

CONCLUSION

CHAPTER 35
Therapy Without Borders:
Bridging Counseling and Psychotherapy Across Cultures 277
Roy Moodley and Bhisham Khina

Index 293

Preface

In mental health care, internationalization and globalization have increased the need for countries to look beyond their borders in order to promote effective health and mental health care. Indeed, in the last decade we have seen numerous governmental and nongovernmental organizations that have evolved to promote and support developments worldwide. However, globalization has generally led to the domination of Western views of mental health as well as the policies and interventions associated with it. Integration of foreign values and ideas has been more apparent in non-Western countries than Eurocentric nations, in part because of the "well-established status and specialty of Western psychological theories as the standard approach to counseling and psychotherapy" (Moodley, Gielen, & Wu, 2013, p. 2). Clearly, as globalization and internationalization continue to intensify, "it is imperative for practitioners, clinicians, educators, and those in training to abandon their sense of self-sufficiency and actively increase their understanding of counseling and psychotherapy practices as they exist across cultures and nations" (Moodley et al., 2013, pp. 2–3).

The counseling profession began this process long ago. Theory, research, and counselor training have focused on issues of immigration, multiculturalism, cultural diversity, and all of the Group of Seven identity categories (race, gender, class, sexual orientation, disability, religion, and age), also known as the "Group of Seven" sociocultural identities (see Moodley, 2011, for discussion). These identities must be seen as fluid, shifting over time in accordance with contextual influences, such as sociopolitical realities, economic possibilities, developmental transitions, personality variables, and cultural histories. Moreover, a holistic approach to understanding one's identities demands that we explore them at three levels: the individual level (uniqueness; like no other individual), the group level (shared values and belief systems with important reference groups), and the universal level (common features shared by all human beings; Sue, 2001). For instance, each case in this text contains features that no other cases share (e.g., a client's developmental background), collective experiences that other cases of similar reference groups share (e.g., shared experiences among Muslim women), and universal characteristics that all cases share (e.g., experience of pain and suffering). At a most basic level, the counselor's own awareness and perceptions of him- or herself as a complex, multidimensional being are critical in working across cultures. Cultural sensitivity, or "cultural empathy" (Ridley & Lingle, 1996), expressed by a counselor is a key ingredient in ensuring that the clinician is culturally competent (Dyche & Zayas, 2001).

As the current high rate of immigration is driving many demographic changes in the United States, Canada, and Europe, counselors and psychotherapists must acquire the ability to interact effectively with people of different cultures, ethnicities, sexual orientations, and religions. These new configurations inevitably bring about different worldviews, belief systems, values, customs, and lifestyles as well as different mental health representations, presentations, enactments of psychological disturbances, and help-seeking behaviors. In order to meet the multicultural and diverse needs of all these varied individual and groups, counselors will need to be much more sophisticated, astute, and complex in the way they formulate and conduct counseling to ensure a culturally responsive service. We believe that the study of an individual case can provide counselors with a breadth *and* depth of knowledge about groups and communities, because

> Each individual is a component part of numerous groups, he is bound by ties of identification in many directions, and he has built up his ego ideal upon the most various models. Each individual therefore has a share in numerous group minds. Those of his race, of his class, of his creed, of his nationality, etc.,—and he can also raise himself above them to the extent of having a scrap of independence and originality. (Freud, 1921, p. 129)

The case studies in this book therefore illuminate the various ways in which counselors and psychotherapists across the globe work with clients in ways that enhance the practice of counseling and therapy. The many different ways in which counseling is understood and undertaken across the various countries represented in this book are described and illustrated through the case studies. Each case study is unique and distinctive, with each offering a rare opportunity for mental health practitioners to get a bird's-eye view of what happens around the world. Therefore, the study of these cases individually and collectively will yield a wealth of information about the theory and practice of counseling and psychotherapy across the globe. Engaging the case study in this way will provide counselors with more than just a comparative analysis of practice; indeed, it will offer process and contextual insights into how current theories of counseling are formulated, modified, and reconstituted within different country contexts. Such an analysis will highlight the weaknesses and strengths of particular theories of counseling and psychotherapy.

As scholars and mental health practitioners bound by ethical standards for the practice of counseling, psychology, and psychotherapy, we are acutely aware of the key ethical issues that may arise when publishing a case studies text. Primarily, striking a balance between protecting a client's anonymity and providing a rich, detailed account of the client's clinical history to make it useful is a common ethical dilemma of case study publication. Furthermore, dual roles of this text's contributors and their associated obligations (acting as both a scholar and a clinician) may result in conflicts, undue influences, and power imbalances that could affect the therapeutic relationship as well as decision-making procedures (e.g., consent of subjects). Although a universal code of ethics has not been formally recognized, it is the duty of our contributors to adhere to the standards and principles adopted by their respective nations to mitigate these risks (for more information about professional regulations in counseling and psychotherapy in various nations around the globe, refer to Moodley et al., 2013).

WHY AN INTERNATIONAL CASE STUDY HANDBOOK IS NEEDED IN A RAPIDLY GLOBALIZING WORLD

During the last four decades, the field of psychology has rapidly expanded in many parts of the world. Stevens and Gielen (2007) estimated that more than one million psychologists are now active around the globe, with American psychologists probably making up less than one quarter of this impressive number. Very large numbers of psychologists can be found not only in European countries, such as England, Germany, Spain, and Russia, but also in Latin American nations, such as Argentina, Brazil, and Mexico (Stevens & Wedding, 2007). Whereas in Argentina, Brazil, and Uruguay psychoanalysis is especially popular among counselors, psychotherapists, and even the general public, in most other nations various forms of cognitive behavior, Rogerian, and interpersonal counseling and psychotherapy are practiced most frequently. It is also noteworthy that in the poorer as well as in many of the economically emerging countries, the more Westernized forms of counseling predominate above all in the big cities, where many of the counselors' clients are educated and somewhat Westernized middle-class women and men. In contrast to this situation, the more traditionally oriented inhabitants of isolated villages and provincial towns are more likely to resort to traditional healers, whose treatment methods rely on explanations revolving around divination and supernatural forces, together with the administration of herbal remedies and other indigenous forms of practicing medicine. The Nigerian case study, for instance, introduces the reader to such a traditional healing approach. Indeed, in many African countries traditional healers tend to outnumber both doctors trained in allopathic (Western-style) medicine as well as psychological counselors and therapists. However, and unfortunately, most counselors (who have been exposed to modern psychological theories) and most traditional healers (who rely on invisible spirits and divine influences) tend to find it difficult to work together for the spiritual, psychological, and medical welfare of their clients. It seems that their ontological and epistemological frameworks diverge so widely from each other that they cannot find common ground for joint professional activities.

On the whole, then, the case studies described in this volume reflect a globalized world in which the field of counseling psychology represents a modern form of consciousness and theorizing about human nature and its potential strengths and weaknesses. At the same time, the studies certainly leave room for a broad variety of cultural influences on both counselor and client that manifest themselves in the form of different expectations in the counseling situation as well as varied family systems; divergent gender roles; culture-specific expectations about the roles of children, students, parents, employers and employees, friends, peers, and dating partners (if any); and so on. Indeed, we as editors like to claim that it is exactly by scrutinizing and meditating upon these highly varied case studies that the reader can learn in detail how general human nature, specific cultural expectations and norms, social institutions, a client's individual character and psychological difficulties, and his or her counselor's interpretations and treatment approach can come together in a series of fruitful encounters evolving over time. The case studies teach us in some detail how an international group of both Western and non-Western counselors conceive of and approach their task of helping a broad variety of clients to achieve less troubled and more fulfilling lives—and, at times, also why counseling can be such a difficult and demanding endeavor.

Besides demonstrating how mental health practitioners in various countries undertake counseling and psychotherapy, this text also attempts to connect ethnicity and counseling as well as the specific cultural practices that are part of healing in those countries. Dyche and Zayas (2001) argued that counselors and psychotherapists who have developed the ability to be culturally empathic are well prepared to practice counseling and psychotherapy with a diverse clientele. This ability entails embracing an attitude and/or skill that effectively

> bridges the cultural gap between clinician and client, one that seeks to help clinicians integrate an attitude of openness, with the necessary knowledge and skill to work successfully across cultures. It involves a deepening of the human empathic response to permit a sense of mutuality and understanding across the great differences in value and expectation that cross-cultural interchange often involves. (Dyche & Zayas, 2001, p. 246)

The counselor of the future will be asked to interact with clients from an almost limitless range of cultural backgrounds. Already the schools of many of the world's great cities, such as New York, Los Angeles, Chicago, Toronto, Vancouver, London, Berlin, and Paris, are filled with the children of immigrants. Take New York City as a striking example: In 2014, more than two thirds of all students in its public school system came from immigrant and minority backgrounds. Consequently, the school counselor in the average New York City public school has to be prepared to see in her office students whose families or parent(s) arrived in the city from some 40 nations spread around the globe. For such a counselor, reading a volume filled with international case studies is not an exotic task, but rather it constitutes an excellent preparation for helping her master her central task—a task that requires her to grasp what the world might look like from the vantage points of her student–clients as well as the students' parents, grandparents, siblings, friends, and peers. International case studies not only tell us how cultural meaning systems work themselves out in detail and on the ground, so to speak, but also teach us how a variety of counseling theories can profitably be applied in a broad range of sociocultural situations that frequently are new to most of us.

How the Book Is Organized

The *International Counseling Case Studies Handbook* is divided into three sections.

Section 1

Section 1 opens with an introduction that outlines the history, philosophy, and process in counseling and psychotherapy around the globe. Chapter 1 discusses ways in which counselors and mental health practitioners can use and maximize the global cases in this text and situate it in their own local communities.

Section 2: Counseling and Psychotherapy Around the World

This section (Chapters 2–34) is divided into five parts representing six continents, or regions. Each region has chapters from some of the major countries where counseling and psychotherapy is undertaken. Countries were selected on the basis of (a) their population size, (b) how well they represent a given region in the world, (c) how well they represent global cultural variability, (d) how well developed their counseling and psychotherapy traditions are, and (e) whether we could find a good author(s) for a chapter on a given country. Regions are presented in alphabetical order, beginning with Africa; followed by Australia and Asia; Central, North, and South America; Europe; and the Middle East. Counseling and psychotherapy scholars and psychology researchers from these countries were invited to submit a case, which was written to the following specifications:

The Client/s
In this section, authors describe the client's diversity in terms of the Group of Seven identities, that is, gender, ethnicity (race), disability, class, age, sexual orientation, and religion. In some cases this section includes a brief description of how the client has constructed his or her subjectivity in terms of the Group of Seven identities. Some authors also comment on the various combinations and intersections of these identities within particular contexts and situations that allow for particular identity performances.

Presenting Issues and Challenges
In this section, authors comment on the client's reason for referral, psychological difficulty, subjective distress, and any clinical observations that they have made.

Case History and Developmental Background
This section requires authors to write about the familial, cultural, social, ethnic, and Group of Seven identities and their contributions to the personality development of the client. Authors of some chapters comment on the relationship between the evolution of multiple identities and the life history trajectories within the context of the respective country's sociopolitical climate.

The Therapy
In this section authors discuss the therapeutic perspectives and the particular approach or modality that was used with the client. The process of counseling and therapy is described in some detail, including the following: interventions; assessment, goals, and therapy treatment; and outcomes. Authors were asked to include introspection and self-disclosure and to reflect on the Group of Seven identities in the clinical process, particularly the use of traditional healing, spirituality, and other alternative healing modalities that support resilience.

Discussion and Analysis of the Case
In this part the authors critically discuss their cases, using theory and ideas from the published scholarship and questioning the use of counseling and psychotherapy as the best modality for the client's particular problems. Authors were encouraged to bring several elements together in their discussion: the Group of Seven identities, problem solving, consciousness raising, and alternative healing modalities. These elements were addressed in a reflective discussion of their work with the client.

Questions
In this section, five questions are posed about the case study. These open-ended questions are designed to stimulate deeper thought and discussion about the

case study as well as how a counselor might handle similar issues with his or her own clients.

SECTION 3

The concluding chapter (Chapter 35) explores some of the main themes and ideas that can be found in the book. An overview of cultural, multicultural, and diversity contexts is discussed, and particular attention is paid to the concepts of individual culture versus the collective culture and the relationship of the self in navigating these spaces. The chapter also looks at the intersection between the body, mind, and spirit, which featured prominently in many cases. Finally, the chapter discusses some key recommendations for counselors and psychotherapists from the lessons learned from the cases in this book.

REFERENCES

Dyche, L., & Zayas, L. H. (2001). Cross-cultural empathy and training the contemporary psychotherapists. *Clinical Social Work Journal, 29,* 245–258.

Freud, S. (1921). *Group psychology and the analysis of the ego* (J. Strachey, Trans.). New York, NY: W. W. Norton.

Moodley, R. (2011). *Outside the sentence: Readings in critical multicultural counselling and psychotherapy.* Toronto, Ontario, Canada: CDCP.

Moodley, R., Gielen, U. P., & Wu, R. (Eds.). (2013). *Handbook of counseling and psychotherapy in an international context.* New York, NY: Routledge.

Ridley, C. R., & Lingle, D. (1996). Cultural empathy in multicultural counseling: A multidimensional process model. In P. B. Pedersen, J. G. Draguns, W. J. Loner, & J. E. Trimble (Eds.), *Counseling across cultures* (pp. 21–46). Thousand Oaks, CA: Sage.

Stevens, M. J., & Gielen, U. P. (Eds.). (2007). *Toward a global psychology: Theory, research, intervention, and pedagogy.* New York, NY: Psychology Press.

Stevens, M. J., & Wedding, D. (Eds.). (2007). *Handbook of international psychology.* New York, NY: Brunner-Routledge.

Sue, D. W. (2001). Multidimensional facets of cultural competence. *The Counseling Psychologist, 29,* 790–821.

About the Editors and Contributors

ABOUT THE EDITORS

Roy Moodley, PhD, is associate professor of counseling psychology at the University of Toronto, Ontario, Canada. He is the director for the Centre for Diversity in Counselling and Psychotherapy. His research interests include critical multicultural counseling and psychotherapy, race and culture in psychotherapy, traditional healing, culture and resilience, and gender and identity. He has authored or edited several journal articles, book chapters, and books.

Marguerite Lengyell, EdD (candidate), is in the Counselling and Psychotherapy Department at the University of Toronto and is currently a psychological associate conducting psychological assessments for children, adolescents, and adults in Toronto, Ontario, Canada. Her academic research interests have focused on ideologies of multiculturalism and their application in the therapeutic process. To be specific, she has had a long-standing interest in mixed race, interracial, and interethnic relationships and children of mixed race or ethnic heritage.

Rosa Wu, PhD, is a registered clinical counselor living and working in Vancouver, British Columbia, Canada. Originally from Taiwan, she has lived in Costa Rica, Panama, Spain, New York, and Toronto and is fluent in English, Spanish, and Mandarin Chinese. Rosa's main research interests include interethnic couple relationships, multicultural counseling competencies, and traditional and alternative methods of healing. She currently teaches in a postsecondary institution and works part-time as a counselor in private practice.

Uwe P. Gielen, PhD, is professor emeritus and executive director of the Institute for International and Cross-Cultural Psychology at St. Francis College, New York. His work centers on cross-cultural and international psychology, Chinese American immigrant children, Tibetan studies, international family psychology, and moral development. He is the senior editor, coeditor, and coauthor of 21 volumes that have appeared in five languages. He has served as president of the Society for Cross-Cultural Research, the International Council of Psychologists, and the International Psychology Division of the American Psychology Association.

ABOUT THE CONTRIBUTORS

Mona M. Amer, PhD, is associate professor of psychology at the American University in Cairo, Egypt. She earned her doctorate in clinical psychology from the University of Toledo and her postdoctoral specialization from Yale University. She is coeditor of the book *Counseling Muslims: Handbook of Mental Health Issues and Interventions.*

Murat Balkis, PhD, is an associate professor in the Department of Psychological Counseling and Guidance at the Pamukkale University, Turkey. His clinical background includes working with college students and dealing with issues related to psychosocial adjustment and academic failure. His research interests include adjustment, homesickness, and procrastination.

Nicole Baudouin, PhD, is a clinical psychologist and therapist. Her research at the National Institute for Studies on Work and Vocational Guidance in Paris, France, deals with the counseling interview, supervision, and psychological processes of vocation. She is the author of the book *Le sens de l'orientation* [The sense of vocation].

Robinder P. Bedi, PhD, is an associate professor in the Department of Psychology at Western Washington University. His research interests include professional issues in counseling psychology, counseling men, and the therapeutic relationship. He specializes in substance abuse counseling and counseling individuals involved in motor vehicle accidents.

Sharon Ziv Beiman, PhD, is a clinical psychologist; works as a faculty member at the College for Academic Studies in Or-Yehuda, Israel; is comanager of Siach-Group, an institute for relational psychotherapy, in Tel Aviv, Israel; serves as chair of the Israeli Forum for Relational Psychoanalysis and Psychotherapy; and is a board member of the International Association for Relational Psychoanalysis and Psychotherapy.

Dounia Belghazi, MD, is a psychiatrist. She graduated from the Medical University at Casablanca, Morocco, and earned a university diploma in cognitive behavior therapy (CBT) and addictology. She trained at CHU in Brugmann, Belgium. She is author of various articles and is currently a PhD student in Casablanca's Laboratory of Mental Health.

Behrooz Birashk, PhD, is associate professor of psychology at Iran University of Medical Sciences, Mental Health Research Centre, and Tehran Psychiatric Institute. He is a member of eight national and international associations. Besides his teaching and research, he is editor in chief of a psychology journal and serves on the editorial boards of eight journals of psychology and psychiatry.

Olaniyi Bojuwoye, PhD, is a professor of educational psychology at the University of the Western Cape, South Africa. He has published many peer reviewed journal articles and book chapters on cross-cultural counseling, African traditional healing, and contextual influences on children's development.

Thierry Bonfanti, PhD, is a professor at the Centro Studi Interculturali of the University of Verona and is on the sociology faculty at the university of Trento. He is a psychologist, psychotherapist, and mediator and is the leading exponent of the nondirective intervention approach in Italy. He has worked in different countries, such as France, Greece, and Spain.

Samuel Jurado Cárdenas, PhD, is full-time professor at the Graduate Studies Division, Faculty of Psychology, National Autonomous University of Mexico. His lines of research and interest include the following: CBT, behavioral medicine, history of psychology in Mexico, and biofeedback.

Doris F. Chang, PhD, is an associate professor of psychology at the New School for Social Research and a research scientist at the Center of Excellence for Cultural Competence, New York State Psychiatric Institute. Her research addresses disparities in the quality of mental health services for racial and ethnic minorities and issues in Chinese mental health.

Maria Damianova, PhD, is an associate professor in the School of Health Sciences at Monash, South Africa. She is a registered counseling and educational psychologist with the Health Professions Council of South Africa.

Andrea L. Dixon, PhD, is an associate professor of counseling at Georgia State University in Atlanta, Georgia. She specializes in multicultural awareness and training and conducts research in these areas and in mattering and wellness across the lifespan.

José F. Domene, PhD, is Canada Research Chair in the School to Work Transition, Faculty of Education, University of New Brunswick, Fredericton. His research interests include social–relational contexts of career development, young adults' health and wellness, and professional issues in Canadian counseling psychology.

Vânia Maria Domingues is a specialist clinical psychologist with more than 30 years of private practice with adolescents and adults.

Carol Zerbe Enns, PhD, is a professor of psychology at Cornell College and is a contributor to the Ethnic Studies program and the Gender, Sexuality, and Women's Studies program. She teaches courses in multicultural psychology and has served as the resident director of the Japan Study Program in Tokyo. Carol's scholarly interests include gender issues, feminism, and feminist psychotherapy in Japan and East Asia.

Yasmine I. Fayad, MA, is an instructor in the Psychology Department at the American University of Beirut, Lebanon. She also worked as a therapist at SKOUN, a nongovernmental organization in Beirut, Lebanon, that provides mental health services to patients with substance abuse problems.

María Fregoso-Vera, PhD (candidate), studies psychology and health and is on the faculty of the Psychology Department at the National Autonomous University of Mexico. For 5 years, she has worked with children who have allergies and their caregivers. She has worked as a teacher at various levels of education, including the college level and higher.

Tony Sam George, PhD, is associate professor and head of the Department of Psychology at Christ University, Bangalore, India. He is also a practicing psychotherapist and works with couples, families, and adolescents.

William B. Gomes, PhD, is a professor of psychology at the Federal University of Rio Grande do Sul, Porto Alegre, Brazil. He has conducted research on psychotherapeutic and counseling effectiveness with Brazilian populations since the early 1990s.

Nanja H. Hansen, MC, is a licensed psychologist in Denmark and a licensed professional clinical counselor in California. She works at Stanford University at the Staff Faculty Help Center. Her clinical interest areas are compassion for self and others, multicultural issues, and life transitions.

Gerard Hutchinson, PhD, is a professor of psychiatry, head of clinical medical sciences, and coordinator of the master's of science in clinical psychology program at the University of the West Indies, Mount Hope, St. Augustine campus, Trinidad and Tobago. He is also the head of Mental Health Services, North Central Regional Health Authority, Mount Hope.

Giel Hutschemaekers, PhD, is full professor in mental health care at the Radboud University Nijmegen (the Netherlands) and is a therapist in a large integrated institute for mental health care in the Nijmegen Arnhem region (Pro Persona). His research is focused on professionalization issues, such as the implementation of evidence-based guidelines and its consequences on professionals' expertise and on patient outcomes.

Shigeru Iwakabe, PhD, is an associate professor in the Developmental Clinical Psychology Program at Ochanomizu University in Tokyo, Japan. He conducts psychotherapy research on client emotional processes, therapeutic failures and impasses, and therapist empathy. He is also interested in cultural issues associated with the practice of psychotherapy.

Naomi James, MA, is a counseling psychologist and trainer at Oasis Africa Training and Counseling Centre in Nairobi, Kenya. She is also head of the counseling department, is in charge of the intern training program, and is head of the psychology department at Oasis Africa Institute of Leadership and Professional Psychology. Oasis Africa provides counseling and psychotherapy services, training, and employee assistance services to organizations.

Roberto E. Javier, Jr., PhD, is a licensed psychologist in the Philippines. He is currently a full professor in the Department of Psychology and is a fellow at the Social Development Research Center of De La Salle University, Manila. He is a board member of the National Association for Filipino Psychology.

Eunsun Joo, PhD, is a professor in the Department of Psychology at Duksung Women's University. She is a certified counseling psychologist in Korea and a certified focusing trainer and coordinator in the United States. She has published numerous articles and books in the areas of culture and psychology, person-centered and focusing approach, and development of psychotherapists.

Nadia Kadri, MD, is a professor of psychiatry. She introduced the first academic training in Morocco on CBT, clinical sexology, and behavioral medicine. She is the author of hundreds of articles published on the national and international levels and of several books on general psychiatry, mental health of women, stigma, CBT, and sexuality.

Bhisham Kinha, MEd, is a counseling psychologist in private practice.

Alla Kholmogorova, PhD, is professor of psychology, head of the Department of Clinical Psychology and Psychotherapy at the Moscow Research Institute of Psychiatry, council member of the Russian Society of Psychiatrists, founder fellow of the Academy of Cognitive Therapy, and head of the faculty of Counseling and Clinical Psychology at Moscow State University of Psychology and Education.

Brigitte Khoury, PhD, is an associate professor in the Department of Psychiatry at the American University of Beirut in Lebanon and is director of the clinical psychology training program. She is also the director of the Arab Regional Center for Research, Training and Policy Making in Mental Health as well as a consultant for the World Health Organization in Geneva, Switzerland.

Lonzozou Kpanake, PhD, is an associate professor in the Department of Psychology at the University of Québec (TÉLUQ), Canada. He received his PhD in psychology from the University of Toulouse, France, and completed his postdoctoral training in transcultural psychiatry at McGill University, Canada. His research has focused on health issues among African populations.

Karen Krause, MD, is head of the ambulatory care clinic for child and adolescent psychotherapy at the Mental Health Research and Treatment Center, Ruhr-Universität, Bochum, Germany. She is a licensed psychotherapist (CBT) for children, adolescents, and adults and is a licensed clinical neuropsychologist. She is a trainer and supervisor for CBT in children and adults.

Eunjung Lee, PhD, MSW, is an associate professor at the Factor-Inwentash Faculty of Social Work, University of Toronto, Ontario, Canada. She is a psychotherapy process researcher focusing on cross-cultural clinical practice. Using case studies and critical theories of discourse analysis, her research explores how clinical theories are signified in sociocultural contexts and how immigration and education policies (re)produce current transnational families.

Del Loewenthal, PhD, is director of the Research Centre for Therapeutic Education and Doctoral Programmes in Psychotherapy and Counselling at the University of Roehampton, London, England. He is an analytic psychotherapist and chartered counseling psychologist. His most recent book (with Andrew Samuels) is titled *Relational Psychotherapy, Psychoanalysis and Counselling: Appraisals and Reappraisals*.

Diego Benegas Loyo, PhD, is a psychoanalyst and researcher of subjectivity and social action. A Fulbright grantee, he participated with the Bellevue Hospital/New York University (NYU) Program for Survivors of Torture. Currently, he is professor of emergencies in psychology at the University Institute Barceló Foundation and teaches at NYU Buenos Aires in Argentina.

Carolina Marín-Martín, PhD, is an associate professor in clinical psychology in the Department at Complutense, University of Madrid, Spain. She works as part-time lecturer of clinical assessment and as a clinical psychologist at the Association for Aid to the 11 March Victims. She is a specialist on posttraumatic stress disorder (PTSD) and addictions problems.

Shafiq Masalha, PhD, is a clinical psychologist and supervisor. He is a senior lecturer at the College for Academic Studies in Or-Yehuda and at the Hebrew University in Jerusalem, Israel. He serves as the president of ERICE, a nongovernmental agency that aims to advance the mental health of children in war areas, especially in the Middle East.

Maria Isabel E. Melgar, PhD, is a clinical psychologist and faculty member with the Ateneo de Manila University in the Philippines. She also serves as the faculty coordinator of the PhD program on clinical psychology. She is the director for counseling and community services at the Fr. Bulatao Psychology Center in Manila.

See Ching Mey, PhD, is a professor at the Universiti Sains, Malaysia. She is an educational and counseling psychologist. She has published 15 academic books, more than 200 international and national academic journal articles, and more than 300 academic papers at national and international seminars. She is the chief editor of the *Journal of Counseling* for the Association of Psychological and Educational Counselors of Asia Pacific and is an editorial board member for 11 international journals and two national journals.

Gladys K. Mwiti, PhD, is a consulting clinical psychologist, a pioneer for transformational and integrative psychology in Kenya, and the founder and CEO of Oasis Africa Center for Transformational Psychology and Trauma Expertise. She is also chair of the Kenya Psychological Association, is both a member and serves on the board of directors for the International Society for Traumatic Stress Studies, and was the 2014 Distinguished Alumni of the Year for the Fuller Graduate School of Psychology.

Rana G. Nashashibi, PhD (candidate), is a counselor, is the director of the Palestinian Counseling Center—Jerusalem, and is a lecturer in counseling theory and practice. She was born and lives in Jerusalem. She earned her bachelor's degree from Birzeit University in 1982 and her master's degree in counseling psychology from Indiana State University (Fulbright Scholar). She was a Humphrey fellow in 1995 at Washington State University and is currently a doctoral candidate at Lesley University in Cambridge, Massachusetts. She has several publication credits.

Lionel J. Nicholas, PhD, is the head of Department of Psychology at Monash, South Africa, and is past president of the Psychological Society of South Africa.

Nadine Pelling, PhD, is a senior lecturer in clinical psychology and counseling at the University of South Australia. She is a fellow of the Australian Counselling Association and was awarded an early career teaching award from the Australian Psychological Society. She teaches, creates scholarship, and maintains a limited private practice.

Maria Adélia Minghelli Pieta, PhD, is a clinical psychologist with a PhD in psychology from the Federal University of Rio Grande do Sul in Brazil.

Vincent Pignatiello, PsyD, is a postdoctoral fellow at the William Alanson White Institute of Psychiatry, Psychoanalysis, and Psychology in New York City. He is also an adjunct professor in the Department of Clinical Psychology at Antioch University New England in Keene, New Hampshire.

Yu Ping, PhD, is clinical psychologist of the Wuhan Mental Hospital for Psychotherapy in China. She received her PhD in psychosomatic medicine and psychotherapy from the University of Duisburg-Essen. She engaged in clinical psychotherapy and research for 8 years, served as vice executive secretary of the Mental Health Association of Hubei Province, and is a member of the standing committee of the Tumors Association of Hubei Province.

Priya Pothan, PhD, holds a clinical psychology doctoral degree from the National Institute of Mental Health and Neuro Sciences, Bangalore, India. She conducts mental health awareness and enrichment programs with schools, corporations, wellness centers, and churches. She currently runs her own psychological clinic and supervises therapists in training and practice.

Jacques Pouyaud, PhD, is lecturer in vocational psychology at the University of Bordeaux, France. He also serves on the board of the Unesco Chair of Lifelong Guidance and Counseling. His researches deal with counseling and processes of self-construction throughout the life course and during psychosocial transitions.

Senel Poyrazli, PhD, is a counseling psychologist in private practice and teaches at the Pennsylvania State University. Her clinical background includes working with a large number of counseling groups and dealing with issues related to relationships, psychosocial adjustment, decision making, depression, and trauma. Multicultural competency training is one of her research areas.

José M. Prieto, PhD, is a senior professor in personnel psychology at the Complutense University, Madrid, Spain. His fields of expertise include assessment and training in occupational settings as well as the nexus between Zen meditation and psychological/spiritual well-being. He lectures and publishes in English, French, and Spanish on psychology and other cross-cultural topics.

Shi Qijia, MD, is clinical professor of neurology and psychiatry and is director of the Institute for Mental Health of Wuhan, at the Wuhan Mental Health Center, China. His primary fields of expertise in psychology include field PTSD therapy, severe personality disorder, eating disorders, and inpatient psychotherapy. He served as president of Mental Health Association of Hubei Province.

Angélica Riveros Rosas, PhD, has been a full-time tenured professor at the National Autonomous University of Mexico since 2008. She has written a test/scale and 18 articles or chapters in peer-reviewed sources. She has advised 10 licensing and master's theses and is currently advising seven doctoral dissertations.

Gargi Roysircar, PhD, is the founding director of Antioch University New England's Multicultural Center for Research and Practice and is a professor of clinical psychology. She conducts research on immigrants, multicultural competencies, cultural personality assessment, and training in culturally sensitive practice. She leads disaster mental health services internationally and is a fellow of the American Psychological Association.

Silvia Schneider, PhD, is professor of clinical child and adolescent psychology and head of the Mental Health Research and Treatment Center at the Ruhr-Universität Bochum, Germany. Her research focus is on the etiology of anxiety disorders in children, their familial transmission, and the treatment of anxiety disorders in children and adolescents.

Wubbo Scholte, PhD, is head of the Addiction Department of De Hoop Mental Health Care and is head of psychotherapy training of the SPON (part of the Radboud University Nijmegen, the Netherlands). His research is focused on the clinical utility of personality assessment.

Wolfgang Senf, MD, is a tenured clinical professor of psychotherapy and psychosomatic medicine and is former director of the Psychosomatic and Psychotherapy Department of Duisburg-Essen University, Germany. He is the former president of the International Federation for Psychotherapy, and he also served as former chairman of German Society for Psychosomatic Medicine and Medical Psychotherapy.

Wiede Vissers, PhD, is mental health psychologist at the Ambulatorium, an outpatient mental health center, and is assistant head of the postgraduate education of mental health psychologists (SPON), both of which are part of the Radboud University Nijmegen, the Netherlands. Her research is focused on remoralization as an outcome measure in psychotherapy research.

Svetlana Volikova, PhD, earned her doctorate in psychology and is a researcher in the Department of Clinical Psychology and Psychotherapy at Moscow Research Institute of Psychiatry, Russian Federation Ministry of Public Health. She is also an assistant professor in the Department of Clinical Psychology and Psychotherapy, Faculty of Counseling and Clinical Psychology, Moscow State University of Psychology and Education.

Caroline Vossen, PhD (candidate), is a clinical psychologist and psychotherapist. She works as a teacher and as coordinator of the ambulatorium for adult patients at the outpatient mental health center of the Department of Social Sciences, Radboud University Nijmegen, the Netherlands. As a researcher, she is preparing her dissertation on cognitive bias medication for patients with common mental disorders.

Humair Yusuf, EdD (candidate), is studying counseling psychology at the University of Toronto, Ontario, Canada. His research interests include representations of illness as well as indigenous healing and spirituality in counseling and psychotherapy. He is the publications editor for the Centre for Diversity in Counselling and Psychotherapy. Currently, he is editing a book titled *Islamic Healing Traditions: Implications for Health and Mental Health.*

Acknowledgments

We want to express our sincere thanks and appreciation to all the expert contributors in this book for the creative and innovative ways in which they undertook writing their respective country chapters. A very special thank you and gratitude goes to all the clients discussed in this book for sharing their many and varied stories, which made this book possible.

During the course of this book's development, there were several contributors who for one reason or another were unable to continue, and others were invited at short notice to take their place to offer particular country chapters. Our special thanks to you for making the effort to meet our deadlines.

Our deepest gratitude to several colleagues, friends, and family who were very supportive of this project: Anissa Talahite, Daniel Harry, Chris Lengyell, Juan Wu, Ingrid Hsing, Irene Wu, Maya Florence, Roisin Anna, Tara Isabelle, and Zina Claude.

We are pleased to acknowledge the support of the Centre for Diversity in Counselling and Psychotherapy, Ontario Institute for Studies in Education, at the University of Toronto; and the Institute for International and Cross-Cultural Psychology, St. Francis College, in New York.

Our thanks to Carolyn Baker, associate publisher at the American Counseling Association (ACA), for all her help and guidance. The team at ACA publications requires special thanks for their help through the production process. Our sincere thanks to Nancy Driver, digital and print development editor.

Part One
WORKING WITH CASE STUDIES

Chapter 1

HOW TO CRITICALLY USE GLOBALLY DISCERNED CASE STUDIES IN LOCAL CONTEXTS

Eunjung Lee

After an initial consultation with a client, some experienced clinicians not only capture a comprehensive picture of the client in context, propose explanatory working hypotheses of the client's presenting issues, and develop customized treatment plans but they also suggest a prognosis of the case. How can they tell the differences among cases after the intake in terms of prognosis? They often note that, "I learned from experience." What does that mean? From years of experience meeting different clients as well as reading and listening to other clinicians' case studies, they develop bit by bit their own inner data files for each unique client in a particular context, which become more elaborate over time, are tested for or against other similar or dissimilar cases, and are validated with successful or unsuccessful outcomes. With time, practice, and intentional professional attention, they develop a frame of reference or organizing principles that identify significant themes in each client's struggles, what works in similar cases, and how to monitor indicators for desirable changes. This inductive process of clinically based knowledge building *is* the case study. Documenting this "disciplined inquiry" of practice (Peterson, 1991, cited in Fishman, 2005, p. 1), selecting appropriate interventions from "case-based reasoning" (Fishman, 2005, p. 11), and transferring the cumulated clinical knowledge to similar cases is the *case study based practice and training* in counseling and psychotherapy. This cumulative clinical knowledge within a clinician is transferrable not only to his or her other cases but also to fellow clinicians' cases through case conferences, workshops, and/or publications. Therefore, the case study is beyond a clinician's hunches or personal clinical wisdom. In reality, it is an inductive, cumulative, and systemic inquiry of human existence and sufferings—a scientific, empirical approach (Lee, Mishna, & Brennenstuhl, 2010). The active pursuit of this wealth of clinical knowledge truly is an accountable practice for a service provider and a necessary quality, especially when serving clients with diverse cultural backgrounds in a global world.

Lee et al. (2010) proposed ways to critically evaluate the case study in clinical practice and proposed case study evaluation criteria. By incorporating these criteria as well as other findings from cross-cultural clinical practice research (Lee, 2010; Lee & Bhuyan, 2013; Lee & Horvath, 2013, 2014), I delineate in this chapter ways to use and maximize a case study approach that is situated in a global context for clinicians in their own local community.

3

Intensive Investigation of a Case Embedded in Real-Life Context

A main purpose of case study is the intensive investigation of the client system/ case under study in naturalistic (not controlled) real contexts, while examining multiple variables using multiple sources of evidence with the aim of providing in-depth rich information (Lee et al., 2010). Providing a thick description of the client in context considering "contextual inclusiveness" (Bergen & While, 2000, p. 932) or "the proximity to reality" (Flyvbjerg, 2006, p. 236) then assists mental health practitioners to "conceptually decide to what extent the case as described" (Fishman, 2005, p. 17) can be applicable to their own cases. Although not exhaustive, the following list is a compilation of areas to consider in developing a rich case study description: the case selection, collection points of clinical information, source of clinical information, intervention procedures and ingredients, interpretation of clinical information, and clients' feedback.

Why is this case selected? The clinicians choose a particular case because it is "typical, extreme/deviant, critical, or pragmatic" (Lee et al., 2010, p. 685) among other cases in their caseloads. This purposeful sampling is referred to as "information-oriented sampling" (Flyvbjerg, 2006, p. 230) to describe the process of maximizing the use of information from the chosen case or "theoretical sampling" (compared with "statistical sampling") to "choose cases that are likely to replicate or extend the emergent theory or to fill theoretical categories" (Meyer, 2001, p. 332). Therefore, the selection of the case itself is informative to mental health practitioners and assists them to reflect on the clinicians' purposeful attention to the case and its underlying cultural and theoretical orientations.

How frequently and over how long a period of time is clinical information collected? One of the great benefits of conducting a case study is an in-depth understanding of the case under study. Accordingly, not only the end product of therapy but also a whole therapy process can be zoomed in and out to monitor the progress and impasses in the clinical processes and, if necessary, to revise the course of the selected intervention. In the description of the case, it is thus important to see whether the clinicians delineate and elaborate the clinical information over time to highlight the clinical processes. The multiple points of clinical data collection then would assist counselors and psychotherapists to make a decision as to whether the interventions caused changes in the case rather than the alternative explanations, such as the changes stemmed from the client's maturation or else the problem itself faded away (Kazdin, 1981).

What is the source of clinical information? It is crucial to indicate sources of clinical information that lead to a clinician's clinical working hypothesis and treatment selection. For example, instead of relying solely on a clinician's observation or a client's verbal indication, for example, "I am depressed," multiple sources of clinical evidence can be collected from multiple subjects (e.g., the client and his or her significant others, the clinician), multiple perspectives (e.g., the client's in-session report vs. homework report, a clinician's observation of the client in individual vs. group sessions), and multiple places (e.g., school, home, therapy sessions). It does not have to be clinicians who contact the multiple subjects and visit multiple places. Rather, clinicians could ask questions pertaining to multiple sources of clinical information, such as the following: "How do you think your partner/children/friends perceive and react to you when you feel depressed?" (multiple subjects); "You look very down and have little energy today. I notice this month you have often looked this way" (a clinician's observation); "Am I getting it right? Do you sometimes feel this way at your school/work?" (multiple places); and "Do you feel the same way that this month is getting harder for you?" (multiple perspectives). In a case study, clinicians may describe these multiple sources of information. If the collected multiple sources of clinical information capture converging changes after the selected intervention, counselors and psychotherapists can have stronger evidence that the changes occurred because of the intervention than if only one source of clinical information is described (Lee et al., 2010).

What are intervention procedures and ingredients? Providing detailed description of the intervention is extremely useful in that it helps mental health practitioners "decide whether the intervention context or content is transferable to their own practice" (Lee et al., 2010, p. 687). Even if some results are less positive, "detailed description can provide information that can lead to altering the intervention" (Lee et al., 2010, p. 687). Gilgun (1994) articulated that clinicians who attempt to replicate interventions described in the case study

> often become frustrated and may doubt their own competence when the particular interventions fail when applied to their practice. If the interventions had been "more thoroughly described, practitioners might have been able to decipher the differences between their interventions and those interventions in research reports and subsequently understand why their interventions and evaluations might not replicate published reports." (p. 374; cited in Lee et al., 2010, p. 687)

Mental health practitioners may ask the following questions to see whether the case study captures detailed description of the selected intervention: Is the target of the intervention/phenomenon of interest similar to my client's?; How often does the intervention occur? (dosage); What constitutes the intervention? (not the brand name of the selected intervention but ingredients and contents of the intervention); Is this intervention applicable to our setting? (context); and Can I use this intervention for my client? (clinician's qualifications and training; Lee et al., 2010). The detailed description of the intervention may help counselors and psychotherapists to imagine their selection and use of the intervention for their own cases. This process may increase potential for their preparedness and attunement to the chosen intervention, which would increase their performance competence in delivering the intervention to the clients and possibly bring more positive outcomes.

What is the clinician's interpretation of clinical information? It is important to make clinicians' working hypotheses, or interpretations of the collected clinical information, as transparent as possible by illustrating a clear "chain of evidence" between the raw clinical case information and the clinicians' interpretations (Lee et al., 2010, p. 687). It is similar to differences between data collection and data analysis when conducting research. Comprehensive clinical information of the client in context using various subjects, perspectives, and places over time is like data collection that attempts a strong power and rigor in data. Clarifying the clinicians' understanding of, working hypotheses of, and critical analysis of the collected clinical information is like the data analysis process and the results section in the documentation of research findings. Clear documentation of the clinicians' interpretation would help counselors and psychotherapists consider alternative points that they have not thought about from the clinical information described. Or it may help mental health practitioners to reinterpret the raw clinical information and/or develop their own ideas and new perspectives, thus building a clinical knowledge base.

What is the client's feedback? Case study researchers argue that subjective data are subject to bias yet provide "the opportunity to develop in-depth and holistic descriptions of the participant's experience and behaviors, an essential feature of case study research" (Yin, 1994, p. 686). Therefore, "guidelines specific to evaluating the usefulness of case studies should include whether they convey the subjective experience of subjects" (Gilgun, 1994, p. 376). Case study is an in-depth study about clinicians as much as it is about clients under study. While reflecting clinicians' cultural values and theoretical orientations, case studies also clarify clinicians' interpretations of clinical information; clinicians say outwardly who they are in terms of personal and professional identities in many aspects of case study. Therefore, a central reference point as to whether the clinical information is comprehensively and exhaustively collected, whether the intervention is appropriately selected, and whether the clinician's interpretation is accurately capturing the client's experiences *is* the client. Every aspect of case study thus should incorporate the client's feedback. A case study should report how the client feedback was pursued and reflected in the course of therapy and evaluation of the case study outcome.

Guiding questions that mental health practitioners could ask include the following:

- Do the clinicians clearly document their working hypothesis/critical analysis/interpretations of clinical information?
- Do the clinicians collect and elaborate the clinical information over time to highlight the clinical processes?
- Do the clinicians describe the multiple sources of information (e.g., multiple subjects, multiple perspectives, and multiple places)?
- Do the clinicians note their rationale of choosing the particular case? What does this choice mean in terms of their cultural and theoretical orientations?
- Do the clinicians provide detailed descriptions of the selected interventions, including, for example, the target of the intervention, the intervention dosage, the intervention contents, context, and clinicians' qualifications and trainings?
- Do the clinicians report how the client feedback was pursued and reflected in the course of therapy and evaluation of the case study outcome?

In a similar manner, counselors and psychotherapists are encouraged to reflect on why they chose a certain case for an intensive case study, how they collected and elaborated their own clinical data over time to capture the intervention process, whether they used multiple sources of clinical information and clarified their own interpretation of clinical information, whether they provided details of their own choice of intervention procedures and ingredients, and whether they clearly incorporated their client's feedback and explained how they did so.

CLARIFYING AND REFLECTING A CLOSE ASSOCIATION WITH THEORIES

Although there have been some variations in terms of how closely the case study should be associated with theories, most scholars agree that one distinctive feature of the case study is its close relationship with theories; thus, case studies contribute toward theory building or theory testing (Bergen & While, 2000; Lee et al., 2010; Yin, 1994). Contrasting this to a statistical generalization of study findings in experimental studies, Yin (1994) highlighted the significance of providing in-depth understanding of the particular case and referred to it as "analytic generalization" in case study. Case study thus contributes generalization of study findings at the level of theory, such as corresponding with other cases or patterns predicted by theory or a deviant or unusual case that promotes an innovative mode of thinking and consequently modifies and expands our knowledge base in current theory (Flyvbjerg, 2006; Gilgun, 1992).

Theoretical approaches that a clinician uses provide the explanatory framework to understand presenting issues, possible potential causes, and plausible progress, and this framework guides the clinician to select specific tasks and techniques in treatment. Whether clinicians clarify their theoretical orientations or not, this guiding framework is fully in action during the therapy process and affects interpretation of outcomes and findings in case study. Clarifying theoretical orientations is even more critical in using global case studies because many counseling and psychotherapy theories are predominantly based on Euro-American Western dominance (Lee & Bhuyan, 2013). Although clinicians in different parts of the world adopt and adhere to a brand name of theory sprung from the Euro-American dominant culture (e.g., psychodynamic approaches, cognitive behavior therapy, emotionally focused therapy), the ways in which they carry and adapt these theories given their years of experience in working with their clients in context are a wealth of knowledge we as clinicians and researchers alike wish to learn from. Therefore, it is important that the clinicians provide a detailed description of therapy theories they select, a rationale of their choice, and how they carry on the selected therapy approaches.

In addressing complex and multiple issues in clients' lives and acknowledging the limitations of adhering to only one particular theoretical orientation, clinical researchers suggest considering and using "more than one theoretical approach or structured model" to facilitate "a flexible therapeutic approach [that] helps the therapist see the strengths and weaknesses" of each theoretical approach (Eells et al., 2011, p. 27). Because one theoretical approach is selected for each case and/ or because of page limits of each chapter, the rationale of the selection and the flexibility of its use in the selected theory should be clearly delineated. Sue (1998) noted the useful concept of "dynamic sizing"—that is, "knowing and using the theories well and also putting them aside to better understand and serve the client" (p. 446). He warned against rigidly adhering to theories and losing sight of comprehensively understanding the *person* of the client. Instead of relying solely on research findings, which are often based on summative populations or groups rather than individuals, more experienced clinicians adopt a more tentative use of language and rely on and reflect on the specific and unique clinical information of the client (Eells et al., 2011). This finding highlights the importance of flexibly using our theories in understanding and working with clients. In the end, clarifying, reflecting, and using a theory in case study is crucial not only in cumulating clinical knowledge while developing the analytic generalizability but also in achieving a goal of finding what works under what contexts and why for this idiosyncratic client—that is, developing *a theory of the client*.

Guiding questions that mental health practitioners could ask include the following:

- Are any alternative and/or traditional theoretical approaches considered as competing theories against the selected ones?
- Does a clinician clarify and reflect on his or her choice of theories and provide the rationale of the selection with respect to this particular client in his or her cultural locations?
- Does a clinician describe any adaptations of the selected theories with respect to this particular client in his or her cultural locations?
- How flexibly and/or rigidly do the clinicians describe their application of the selected theories?

In a similar manner, counselors and psychotherapists reading this book are encouraged to clarify and reflect on their own theoretical orientations and contemplate how well the clinicians' theoretical approaches fit with their own positions in working with a particular client. They are also encouraged to think about ways they may do the dynamic sizing to use theoretical approaches similar to the ones in this book.

Considering the View of Culture and the Intersectionality of Multiple Diversities

Case studies in this volume come from different times (e.g., past or present, a certain political era) and places (different countries, rural or urban, etc.). Even in the same case, a client and clinician may come from different backgrounds. In a similar manner, each mental health practitioner is situated in a unique time and place where culture or diversity is understood in his or her own unique contexts. In reading case studies in global contexts such as this volume, it is crucial to keep in mind how culture or diversity is described in each case—that is, how each clinician is considering and presenting similarities and differences between the client and the clinician and how the reader's (i.e., the mental health practitioner's) view of culture and diversity is similar to or different from the views conveyed in each case study. In that way, the case study "there and then" can be transferred to valuable examples for mental health practitioners to understand their own cases "here and now."

Soon after beginning to read the case study chapters, mental health practitioners will realize that many of the cases do not specifically indicate or discuss culture or diversity per se, except American, British, and Canadian case studies, where culture and diversity issues have been marked to be visible as politically correct and ethically responsible practice. In most of the case studies, culture and diversity issues are presented in a more or less implicit and nuanced manner. Therefore, readers should pay special attention to the case studies, carefully reviewing them in order to get a glimpse at how clients and clinicians in the real world—where culture and diversity matters are less visibly present than in practice discourse—address and work through their culturally embedded clinical issues. It is not uncommon to come across practice guidelines in American, British, and Canadian multicultural literature that invite diverse clients to explain their own cultural values, customs, and ideas and that suggest a clinician take a learner's position to get some knowledge of his or her client's culture (Lee & Bhuyan, 2013). Although useful, this approach is limited in that many clients who are bombarded with life stressors and psychological sufferings at the time of contacting clinicians struggle to explain more or less pervasively embedded cultural values and ideas. Besides, this approach is onerous in that it puts the responsibility of educating the clinician about one's culture onto a client, who is already vulnerable with presenting issues, for the convenience of a clinician. Studies on cross-cultural dialogues vividly illustrate that clinicians have often missed cues of cultural ideas and values that clients bring to their attention in clinical encounters (Lee & Bhuyan, 2013; Lee & Horvath, 2013, 2014). Therefore, it is invaluable to carefully review and use the case studies with embedded cultural values in a nuanced manner so we can develop our eyes and ears to tease out implicit cultural meanings. Then we can further consider effective ways to communicate our understanding of the embedded cultural meanings to clients in an explicit manner that will foster therapeutic engagement (Tsang, Bogo, & Lee, 2011).

In multicultural literatures, culture is often described as the background information of the person—something external rather than internal or psychological—which erroneously leads to the assumption that understanding the client's cultural group information (e.g., learning about between-group differences, such as Asian Canadian) may lead the clinician to better understand the client (e.g., adding the within-group individual differences, such as a third-generation, single Korean Canadian female). Yet, in a case study, it is crucial to be "client-specific" (Ho, 1995, p. 17) rather than cultural-group-specific. In this regard, Ho (1995) proposed the very useful concept of "internalized culture," translating the sociopolitical concept of culture into the psychological concept (Lee, 2010). It is defined as "the cultural influences operating within the individual that share (not determine) personality formation and various aspects of psychological functioning" (Ho, 1995, p. 5). To name a few, examples include child raising practices, preferences of marriage type and age as well as couple's relationship (e.g., romantic love, arranged marriage), how emotions are addressed (e.g., expressing or repressing anger, guilt, love), and normative human development cycle (e.g., appropriate type of dependence, independence, or interdependence as a male adolescent).

In an era of fast-growing global mobility and global population, the boundaries of group cultural membership are increasingly more fluid than earlier treatment models present, and "different cultural systems are internalized and coexist within the mind" (Ho, 1995, p. 13). In addition, at any given moment multiple cultural identities exist for both the client and the clinician, some in the foreground and others in the background. Because the client and clinician respectively bring their own multiple introjected or internalized cultural views (i.e., values, attitudes, and conventional ways of behaving within a culture) into the therapeutic encounter, it is crucial for clinicians to clarify and address the internalized multiple similarities and differences between client and clinician (Tsang, Bogo, & George, 2003).

Guiding questions that mental health practitioners could ask include the following:

- How does the clinician describe multiple cultural factors or Group of Seven identities in the case study?
- How do you think the cultural norms and values that clients and clinicians convey influence processes and paths of therapy, therapy relationship, and outcomes?

- What aspects of internalized culture have been noted or dismissed? How and by whom?
- What multiple and fluid aspects of culture within the therapy dyad have you observed?

In a similar manner, counselors and psychotherapists are encouraged to reflect on their own internalized culture and multiple cultural identities while reading case studies. For example, they should consider their initial reactions to particular presenting issues, contents that clients talk about, and/or ways that clinicians address issues. Consideration should include not only negative reactions but also positive ones, such as feeling comfortable and accustomed to ways that the therapy unfolds and is described in a certain case study. Clarifying counselors' and psychotherapists' own internal and multiple cultural views and ideas would help in making a decision as to whether the case study is applicable and receptive to their practice.

CONCLUSION

Seasoned clinicians spend hours, days, and years listening to a wide range of stories from various clients or, in a quantitative research term, numerous subjects. So-called well-validated, evidence-based treatment approaches have a number of subjects far below the wealth of these clinical data files if compiled systemically. For example, case study books such as this volume of systemically compiled case studies then move from a valuable but fragmented single case study to create what Fishman (2005) called a "case database." This case database that preserves the individual uniqueness of each case is qualitatively different from other experimental studies that merge "individual case information into group data and, in the process, strip away individual context and reduce qualitatively complex processes to numbers" in order to achieve generalization (Fishman, 2005, p. 34).

Case study is not looking at clients under a microscope and positioning them as "others" to be studied and changed. This guideline is thus intended to move the dynamics of the observer–observed the other way around, encouraging mental health practitioners to be mindful of how clinicians "own their own perspectives" (Fishman, 2005, p. 12)—including their multiple cultural values, theoretical orientations, and preference of techniques and personal anticipations—and consider the role these play in the therapy process and outcomes. This ontological shift in rethinking case study is even more crucial when we review case studies from around the world. In a similar manner, mental health practitioners are encouraged to observe not only the clinicians' reflections on the case presented but also their own reflections, for example, considering their own cultural/theoretical perspectives and details of their clients' contextual information when contemplating the transferability of the cases discussed in this book. In this way, cases from different countries and their presentations of suffering and coping can help mental health practitioners who work with clients originally affiliated with or emigrated from these countries, but they can also help practitioners understand some clients in their caseload here and now who exhibit similar issues.

REFERENCES

Bergen, A., & While, A. (2000). A case for case studies: Exploring the use of case study research in community nursing research. *Journal of Advanced Nursing, 31,* 926–934.

Eells, T. D., Lombart, K. G., Salsman, N., Kendjelic, E. M., Schneiderman, C. T., & Lucas, C. P. (2011). Expert reasoning in psychotherapy case formulation. *Psychotherapy Research, 21,* 385–399.

Fishman, D. B. (2005). Editor's introduction to PCSP: From single case to database: A new method for enhancing psychotherapy practice. *Pragmatic Case Studies in Psychotherapy, 1,* 1–50.

Flyvbjerg, B. (2006). Five misunderstandings about case-study research. *Qualitative Inquiry, 12,* 219–245.

Gilgun, J. F. (1992). Hypothesis generation in social work research. *Journal of Social Service Research, 15,* 113–135.

Gilgun, J. F. (1994). A case for case studies in social work research. *Social Work, 39,* 371–380.

Ho, D. Y. F. (1995). Internalized culture, culturocentrism, and transcendence. *The Counseling Psychologist, 23,* 4–24.

Kazdin, A. E. (1981). Drawing valid inference from case studies. *Journal of Consulting and Clinical Psychology, 49,* 183–192.

Lee, E. (2010). Revisioning cultural competencies in clinical social work practice. *Families in Society, 91,* 272–279.

Lee, E., & Bhuyan, R. (2013). Negotiating within Whiteness in cross-cultural clinical encounter. *Social Service Review, 87,* 98–130.

Lee, E., & Horvath, A. O. (2013). Early cultural dialogues in cross-cultural clinical practice. *Smith College Studies in Social Work, 83,* 185–212.

Lee, E., & Horvath, A. O. (2014). How a therapist responds to cultural versus non-cultural dialogues in cross-cultural clinical practice. *Journal of Social Work Practice, 28,* 193–217. doi:10.1080/02650533.2013.821104

Lee, E., Mishna, F., & Brennenstuhl, S. (2010). How to critically evaluate case studies in social work. *Research on Social Work Practice, 20,* 682–689.

Meyer, C. B. (2001). A case in case study methodology. *Field Methods, 13,* 329–352.

Sue, S. (1998). In search of cultural competence in psychotherapy and counseling. *American Psychologist, 53,* 440–448.

Tsang, A. K. T., Bogo, M., & George, U. (2003). Critical issues in cross-cultural counseling research: Case example of an ongoing project. *Journal of Multicultural Counseling and Development, 31,* 63–78.

Tsang, A. K. T., Bogo, M., & Lee, E. (2011). Engagement in cross-cultural clinical practice: Narrative analysis of first session. *Clinical Social Work Journal, 39,* 79–90.

Yin, R. K. (1994). *Case study research: Design and methods. Applied social research methods series* (Vol. 5). Thousand Oaks, CA: Sage.

Part Two

Counseling and Psychotherapy in Africa

Chapter 2

COUNSELING AND PSYCHOTHERAPY IN EGYPT: OMAR'S STORY

Mona M. Amer

INTRODUCTION

Egypt is an Arabic-speaking country located at the northeast tip of Africa. Centuries of intercultural trade and negative economic consequences of colonization have produced a nation riddled with socioeconomic tensions and cultural inconsistencies (Amer, El-Sayeh, Fayad, & Khoury, 2015). These contradictions are quite visible. For example, in the capital city of Cairo, 60% of residents—a large proportion of whom are migrants from the rural governorates—live in abject informal settlements, including slum and squatter areas (Kipper & Fischer, 2009). These settlements are often nestled against lavish high-rises and gated communities that cater to the urban elite, who have adopted some of the languages, worldviews, and traditions of European and American cultures.

Psychotherapy and counseling in Egypt reflect these class distinctions and intercultural exchanges with the West. Competent psychotherapists typically work in the larger cities, serving mostly those from the upper and middle classes. Mental health models and interventions are largely imported from Europe and the United States, without systematic efforts to empirically assess their effectiveness or foster indigenous techniques. There are no comprehensive psychotherapy training programs at Egyptian universities that combine formal didactic instruction with intensive supervision, and there is minimal oversight and regulation of the professions. As a result, many therapists develop their skills in a patchwork fashion, borrowing from different theoretical models on the basis of trial and error and consultation with senior clinicians (Amer, 2013).

The eclectic nature of therapy in Egypt is illustrated in this chapter with the story of Omar. The chapter demonstrates how issues of diversity—particularly class, gender, age, and religion—intersected with his presenting problems and the therapy process. Like many practitioners in the larger city centers, the therapist in this case example had been influenced by Western models, and she changed therapy format and focus more than once during the process in order to support Omar's needs.

THE CLIENT

Omar is a 36-year-old heterosexual husband and father of two boys, ages 12 and 8. Throughout his life, he has identified himself first and foremost as Muslim; and he is keen to pray the five daily prayers and attend Friday congregational prayers. However, beyond these rituals he has not participated in many Islamic practices or focused on his religion. During his childhood, Omar lived many years in an international compound in Kuwait; later, he relocated to Cairo, where he attended English-language schools. As a result, he has been affiliated with the transnational ("third culture") community, without opportunity to nurture a sense of Egyptian nationalism or Arab identity.

PRESENTING ISSUES AND CHALLENGES

Omar's attachment to Egypt was wavering at the time when he sought therapy. He was considering immigrating to another country to escape feelings of frustration and hopelessness across multiple domains of his life, including work and family. His private furniture design and import business had not seen any significant transactions in more than 6 months. Aside from the economic downturn affecting the nation as a whole, Omar attributed his work challenges to difficulties expressing himself in Arabic and understanding the subtle indirect communication styles common in Egypt. He also complained that opportunities were monopolized by businessmen who were older and more established, and that buyers and colleagues often missed meetings or did not pay him according to schedule.

Financial constraints had affected the social status of Omar's family. Omar and his wife, Aleya, were urban Cairenes who had studied in foreign language schools, and therefore they could be described as upper-middle class. Moving to a gated community in a New Cairo suburb 4 years ago additionally elevated their social status. Because of the salience of classism in Egyptian society, this was an aspect of identity that Omar and Aleya invested a great deal of effort to preserve and exhibit. However, such appearances of affluence had been more difficult to maintain in recent months.

The family's financial pressures had begun to affect their relationships at home. Omar had felt increasingly defective in his ability to support his family as the man of the house. He compensated by asserting greater control and dominance, leading to frequent arguments with Aleya. The conflicts often intensified to Omar shouting, and twice he shoved his wife. Both of them showed little frustration tolerance toward their children, reacting harshly toward behaviors (such as bickering) that would be appropriate for their ages. At the time of Omar's self-referral, the boys' behaviors had escalated to what Omar perceived as "out of control" and "extremely disrespectful." He was concerned that the boys' acting out would be noticed in public settings, causing embarrassment to the family's reputation and cultured image—an image that Omar had valued since he was a child himself.

CASE HISTORY AND DEVELOPMENTAL BACKGROUND

Although Omar was born in Cairo, from the ages of 4 to 12 he was raised in Kuwait. He lived with his parents in a private compound with neighbors from diverse nationalities. He did not have any siblings; however, he was social, joining friends in activities such as swimming and tennis. His mother was a homemaker who was devoted to caring for Omar and his father. This model of the wife showing deference to the husband influenced Omar's gender-role concepts. His father worked for a petroleum company that funded their living and educational expenses, making it possible for Omar to attend the highest ranking international school.

When the family returned to Egypt, Omar joined a school that followed the American curriculum. The majority of the students were Egyptian, however, and many of his classmates scoffed at his Arabic and English accents, presumably out of jealousy that they could not quite master the Americanized accent that he had gained in Kuwait. Omar did not share the same interests with many of his peers. This period of difficulty ended when he enrolled in a private English-language university that had a more diverse student body, including those who had also been raised in the transnational culture. He spent his free time and weekends with his new friends at one of the exclusive sporting clubs.

After completing his bachelor's degree in economics, Omar established his own furniture business. At the time when he was starting the company, he was introduced to Aleya through his social network, and they were married a year later. Aleya was impressed with Omar's entrepreneurship and charisma. Omar felt comfortable interacting with Aleya because she also spoke other languages and came from a family with a good name. Her father's family had been well-known for their success in numerous businesses since the time of the British occupation of Egypt. After graduating with a French literature degree from Cairo Central University, Aleya was offered a job at one of her father's textile companies for a moderate salary.

THE THERAPY

In his first meeting with Rasha, the therapist, Omar mentioned that he had chosen her to be his therapist upon the recommendation of his friends because he was searching for a psychologist who understood English and had some exposure to Western cultures. Rasha had completed a bachelor's degree in psychology at an elite private English-language university in Cairo. She subsequently earned a diploma in clinical psychology (focused mostly on psychological testing) from Cairo Central University, followed by a master's degree that primarily entailed a research thesis. She had gained most of her therapy skills from consulting with senior practitioners and attending practical training workshops. She was currently enrolled in an online counseling doctoral degree offered by a U.S. university.

Omar met with Rasha over 8 months, with numerous appointment cancellations throughout this time. The therapy process could be viewed as divided into three phases. The first phase focused on Omar's feelings of inadequacy at work and at home and his fantasies of immigrating and leaving these frustrations behind. The therapist helped him articulate his ideals of what makes a successful businessman (largely drawn from rich and powerful characters he had viewed on Egyptian TV series) and how he could build his repertoire of skills to perform better at work. He also expressed frustration about the double bind of being too young to be respected compared with more distinguished businessmen and yet too old to begin reestablishing his business in another country. Integrating a dynamic approach to the work, the therapist helped Omar gain insights into how his experiences paralleled the feelings of frustration and not living up to model standards that he felt in his relationship with his father.

When Omar's complaints about tensions at home persisted, the therapist invited the family to session. Omar agreed, with the stipulation that the emphasis be on parenting strategies, as he was not willing to discuss marital issues. Rasha agreed to these conditions. During this second phase of the therapy, Rasha met several times with Omar and Aleya as well as with the children. Rasha became more appreciative of the high levels of stress affecting the family. Omar spent long hours of frantic high-tension work at his office, often returning home near midnight. In turn, Aleya shouldered the responsibility of caring for the children's schooling needs and extracurricular activities after she returned from work and on the weekends. Omar felt increasingly marginalized as the man of the house and was angry that Aleya did not follow through with his commands on how to parent in his absence. For example, a topic of frequent conflict was that Aleya did not require their eldest son to pray the daily prayers, which Aleya did not believe to be a priority. Aleya was angry at not being treated as an equal in the decision making.

Many sessions focused on stress management, including behavioral techniques for recognizing and reducing emotional flooding. Parenting techniques were discussed, and the therapist normalized much of the children's behaviors. She explained that behaviors that were perceived to be disrespectful—such as disagreeing loudly or slouching when sitting—were not surprising given their upbringing. The boys attended English-language schools and watched American TV shows, and yet the parents unreasonably expected them to interact according to traditional Egyptian standards for child behavior. Moreover, the parents' high levels of stress led them to overreact to the children's behaviors, so the boys were acting out in response to this high-tension environment. The parents agreed with these observations and negotiated practical agreements to reduce stress. For example, Omar arrived home early one day a week, giving Aleya a chance to take a break from the strains of parenting.

Over time Omar and Aleya showed greater willingness to explore their marital struggles, and the therapy transitioned into the third phase. Although the therapist had originally conceptualized the marital dyad to be the main source of family conflict, it was not until the focus was taken off this relationship and instead concentrated on relieving general family stress that the couple became more open to discussing their relationship. They revealed that their marital problems had become so intense in recent years that their parents and siblings had become involved. After family meetings were not successful in resolving the conflicts, Omar's mother had pressured the couple to seek support from a sheikh (religious leader). The sheikh advised Aleya to cover her hair and be more obedient to her husband in order to save the marriage. This advice angered Aleya, who felt unfairly blamed.

In sessions with Omar and Aleya alone, much of the discussion related to these kinds of tensions in gender roles. For example, Aleya felt marginalized both at home and at work, and she wished to be treated as an equal partner. Contradictions in Omar's values were explored. While he expected Aleya to be subservient to his commands, he showed deference toward other women, including the therapist. Although he presented himself as a Westernized businessman at work, he wanted to be treated as the traditional man of the house at home. Omar was largely unwilling to acknowledge these contradictions, but Aleya expressed satisfaction that at least she had a chance to share her voice in session. The couple's visitations became less frequent at the time of their children's end-of-the-year examinations. During the children's summer break the family traveled to London for a vacation, and although Omar promised to resume therapy after their return, he did not contact the therapist again.

DISCUSSION AND ANALYSIS

The ease with which Omar initiated and ended therapy may seem unusual within the Egyptian context. For many Egyptian men, admission of psychological distress may be seen as undermining their masculinity (Okasha, 2004), and it is common for men to refuse therapy to avoid shame and blame. In Omar's situation, however, coming to therapy was consistent with the cultured Western image that he wished to portray. He was not suffering from any disability or mental illness that would have made therapy a sign of weakness. His willingness to bring his wife and children to session moreover suited his image as the leader of the family; he requested that all contacts be made through him and spoke about the therapy as if it was a provision he was giving to his family, similar to food or money. He wanted to ensure that he was obtaining the highest class product and as such was reassured that the therapist had had some exposure to American culture. It would have been expected for Omar to resume therapy after the family trip to London as a show of respect to an authority figure (the therapist) and in light of his complaints about other Egyptians not keeping to promised appointments. However, he may have been unwilling to face continued exploration of his contributions to the marital discord.

Omar's family vacation to London at a time of financial constraints is an example of the contradictions that he showed in negotiating multiple aspects of his identity. He was maintaining the image of the urban socialite while struggling to make an income in a nation that he had never quite felt attached to. Omar's educational training in the Americanized transnational culture had provided him with the entrepreneurial skills and confidence to establish his own business. At the same time, it made it difficult for him to communicate within the high-context Arab culture (Samovar, Porter, McDaniel, & Roy, 2013), in which messages are often subtle and time orientation is less precise. This difficulty in communication negatively affected his success at work, leading to financial pressures and fears of losing his family's social status. He also felt small and inconsequential compared with his older and more successful business colleagues.

Omar felt unable to maintain control over his financial status, wife, and children. In response, he had reacted by becoming increasingly authoritarian; for example, he insisted that the family comply with religious regulations although he, himself, was not highly religious. Thus, although religion could have been a source of support and resilience to the family, instead it was perceived by Aleya to be a burden, particularly after the sheikh they visited had endorsed the traditional marital gender roles that Aleya disagreed with. Aleya reacted to Omar's increased authoritarianism by becoming angry and confrontational. Omar and Aleya were consumed by their marital conflicts and stress and in turn had become impatient and harsh with the children, who reacted to the tensions by engaging in more disruptive behaviors. This behavior contributed further to Omar's experience of losing his grasp over his family, and thus this cycle continued.

Because Rasha had not been trained in family systems therapy, she may not have recognized this example of circular causality and other systems dynamics, such as the positive feedback loops that contributed to the family distress. Had family therapy been used, Omar and his wife may have gained greater insight into the transmission of cultural values and practices (such as gender roles) from their families of origin and how the tensions within their own marital dyad could not realistically be isolated from tensions with the children. Instead, most of the techniques used with the family were based on individual therapy, primarily cognitive behavior therapy. The therapy techniques used in this case are not unusual in Egypt, where the central importance of family means that family members often attend therapy sessions even though there are no institutionalized family therapy training programs. Many therapists in Egypt instead depend on their own creativity and self-learning to find ways to effectively serve their clients, including extrapolating individual therapy concepts and techniques to relational issues. It is not uncommon for a therapist to use eclectic approaches or to shift therapy styles midprocess.

One of Rasha's strengths as a therapist was her attunement to cultural sensitivities. For example, she understood the importance of maintaining alliance and therefore did not pressure the couple to discuss their marital concerns. She was not surprised that the couple had previously chosen to reveal those same concerns to other persons who were not professionals. Interventions from family and religious supports are common in in the Arab world (Lambert, 2008). Although the therapy terminated without resolution of the marital problems, it is likely that even if Omar had resumed therapy, he would have continued to place boundaries on exploring sensitive marital issues, such as those related to intimacy. Self-disclosure and exploration of intimacies may be avoided by Arab clients (Dwairy, 2006).

CONCLUSION

In many ways, Omar's case represents the intercultural complexities of living in a diverse nation such as Egypt. Omar had faced numerous stressors adjusting to different cultural contexts as he was growing up in Kuwait and Egypt, and he continued to face subtle intercultural challenges communicating with other Egyptians within his own nation of birth. He also showed contradictions regarding gender, religion, nationalism, and other aspects of his identity. These contradictions emerged during the therapeutic process because they were fueling some of the tensions of the family context. Although the family did not continue therapy, they did benefit from gaining greater awareness of how stress was negatively affecting the family dynamics. They were supported by gaining some practical strategies to reduce tension, which allowed the family members to interact in more positive ways with one another.

QUESTIONS

1. What privileges did Omar gain through his education in the transnational culture that positively affected not only his social status but also his ability to use therapy?
2. How would the therapeutic conceptualization, focus, and techniques have differed if the therapist had been trained in family systems therapy?
3. What were the benefits and drawbacks of the shifts in therapeutic modalities and topics of focus across the three phases of Omar's therapy?

4. If you were Omar's therapist, how would you have conceptualized and treated him differently on the basis of your own therapeutic orientation?
5. What kinds of therapy techniques could have better supported Omar in exploring the incongruities in his national, religious, and gender identities?

REFERENCES

Amer, M. M. (2013). Counseling and psychotherapy in Egypt: Ambiguous identity of a regional leader. In R. Moodley, U. P. Gielen, & R. Wu (Eds.), *Handbook of counseling and psychotherapy in an international context* (pp. 19–29). New York, NY: Routledge.

Amer, M. M., El-Sayeh, S., Fayad, Y., & Khoury, B. (2015). Community psychology and civil society: Opportunities for growth in Egypt and Lebanon. *Journal of Community Psychology, 43*, 49–62.

Dwairy, M. (2006). *Counseling and psychotherapy with Arabs and Muslims: A culturally sensitive approach*. New York, NY: Teachers College Press.

Kipper, R., & Fischer, M. (Eds.). (2009). *Cairo's informal areas: Between urban challenges and hidden potentials. Facts. Voices. Visions*. Zamalek, Cairo: GTZ Egypt.

Lambert, L. (2008). A counselling model for young women in the United Arab Emirates: Cultural considerations. *Canadian Journal of Counselling, 42*, 101–116.

Okasha, A. (2004). Focus on psychiatry in Egypt. *The British Journal of Psychiatry, 185*, 266–272.

Samovar, L. A., Porter, R. E., McDaniel, E. R., & Roy, C. S. (2013). *Communication between cultures* (8th ed.). Boston, MA: Wadsworth.

Chapter 3

COUNSELING AND PSYCHOTHERAPY IN WEST AFRICA: MAZABALO'S STORY

Lonzozou Kpanake

INTRODUCTION

Togo is a West African country with approximately 7 million people. It is a multi-ethnic society encompassing a wide variety of cultures that reflect the influences of its many ethnic groups, the largest and most influential of which are the Ewe, Kabye, Kotokoli, and Ouatchi. In terms of religion in Togo, most people have indigenous beliefs (e.g., Voodoo), yet there are also significant Christian and Muslim minorities. Though French language is commonly used in public life, it is only the fourth most-spoken first language, behind indigenous Africans languages, such as Ewe, Kabye, and Kotokoli (Central Intelligence Agency, 2013).

When exploring the worldview of ethnic groups in Togo, Blier (1996) found them to be fundamentally spiritual and collectivist. That is, their worldview draws no sharp boundaries between the individual and the group but instead stresses the collective as the essential frame of reference and source of meaning. The interdependence of the person and his or her kinship gives rise to an understanding of mental illness as a failure to maintain channels of connection with the person's communal agency. Thus, the ill person is not responsible for the affliction, because the individual is not an isolated entity but, rather, an embodiment of the social order.

In West African cosmology, humans are a link in the cosmic chain of events that summons lower orders (minerals, plants, and animals) to join higher ones (spirits, ancestors, and God). West Africans incorporate invisible entities into their daily life. These spiritual entities constitute forces that constantly influence the course of the person's life through beneficial or harmful events. Ancestors are the closest links that the person has with the spiritual world. The place of ancestors in the person's life reflects the belief that the dead person does not wholly disappear. The ancestors are the "living dead," members of the kin who have died but continue to live as "shades." As such, they have a profound influence on the individual's daily life. Ancestors are guardians of family affairs, traditions, and ethics and are enforcers of the social order (Vontress, 2005). They act as the guide, the watchperson over the individual, offering protection from seen or unseen malevolent beings, illness, social misfortune, and destroyers of the kinship.

In exploring the understanding of mental health issues among African populations, research has identified a general tendency for mental illness to be attributed to supernatural spiritual activities (Vontress, 2005). In line with these explanations, African patients construe their distress in cultural idioms that implicate entities of the invisible world. The phenomenological world of Africans is holistic, with no clear boundary between the self, the kinship, and the spiritual world; thus, balance is a pivotal concept.

In this chapter, I present a case where a culturally adapted therapy was used with a young adult from Togo who presented with anxiety and somatizations. The client, Mazabalo, is described, with a focus on his understanding of his illness and the healing process. The chapter concludes with an emphasis on key aspects of the therapeutic process.

THE CLIENT

Mazabalo was a 27-year-old man who attended University of Lomé in Togo, where he was completing a bachelor's degree in law. When he came to consult some 5 years ago at the mental health clinic of University of Lomé Teaching Hospital, he was in his senior year in the law program. He lived with his uncle and several other relatives. He was heterosexual, unmarried, and had no visible disabilities. He was from the Kabye ethnic group in the northern regions of Togo, had received Catholic baptism, attended church regularly, and self-identified as a Christian.

PRESENTING ISSUES AND CHALLENGES

As the university final examinations date approached, Mazabalo started to feel quite anxious and experienced difficulty with concentration, headaches, and sleep disturbances. When his suffering started he felt it was a manifestation of malaria, a disease he had experienced numerous times. As was his habit, he bought antimalarial drugs in a local market stall and took them, but no changes occurred. One week later, he consulted a general physician, who recommended a blood test. Finding nothing wrong with him, the physician prescribed some vitamins and referred him to the mental health service. When Mazabalo came to see us at the mental health service, his most troublesome presenting concern was chronic headaches. He was received in consultation by a team composed of five counselors. The counseling team's orientation takes into account social and cultural contexts to provide valuable counseling services.

CASE HISTORY AND DEVELOPMENTAL BACKGROUND

Mazabalo was born in a polygamous family. His father was a 55-year-old man who was a primary school principal and had five wives and 21 children. Mazabalo's mother was a 46-year-old woman who was a midwife and the first wife. Both parents lived and worked in Tcharé, a mountain village in the northern part of the country located 420 kilometers north of Lomé, the capital city of Togo. Mazabalo's kin are originally from that region (Kara region), the homeland of the Kabye ethnic group. Mazabalo was raised there, like members of his kin, until he attended the country's only university, which is located in the capital city. Like other members of the clan, Mazabalo had followed all the rites of passage required for each developmental stage and had participated in many of his traditional ethnic group's ceremonies.

Mazabalo's father was diagnosed with a metastatic bone cancer. Although he did not deny this diagnosis, he and his family consulted a traditional healer, who attributed his sickness to sorcery action from Bidjada, his third wife. From that time on, Mazabalo's father resided in the traditional healer's home, where he was receiving treatment. He was living there with his fifth wife, who was in charge of cooking and providing personal care to him. After 5 months, this fifth wife had a heart attack and died. That death was attributed to Bidjada's sorcery action aimed at making Mazabalo's father more vulnerable.

THE THERAPY

It became evident to the counseling team at the outset that Mazabalo's symptoms began when his father was admitted to the hospital suffering from tibia pain caused by cancer. Using family systems questions consistent with West African cultural context, we discovered how close Mazabalo was to his maternal side of the family. We wondered if consulting with some members of his maternal lineage would be beneficial; among the Kabye, it is believed that the person "belongs" to his maternal lineage. Mazabalo agreed, and invitation was extended to three family members.

Mazabalo attended the following session accompanied by the elder of his maternal lineage as well as one uncle and one aunt. He said he could not take the final examination because his headaches had been so intense that he was not capable of concentrating and reading. He felt very anxious about his education and angry with himself for not being able to take the examination, though he felt much more anxious for his life. During this session the accompanying family members told us how all the members of the clan were proud of Mazabalo's educational achievements; he was not only the first of the clan to get a university degree but the first to complete elementary school. He was aspiring to become a magistrate. The elder of the clan said, "He is the one who would raise our *djedjewiye's* [clan's] name."

When asked about their feelings toward the difficulties Mazabalo was facing in his educational life, the family's elder responded, "The rest of it is in the hands of ancestors, and they will not accept that their names be annihilated." When asked for clarification, Mazabalo's uncle stated that "some turmoil is happening in the djedjewiye, and we have to react before it becomes too late." He then disclosed the illness of Mazabalo's father, the death of one of Mazabalo's stepmothers, "and now the blockage of our child's promising future, all in a 5-month period." He added, "All that is too much to keep sleeping, so we went to ask [a traditional healer]. It was revealed that there is a person that integrates the clan who is responsible for those bad things." When asked for further clarifications about Mazabalo's stepmother's responsibility in the sicknesses and the death among the family, Mazabalo's uncle explained, "After a violent quarrel with her husband, Bidjada, whose eyes see [meaning she has supernatural powers enabling her to see the invisible world], told her husband she would make him suffer for the rest of his life. Our brother-in-law [Mazabalo's father] started feeling pain in his right leg the following day." We assessed how much credence the family gave to this interpretation. Mazabalo's uncle stated that Bidjada's responsibility had been established by two traditional healers they consulted independently. He added, "These healers told us that several members of the family, including Mazabalo, his father, and his stepmother who died are in fact victims of *Kamtou*; that woman [Bidjada] has captured their *Kalizo* [souls] and confined them at the bottom of Kara river." Kamtou is a popular practice among the Kabye consisting of a witch person capturing another person's Kalizo and confining it in a relatively unattainable place (e.g., the bottom of a lake or river or inside a grave). From that moment, the person who is a victim of Kamtou becomes sick and may die unless his or her family consults a traditional healer, who would determine the cause of the illness and perform appropriate rituals to release the captured Kalizo. The sick person recovers when his or her Kalizo gets back to him or her.

The counseling team asked Mazabalo how much he believed in such narratives. He stated, "Jesus said, 'If forces of Goodness exist, therefore forces of the nether world exist too.' I am a Christian, and I know the devil exists." One member of the clinical team asked Mazabalo if he wanted to be involved with his family in a traditional healing, and he declined. Mazabalo expressed concern about the embarrassment that would be brought upon members of his church if his participation in a traditional healing became public knowledge within his Christian community. He could even be excommunicated from his church. He also stated that he believes in Jesus Christ and is certain that Jesus Christ is "stronger" than satanic forces. Mazabalo then elaborated, "Actually, as a Christian I cannot engage in these traditional healing procedures. I believe they are powerful. A couple of years ago I witnessed a neighbor recover from Kamtou, but because I am now a Christian, I cannot continue in that way." We (the counseling team) helped Mazabalo find a compromise, in which he would not participate in the traditional healing ceremony himself but would delegate his maternal uncle to make all the traditional healing ceremony requests. In addition, he had the idea of "organizing with other members of the clan who are Christians, 1 week of fasting and prayer in order to implore God's protection against the current turmoil in the family."

In the following session, 1 month later, Mazabalo reported that the elders of his kin and two traditional healers performed the *Kalizo kpèzeou* [soul releasing] ceremony, as expected. He also said, "The traditional healers had requested that in order to strengthen their intervention, the family has to perform a ritual slaughtering of a white ram to beg for Mazabalo's founding ancestor's protection." In addition, Mazabalo, one of his aunts, and two of his cousins who are Christians organized a *novena* [9 days of prayers] and requested one Sunday worship to protect the whole family.

We (the counseling team) encouraged Mazabalo in his attempt to have some control over his life through spiritual actions. Furthermore, using cognitive restructuring techniques, we helped him learn to accept the idea that African ontological beliefs can coexist with Christianity.

One month later, at the tenth session, when asked about what had improved since the first session, Mazabalo responded that he had noticed improvements in anxiety, concentration, and sleep and reported "feeling full of serenity because I know I am now on the right way." When invited to return in the next month for additional support, he said, "I feel stronger now, I am winning the battle." In sum, he felt ready to end the counseling.

DISCUSSION AND ANALYSIS

Human beings do not exist in isolation; each of us lives and grows up in some specific social and cultural setting. That setting is the context in which we develop our ideas about our way of being in the world. This cultural context influences the system of meanings we confer on mental illness, our experience of mental illness, our help-seeking behavior, and our expectations of recovery. Analysis of this case points out the influence of West African ontology, which provided a framework to the client and his kin group—an understanding of the cause of the illness for which they consulted as well as their expectations for recovery. Consistent with this population's worldview, the meanings of affliction could not be understood independently of the client's kin group, his spiritual world, and his individual self-projects. These agencies, which are interconnected with the client, are inextricably interdependent. Mazabalo's illness was not a manifestation of his individual self alone. As such, psychotherapy that centered only on Mazabalo's self-history would likely lead to failure to fully understand what was involved in this case. By considering the cultural context of the case, the clinical team discovered that in the client's view, as with his family's view, he was not responsible for his sickness. Rather, he was one of the victims of Bidjada's malevolent actions. That is, Mazabalo's problems were a manifestation suggesting there were disturbances in his kin's social order. Ignoring such a significant causality of the client's illness would have led to inappropriate therapeutic goals. Following the lead of the client's spiritual engagement, the clinical team recognized and honored his spiritual agency, which was also used in the recovery procedures. Entities of the spiritual agency involved in this case were God, who was petitioned through the novena, fasting, and Sunday worship, and ancestors, who were petitioned through traditional rituals. As explained earlier, both Christian and African traditional worldviews coexist harmoniously within many Christians in West Africa.

Such an intervention may have positive effects on the patient health because it has addressed the fundamental need to establish, repair, and maintain links to family, community, and the spirits that are essential for the African concept of the healthy person. The intervention attempted to identify the nature of the patient's person disconnectedness and then to help him engage his self, his spiritual agency, and his social agency in order to reestablish the oneness and harmony within his person's agencies. This task was accomplished by involving his kin-group members in the therapy process, by supporting his spiritual projects, and by promoting self-enhancement. In African cultural context, such an approach is more readily understood and accepted by patients because it fits with the African cultural worldview. The present case shows the nature of the phenomenological world among African people, which is fundamentally holistic, with no clear boundary between the self, the social world, and the spiritual world. In addition, it shows that reestablishing connectedness within the person promotes his or her psychic function, and the balance between the client's social and spiritual agencies is a pivotal concept of recovery.

Furthermore, analysis of African traditional healing practices—services that 70% to 90% of African people rely on for treatment of mental illness (Mkhize, 2004)— shows that their healing principles rely on the cultural framework discussed earlier. In fact, within African traditional healing paradigms, medicine, spirituality, and community are virtually inseparable (Blier, 1996; Hammon-Tooke, 1989; Vontress, 2005). Traditional healing goals of wholeness and harmony within the person are achieved through family involvement in the healing ceremony, which represents a form of conflict resolution for anomic and fragmented kinship, and through rituals that are devised to manage the person's connectedness with his or her spiritual entities.

The therapeutic function of traditional healing in restoring the African person's equilibrium and balance has been analyzed in a psychodynamic perspective (Weinrich 1989/1990). Writing from a post-Jungian perspective, Hillman (1995) found an analogy between animal sacrifice performed during healing rituals and the symbolic sacrifice of the individual's ego, which saves the person from an overwhelming or inflated ego. This deflation of the ego helps to reset the balance in the disturbed person and to recover the totality of personhood, which extends well beyond the individual ego.

CONCLUSION

African cultural systems of thoughts, values, and social norms are fundamentally distinct and different from other cultures. For decades, the approach toward mental illness in West Africa has been dominated by Eurocentric worldviews, with potential biases, such as misdiagnosis of mental illness and inappropriate therapeutic goals for African clients. In fact, not taking seriously African people's ontology and worldview can severely limit the ability of counseling and psychotherapy to evolve or grow. West African cultural ontology and worldview lie behind West African people's notions of health, illness, and recovery. In counseling with African clients, this framework suggests the value of an approach that emphasizes the two fundamental psychic processes inspired by African traditional healing: establishing links and containment. To work in this mode, clinicians should consider the following in the healing process: (a) involvement of the patient's family and community members, (b) respect of the patient's spiritual narratives as objective realities, and (c) African ontology. Such a therapeutic approach would stress the whole person's change, rather than aiming to produce an internal reorganization of the client's inner self.

QUESTIONS

1. How could a therapist involve an African client's family in counseling?
2. How could a therapist work with an African client's supernatural entities?
3. Does therapist–client cultural match enhance counseling efficiency?
4. What can therapists learn from African traditional healing practices?
5. How could therapists integrate African traditional ontology into counseling?

REFERENCES

Blier, S. P. (1996). *African vodun: Art, psychology, and power*. Chicago, IL: University of Chicago Press.

Central Intelligence Agency (2013). *The World Factbook: Togo*. Retrieved from https://www.cia.gov/library/publications/the-world-factbook/geos/to.html

Hammon-Tooke, W. D. (1989). *Rituals and medicines*. Johannesburg, South Africa: Donger.

Hillman, J. (1995). *Healing fiction*. Woodstock, CT: Spring.

Mkhize, N. (2004). Psychology: An African perspective. In D. Hook (Ed.), *Critical psychology* (pp. 24–52). Lansdowne, Cape Town, South Africa: UCT Press.

Vontress, C. E. (2005). Animism: Foundation of traditional healing in sub-Saharan Africa. In R. Moodley & W. West (Eds.), *Integrating traditional healing practices into counseling and psychotherapy* (pp. 124–137). Thousand Oaks, CA: Sage.

Weinrich, H. (1989/1990). African spirit beliefs in the light of Jungian thought. *Harvest, 35,* 168–180.

Chapter 4

COUNSELING AND PSYCHOTHERAPY IN NIGERIA: DAYO'S STORY

Olaniyi Bojuwoye

INTRODUCTION

Nigeria is the largest West African country, with more than 400 heterogeneous ethnic groups, making it the most ethnically diverse country in Africa. Although there are commonalities in traditional and cultural practices among these heterogeneous ethnic groups, Nigerian cultures have been largely infiltrated by foreign Western cultural influences, leading to drastic conflicts. Nigeria is also experiencing a number of economic and political problems because of deterioration in nearly all areas of Nigerian public life.

Traditional cultural psychotherapeutic practices in Nigeria have been in existence since time immemorial, although Western-oriented models of counseling and psychotherapy have also taken root, especially in educational and health settings. However, Nigerian traditional psychotherapeutic and related cultural practices continue to flourish, servicing more than 60% of the population (Bojuwoye, 2001; Pelzer, 1995). Relying on indigenous knowledge and cultural practices transmitted from generation to generation, mostly verbally, traditional psychotherapeutic practices have evolved unique methods and strategies for diagnosis, treatment, prevention, and elimination of physical, mental, and social ill health and/or diseases, thereby bringing well-being to the people (Adekson, 2003). The various paradigms of illness and health that are bound to cultures, social constructions, and worldviews also inform various cultural models and approaches to psychotherapeutic practices for the delivery of physical, mental, social, and spiritual health. In terms of actual practice, the theories informing treatment methods are primarily eclectic, with varying aspects of cognitive behavior therapy, family therapy, humanistic methods, relaxation techniques, hypnosis, and analytic-oriented sessions, especially in settings outside of education (Pelzer, 1995). However, in educational settings, emphasis has generally tended to be more on relationship-centered therapies. A major factor responsible for the use of relationship-centered therapeutic approaches (such as psychodynamic approaches) is their close association with the collectivist group- and family-oriented traditional psychotherapeutic approaches (see Bojuwoye, 2013; Bojuwoye & Mogaji, 2013). Adekson (2003) reported on widespread uses of cultural approaches to therapy similar to Carl Rogers's client-centered psychotherapeutic model. Sociocultural group psychotherapeutic practices also feature prominently in hospital settings (especially in cases of marital and family problems) as, by virtue of African general group awareness tendency, individual approaches may not succeed with the people (Pelzer, 1995).

This chapter discusses the case of traditional cultural counseling with a client named Dayo. The discussions feature analysis and explanations of the traditional counseling treatment modality that Dayo underwent.

THE CLIENT

Dayo is a 44-year-old heterosexual male of Yoruba decent who is employed, married, and has four children—two sons, 18 and 8, and two daughters, 15 and 12. With his current earnings, Dayo could be described as having a middle-class socioeconomic status. Moreover, his wife, a 40-year-old elementary school teacher, also contributes significantly to the family income.

PRESENTING ISSUES AND CHALLENGES

Dayo presented with illness that he could not quite name but described in many complaints. He reported feeling generally unhappy, down, and miserable and had lost interest in many things he used to do. Other illness symptoms he reported included having a headache; experiencing general body weakness; and feeling confused, worthless, and unappreciated. Dayo also suffered from sleep problems.

Not being able to name or describe exactly what was wrong with him or why he was experiencing ill health made Dayo very anxious. In Dayo's culture, when a person is experiencing ill health, the tendency is for the person to be preoccupied with a search for explanations and reasons for the ill health. The challenge confronting Dayo, therefore, was finding satisfactory explanations for his ill health or getting somebody to explain to him why he was unwell, especially so soon after being promoted to a higher job position. It was this search for explanations that was causing him anxiety.

CASE HISTORY AND DEVELOPMENTAL BACKGROUND

Born into an extended family in a rural village community, Dayo is the second child of his mother but the sixth of the eight children of his polygamous father. Dayo's mother was the younger or junior wife of his father's two wives. The father died when Dayo was about 10 years old and about 3 years into his primary school education. By cultural practices, the death of his father meant that financial support for Dayo (including schooling) had to be borne by his older siblings and other older extended family members (grandparents, uncles, aunts, and even the entire village community). Despite his financial difficulties, and with encouragement from his mother, Dayo successfully completed a high school education after which he won government scholarships to study at the university. He was the first with a university education in his extended family and even in his poor rural village community. He was employed immediately after graduation from the university at a government department in the state capital, the main city in his province of birth.

Dayo was also doing well in his job and recently was promoted to a new higher job position after a competitive interview in which five other colleagues were also involved as candidates for the same position. The new appointment came with higher status, increased salary, transportation and housing allowances, as well as other benefits. However, the new position also came with extra responsibilities (several meetings to attend, reports to write, and frequent travel), all of which occupied most of Dayo's time, making it impossible for him to partake in his usual leisure-time social club activities with his friends. His frequent travel out of town also meant spending less time with his family and not being able to attend his church as regularly as before; in addition, he was completely unavailable to members of his extended family and the rural village community.

Dayo's new lifestyle and behavior had attracted a lot of criticism. The loss of regular contact with his friends and colleagues was interpreted as Dayo's arrogance, now that he was occupying a higher position or higher status than them. Members of his extended family, church, and rural village community also frowned upon and rebuked Dayo for his inability to devote time for meetings with them and for his apparent stoppage of his advocacy, philanthropic, and community leadership-role activities that he used to perform. Members of his church and rural village community failed to understand why he no longer was able to play his leadership role, particularly his role as a provider for and defender of the community—a traditionally perceived male gender role he was expected to uphold. With his new lifestyle or behavior pattern being incorrectly and unfairly misinterpreted by those associated with him and his not being able to meet his "supposed" traditional roles, Dayo was left feeling unhappy, frustrated, guilty, worthless, and anxious. The various roles and identities expected of Dayo presented him with serious challenges to his effective functioning, especially as they conflicted with one another and tended to tear him apart.

THE THERAPY

As a well-educated person, Dayo first sought help from the government hospital offering mainstream Western-oriented services. The results of his consultation with a Western-oriented biomedical practitioner revealed that Dayo might be suffering from malaria fever to which he might have succumbed as a result of his apparent deep depression. Both his fever and the general feeling of unhappiness were thought to be responsible for his general weakness and sleep problems. He was treated with an antimalaria medication for the fever. However, Dayo's nightmares refused to go, and he became emotionally very restless. Adding to his anxiety was the feeling of isolation he was experiencing as he perceived his friends and community members to have abandoned him.

Therefore, not satisfied with the Western-oriented model of diagnosis and treatment, Dayo, in the company of an older extended family member, consulted a Yoruba traditional healer (also referred to as *Babalawo* or *Ifa* priest) for assistance.

The traditional healer began his assessment with an observation of the client. Traditional healers have very good clairvoyant abilities. A physical examination was conducted by touching the client's body to gather information about how he was feeling. This examination was followed by an interview, which featured questions focusing on the client's physical health, family relationships, and community and workplace relationships. For further assessment and diagnosis, the traditional healer also consulted his cultural healing instruments and recited traditional divination poems—the Ifa oracle, a metaphorical dialogue that includes proverbs and stories on a variety of human relationships, decision-making situations, and lifestyle choices as well as incidences capable of promoting or hindering effective human functioning. This process was an attempt to gather information from the spiritual world on the client's ill health, which the healer reported was associated with troubled or ruptured human relationships. Apparently, the client must have been inflicted with the ill health by people who were envious of his new job status. To get well, Dayo would need to fortify himself against evil agents and also appease the people who were not happy with his current lifestyle and behavior.

To treat the physical ailment (fever), the healer prescribed a cleansing treatment to get rid of the malaria and the weakness. Dayo was given an herbal concoction to drink and to bathe and cleanse the inner and outer parts of his body. To further fortify against Dayo's discomfort, the healer made some incisions on his (Dayo's) body to let out some contaminated body fluid or blood. Some black powdery object was also rubbed on the incisions for the body to generate further immunity against the foreign agents that were causing the ill health. The actual therapeutic treatment was through the prescription of a ritual involving animal sacrifice. The ritual is essentially a group procedure for the rebuilding of relationship networks and involves the slaughtering of a bull for a feast with friends, colleagues, other associates, and community members.

DISCUSSION AND ANALYSIS

Traditional Africa's theory of ill health is incorporated with an intentional stance, because the traditional belief is that nothing happens in nature by chance and that whatever happens to humans must have meaning and purpose (Ray, 1993). The lack of a satisfactory explanation for ill health, therefore, causes people to be filled with thoughts of being overpowered by a "higher power." Pillay and Wassennaar (1996) also offered the explanation that when people in Africa have ill health and experience medical conditions or other negative life events that they have no direct control over or do not fully understand, they become obsessed with thoughts of being controlled by someone "out there."

The client's choice of a traditional healer tells us much about the African help- or health-seeking behaviors, which largely favor traditional mental health practitioners. The patient's difficulty with accepting Western-oriented practice may be connected with the perception that it is not being operated within the perspectives of his cultural realities. To be effective, psychotherapeutic practice must operate from within the perspectives of the client's cultural realities. In this case, therapy operated within the client's cultural reality that stressed the importance of finding the meaning of ill health; in addition, the therapy touched on the metaphors associated with ill health and the care patterns that shape the experiences and social relations of the sufferer.

Some aspects of the traditional and cultural approach to healing paralleled those of Western-oriented psychological practice, as the healer started by conducting an assessment through observation and interview to gather information so that he could arrive at some hypotheses about the client's illness. Use of cultural tools such as divination and poems (i.e., the Ifa oracle, a body of knowledge or traditional oral literature) helped the healer to gain spiritual insight into and better comprehension of his client's problem and to arrive at culturally appropriate diagnosis and treatment. In many sub-Saharan communities, conceptualization of ill health takes into account not only the physical but also sociocultural and spiritual factors; AIDS, for instance, is considered to be spiritual in nature (Pelzer, 1995). It is generally the standard practice in many non-Western traditional therapeutic practices to make recourse to the spiritual realm for information to aid in the diagnosis of ill health.

In this client's therapy, the model of intervention was informed by the traditional conception of ill health—which is considered to be multidimensional in nature—and this conception informed the design of a holistic intervention model. It involved interactions and integration of body, spirit, and mind as well as integration of the individual with his environment (see Atherton, 2007).

The traditional healer's first attention was on the client's physical health; therefore, the healer prescribed herbal medicine to cure the physical ailments—the fever and body weakness. The prescription of an herbal concoction for the treatment of the client's physical ailment presupposes that pathogens or foreign object intrusions might have been responsible for the illness of the client (see Mpofu, 2000).

A major aspect of the African traditional psychotherapeutic practice relies on the theory that illness is externally caused and that it is essentially associated with human relationships. This belief is explained by Dryden (1984), who suggested that some traditional cultures view ill health as largely extrapsychic rather than intrapsychic and as acute or chronic disturbances in the balance of emotional forces in the individual's important relationships structure. Indeed, both the traditional healer and the client in this case study believed that some relationships had been ruptured as a result of the client's new job position, lifestyle, and behaviors, which isolated the client from people associated with him. Simply put, one's behavioral patterns and or lifestyle choices can lead to disruption in relationships with other people, which can in turn result in ill health.

Healing, from an African perspective, goes beyond symptom removal (as in the biomedical model) to addressing deeper contextual as well as emotional and spiritual causes of ill health. Thus, in contrast to the Western-oriented counseling model that emphasizes one-on-one consultative therapeutic process, cultural counseling comprises (a) a series of activities or services that may be largely educational or information-based, (b) attitude development, and (c) skills building. An important concern in healing or traditional counseling process is to provide the patient with information on human interpersonal relationships responsible for illness and health. Healing also includes helping the patient to come to terms with and appreciate the structures of and forces in nature, which, although they may be impinging negatively on people's health, are nevertheless essential parts of the essence of life, not to be wished away but to be negotiated and accommodated or embraced (Bojuwoye, 2001). Patients are made aware of the fact that community is an essential part of human life. Thus, with ill health being socially constructed, the belief is that it is by achieving social health that the body can have enough resources to address other health problems (especially physical health problem) affecting the individual. Therefore, treatment involves rearranging the individual's social networks in order to disrupt the social order that is perceived to be causing the ill health.

In addressing the disruption in the client's relational experiences, the traditional healer prescribed a treatment that is understood by the culture to provide healing. This treatment involved communal spiritual experiences, or the establishment of good social networks, by performing animal sacrifice. African traditional psychotherapeutic or counseling practice is essentially collectivist or by group, and its basic principle is to change the dynamics of human relationships from being competitive to being collaborative. The process largely revolves around education, information sharing, and skills building on human interpersonal relationships. As people come together to share meals, dance, and sing together, they learn more about themselves and about how best to relate with each other. By so doing, their spirits are freed from the contamination of destructive negative emotional feelings as their relational experiences facilitate self-discovery and the creation of a pleasant, positive, appreciative, and affirmative environment (Atherton, 2007). The collective consensual actions involved in people sharing a feast enhance group consciousness (solidarity), promoting acceptance and appreciation of one another.

Indeed, behavior is displayed in cultural context, and it is only meaningful when understood from within that context. Therefore, therapists who work with minority cultural groups in the West need to be familiar with and have a better understanding of the contextual cultural factors influencing their clients. Understanding cultural norms related to their clients' behaviors can help therapists avoid generalizations and stereotypes and instead design culture-infused intervention strategies that are meaningful to their clients. Culture-centered therapy should focus on culturally learned expectations and values that control behavior as well as dimensions of cultures such as ethnicity, gender, sexual orientation, age, religion, socioeconomic status, social class, and other dimensions that are relevant for the individual client (Arthur & Collins, 2010).

In the present case study, integrating principles of African cultural psychological services—such as those associated with relationship-centered approaches—encouraged group awareness and interactions and proved to be an effective way to deal with the client's ill health.

CONCLUSION

Although the discussion of this case focused mainly on the client's consultation and treatment with a traditional and cultural healer, it is important to remember that there are many Western counseling and therapy approaches in Nigeria. All approaches, however, have infused the cultural and traditional methods in some form or another. Because ethnic culture influences people's worldview and the ways in which they think, feel, and behave, it has a major influence in their help-seeking behaviors as well. Moreover, cultural influences on people's beliefs about illnesses contribute significantly to how clients present and represent their emotional and/or psychological difficulties. It is therefore important to infuse cultural knowledge and skills as well as traditional healing methods into a treatment of wellness for all clients, especially in the diaspora.

QUESTIONS

1. What alternative explanations can be offered, especially from the perspectives of culture, for Dayo's psychological difficulties?

2. How credible is the contention that his socioeconomic condition can be used to predict Dayo's psychological discomfort?
3. What are the limitations of the traditional healing strategies for treating Dayo?
4. In what ways are the assumptions of multiple identities by Dayo responsible for his psychological difficulties?
5. What are the advantages of the holistic approach of African traditional psychotherapeutic practice?

REFERENCES

Adekson, M. O. (2003). *The Yoruba traditional healers of Nigeria.* New York, NY: Routledge.

Arthur, N., & Collins, S. (2010). Introduction to culture-infused counselling. In S. Collins & N. Arthur (Eds.), *Culture-infused counselling* (pp. 3–25). Calgary, Alberta, Canada: Counselling Concepts.

Atherton, K. (2007). *Holistic healing* (Report published by Pindari Herb Farm). Retrieved from http://pindariherbfarm.com/healing/holiheal.htm

Bojuwoye, O. (2001). Crossing cultural boundaries in counselling. *International Journal for the Advancement of Counselling, 23,* 31–50.

Bojuwoye, O. (2013). Integrating principles underlying ancestral spirits beliefs in counseling and psychotherapy. *Ife Psychologia, 21,* 74–89.

Bojuwoye, O., & Mogaji, A. A. (2013). Counseling and psychotherapy in Nigeria: Horizons for the future. In R. Moodley, U. P. Gielen, & R. Wu (Eds.), *Handbook of counseling and psychotherapy in an international context* (pp. 40–50). New York, NY: Routledge.

Dryden, W. (1984). Therapeutic arenas. In W. W. Dryden (Ed.), *Individual therapy in Britain* (pp. 1–22). London, England: Harper & Row.

Mpofu, E. (2000). Rehabilitation counselling: Issues in professionalization and identity. *Rehabilitation Education, 14,* 199–205.

Pelzer, K. (1995). *Psychology and health in African cultures: Examples of ethno-psychotherapeutic practice.* Frankfurt, Germany: IKO Verlag.

Pillay, A. L., & Wassennaar, D. (1996). Hopelessness and psychiatric symptomatology in hospitalized physically ill adolescents. *South African Journal of Psychology, 26,* 4–51.

Ray, C. B. (1993). Aladura Christianity: A Yoruba religion. *Journal of Religion in Africa, 23,* 266–291.

Chapter 5

COUNSELING AND PSYCHOTHERAPY IN MOROCCO: T.M.'S STORY

Nadia Kadri and Dounia Belghazi

INTRODUCTION

The practice of counseling in Morocco may have begun with the *maristans* (a word of Persian origin denoting a place for clients) at the turn of the century. Originating from an Arab-Muslim tradition, these maristans were the only available public health institutions in Morocco during the early 20th century. In the beginning, these establishments received clients without making a distinction between physical and mental disorders. The more notable ones were the maristans of Fès Marrakesh and Salé. Those institutions served as refuges for the mentally ill and contained various facilities. Music therapy was known to have been practiced there.

In Morocco, the practice of modern psychotherapy goes back several decades and has been associated with psychiatry and psychology. It was first practiced in the 1950s by French psychiatrists during the colonial period. The training of Moroccan psychiatrists (mainly in France and some in Morocco), however, started in the mid-1970s. The most available psychotherapies in Morocco are psychoanalytic, cognitive behavior, and systemic therapies. Moroccan mental health professionals are increasingly interested in psychotherapy techniques, especially with the growing evidence of their effectiveness (see, for discussion, Kadri & Bennani, 2012).

This chapter discusses the therapy of a young Moroccan man suffering from personality disorder who was being treated with cognitive behavior therapy (CBT) and schema therapy (Beck, 2004). We used CBT according to a specific model that focuses on early cognitive schemas. The model encompasses five therapy axes: cognitive methods, affective methods, interpersonal methods, behavioral methods, and consolidation skills (Cottraux, 2011). At every stage of the therapy, we first took into account the client's cultural specificities so that we could establish a good therapeutic alliance. Then, we focused on understanding his functioning and decoding what made the dysfunction continue.

THE CLIENT

T.M. was a 25-year-old male from Morocco who lived with his parents and grew up in a wealthy family as the youngest of three siblings. His father was a businessman, and his mother was a housewife. He identified as a Muslim Arab and as a heterosexual. He had no physical disabilities.

PRESENTING ISSUES AND CHALLENGES

The client reported symptoms that could be coded on Axis I of the *Diagnostic and Statistical Manual of Mental Disorders* (4th ed., text rev.; American Psychiatric Association, 2000), namely, suicidal depression and anxiety disorders. At this stage the real challenge for the client was to hear that all these symptoms were secondary to a deeper disorder, an operating mode that turned dysfunctional. Indeed, this symptomatology is the complication of a personality disorder. However, the stigma surrounding mental illness in Moroccan society and the shame that clients and their families may feel means that it is much more tolerable for them to believe that they suffer from organic pathology than mental illness.

CASE HISTORY AND DEVELOPMENTAL BACKGROUND

T.M. comes from a traditional Moroccan family that belongs to a wealthy social class. He is the youngest of his siblings. T.M. has had a very symbiotic relationship with his mother. They have had some moments of great reconciliations and others of aggressive remoteness. His mother holds important "magical–religious" beliefs, and she probably suffers from generalized anxiety disorder.

As a child, T.M. was shy and self-contained. His teenage years were difficult as he had little self-confidence and no friends. He started developing anxiety attacks, bulimia, and compulsive masturbation.

T.M. consulted his first psychiatrist at the age of 13. He described a state of ill being and lack of confidence. His schooling was tumultuous, and his social relationships were likewise extremely complicated.

T.M. indicated that he experienced weird things. He saw writings of *Jin* [demons] on the walls and was convinced he had been bewitched and was inhabited by a Jin. These strange things were also accompanied by bodily sensations in specific areas, usually in the genitals. They occurred in situations where he felt discomfort or anxiety. These sensations returned in a stereotypical manner. Together with his mother, T.M. consulted a *fkih*, a type of traditional healer or exorcist. The fkih urged him to read some verses from the Koran, to pray a lot, and to brush his body with oil and honey. Moreover, the fkih recommended regular sessions to remove the Jin. During the follow-up, T.M. met a young fkih with whom he underwent several *Saraa* healing sessions. His belief in Jin allowed him to assign meaning to his unhappiness, but it also made him understand that this would not solve his problems.

T.M.'s academic and professional paths were disrupted. At the beginning of the follow-up, he was dropping out of school. Subsequently, he reenrolled in a school for vocational training in pastry. He graduated from pastry school and even took up internships abroad (in France and Belgium), with great success. However, once he was back in Morocco, he could not fit in with the internship settings or Casablanca's pastry companies. He said his employers did not recognize his talents. Consequently, he resigned after a few months of work and started working alone as a pastry craftsman. He made beautiful wedding cakes, and eventually his reputation grew, and he started to receive many orders. However, T.M. still had two problems. First, he could not satisfy his customers because he constantly canceled orders. His professional performance was frequently disrupted by his emotional states. When he was in a negative phase, he saw everything in black; he would withdraw and stop working. As a result, he could not expand his business because he could not find partners. In fact, he consistently lashed out to potential partners and broke all possible associations with them.

The course of T.M.'s romantic relationships was typically disastrous, and he suffered enormously because of this. Although he had a lot of success initiating relationships with girls, his involvements always ended badly. Even when things were going well, T.M. felt his girlfriends did not pay attention to him or meet his demands. He systematically concluded that they no longer wanted him, and so he would respond by withdrawing from these relationships or attacking them before the breakup. This behavior would result in feelings of sadness, dark ideas, and suicidal ideation. He never questioned himself and always assumed the victim role.

Throughout his history, it emerged that the most important goal for T.M. was to reduce his depressive symptomatology. He also agreed to consult a psychiatrist. What T.M. always put forward during the interviews was that he felt deep sadness and experienced anxiety attacks with sensations of heaviness, palpitations, and intense headaches. He also suffered from binge eating and compulsive masturbation. He considered himself incompetent and doubted his own abilities. He blamed his family and society for his failure at school. He discontinued his studies because he felt desperate. He no longer had energy and was disgusted with life. Crying a lot, he verbalized dark ideas and a desire to die.

THE THERAPY

As our focus in the current chapter is on the psychotherapeutic field, we do not go into detail on the client's medical care. From the beginning T.M. was followed in outpatient care consultation. He was under medical treatment (antidepressant and antianxiety treatment). He was not hospitalized because he and his family refused to do so. It is important to stress that his family was very supportive and present during these difficult phases.

The first step involved addressing the critical issue by appropriately assessing the risk of suicide. Thus, the first stage of the treatment was to reduce the risk of suicide and treat depression with antidepressant and anxiolytic medication. In addition, we used CBT that focused initially on depression. Through functional analysis of T.M.'s problematic situations, we verified his cognitive distortions. Subsequently we diagnosed him with borderline personality disorder of the avoidant/dependent type.

The main challenge was to develop a positive and strong therapeutic relationship with T.M. to persuade him to accept the idea that his depression was secondary to a deeper personality disorder. However, the client's cultural beliefs made this task extremely difficult. Both the client and his mother believed that his problems were attributable to the Jin and bad luck. They thought he was bewitched and must therefore be treated by an exorcist.

We had to follow the client's lead and allow him to try his approach in alleviating his ill-being by consulting a fkih. He followed all the procedures recommended by the fkih until he realized they did not solve his problems. At this stage, we had established a strong enough therapeutic relationship to jump-start the therapy. It took an immense effort in close collaboration with the client in order to explain all the steps of therapy. We implemented CBT centered on early cognitive schemas.

We used the relational fluctuations to highlight the client's cognitive schemas and to implement corrective emotional experiences. The therapy lasted 3 years. We used cognitive, emotional, interpersonal, and behavioral methods as well as those intended to consolidate his progress. The sessions were structured according to the classical model of CBT.

During the cognitive work, a large part of the therapy was based on the client's life scenario. We asked T.M. to relate his story in order to see how his unconditional personal convictions and beliefs were built. The functional analysis of his problems made the automatic thoughts stand out and underlined the links between thoughts, emotions, and behaviors. T.M. used Beck columns extensively. The work on the modification of the cognitive distortions was complicated for T.M. He had difficulties finding the abusive nature of his belief system. The dichotomous thinking was the basis of his earlier schema. All CBT's techniques were used: advantages, disadvantages, questioning, role playing, and problem resolution.

During the therapy, we had to do specific work to manage T.M.'s suicide attempts. He made two serious suicide attempts in a short period of time because of breakups with his girlfriends. During these phases, the sessions were longer and more frequent. Recognition of and empathy with the client's suffering was the key to keeping a strong therapeutic alliance. We never directly condemned T.M.'s suicidal gesture. When he felt ready, we began working on crisis management as based on a functional analysis of his suicide attempt. The client sought to discover the negative elements of his behavior. He made a list of all the alternatives that could reduce his pain without resorting to suicide. The therapy worked well in that the client did not attempt suicide during the last breakup. After his second suicide attempt we resumed this work from the beginning. We focused on problem-solving techniques and the management of his impulsivity.

It should be noted that despite the fact that T.M. does not consider himself as a very religious person, the fact that suicide is a sin in Islam helped him to reconsider it as a solution to his suffering. He said that if he wanted to escape the hell on earth it is not to live it in the afterlife.

T.M. had undergone a number of practical experiences to test his unconditional beliefs. The behavioral methods enabled the client to make significant progress, especially in his professional life. His decision to redirect and become a pastry chef after his failure at school undermined his belief "I am incompetent." He had not only succeeded in his training but had become a recognized pastry craftsman. This progress was reinforced in the course of therapy. T.M. evaluated his behavior in all kinds of difficult situations. He did a great job finding alternative behaviors more suited to the circumstance. These new behaviors gave rise to positive reactions from his social environment that generally encouraged the client to invest himself in the therapy and in making changes.

T.M. often felt overwhelmed by his emotions and had trouble managing them. He would resort to inappropriate behaviors. It was hard for him to recognize his emotions. In a culture that forbade men to be sad and cry, T.M. took refuge in feelings of shame and anger. His relationships with women were complicated because he wanted to live up to the image that society provided—the man playing the dominant role. T.M. rapidly found himself in situations of emotional dependence that he could not bear. These situations filled him with a lot of anger. Indeed, it was while in this state of emotional fragility that T.M. became aggressive toward his lovers and toward himself. The role-play was an interesting technique that allowed him to change his negative roles. It also allowed him to determine whether he had changed his schema by playing the devil's advocate. Gradually, T.M. succeeded in recognizing his emotions better, which in turn reduced his impulsive behaviors.

At this stage of the therapy, T.M. judged the progress of the therapy very positively. He felt a significant decrease in his anxiety, and his mood had significantly improved. His social relationships remain complicated, and he continues to experience difficulties in managing them. Nevertheless, T.M. no longer engages in impulsive and aggressive behaviors. Actually, he focuses his work on the realization of the alternatives introduced in the course of the therapy. His ultimate goal is to develop his business and establish a stable and loving relationship.

DISCUSSION AND ANALYSIS

Research generally supports the conclusion that CBT is an effective treatment modality for reducing symptoms and enhancing functional outcomes among clients with borderline personality disorder. We have chosen to use this approach to help our clients. But from the first interviews some legitimate questions have emerged. Is this therapy adapted to a non-Western culture? Is its application universal, or must it take into account the cultural, societal, and religious specificities of a North African, Arab and Amazigh, Muslim country such as Morocco?

Our case study has shown that the answer cannot be dichotomous. CBT is perfectly suited to multiculturalism in the sense that its principle is to stay focused on the client. The goal is to cultivate the client's personal power and his or her ability to work on understanding his or her cognitions, emotions, physical symptoms, and behavior to better interact with his or her environment. But to get there, the cultural subtleties of this environment must be introduced.

Among the innumerable manifestations of cultural differences that can be identified throughout the world, Sue and Sue (2013) brought together four dimensions inherent in psychotherapeutic work: the nature and the establishment of the therapeutic relationship, the standards for verbal and nonverbal communication, cultural particularities related to the expression of distress, and the place of rational thought.

The nature and the establishment of the therapeutic relationship must consider certain parameters. In Morocco, a patriarchal society, a female therapist may be a problem or at least a source of discomfort for a male client. The question of the age of the therapist can be very important in a culture where respect for the older person, who is considered to be wiser and more experienced, is fundamental. The therapist's youth can be a detriment. The client's social level also affects the nature of the therapeutic relationship. The clients of a high social status are more likely to work in collaboration with the therapist, whereas in modest social circles a more directive relationship is generally warranted; the therapist is seen as the expert. Finally, to a lesser extent, the foreign nationality of the therapist, especially the European one, can give the therapist more credibility. In the collective imagination, foreign doctors are more competent. This belief is paradoxically not the case for Moroccan clients living in Europe, however, who feel more understood by a therapist of the same origin.

On the verbal and nonverbal communication, it seems to us that there are no special codes. However, the therapist will be more appreciated if he or she shows warmth and empathy in his or her communication style and uses a certain vocabulary and expressions in some sensitive topics (such as intimate life, sexuality) instead of an overly direct terminology. It is best to maintain professional boundaries and meet in an office. Finally, it is best if the counselor wears professional attire.

Somatization is the most common expression of distress in Morocco. It is much easier to talk about physical suffering than mental distress because mental illness is still highly stigmatized in Morocco. Apart from some illnesses, such as schizophrenia, most mental illnesses (such as depression and anxiety disorders) are not recognized. They may even be considered as a lack of religiosity, a weak belief in God. Verbal communication of emotions is almost nonexistent; talking about emotions is not a part of Moroccan culture. As for men, it is unacceptable to show emotions (a man does not cry) or suffering because it is synonymous with weakness. They will report more irritability, physical complaints (headaches, muscle cramps), general fatigue, and insomnia, whereas women may be more emotionally expressive (e.g., tearfulness and even moments of hysteria). This expressive suffering is common, and if the woman loses consciousness, it is customary to revive her by putting keys in her hands and making her feel an onion. These practices tend to disappear gradually as the society becomes more literate.

Cognitive restructuring is fundamental in CBT. But relying solely on rational thought and Western logic may be unsuccessful with clients who belong to Eastern cultures. In addition to rationality, Moroccans also have mystical, spiritual, and religious dimensions that must be taken into account. Furthermore, the belief in the Jin, the evil eye, jealousy, destiny, and witchcraft is not considered irrational; it is completely acceptable. This type of thinking is not to be blamed or derided because the quality of the therapeutic relationship and the success of the therapy are at stake.

CONCLUSION

In this case study, it was more difficult to change the client's assumptions that arose from cultural or religious histories. They were positively reinforced by society and the social environment of the client, making it difficult to highlight the nature of the client's thoughts together with their negative consequences. In this regard, it was important to be careful in how to address these issues. Hence, we chose to accept that T.M. went to the fkih and performed the rites recommended by the fkih. This example shows the importance of understanding the client's cultural beliefs and his or her help-seeking behaviors. Therefore, this case study strongly suggests that when the therapist and client share the same background, a culturally sensitive and adaptive therapeutic approach can be more easily attained.

QUESTIONS

1. T.M. experienced weird things, such as seeing writings of Jin on the walls and having bodily sensations, especially in the genital areas. Are these psychotic symptoms? How do cultural and magical beliefs interfere in psychopathology?

2. As mentioned in the text, "We had to follow the client's lead and allow him to try his approach in alleviating his ill being by consulting a fkih." Rather than strengthening the therapeutic alliance, might this action have caused the opposite effect?

3. "T.M. often felt overwhelmed by his emotions . . . In a culture that forbade men to be sad and cry, T.M. took refuge in feelings of shame and anger." Would T.M. need an emotional therapy? In a broader context, would an "emotional" education that was based on the recognition and acceptance of emotions be sufficient to avoid this problem?

4. What other therapy could we engage in with the client so that he could master and regulate the negative consequences of his behavior, considering depression and anxiety as a complication of the personality disorder?

5. Is it ethical for a doctor to impose what the patient must believe or not?

References

American Psychiatric Association. (2000). *Diagnostic and statistical manual of mental disorders* (4th ed., text rev.). Washington, DC: Author.

Beck, A. (2004). *Cognitive therapy of personality disorders*. New York, NY: Guilford Press.

Cottraux, J. (2011). *Les psychotherapies conportementales et cognitives* [Behavioral and cognitive psychotherapies]. Issy-les-moulineaux, France: Elsevier Masson.

Kadri, N., & Bennani, J. (2012). Counseling and psychotherapy in Morocco: The renewal of an ancient tradition. In R. Moodley, U. P. Gielen, & R. Wu (Eds.), *Handbook of counseling and psychotherapy in an international context* (pp. 51–59). New York, NY: Routledge.

Sue, D. W., & Sue, D. (2013). *Counseling the culturally diverse: Theory and practice* (6th ed.). New York, NY: Wiley.

Chapter 6

COUNSELING AND PSYCHOTHERAPY IN SOUTH AFRICA: MR. DLAMINI'S STORY

Lionel J. Nicholas and Maria Damianova

INTRODUCTION

South Africa combines a history of extensive early engagement with international psychology with enduring traditional beliefs about alleviating or curing mental health problems. In light of the cultural and religious diversity in South Africa, the counseling interventions available to individuals and communities encompass professional psychological services, religious support, or traditional healing. Counseling and psychotherapy programs in South Africa expose their students and interns to the mainstream psychological theories and offer electives linked to the particular expertise of the trainers and teachers. The subsequent practice includes, among others, eclectic, psychodynamic, cognitive, behavioral, person-centered, or narrative approaches. A range of family therapy models, hypnotherapy, and strategic therapy are presented at workshops and conferences providing specialist training for psychologists. Although no particular paradigm is singled out as the most useful or preferred one, integrative psychotherapy was followed in the case presented below because of its high responsiveness and sensitivity to multicultural dynamics (see, for discussion, Cooper & Nicholas, 2013).

Almost 80% of the South African population of 50.6 million are Black African, many of whom hold traditional beliefs about health and mental health while also using Western health and mental health services. Only 0.3% of the South African population indicate traditional African beliefs as their religion, and there are approximately 20,000 traditional healers who are regulated by the Traditional Health Practitioners Council of South Africa (Ramgoon, Dalasile, Paruk, & Patel, 2011). In its quarterly tracking of perceptions of government, the Government Communication Information Services (2011) reported that 14% of the population consulted traditional healers. Nicholas, Damianova, and Ntantiso (2012) surveyed first-year students from various disciplines and found that only 10 of 567 expressed a preference for assistance from traditional healers. Robertson (2006) surveyed 349 adults who had consulted traditional healers and found that more than 90% of them were satisfied with their treatment and would consult traditional healers again. Traditional healers intuitively interpret behaviors and experiences in the context of relationships with ancestors and bewitchment. Gobodo (1990) agreed that although it is important to recognize cultural diversity in South Africa, it would be a mistake to overdiagnose culture. Edwards (1986) found that traditional healers and psychologists, while working from different theoretical orientations, held significantly similar views about diagnosis and treatment. He also found that patients viewed traditional healers and psychologists as more or less equally helpful.

This chapter examines the counseling and psychotherapeutic dynamics pertaining to the case of Mr. Dlamini (a fictitious name used to protect the client's identity), who sought professional psychological assistance in relation to neurological and neuropsychological complaints. Although Mr. Dlamini is a traditional leader, he expressly wanted psychological intervention, and as a result, the therapy was conducted within a Western paradigm. On the basis of a comprehensive, multidisciplinary assessment it was revealed that his symptoms were of psychogenic origin, and accordingly the client received counseling informed by the integrative psychotherapy approach.

THE CLIENT

Mr. Dlamini is a Black male of South African origin, in his mid-30s, with a strong Christian affiliation combined with traditional religious beliefs and traditional cultural values. He is married and has a young child. He has an engineering degree and is a manager in a large company.

PRESENTING ISSUES AND CHALLENGES

Mr. Dlamini first began experiencing involuntary head movements and impaired gross motor coordination of his lower limbs 15 years ago. There were instances when he felt he was unable to synchronize his leg movements, resulting in loss of stability when walking, but the results from the neurological, electroencephalography, and magnetic resonance imaging examinations conducted at the time showed no abnormalities. His difficulties persisted, and he also noticed he was extremely forgetful, and his mood was becoming unstable. He was then referred for a neuropsychological assessment with a specific query regarding his neurocognitive functioning. Prior to this referral, he had further neurological, magnetic resonance imaging, and electroencephalography examinations, which again revealed no apparent abnormalities.

In the intake interview Mr. Dlamini stated that in the last 2 to 3 years his memory and concentration difficulties had increased. He was frequently distracted at meetings and could not recall issues that had been discussed. The involuntary movements of his head, stiffness in his neck, and unstable gait had become more pronounced and frequent. He experienced further deterioration in his concentration, was easily distracted, and had difficulties recalling information pertaining to work, people, and events. He reported a strong sense of insecurity and sadness, which was at times associated with the death of his father. He often felt anxious about his performance at work and in other social domains. He therefore avoided speaking in public, although he was expected to do so in light of his responsibilities at work, in the community, and at various family and church gatherings. For the last 2 years, he had frequently experienced emotional instability and high levels of anxiety. Mrs. Dlamini had noticed that her husband was often withdrawn and would feel uncomfortable expressing his feelings and thoughts. These difficulties interfered with his performance at work and led to tensions in the relationship with his wife. Mr. Dlamini became increasingly concerned that he was not fulfilling his obligations and was disappointing his colleagues and superiors at work, his family, and his community.

CASE HISTORY AND DEVELOPMENTAL BACKGROUND

In view of Mr. Dlamini's presenting problems and referral question, a detailed medical, developmental, family, educational, and employment history was obtained. Mr. Dlamini reported that he was not aware of any delays in reaching his developmental milestones. He had average to above average academic performance at school, and after completing his tertiary education, he had gone on to have a successful career at large companies where he held senior positions. The predominant language of his education and employment has been English. His home language is one of the African languages officially spoken in South Africa.

Mr. Dlamini is the eldest of three children, and after the death of his father a couple of years ago, he took on the role of the traditional leader in a small indigenous community within South Africa. As a child he always strived to gain the approval of his father and other authority figures and recalled being terrified when he did not meet their expectations. There were instances when corporal punishment was used, and he recalled the resulting pain and humiliation. He described himself as always feeling anxious to be accepted and to perform well—whether at school, at work, in his church, or in the community. He enjoys spending time with his family, and after the birth of his first child, became even more motivated to ensure that his family is well protected and looked after. In addition to his strong sense of responsibility toward his own family, he also supports his mother, siblings, and extended family and contributes to their financial sustainability. He is actively involved in various initiatives at his church and has significant responsibilities in organizing the activities of the congregation.

Prior to experiencing the initial symptoms, Mr. Dlamini had no apparent medical or psychological concerns, and at the time of the intake he was not taking any medication. He has no family history of psychiatric or neurological disorder and although at university he used to drink, he stated that since then he has not been consuming alcohol. He has never used drugs and is a nonsmoker.

THE THERAPY

The results of the comprehensive neuropsychological and psychological assessment, undertaken in light of the referral, indicated that Mr. Dlamini's memory and cognitive functioning were inclusive of capacities primarily clustered within the average to above average level, with specific vulnerabilities pertaining to verbal associative learning and processing speed. His personality profile on the NEO Personality Inventory—Revised (Costa & McCrae, 1992) revealed high Neuroticism, low Extraversion, average Agreeableness, very low Openness to Experience, and very low Conscientiousness. On the Beck Depression Inventory (Beck & Steer, 1993a), his functioning was within the mild range, reflecting a wide range of mild to moderate symptoms. His overall anxiety level on the Beck

Anxiety Inventory (Beck & Steer, 1993b) was within the mild range, with a broad scope of symptoms rated at minimal or moderate level. Thus, the assessment findings suggested that emotional and personality factors were implicated in Mr. Dlamini's condition, and these included susceptibility to psychological distress; anxiety and depression; diminished interest and engagement in social interactions; limited involvement in novel experiences; as well as low personal organization, persistence, control, and motivation in goal-directed behavior. Significantly, symptoms of complicated grief associated with the death of Mr. Dlamini's father were also indicated in the assessment process. Thus, it was concluded that Mr. Dlamini's presenting issues (difficulties related to concentration, memory functioning, motor control, and physical symptoms) were most likely psychogenic in nature; therefore, he was advised to begin individual counseling to deal with past emotional experiences and bereavement, with a focus on enhancing his coping strategies regarding the multiple expectations in the family, at work, and in the community. The integrative psychotherapy approach was followed as it was considered the most relevant to the individual characteristics and the multicultural dynamics involved in this case.

The counseling process revealed that a central theme in Mr. Dlamini's reflections on his life was the relationship with his father. Mr. Dlamini grew up experiencing apprehension and anxiety that he was not meeting the expectations of his father. Despite striving to achieve and be seen as successful, he rarely received any positive feedback from his father, leaving him insecure and doubtful of his capacities and his fitness to be, as the eldest son of a traditional leader, the pride of the family. Mr. Dlamini had hoped that as an adult man he would be able to change the relationship with his father and act more confidently; however, he could not accomplish this change as his father died unexpectedly. Mr. Dlamini reached the hospital after his father had passed away and so did not have the chance to say a final goodbye; as a result, he felt strong guilt and a sense of failed responsibility. His mourning process was marked by these feelings as well as by his strong need for parental acceptance and approval, which was at the core of his personal aspirations and main relationships but which remained unfulfilled. The complicated grief process also included repression of feelings of loss, sadness, anger, fear, confusion, and insecurity. It was particularly difficult for Mr. Dlamini to acknowledge and express anger toward his father because relating to him with respect and compliance had always been the normative standard in his upbringing.

Mr. Dlamini had an excessive sense of responsibility to follow in his father's footsteps and play a leading role in the community and in the family. However, the expectations and demands of his community, family, church, and work pulled him in different directions, and he did not know which way to turn. Not only was he uncertain how to reconcile these expectations but he constantly doubted his abilities to deliver results to the satisfaction of others. His anxiety was also related to his endeavors to preserve his traditional values while maintaining efficient performance at organizations driven by business principles and Western institutional culture.

The reflections gained in the counseling process were that Mr. Dlamini (a) had been dissociating from significant psychological discomfort related to a history of emotional distance between him and his father; (b) suffered from exacerbated anxiety and insecurities associated with his perceived or real failure of high parental expectations; (c) experienced a complicated grieving process, including repressed feelings of anger and sorrow; and (d) had tensions emanating from his helplessness to unite traditional belief and values systems with personal aspirations and goals.

DISCUSSION AND ANALYSIS

Informed by the integrative psychotherapy approach, the counseling intervention with Mr. Dlamini focused on goal consensus, collaboration, and working alliance and empathy (Norcross & Beutler, 2011). By overcoming the limitations of single-school therapies, which do not always accommodate diversity, the integrative therapeutic approach has cultural sensitivity and relevance at its core and is perceived to place strong emphasis on the process of change (i.e., how) versus the objective of change (i.e., what).

The client's subjective complaints of movement disorders and head twitching—the primary reason for his seeking professional help—may be understood when accounting for the role of gender and religion (traditional beliefs) in the intrapersonal and interpersonal dynamics manifested in this case.

A significant aspect of these dynamics is the role of traditional leader that Mr. Dlamini had to take on by obligation after the death of his father. This position is traditionally passed on from father to son. Initially, Mr. Dlamini experienced uncertainty and hesitation about this duty, particularly in view of the fact that his mother expressed concerns that he might become the object of witchcraft, which could hamper his health and that of his immediate family. The belief that witchcraft may result in misfortune and ill health is deeply embedded in the system of traditional beliefs (Cooper & Nicholas, 2013), and despite the fact that his mother is an educated person, she obviously has adopted this belief. In traditional communities, the mother plays the leading role in running family affairs. Thus, his mother's concerns about witchcraft had a significant impact on Mr. Dlamini's views, and he postponed assuming his role as traditional leader for 3 years. By initially not accepting this role, Mr. Dlamini felt that he was not fulfilling his father's wishes and was letting him down. Although Mr. Dlamini was motivated to achieve a similar status of respect, he also wanted to break the pattern of subordination that pervaded the relationship with his father and was beginning to be replicated in the relationship with his uncle, who in the interim acted as the traditional leader.

Mr. Dlamini found himself torn by competing concerns: uncertainty about taking on the role because he questioned his own readiness and competence; concerns about the risk that he might be subjecting himself and his family to if they were bewitched; a strong sense of duty to obey tradition; and a desire to prove himself, be as powerful and respected in the community as his father used to be, and be superordinate, not subordinate. These tensions were exacerbated by a complicated grief process. A particularly important event during this period of decision making was the birth of Mr. Dlamini's child. Among male Black Africans, the responsibility to provide for their family is considered essential and is at the core of their identity. Thus, his new role as father enhanced Mr. Dlamini's motivation to ensure that he was able to provide a safe and secure upbringing for his child and that his family was well looked after. This motivation, however, both encouraged and hindered him from accepting the position as traditional leader. The high status and power associated with such a role would enhance his family's reputation in the community, but this status could also result in bewitchment that he feared could harm him and his family.

Gender-role delineations within the traditional belief system were also implicated in Mr. Dlamini's presenting issues. As a male, who is expected to be the main provider and protector of the family, it was more "acceptable" to both Mr. Dlamini and others to have neurological rather than psychological issues. Being physically, rather than mentally, "ill" appeared to have been a safer option as the latter is in direct conflict with the social expectation of high personal integrity that Mr. Dlamini aspired to fulfill as a traditional leader in his community. Within the framework of traditional community and family value systems, having a neurological issue was less likely to result in others' labeling the individual as "mad." Psychological dysfunctions and related interventions can be perceived as threatening because they entail reexamining and reliving experiences of pain and trauma that occurred in a person's distant or recent life history. The dissociative mechanisms at play were likely to have been exacerbated by factors related to both his gender role and traditional beliefs.

It is important to note there was no congruence on the Group of Seven identities between the client and the psychologist (White, middle-aged female of non-South African origin, with no strong religious background or affiliation), and this had to be taken into account when reflecting on the dynamics of this case and the potential impact of cultural sensitivities (Gobodo, 1990). With cognizance of the possible constraints from this incongruence, the psychologist suggested a referral to another therapist, but Mr. Dlamini chose to continue counseling with her. Following treatment, Mr. Dlamini reported that the initial symptoms had gradually subsided. The change processes outlined within the integrative psychotherapy framework—that is, consciousness raising, self-reevaluation, emotional arousal, environmental control, and contingency management—were accomplished.

CONCLUSION

Mr. Dlamini's symptoms were found to be an expression of significant psychological discomfort that originated from the following: complicated grieving process; strong aspirations for gaining approval and acceptance from internalized and present authority figures, particularly his father; excessive sense of community and family responsibility; powerful desire to meet the expectations of authority figures; and fear of failure as well as difficulties integrating his traditional values with Western cultural and religious affiliations. These dynamics were influenced by this client's motivation to adhere to the traditional belief systems and gender roles, which in part were in dissonance with his personal views. This case shows the significance of cultural sensitivity in understanding the dissociative and defense mechanisms underlying a client's symptoms.

QUESTIONS

1. What role did the client's gender and affiliated sociocultural status play in the expression of symptoms as neurological, rather than psychological?
2. How would disruption of any aspect of the diversity matrix lead to destructive behaviors?

3. To what extent did the client's subjective experience of neurological incapacitation serve as a coping and/or defense mechanism?
4. Could the intervention be based on a different therapeutic approach? Justify the choice, or the lack thereof, of an alternative approach.
5. What were the therapeutic challenges and dilemmas in this case? Were they addressed and resolved?

REFERENCES

Beck, A. T., & Steer, R. A. (1993a). *BDI: Beck Depression Inventory*. New York, NY: Psychological Corporation.

Beck, A. T., & Steer, R. A. (1993b). *Beck Anxiety Manual*. San Antonio, TX: Psychological Corporation.

Cosat, P. T., Jr., & McCrae, R. R. (1992). *Revised NEO Personality Inventory (NEO-PI–R) and NEO Five-Factor Inventory (NEO-FFI) professional manual*. Odessa, FL: Psychological Assessment Resources.

Cooper, S., & Nicholas, L. (2013). Counseling and psychotherapy in South Africa. In R. Moodley, U. P. Gielen, & R. Wu (Eds.), *Handbook of counseling and psychotherapy in an international context* (pp. 61–71). New York, NY: Routledge.

Edwards, S. D. (1986). Traditional and modern medicine in South Africa: A research study. *Social Science & Medicine, 22*, 1273–1276. doi:10.1016/0277-9536(86)90194-2

Gobodo, P. (1990). Notions about culture in understanding Black psychopathology: Are we trying to raise the dead? *South African Journal of Psychology, 20*, 93–98. doi:10.1177/008124639002000204

Government Communication Information Services. (2011). *Public perceptions on social human development issues in South Africa*. Pretoria, South Africa: Author.

Nicholas, L., Damianova, M., & Ntantiso, M. (2012). A comparison of South African and international first-year students' counseling needs and preferred counseling sources. *Australian Journal of Guidance and Counselling, 23*, 106–114. doi:10.1017/jgc.2012.21

Norcross, J. C., & Beutler, L. (2011). Integrative psychotherapies. In R. J. Corsini & D. Wedding (Eds.), *Current psychotherapies* (9th ed., pp. 502–535). Belmont, CA: Brooks/Cole.

Ramgoon, S., Dalasile, N. Q., Paruk, Z., & Patel, C. J. (2011). An exploratory study of trainee and registered psychologists' perceptions about indigenous healing systems. *South African Journal of Psychology, 41*, 90–100.

Robertson, B. (2006). Does the evidence support collaboration between psychiatry and traditional healers? Findings from three South African studies. *African Journal of Psychiatry, 9*, 87–90.

Chapter 7

COUNSELING AND PSYCHOTHERAPY IN SUB-SAHARAN AFRICA: KARIMI'S STORY

Gladys K. Mwiti and Naomi James

INTRODUCTION

Sub-Saharan Africa contains a multiplicity of cultural and psychological themes that are undergoing rapid change because of global Westernization (Hoogvelt, 1974; see also Mwiti & James, 2013). Western psychology has been viewed as an effort to negatively influence the African way of life through direct translation of diagnosis and intervention (Nyasani, 1997). However, Thairu (1975) argued that this reality has helped social scientists to adopt an eclectic model of psychotherapy, one that appreciates different African identities free from the control of Western psychological theory. The Oasis Africa's Transformational Psychology model uses the analogy of the African three-legged stool (Mwiti & Dueck, 2006) with three intertwined systems: (a) Western theories of psychology, (b) a spiritual worldview, and (c) an indigenous African worldview.

This chapter discusses the therapy of Karimi, who presented with posttraumatic stress and complicated grief reactions. The process of counseling for Karimi was to find meaning from her loss. Traumatized clients struggle to find the purpose or meaning of their loss (Davis, Wortman, Lehman, & Silver, 2000). Common in African mourning, nuclear and family connections deal with the shared traumatic loss and thereby enhance recovery.

THE CLIENT

Karimi is a single 26-year-old Kenyan woman of the Meru tribe who lives with her single 40-year-old sister; other distant family members live in rural areas. Spiritually a committed Christian, Karimi works in information technology for a mobile telephone company.

PRESENTING ISSUES AND CHALLENGES

Karimi presented with posttraumatic stress and complicated grief reactions. Her job evaluation indicated symptoms of work stress and diminishing productivity. At intake, Karimi narrated that her parents were killed in a road accident 2 years before.

Because she could not live alone anymore, she was now living with her older sister, Norah. Karimi reported never receiving any psychological help after the incident.

CASE HISTORY AND DEVELOPMENTAL BACKGROUND

Karimi lost her parents as she and they drove together to a wedding away from Nairobi. A truck hit their car, pushed it off the road, and it rolled downhill. Trapped in the wreckage for many hours, Karimi remembers her mother's call for help and an eerie silence after the screams stopped. She remembers pain from her shattered leg, the cold of the freezing rain, and trying to come to terms with the reality of the disaster.

In the hospital, Karimi learned both her parents were dead. After discharge, Karimi was too distraught to go back to her apartment and had nightmares, poor appetite, and guilt at her inability to help her parents. A committed Christian, Karimi was angry with God and refused to go to church any more. She wanted to die. Eventually, she resumed work, but her job performance soon deteriorated. She would not take public transportation, walked to work, was withdrawn, and was losing weight from poor appetite.

Her sister Norah was always angry with Karimi, claiming the young woman's symptoms were imaginary. She made Karimi do all the household chores, including going to the market every Saturday morning. Walking to the market, the smell of petrol made her nauseated and brought back memories of the accident. Hospitalized for several weeks after the accident, Karimi had missed her parents' funeral. However, for these past 2 years, she had refused to visit the grave, arguing that she could not face the fact that she would never see her parents again. Her old aunt was angry and claimed that someone may have looked at Karimi with an evil eye. If not, why were so many bad things happening to her? At this point, her employer called our clinic. Karimi's job evaluation was once again wanting, and it was only a matter of time before she lost her job.

THE THERAPY

Karimi came to therapy with posttraumatic stress symptoms that were affecting her work and social relationships. Naomi James (coauthor) conducted the intake interview. Karimi presented with complicated grief reactions and poor functioning at work. After signing the treatment contract, Naomi explored Karimi's background and presenting problem. The client stated, "I want to get well. My work is suffering. I have lost friends. I also want to be able to live freely on my own again." During the intake interview Karimi did not indicate any history of psychiatric illness, and her medical history indicated no physical ailments. The client was taking medication for pain; her company's clinic nurse supplied the medicine and also offered moral support. Karimi's showed a great deal of anxiety, with signs of helplessness and worthlessness.

When I (Gladys K. Mwiti) met Karimi, I repeated the assurance of confidentiality. I explored her developmental and trauma history and issues surrounding the accident, coping methods, and current support systems. She narrated the feelings of guilt and symptoms of hyperarousal she experienced after the accident. I carried out an assessment for posttraumatic stress disorder, and her total scores were above average for posttraumatic stress. Because of the client's arousal level, deficient sleep, and poor appetite, I referred her for psychotropic medication evaluation.

The following week, she had seen the psychiatrist and was sleeping better with medication. Together with the client, we created treatment objectives from her main outlined goal of "getting well, restoring and improving work output, rebuilding social connections, and independence."

Karimi experienced complicated grief reactions presenting as prolonged state of grief and helplessness to integrate her parents' death into her life. Because she was withdrawn and mainly housebound, she had lost most of her friends. Karimi's faith was shaken, and she was left wondering how true her aunt's analogy of a curse was as the reason for all the happenings.

Karimi was consistent in therapy and completed her homework as assigned. Within the first three sessions, the intake and assessment were completed to determine nature and severity of Karimi's trauma symptoms. Throughout the course of treatment, I provided her with trauma psychoeducation to enhance her coping, maintained therapeutic engagement, and modeled nonavoidance. I also used psychoeducation after she shared the story of the accident to normalize her symptoms and help her to understand treatment procedures.

During the next two sessions, I began work on the client's hyperarousal and avoidance symptoms, using trauma focused cognitive behavior therapy to begin work on specific memories related to the accident. Dealing with her phobic avoidance of public transportation was of particular attention in order to enhance her day-to-day functioning. I first taught Karimi and modeled several relaxation techniques. These techniques have the benefit of lowering arousal and reducing physical tension that were most probably contributing to the client's fatigue. I explained the relationship between progressive muscle relaxation (PMR) and stress and that she could use the same technique alone at home, while walking, or even when approaching the object of her avoidance: the transport *matatus* [minibus] that she needed to ride to the office or market.

I indicated that she could use the nausea and tension she experienced each time she smelled petrol fumes as a cue to use PMR. Using a scale of 1 to 10, she learned how to use subjective units of distress (SUDS) to rank her distress and triggered memories. Achieving desensitization on public transportation involved using a colleague at work to help her achieve graded actions. She began sitting at the bus stop near passing vehicles, using PMR to relax, avoid nausea, and lower her distress. Later on, they took short matatus rides together.

Cognitive restructuring was used to help her work through and analyze her strengths, weaknesses, opportunities, and threats by realistically acknowledging her abilities and working through her weaknesses and opportunities. She was receiving strength to deal with her threats, such as her sister's complaints and challenges at work. Later on, I used the psychodynamic–interpersonal skills model to explore and listen to Karimi's worries and concerns. She identified her interpersonal difficulties responsible for precipitating and maintaining the symptoms of stress and feeling oppressed as she lived with her older sister. I shared my formulation with the client that this sibling distance was contributing to some of her symptoms because the two had never been emotionally close given that they were born many years apart.

Norah, Karimi's sister, was invited to attend therapy. In a joint session, Norah narrated positive changes that she had witnessed in Karimi since she began therapy. She added that she was now able to understand the impact the accident had on

Karimi. Eventually, Norah owned up to the fact that she, too, missed her parents and was angry that they had both died, leaving the care of Karimi in her hands.

In future joint sessions, I explored closure and reconnecting with their extended family through indigenous cultural rituals to bring resolution to their parents' death and memorialize their departure. How did the rituals fit into Karimi's Christian faith? That week, Karimi's homework was to meet with her pastor, sister, and family elders to discuss the rituals they could observe to remember and honor their parents. They decided to memorialize the departed through the unveiling of the cross at the grave and a feast of remembrance and thanksgiving served in their traditional homestead where the graves of the departed were located. In therapy, I reviewed what facing the grave for the first time would mean to the client. She remembered the need to use triggers as cues to do PMR or some other relaxation techniques learned in therapy.

On memorializing day, in the company of her sister, family, and friends, Karimi was able to visit her parents' grave for the first time. Later in therapy, she reported that a heavy weight was lifted from her heart. At home, friends and family had eaten together and shared memorable things about the departed couple. The two women brought back pictures of her parents, some shared by relatives and friends, and began to create an album of memory. Karimi's aunt, who had threatened the young woman that she might be cursed, joined the family and remembered the departed couple in amazing ways. Listening to the family and friends gathered to memorialize her parents, she realized that their death was not a waste after all. The narratives and telling and retelling of stories about her parents increased Karimi's sense of meaning and adjustment.

In therapy, continued trauma psychoeducation involved training to sustain healing. I discussed the need to exercise, rest, drink lots of water, maintain a healthy diet, and ensure that she gradually restored her leisure activities. Through treatment, I repeated trauma severity assessment several times as well as the SUDS. There was a consistent decrease in symptom severity. When I started considering termination, her sleep and eating patterns were almost back to normal as was her appetite. Post-traumatic stress disorder symptoms had reduced considerably to a score of either 1 (*slight problem*) or 0 (*not a problem*).

Karimi was now ready to discuss matters of faith by exploring her survivor guilt and helplessness to save her mother. She began to realize that because she, herself, had been pinned in the wreck, she could not have helped anyone; she also came to understand that the accident was beyond her control and that the perpetrator was the person to blame. Karimi asked if we could pray together so that she could let God carry her helplessness. Praying aloud, she told God that she knew that she was not to blame and asked forgiveness for allowing helplessness and loneliness to dictate her life. That day Karimi declared that she would resume daily Bible reading and prayer. Her church attendance was becoming more regular.

The final therapy process involved Karimi's planning to move out of her sister's house to her own apartment. I saw Karimi for a few more sessions. Her nightmares were gone, and she was concentrating better at work. She was able to take public transportation when with workmates. During our final session, she reported that she had placed her parents' picture on a central place in her apartment.

DISCUSSION AND ANALYSIS

This client narrated her trauma memory interspersed with interventions of anxiety and stress management, with particular attention to relaxation exercises and desensitization related to symptoms of avoidance. Rather than avoiding triggers of her trauma reactions, Karimi received trauma psychoeducation through each phase of treatment. The process of healing and adjustment included understanding the impact of the traumatic incident, that is, experiencing a near-death accident; dealing with hyperarousal; reexperiencing the accident through nightmares, loss, and grief; experiencing emotional distancing from her sister; suffering from social withdrawal; living with the fear that she was somehow responsible for the accident; and having poor work performance. Homework helped the client to apply a personal analysis examining strengths, weaknesses, opportunities, and threats so as to understand self, family, organization, community, and other focuses of change. In therapy the client created a personal, family, organizational, and community plan for change. She learned how to use SUDS within a regular relaxation program. Sustainable change is maintained through social supports of family and social/work connections undergirded with expert help from therapy with consistent monitoring and evaluation.

Karimi learned interpersonal skills that assisted with resocialization. Cognitive restructuring helped her change her perspective, especially in her sense of value and in understanding her sister's fears that kept the older woman from wholly accepting the client. Recommitment to Christian spiritual values and disciplines helped restore meaning. Finally, African indigenous community interconnectedness as well as rituals of memorializing the departed and celebrating life with the community placed the client in a web of caring connections. These connections began to enhance resiliency and sustain the healing.

Challenges in working with indigenous clients from a different cultural group exist. Indeed, as is common in Kenya, the communication and conversations seamlessly weave together English, Kiswahili, and Ki-Meru.

The Oasis Africa's Transformational Psychology model incorporates understanding of wholeness and health as it relates to an individual's identity. The goal of this model is to reclaim and restore the individual within a cushion of community belonging. The process involves integration of Western psychotherapies with African indigenous methodologies, religious coping, and social support to create an integrated multidisciplinary eclectic approach to psychotherapy. The individual's resiliency is a combination of indigenous cultural values, the quantity and strength of social connections, and the level of spirituality that embraces matters of faith and the interconnectedness of the individual with others and with God. This approach acknowledged Karimi's African-shared values of her identity: sociality, patience, tolerance, sympathy, acceptance, and spirituality. Through patience with her older sister and endurance from her spirituality, she was able to identify the values they shared. As African girls and daughters of the same mother, they valued certain psychological and moral characteristics that define African ethnic shared values, for example, hospitality, friendliness, and *ubuntu*, where one seeks the common good emphasizing the community versus the individual (Makgoba, 1997).

Integrative psychology as used in this case study combined the person-centered approach to establish a therapeutic alliance, whereas narrative psychother-

59

apy helped construct Karimi's story (Kelley, 2002; Reyneke, 2004). The use of psychodynamic–interpersonal skills offered an opportunity to explore and listen to the client's worries and concerns, whereas trauma-focused cognitive behavior therapy was used to work with the client's trauma symptoms. The therapy identified self-defeating thoughts, actions, and feelings that were compromising coping. Throughout this case, best practices were used to integrate Western psychological theory and indigenous psychologies and therapies (Papadopoulos, 2008). This approach kept at the fore Karimi's needs and adopted solutions shaped by an understanding of her psyche, its experiences, as well as its cultural and ethnic calabashes where her individual personality had been brewed.

CONCLUSION

In delivering psychotherapy to African clients, therapists should use an integration of several models of psychotherapy as informed by Western psychological theory, the client's African indigenous value systems, and the client's spiritual beliefs and coping styles. Knowledge of psychological theory and selection of appropriate psychotherapeutic interventions are required to integrate approaches that meet the client's needs. The needs of an African indigenous client go beyond individual coping to call for community engagement in sustainable healing. Finally, matters of disciplined spirituality connect the human to the Divine for care and sustenance.

QUESTIONS

1. What personal diversity factors worked to shape Karimi's response to the traumatic incident?
2. How do Karimi's diversity factors enhance her coping and resilience?
3. Instead of an integration approach, we could have chosen to use one therapeutic orientation, for example, trauma-focused cognitive behavior therapy. Would this approach have led to the full resolution of the client's presenting problem?
4. Critically examine this case and discuss its strengths and limitations.
5. Discuss how you could have worked with the client using your own therapeutic orientation.

REFERENCES

Davis, C. G., Wortman, C. B., Lehman, D. R., & Silver, R. C. (2000). Searching for meaning in loss: Are clinical assumptions correct? *Death Studies, 24,* 497–540.

Hoogvelt, A. (1974). Modernization and individual modernity: Structural convergence and psychological syndromes. *Africana Research Bulletin, 4,* 23–37.

Kelley, P. (2002). Narrative therapy. In A. R. Roberts & G. J. Greene (Eds.), *Social workers' desk reference* (pp. 121–124). New York, NY: Oxford University Press.

Makgoba, M. W. (1997). *MOKOKO: The Makgoba affair—A reflection on transformation.* Florida Hills, South Africa: Vivlia.

Mwiti, G. K., & Dueck, A. (2006). *Christian counseling: An African indigenous perspective.* Pasadena, CA: Fuller Press.

Mwiti, G. K., & James, N. N. (2013). Counseling and psychotherapy in sub-Saharan Africa: Brewed in an African pot with Western seasoning. In R. Moodley, U. Gielen, & R. Wu (Eds.), *Handbook of counseling and psychotherapy in an international context* (pp. 72–82). New York, NY: Routledge.

Nyasani, J. M. (1997). *The African psyche*. Nairobi, Kenya: University of Nairobi and Theological Printing Press.

Papadopoulos, R. K. (2008). Systemic challenges in a refugee camp. *Context, 98,* 16–19.

Reyneke, R. P. (2004). Die benutting van narratiewe beginsels tydens gemeenkapsontwikkeling [The use of narrative principles during community development]. *Maatskaplike Werk* [Social Work], *40,* 125–137.

Thairu, K. (1975). *The African civilization*. Nairobi, Kenya: Kenya Literature Bureau.

Part Three

Counseling and Psychotherapy in Australia and Asia

Chapter 8

COUNSELING AND PSYCHOTHERAPY IN AUSTRALIA: CYNTHIA'S STORY

Nadine Pelling

INTRODUCTION

Australia epitomizes diversity. Not only do the country's original inhabitants, Aboriginal and Torres Strait Islander people, call Australia home but so do immigrants from more than 200 countries; more than a quarter of the 23 million people were born overseas. Religions practiced by Australians include Christianity, Judaism, and Buddhism. Although Australia's neighbors are mainly Asian, the country keenly follows both European and North American educational and popular trends.

Australia has a universal health care system. The most prevalent mental health issues experienced in Australia are anxiety, depression, and substance abuse. A government subsidy exists for private psychological treatment when a client is referred by a general medical practitioner. The subsidy is highest for clinical psychologists and lower for general and counseling psychologists. Some not-for-profit organizations—those serving 100 or more couples a year—will soon have limited access to funding for couples counseling in a planned trial of subsidized relationship counseling, if this proposed measure remains in the enacted government budget. Private counseling and counselors are not subsidized, although lobbying exists. Psychology is legally regulated, whereas counseling is voluntarily regulated.

The majority of therapists are female and between the ages of 49–53. Counselors tend to be married, heterosexual, and live in urban environments as well as report being Christian and Caucasian. The most predominant therapy theories include eclecticism with cognitive behavior and narrative influences. Most therapists have an honors/bachelor's or a master's degree (Lack & Pelling, 2009). Regardless of theoretical leanings, when government subsidies are involved only approved strategies are allowed. Approved strategies include psychoeducation, motivational interviewing, cognitive behavior therapy (CBT), interpersonal therapy for depression, and narrative therapy (with Aboriginal and Torres Strait Islander people; see, for discussion, Brown, 2013).

CBT is an empirically supported treatment for both anxiety and depression. It is short term and problem focused, and it merges behavioral and cognitive therapeutic approaches. Through CBT, clients become aware of maladaptive cognitive–affective–behavioral connections and identify and experience alternative patterns. Problem-solving and relaxation training are included within CBT strategies along with identifying and disputing cognitive distortions; in addition, behavioral techniques such as activation and rehearsal are used. Goals include symptom reduction and improvement of quality of life (Craske, 2010).

This chapter discusses therapy with a Caucasian Australian woman of Jewish heritage presenting with both anxiety and depressive symptoms.

THE CLIENT

Cynthia is a 61-year-old Caucasian woman. She is heterosexual and is in a committed long-term relationship. She lives alone. She is Jewish but not active in the structured practice of her faith. Her parents were Nazi Holocaust survivors, and most of their relatives were "wiped out" during that time; as such, Cynthia is a child of survivors (COS). She is child-free and the sole surviving member of her family. Cynthia is middle-class educationally, occupationally, and financially. As a teacher, Cynthia supports herself by engaging in relief teaching.

PRESENTING ISSUES AND CHALLENGES

Cynthia presented with signs and symptoms of both anxiety and depression. She presented as physically agitated. Her symptoms fulfilled the criteria for generalized anxiety disorder in that for more than 6 months she had experienced excessive anxiety and worry, more often than not, which was difficult for her to control. As a result, she found herself "on edge" as well as tense, and she experienced sleep disturbance. In addition, Cynthia met the criteria for dysthymic disorder in that for an extended period she noted low self-esteem and difficulty making decisions. Her general practitioner (GP) doctor noted depression, and Cynthia had been taking antidepressant medication for years. As generalized anxiety disorder is not diagnosed when symptoms occur exclusively during a mood disorder, the diagnosis applied was dysthymic disorder.

CASE HISTORY AND DEVELOPMENTAL BACKGROUND

Cynthia was previously a cigarette smoker. Her GP also noted a history of binge alcohol use as well as some hazardous use, which was modified as early as 1999. Cynthia noted choosing to abstain from alcohol approximately 8 months prior to our first meeting. Historical information obtained indicated that her parents were probably depressed but were not treated. Cynthia reported taking Zoloft for more than 12 years. Although she was of small size and healthy weight, she indicated formerly being overweight.

Cynthia was educated as a teacher and had been employed in the education field as a teacher/relief teacher for years. Cynthia started on her doctor of philosophy degree (PhD) years ago in linguistics but found this pursuit isolating and depressing and thus withdrew from study about 10 years ago. Cynthia was an only child and cared for her parents as they aged. The Nazi Holocaust effectively eliminated the majority of her family members, meaning her family was without regular familial supports even more than most immigrants in their adopted home of Australia. She noted periods of social isolation in which she saw friends intermittently every few months.

THE THERAPY

The stated goal for treatment was to "get rid of the dark cloud" overshadowing Cynthia. When I first met Cynthia, she noted that she feared the "worst will happen" in life and that she would "not be able to handle it"; thus, she often felt as though the "sky is falling in." She indicated that she often woke during the night thinking about "doing work well." Cynthia noted her goal for treatment was to lower her anxiety.

It was clear from the outset that Cynthia engaged in negative self-talk. She described her anxieties and fears and then called them "stupid" and "silly." Moreover, despite being well educated and clearly intelligent, she was viewing her decision not to proceed with her PhD as a failing. As a consequence, having already discussed the link between thoughts, feelings, and behaviors, we designed a homework activity. To be specific, she was to write down her feelings, her accompanying thoughts, and the situations in which these occurred. The goals were to demonstrate the connection between thoughts and feelings for Cynthia as well as to identify her main cognitive distortions.

Our second meeting was a few weeks later. Cynthia had recorded a great deal of information relating to her life situations, feelings, and thoughts. Cynthia noted that she was now acutely aware of the connection of her thoughts to her feelings both positive and negative. We reviewed her homework in detail, and I invited Cynthia to help me examine trends in her thoughts and feelings and their connections.

Standard thinking distortions were identified and discussed throughout our work together as they connected to our session content. Our discussions were colloquial in manner and generally did not use CBT terminology. Cynthia is conversant in linguistics and noted ruminative thoughts. I believed that a focus on conversational language and easily remembered maxims designed to promote health and realistic thinking would encourage their adoption. Thus, at the end of each session, we summarized our work in an easy-to-remember saying. Because the bulk of our work consisted of identifying and disputing various categories of cognitive distortions, a number of these distortions are discussed here, accompanied by a brief description of how they were addressed.

Fortune Telling (jumping to conclusions and arbitrarily predicting things will turn out bad) and Catastrophizing (e.g., what could happen will be so awful that it cannot be endured) were two cognitive distortions causing distress. To be specific, Cynthia noted one of her main fears was "ending up in a wheelchair" and as a result being "dependent on others," which would be awful. She maintained this fear despite the fact that she had no physical ailments relating to likely wheelchair use and knowing the "silly and stupid" nature of her fear.

In response, we discussed examining the evidence for her fear of becoming wheelchair reliant. We noted it would be an idea to count how many people she encountered over a few weeks using a wheelchair to judge how common that might be in reality. As expected, Cynthia did not encounter large numbers of wheelchair-using people. The unlikelihood of her fear coming true was disputed and her anxiety lessened. The accompanying concern regarding being "dependent on others" and how awful that would be was examined. We discussed how there are different levels of being dependent as well as interdependent. Thus, thinking in moderation was encouraged in contrast to dichotomous thinking.

Mental or Negative Filtering (dwelling on negatives and ignoring or discounting positives) was another cognitive distortion causing Cynthia distress when combined with Magnification and Minimization (blowing things out of proportion and shrinking importance inappropriately, respectively). These cognitive distortions were actively involved in the production of her financial and work anxieties. When discussing her financial challenges, Cynthia would move quickly from a superficial listing of fears to the reasons she "shouldn't" be thinking like that and why she "ought" not be concerned as she "knew others were worse off" than she. Her financial fears led to fears of not gaining enough work, and then work subsequently gained a place of prominence in her life. She was engaging in a ruminative cycle of concern and self-denigration regarding being concerned.

In response to the intertwined ideas that Cynthia would be in great financial need as she got older and that she was "silly" to scare herself with such thoughts, we examined the evidence for both. Was Cynthia likely to be in great future financial need? No. She had her own home and income from her teaching activities. In Australia, we also have a welfare system that provides assistance with the cost of living even when you own your own home and/or have assets. Conversely, was Cynthia "silly" for being concerned about finances? No. It would be "silly" not to be concerned about finances when one is past 60 and has no family upon which to rely. By focusing on the details of both her financial need and resources in a slower and more measured manner, we were able to properly challenge her distressful ruminations about finances and halt labeling herself as "silly." Cynthia had a need to be thoughtful and purposeful financially. She needed to respond, not react, to financial concerns. Again, in our work we affirmed the middle ground as a more realistic depiction of her concerns.

Cynthia's self- and situational descriptors were replete with "should statements" (criticizing oneself with should, must, and ought statements) mixed with all-or-nothing thinking (seeing things in dichotomous categories and wanting to be perfect). She wondered whether she "should" revisit her unfinished PhD but did not want to do so. She "must" maintain her connections with friends and acquaintances but had not done so. She "ought" to enjoy life more but wondered what that meant for her financial security. She "should" make herself financially secure by developing the land upon which her house is located but liked living in her home as is. Her dichotomous thinking and propensity to question her "best" course of action were directly related to her being unable to move forward.

How could Cynthia move forward and make needed life decisions? We reiterated that Cynthia was the expert on herself and only she knew what was going to be best for her and her situation. We focused on how and on what basis she could make her needed decisions. We noted that decisions can be based on status, finances, emotional comfort, physical health, and relational impact. I encouraged Cynthia to focus on what she wanted and what was important to her instead of on what she did not want. We discussed how any decision will have negative and positive results, and accordingly there was no one perfect solution to any problem.

In response to Cynthia's self-recriminations, we challenged the standards she expected of herself and examined her self-definition as lacking. We reframed supposed weaknesses as humanity. We discussed changing her standard from perfection to acceptable, and this allowed forward movement and self-acceptance.

Behaviorally, we reviewed breathing techniques, progressive muscle relaxation, and imagery to reduce tension. Hypnosis reinforced Cynthia's ability to identify her cognitive distortions and healthy alternatives as well as her experience of relaxation. One such hypnosis session involved a camel trek through the red center of Australia over various terrains in a methodical and purposeful manner. This hypnosis session used a dream holiday discussed by Cynthia and was thus very personal.

After our fifth session, Cynthia noted being "over" her wheelchair fear and being more purposeful regarding her work activities. She had left the idea of finishing her PhD in the past and was not chastising herself for this decision. She was allowing herself to be human and was enjoying life more. She noted being busy in her garden, had connected with a female rabbi at a local synagogue, and was reporting social contacts.

DISCUSSION AND ANALYSIS

Cynthia was a compliant and engaged client. Although she was depressed as well as anxious, overwhelmed by negative thoughts, and historically engaged in a variety of unhealthy coping activities and habits, she also had hope. She had hope that she could feel and be different. She simply did not know how to feel and be different despite the fact that she had already started to take action by moderating and then ending her own overeating as well as alcohol and nicotine abuse. By connecting her thoughts and feelings and examining her alternatives to negative self-talk, Cynthia was able to change her perception and attitude toward herself and her circumstances; as a result, her feelings moderated, and a variety of healthy activities became possible to her, which thus reinforced her positive changes.

Cynthia benefited from a number of the helpful 6 Cs in therapy, which draw on some of the scholarship surrounding common factors (Grencavage & Norcross, 1990). To be specific, the following Cs were used: connection, choosing, contingency, conditioning, consciousness raising, and catharsis. First, Cynthia was connected to both the therapist and her GP, and thus a strong therapeutic alliance was forged. Second, Cynthia was empowered to change her feelings by changing her thoughts after examining them for usefulness. Cynthia was asked to choose for herself what thoughts to encourage and to evaluate for herself the impact they had on her feelings and behaviors. Her coping skills, healthy relaxation techniques, or unhealthy habits were also reframed as choices that Cynthia could make daily. Behaviorally, Cynthia gained some measure of control over her anxious feelings through practicing various breathing and relaxation techniques, and she learned that her feelings, thoughts, and behaviors were influenced by aspects of conditioning and contingency. Psychoeducation in terms of healthy self-care and life-balance goals raised her conscious awareness regarding the need for fun in her life and the choices regarding those opportunities available to her. Finally, Cynthia was able to express her feelings and have them accepted and understood in her own context, allowing for a cathartic release. However, Cynthia benefited most from an increase in (a) her conscious understanding regarding how her own thought processes affected her mood and (b) her ability to adjust her thoughts to purposefully moderate her mood via identifying cognitive distortions and practicing their alternatives.

The CBT approach worked well with Cynthia, who was engaged in therapy and was personally thought- and language-oriented, as demonstrated by her interest in linguistics. She demonstrated a high level of self-awareness and easily learned the skills required to challenge her cognitive distortions and encourage relaxation. The way in which Cynthia and I, her therapist, worked together addressed Cynthia's negative mood and anxieties as well as her cognitions and behaviors. Her cognitions were moderated and made more realistic and less negative. Her behaviors became more purposeful and focused on balance and what would promote health.

Therapy indirectly addressed diversity issues. Cynthia's age related to her future financial fears, and the realistic nature of financial concerns at such an age were affirmed. Her child-free status and her living alone affected her anxiety regarding possibly needing care in the future. Women tend to live longer than men, and with no children Cynthia would have to support herself in her later years. Her middle-class status and professional standing helped to buffer the impact of such factors. It was interesting that when I attempted to directly use Cynthia's religion metaphorically in one of our hypnosis sessions, it was not recognized. Even when I brought up stories from the Tanakh (what Christians call the Old Testament), Cynthia did not notice. When I subsequently discussed the metaphors that came up in therapy—for example, Moses in the desert and flowing water from a rock once struck—it was clear that Cynthia's religion was not central to her experience. This situation was not surprising as research has indicated that COS tend to identify less with feelings of being Jewish (Baron, Eisman, Scuello, Veyzer, & Lieberman, 1996). Luckily, the imagery used was nonetheless relaxing. Exploring Cynthia's status as a COS and linking a possible survivor syndrome to her depressive and anxious symptoms was an option in her therapy (Baron, Reznikoff, & Glenwick, 1993; Phillips, 1978).

Cynthia's parents were Nazi Holocaust survivors, and she, herself, was a COS. In her writing about the Second Generation, Bendor (2008) noted the importance of cognitively reframing one's experience from victim to victor. Cynthia did this reframing in her therapy in the here and now. Cynthia clearly noted how it was not enough to be a mere survivor. Indeed, Cynthia was on the earth to thrive! Perhaps a greater focus on Cynthia's COS status would have enhanced therapy, or perhaps it would have unduly focused on the negatives of human nature and circumstances.

CONCLUSION

Cynthia's case is quintessentially Australian. First, it focused on anxiety and depression. Second, it involved a client and a psychologist in private practice with government-subsidized services. Third, it was time limited, addressed the referral reason, and used an efficacious therapy approach. In addition, Cynthia's case is specifically multicultural by virtue of the differing characteristics of both the client and therapist.

QUESTIONS

1. What impact do you think Cynthia's COS status had on her (a) mood and (b) fear of becoming wheelchair bound, which would result in a dependency upon others?
2. How did the treatment honor Cynthia's family history?
3. How do you think treatment would have proceeded had the therapist and Cynthia focused on Second Generation issues versus cognitive distortions?

4. In Australia we have what is known as the "Stolen Generation" (a generation of Indigenous children, now adults, forcibly taken from their homes to be raised in the dominant majority culture) to which Second Generation issues relate. Can you think of any cultural or religious groups to which Second Generation issues could be pertinent where you live?

5. Make an argument that Cynthia could have been diagnosed with either an anxiety or somatoform disorder. Why did the therapist therefore diagnose dysthymia versus an anxiety or somatoform disorder?

REFERENCES

Baron, L., Eisman, H., Scuello, M., Veyzer, A., & Lieberman, M. (1996). Stress resilience, locus of control, and religion in children of Holocaust victims. *Journal of Psychology, 130,* 513–525.

Baron, L., Reznikoff, M., & Glenwick, D. (1993). Narcissism, interpersonal adjustment, and coping in children of Holocaust survivors. *Journal of Psychology, 127,* 257–264.

Bendor, S. J. (2008). Strong at the broken places: Diverse voices from the second generation. *Journal of Jewish Communal Service, 83,* 243–249.

Brown, J. (2013). Counseling and psychotherapy in Australia: Championing the egalitarian society? In R. Moodley, U. Gielen, & R. Wu (Eds.), *Handbook of counseling and psychotherapy in an international context* (pp. 171–181). New York, NY: Routledge.

Craske, M. (2010). *Cognitive–behavioral therapy.* Washington, DC: American Psychological Association.

Grencavage, L. M., & Norcross, J. C. (1990). Where are the commonalities among the therapeutic common factors? *Professional Psychology: Research and Practice, 21,* 372–378.

Lack, C. W., & Pelling, N. (2009). Who are Australian counsellors and how do they attend to their professional development? In N. Pelling, J. Barletta, & P. Armstrong (Eds.), *The practice of clinical supervision* (212–221). Bowen Hills, Queensland, Australia: Australian Academic Press.

Phillips, R. E. (1978). Impact of Nazi Holocaust on children of survivors. *American Journal of Psychotherapy, 32,* 370–378.

Chapter 9

COUNSELING AND PSYCHOTHERAPY IN CHINA: YANG'S STORY

Shi Qijia, Yu Ping, Doris F. Chang, and Wolfgang Senf

INTRODUCTION

China is one of the oldest countries in the world, with its history dating back more than 5,000 years; it has 56 different ethnic groups, the largest population on the earth, and a great difference between regions and ethnic groups. On May 12, 2008, an 8.0-magnitude earthquake devastated the Wenchuan County of China's Sichuan Province, leading to the tragic loss of more than 68,000 lives, including some 5,000 school children. This tragedy has had a major impact on the role of counseling and psychotherapy in China.

The growth of counseling, psychotherapy, and psychology has been on the rise. In this emerging field, there are many different counseling and psychotherapy approaches that have been introduced, such as psychoanalysis, cognitive behavior therapy, humanistic psychotherapy, family therapy, and so on (see, for discussion, Chang, Cao, Shi, Wang, & Qian, 2013). In recent years, China has begun to show interest in interpersonal psychotherapy (IPT) as a treatment (Miniati et al., 2014). Chinese therapists have been attempting to improve their patients' social functioning, help them rebuild an emotional connection with other people, and face the challenges in their daily life through IPT.

In this chapter, we discuss the case of Yang, who presented with posttraumatic stress disorder (PTSD) on the basis of diagnostic criteria from the *Diagnostic and Statistical Manual of Mental Disorders* (5th ed.; American Psychiatric Association, 2013) following the death of her child in the earthquake and her subsequent pregnancy. Her trauma experience and struggle are typical of a special group of survivors referred to by the media as "mother in the quake-hit area." We discuss her therapy and explore how therapy helped her recover from the tragedy and face the challenges of raising the new baby.

THE CLIENT

Yang is a 41-year-old married heterosexual Chinese female worker from a small town in southwestern China that sustained heavy damage in the earthquake. She was the mother of an 18-year-old son who died when his school collapsed during the earthquake. When she initiated treatment 1 year after his death, Yang was 6 months pregnant with her second child. Like most other Chinese, she would be considered working class and does not identify with any religion.

PRESENTING ISSUES AND CHALLENGES

Yang's presenting issues appeared to stem from experiences of trauma and loss surrounding her primary identity as a mother. For a year following the death of her son, Yang reported that she felt depressed, had difficulty sleeping and had nightmares, and cried frequently at night for no reason. Furthermore, she reported difficulties getting along with her husband and neighbors. At the time she presented, she experienced major challenges on how to face and raise her second child because she was still disturbed by the memory of her dead son. Not only did she think she would not be able to overcome her grief, but she also had many reasons to fear for her new baby.

CASE HISTORY AND DEVELOPMENTAL BACKGROUND

Yang grew up in the village and was brought up with her older sister in a traditional close-knit Chinese family. The traditional idea of a Chinese family, especially in the rural area, dictates that only boys could carry on the family line. Yang reported feeling significant pressure, which she attributed to her father's continual dissatisfaction with her and her sister's female gender. So Yang's son had a special meaning for her because there were only girls in her original family.

Her deceased son, Daiyang, was a high school student who was described as intelligent, diligent, and healthy. He loved drawing and music and excelled at calligraphy. Yang believed that it was her son's diligence that led to his death, as he was studying in the classroom when the earthquake hit, whereas his classmates were enjoying their free period on the playground. Yang was very close to her son, relying on him for daily activities as well as emotional support.

After Yang received the news about her son's death, she rushed to the school. So many children had died that there was not enough room to lay their bodies in a sheltered area. Her son's body was laid outside exposed to the elements and was soaked by the pouring rain. For a long time afterwards, Yang had frequent dreams of her child telling her, "Mom, I am so cold!"

Since the earthquake, Yang had experienced frequent flashbacks of the scene of her son's death, which made her feel miserable and anxious. She avoided any news that was earthquake-related and was unwilling to speak of the event. She reported significant memory difficulties, anhedonia, and sleep difficulties. Despite China's One-Child family planning policy, families who lost children in the earthquake were given special permission to have another child. Many mothers in the quake-hit area such as Yang were allowed to get pregnant again. Initially, her husband did not want another child; however, Yang insisted and conceived in December 2008, 7 months after her son's death. She reported nausea and loss of appetite related to the pregnancy, which lasted throughout the first trimester.

Although she reported substantial social support from her neighbors and colleagues at work, after her son's death, she argued frequently with her husband and neighbors and felt affectively numb.

THE THERAPY

Yang's long history of PTSD symptoms and interpersonal problems made her a good candidate for IPT, which differs theoretically and technically from other PTSD treatments in that it aims to reduce the impaired interpersonal function resulting in PTSD rather than exposing the client to traumatic events so that he or she can reprocess them. Our ITP for the PTSD comprised seven weekly 50-minute sessions. The therapist largely devoted the initial two sessions to an "interpersonal list," collecting information to recognize current relationships, understand overall patterns of interpersonal activities, and connect relationships to symptoms. Then the therapist drew up the case, gave the diagnosis—which focused on interpersonal problems—and discussed this planning with the patient. Sessions 3 to 7 focused on completing mourning and resolving the interpersonal problem area (e.g., lack of relationship). The therapist also provided some relaxation exercises as a complementary skill. The final sessions focused on dealing with separation, an important interpersonal event for the patient from the beginning of the time-limited therapy.

The therapist initially focused on exploring Yang's feelings about her son's death. In the third session, Yang stated that she did not want her new baby to know of the existence of her deceased son. She became intensely emotional and was aided by the use of relaxation techniques in session. The fourth session was spent entirely in silence, with the therapist and patient sitting quietly without speaking. This session appeared to mark a turning point in the relationship, and Yang began to more fully trust the therapist. She remarked, "I didn't know that a relationship between two people could be like this until I met you." At the time, the therapist described the moment as a shared emotional "field," with two individuals both immersed in mourning.

After Yang was finally able to accept the fact of her son's death, the treatment targeted her relationship with her husband and significant others and finally her expectations of the baby and their future. Although she initially complained about her husband's lack of understanding, she began to see that they were lacking in communication skills. The therapist assisted her in recalling happy memories from their relationship and viewing the relationship as a resource. She gradually reported improvements in her mood and relationships with others, although her memory difficulties persisted. After several weeks, she reported finally taking down the portrait of her deceased son that had occupied a prominent place in her home.

In the final session, the therapist explored Yang's feelings about her growing baby. She reported relief that her psychological state and relationships had improved, as she had been concerned about adversely affecting her baby. Although she had withdrawn from her extended family following the death of her son, Yang began to view them as sources of support. She decided to initiate contact with them as she made plans for the upcoming birth of her baby. Follow-up interviews were conducted twice by telephone.

DISCUSSION AND ANALYSIS

Because of the One-Child family planning policy in China, the single child in the family means a great deal to that family, especially to mothers. Furthermore, in Chinese culture, there are gender differences in the social life. Because of the influence of the division of labor and socialization, males have some power of domination and control; at the same time, influenced by Chinese traditional culture, especially advocated by Confucian culture of "male superiority to female" and "Three Obediences and Four Virtues," the social value of females is devalued. Therefore, a boy is viewed as more valuable than a girl, as boys are considered important for maintaining continuity between generations and guaranteeing that parents will be cared for in their old age, particularly in villages and towns. For these reasons, Yang experienced the loss of her son as catastrophic. Her identity status as a common worker from a remote village was also critical in understanding her loss experience. As is typical of many villagers, Yang and her husband had invested in their son's education as a path toward upward mobility for their whole family. Reflecting these efforts, her son excelled in high school, and his achievements were a source of pride for Yang and her family. Like most Chinese families, this one-child relationship is vulnerable. When parents lose their children, they may lose everything in their lives. In this context, Yang's response to her son's death may not be considered atypical.

Other women who have lost their children have also reported feelings of sadness, hopelessness, anxiety, and fear. Some have even reported obsessive thoughts or have found themselves preoccupied with thoughts of death. Accompanying these difficulties is often a strong sense of guilt and shame. In the quake-hit areas, however, rebuilding efforts have emphasized other infrastructure projects, and mental health treatment is limited and difficult to obtain.

As a result, these women and their infants represent a particularly vulnerable group. Deterioration in self-care may translate into failure to obtain proper prenatal care and engagement in dangerous or self-destructive behaviors. There is also concern that the attachment process may be disturbed in these distressed mothers and their children, which would adversely affect infant development. As a result, it is of critical importance to provide special assistance to these mothers of the quake-hit area.

In China, for the mother, having a son increases her status and power within her husband's family. Milestones of separation include when the child turns 18, when he or she enters adulthood, when the child moves out of the natal home, and when parent or child dies—the ultimate separation. For Yang, the best way to deal with the loss of her child was to give birth to a new one. However, her pregnancy sparked feelings of guilt regarding her first-born, producing an intense emotional reaction to the pregnancy beyond the normal range. The establishment of a stable and secure therapy relationship was deemed a necessity for successful treatment and recovery. Thus, the therapist focused Yang's feelings toward her growing baby and her resources for support.

Although IPT was initially used as a treatment for depression (Weathers, Keane, & Davidson, 2001), it has been successfully applied to other problems such as PTSD (Krupnick et al., 2008). In recent years, China has begun to show interest in IPT as a treatment that may be applicable to the Chinese. There are several reasons why we chose to administer IPT for this patient in particular. First, Yang lacked an emotional connection with her husband and reported a significant decline in social functioning in general. Although she was immersed in sorrow over the death of her son, she was facing the challenges and demands of raising a new baby. Therefore, the priority was to reestablish a supportive social support network.

Because IPT is a brief, time-limited intervention, it was suitable for the limited resources available in the quake-hit area. From the perspective of IPT, it was important to address the client's complicated grief reaction. Strategies included helping the patient express her feelings about the death of her son, develop a coherent narrative of her loss experience, and conceptualize her well-being and recovery within an interpersonal framework. In attempting to promote emotional expression and acceptance, the therapist encouraged Yang to talk about her child, using his photo and belongings to facilitate her emotional expression. The therapist also encouraged her to engage in activities that would help her complete the mourning process, such as visiting her son's gravesite. Role-plays were used to explore what Yang would say if she saw her son again. In the final session, Yang showed her son's calligraphy to the therapist, recalled her son's many achievements, and discussed how to tell the new baby the story of his older brother. This was taken as evidence that Yang was finally able to accept the fact that her child had died and had begun to plan a new life.

To develop a coherent narrative of Yang's loss experience, she and the therapist discussed what to do with the portrait of her deceased son and whether or not to let the new baby know of his brother's existence. After some time, Yang decided to take her son's photo down from the wall because she thought it would help her recover from the loss more quickly. The therapist encouraged her to talk to her second child about the older brother's death to complete the normal process of mourning and role conversion. To conceptualize recovery and well-being within an interpersonal framework, the therapist engaged Yang in discussions about her relationship with her husband. As that central relationship improved and her symptoms slowly abated, the therapist helped Yang to understand the relationship's importance in her life. This process led to further discussions about the quality of her relationships with colleagues and relatives as well and their connection to her overall functioning and well-being.

In the latest follow-up interview, Yang stated that her symptoms and her relationship with her husband had shown significant improvement. She had also begun to chat with her colleagues at work again. The seven treatment sessions of IPT for PTSD offered Yang a chance to understand herself through her emotional and interpersonal patterns subsequent to her son's death. Formal exposure techniques were displaced by the IPT that focused on the patient's feelings in present interpersonal relationships through determination and communication analyses. Her PTSD symptoms seemed to decrease through the processes of understanding emotions and relationship patterns and the rebuilding of social support.

Yang's story emphasizes the characteristic of IPT that makes it potentially useful to patients with PTSD. The IPT interpersonal list could help patients explore their defective relationships over the core symptoms of PTSD that may adversely affect functioning. Yang struggled with her interpersonal relationships and her new baby. The more she discussed these struggles, the more she realized there was a connection between her relationships and her PTSD symptoms. The therapist gave her an opportunity to observe her interpersonal relationship not only with her husband but also with other significant people, which helped Yang recognize her guilt arising from her son's death and her new pregnancy.

CONCLUSION

Through the use of IPT, Yang was able to accept and mourn her dead son from her heart and emotions; it was indeed a very painful tragedy. She was able to re-establish a good relationship with her husband and significant others who were seen as important supportive resources for her daily life in the future. After dealing with her trauma, Yang was able to understand her guilt regarding her dead son and began to think about how to bring up a new baby. The short-term goals of IPT for this client included the following: (a) understanding trauma and creating a connection between symptoms and emotions; (b) establishing links among symptoms, feelings of grief, and interpersonal relationships; and (c) confirming the client's interpersonal relationship problems, such as role conflict, role change, and lack of relationships.

Over the last century, counseling and psychotherapy have undergone significant development in China. Different methods, such as psychoanalysis, cognitive therapy, and IPT, have been empirically proven to be effective in treating mental illness. Although the long-term efficacy of IPT for PTSD clients in the West has yet to be verified, the research in China has been ongoing, and the results will be assessed for its future development. Chinese psychological treatments, however, continue to face many problems when compared with Western approaches to therapy, such as those related to short-term therapies and problems of localization, among others.

QUESTIONS

1. Is this client's anxiety related to her age as an older mother?
2. Is pregnancy a risk factor that could increase the prevalence of PTSD with altered hormone levels?
3. Does women's status in the family and society affect their ability to cope with crisis?
4. How does length of treatment time influence the therapeutic effect?
5. What other methods could be used to improve the client's situation?

REFERENCES

American Psychiatric Association. (2013). *Diagnostic and statistical manual of mental disorders* (5th ed.). Arlington, VA: Author.

Chang, D. F., Cao, Y., Shi, Q., Wang, C., & Qian, M. (2013). Counseling and psychotherapy in China: Building capacity to serve 1.3 billion. In R. Moodley, U. Gielen, & R. Wu (Eds.), *Handbook of counseling and psychotherapy in an international context* (pp. 182–192). New York, NY: Routledge.

Krupnick, J. L., Green, B. L., Stockton, P., Miranda, J., Krause, E., & Mete, M. (2008). Group interpersonal psychotherapy for low-income women with posttraumatic stress disorder. *Psychotherapy Research, 18,* 497–507.

Miniati, M., Callari, A., Calugi, S., Rucci, P., Savino, M., Mauri, M., & Dell'Osso, L. (2014). Interpersonal psychotherapy for postpartum depression: A systematic review. *Archives of Women's Mental Health, 17,* 257–268.

Weathers, F. W., Keane, T. M., & Davidson, J. R. T. (2001). Clinician-Administered PTSD Scale: A review of the first ten years of research. *Depression and Anxiety, 13,* 132–156.

Chapter 10

COUNSELING AND PSYCHOTHERAPY IN INDIA: RADHA'S STORY

Priya Pothan and Tony Sam George

INTRODUCTION

India is an ancient land. Its area makes it the seventh-largest country in the world, and its diversity makes India a pluralist melting pot of various religions, languages, and customs. With rapid social changes evoked by globalization, family and couple systems face new stressors and possess fewer social support resources than before. Nevertheless, deeply rooted cultural expectations and social norms are still reflected in the tension that the average Indian faces in meeting the challenges of globalization. Counseling and psychotherapy in India are going through an important phase of maturation and development. However, manpower development is largely inadequate in the Indian mental health sector, with only 0.301 psychiatrists, 0.047 psychologists, and 0.033 social workers per 100,000 health professionals (Mental Health Atlas, 2011). Counselors and psychotherapists have tried and tested various theoretical and practice models among diverse clientele in India. Although the practice of counseling and psychotherapy tend to incorporate different formats of Western psychotherapy in an eclectic format, the reinvention of ancient Indian healing practices has added a new dimension to the clinical practice (see, for discussion, George & Pothan, 2013).

This eclectic format is demonstrated with a case illustration in which a combination of cognitive behavior models as well as a person-centered approach were emphasized. In Indian collectivistic society, the identity of self is largely relational (Roland, 2005), and psychological difficulties frequently manifest in the context of couples or family difficulties. A relational self, although applicable to both sexes, is more strongly descriptive of the self-construct of Indian women (Kumar, 1991). Hence, systemic frameworks are kept as the overarching principle in this case, with the added inclusion of indigenous healing approaches.

In this chapter, we discuss the case of Radha, who presented with depression and infertility. She was having marital difficulties, which heightened with her in-laws' infertility-based accusations. Considering that the issues the client presented with in the following case were linked to her particular situation (a woman with a disability in a patriarchal culture and living in a conservative Indian family), we decided to look at models that value systemic influences yet do not negate the personal meaning-making process of the client and her immediate family. The present challenges for counselors and psychotherapists in India are also evident.

THE CLIENT

Radha is an educated 32-year-old woman who has an engineering degree and works in a software multinational Company in Bangalore. She comes from a Brahmin upper-middle-class family in Tamil Nadu, Southern India. She is a practicing Hindu and strongly believes in the notion of karma, which assumes that the sum of a person's actions in this and previous states of existences decide the person's fate in this life. She has been married for 4 years and resides with her husband and his family (including his parents, his unmarried sisters, and his married brothers and their spouses and children) in Bangalore. Her husband is a North-Indian and works as a software professional in the same company.

PRESENTING ISSUES AND CHALLENGES

Radha presented to a female counseling psychologist with distress arising out of marital difficulties and female infertility. She found it difficult to deal with the hostility and blame projected onto her by her in-laws. She was accused by her mother-in-law of not revealing her "disability" before the marriage, although the client affirmed no prior knowledge of her infertility. Because of these accusations and her husband's wavering support, she perceived abandonment. She reported that she was starting to feel less self-sufficient and self-controlled, and that she experienced several moments of uncontrolled emotions of anger, fear, and sadness. She noted that small provocations or self-errors led to crying, and this had become more frequent over the last month. She also found herself believing that she was not a "worthy wife" as she was unable to create progeny, function independently, and carry out the roles required at home and the workplace. She tended to question herself and her abilities and found it difficult to concentrate on the task at hand. Her husband informed the counselor that he was becoming increasingly irritated with her reactivity.

CASE HISTORY AND DEVELOPMENTAL BACKGROUND

Radha had relocated with her mother from Dubai to India at the age of 16 to further her education. She recalled that she was upset to leave her father and viewed her mother as an excessive perfectionist. She found solace in the prayers and practices of Hinduism.

At the age of 28, Radha met her husband at her workplace and found him to be confident, loyal, and protective. However, his parents opposed the marriage, citing cultural incompatibility as he came from a nonvegetarian Sindhi community background. Her husband requested that she adjust to living with his family as he was the only son. She married him and learned to adjust to their cultural and dietary practices. She continued to do her Brahminical pujas but would not insist on her husband and his family joining her. (Brahminicial pujas are religious daily prayer rituals offered by Brahmins—a caste in Hindu tradition—as a form of worship; e.g., one may light an incense stick or a lamp while chanting a prayer to a deity.) Radha viewed her in-laws as pleasant and foresaw no future difficulties.

However, around a year and a half ago when she and her husband tried to conceive, her mother-in-law started to taunt her and had recently accused her of "cheating her son by not contributing to the maintenance of their family line." Radha felt rejected and disgraced at her husband's lack of support, and she felt lonely and confused. She believed in the karma theory that her earlier life behaviors had led to this infertility and she deserved to be punished. She looked at expectant mothers as blessed and felt hopeless. Radha sought magical–religious treatments by visiting several pilgrim sites and carried out several pujas that were based on the traditions of her husband's family and her own family of origin.

THE THERAPY

The focus of counseling was to alleviate Radha's psychological distress, help her redefine her identity, and explore alternatives to infertility in the individual and marital context. Radha attended 15 individual sessions and five couples counseling sessions over 6 months. She was initially resistant to attend sessions and stated that she wanted a fast cure.

The first two sessions predominately involved allowing Radha to vent within a cognitive behavior therapy focus. She felt frustrated with her life and kept mentioning that she should have stayed with her father in Dubai rather than coming to India and dealing with all these difficulties. She blamed herself for choosing her spouse, not realizing that she was infertile, which caused distress to her in-laws and her family. The counselor helped her look at herself in a more neutral perspective and taught her how she could stop the negative thoughts of blame and rejection. She found writing out her thoughts helpful, and she continued doing so every time she felt excessively preoccupied with these thoughts and when she felt overwhelmingly hopeless.

By the fourth session, she noted that her hopelessness and sadness had reduced, but she had strong moments of anger at herself. The counselor also found that Radha had withdrawn from participating in household work and kept ruminating about her difficulties. She was then assigned a daily activity schedule that kept her busy with household tasks and created effective personal time. She was asked to consciously shift her focus away from visiting pilgrim sites and to instead engage in tasks that she enjoyed. Radha spontaneously thought of doing gardening as she remembered that she used to care for a garden when she was 14 or 15 years old and described that period as the happiest time of her life. She was encouraged to also add a present-day task that she liked, and she responded with the hobby of photography. She was encouraged to do the tasks with pleasure and to try to accomplish more from these two hobbies.

By the end of the sixth session, Radha sounded excited to talk and show photographs of the plants she took under different light settings and also reported that other people had appreciated her for these efforts when she had posted some photographs on a social media website. As she gradually began to feel more confident and calm, she was also asked to broaden her coping to include problem solving, distractions, and socialization to cope with irritants at work and home. She was able to tune out her in-laws' reactions to her infertility and become mindful only of the task at hand.

Because traditional healing practices and spirituality are also important aspects of healing in India, in the fourth session the counselor suggested that Radha practice Pranayama (breathing control exercises), yoga, and meditation to create a sense of relaxation. The client mentioned that she had met two women who had an impact on her life; in addition, her sense of abandonment and unworthiness had started to decrease. One of the women had attended counseling herself and had found it beneficial. This knowledge increased Radha's willingness to work with the counselor and challenge herself with intrasession therapy tasks.

As storytelling and language are important aspects of Indian culture, a narrative therapy approach was followed. Radha reflected on how she saw women as childbearers and was critical toward them. She discovered that she had anger at how her mother took her away from her father for academic purposes and then frequently critiqued her; she realized that she still felt anger toward her mother for doing so. She then understood how she always wanted to please her father and that became generalized to seeking out others' approval; one form of approval was to have a child. When asked to describe herself, she found that the characteristics she frequently noted as her core characteristics were "caretaker," "critical," and "responsible." She recognized how her identity was rooted in her negative view of equating the status of a woman to a mother and how Indian families focus on childbearing with approval and satisfaction. Hence, she slowly grasped how her view of life was linked to the meaning she attributed to infertility in her sociocultural milieu. Radha was then asked to reauthor her life by redefining her sense of self and her identity as a person and through that gain a deeper understanding and care for herself as a person. She found this process very hard and wanted to stop coming for sessions. She then chose new identity words of "independent," "warm," "supportive," and "decisive" to characterize her new sense of identity and kept trying out the usage of these adjectives in her daily life. Learning how to accept the notions of others while maintaining her new identity was a process that she struggled with over a few sessions.

Radha then looked again at the concept of karma in her life and viewed it from a less judgmental perspective. She became more competent, calmer, and comfortable with herself and then was seen for three follow-up sessions to maintain the gains. She also reported in one of the follow-up sessions how she was able to tell a close friend how to look again at her own life and believed that this was something her old self would never have been able to do. She started to use photography to further her new narrative and took photographs from new and different angles to symbolize her self-related changes.

DISCUSSION AND ANALYSIS

According to a 2010 report by the International Institute of Population Sciences, infertility is growing at an alarming rate, especially in metropolitan areas. It has been estimated that, globally, of the 60–80 million couples suffering from infertility, about 15–20 million are in India alone (Times of India, 2012). Despite this rise in infertility, the cultural notions in India view motherhood as the main role of a women and as a source of pride. Radha's earlier adjustment to living with her husband's family indicated that she had been able to cope with different practices and customs. Coping with diversity is commonly seen in India and is often tolerated. However, with this particular client, one could see that her frustration tolerance broke at the diagnosis of infertility and the family's reaction to it. Her gynecologist's referral of her to a counselor after the diagnosis of female infertility indicated the difficulties Radha was having coping with this diagnosis in Indian society. Seventy percent of infertile couples in South Asia note that in-law interactions with the infertile wife are characterized by nagging, threatening divorce, or considering them inauspicious (Sudha, Reddy, Reddy, & Reddy, 2011). Hence, a similar client in the Western culture may have had difficulties primarily dealing with the concept of infertility, rather than this client who found it more difficult to cope with the familial reactions to her infertility. Jejeebhoy (1998) wrote, "In the South Asian setting, which prizes reproduction and in which women typically gain prestige and security in their husband's homes only after they have produced a son or two, few are unaware of the devastation infertility can cause for women's lives" (p. 20). Hence, the level of despair and rejection reported by the client is commonly evidenced in Indian families, and this is accentuated by the traditional belief of a woman performing the entwined roles of a wife and a mother. Thus, the client internalized her in-laws' reactions and also rejected herself as a wife and as an individual.

The client needed to be able to take another look at her herself and the concept of infertility within her sociocultural milieu. As opposed to Western formats of counseling and psychotherapy, individuation per se from her in-laws would not help the client. In addition, as childless women are stigmatized and not allowed to participate in various auspicious ceremonies, especially those involving childbirth and naming (Barua, Apte, Pande, & Walia, 2013), this religious ostracism made the client feel alienated and alone—especially as religion was an important aspect of her lifestyle and coping patterns. Her belief in karma, frequent visits to temple, and fear of subsequent ostracism made her feel pressured and reactive. The narrative format, with its emphasis on story-telling, also finds a strong base in the Indian religious mythology, and the client was able to find strength from reusing a familiar style to readdress self. In taking another look at religion, she was able to draw strength from its practices and find a balance between acceptance of her infertility and her religion.

Familial support is also considered important to the recovery process of mental illnesses in India. In the patriarchal society of India, infertility is often viewed as the wife's difficulty, and she alone has to find a solution to her problems. The marital sessions allowed the couple the chance to strengthen their marital bond, deal with the infertility as their joint difficulty rather than just the wife's problem, enhance their sexuality, and support each other. Even with current socioeconomic changes, the traditional gender roles of the husband as breadwinner and the wife as nurturer continue to exist, and the client's failure to provide a child meant failure of her role. Sexuality is also a less discussed topic, and the couple had found it hard to be sexually intimate and discuss their fears after the diagnosis of infertility. The counselor's suggestion to use traditional healing practices, especially Pranayama, greatly helped the client, as she used these practices as for preventive coping.

Handling the sensitive issue of infertility was challenging for the counselor, especially dealing with the ingrained cultural resistance to infertility and the client's value system that contributed to her own psychological state. By having the client use narrative work and redefine herself, the counselor had to maintain a fine balance in helping the client find her new values within the Indian context. The counselor's gender also became an important issue as gender-role expectations aggravate the situation for women (Barua et al., 2013) and often make the counselor feel hopeless against the strong gender roles prescribed in a collectivistic society. The support of the husband despite the in-laws' resistance was a strong factor for therapy success, and the counselor was hopeful in this situation. However, other similar cases in India do not necessarily have the same positive outcome.

CONCLUSION

Radha's case reflects a number of important issues that counselors and psychotherapists might consider in India. With changing family and work structures, shifting gender roles, reduced social support, and greater cultural confluence, therapists must possess multiple tools to handle issues that emerge from the intersections of these factors. Classical approaches to counseling and psychotherapy are indeed useful but require contextualization and an understanding of eclectic practice. Systemic perspectives are useful in counseling and psychotherapy practice because of the close interaction of extended family in a couple's functioning. Along with eclectic practice, integration of alternative systems of care, such as traditional healing practices, is seen as essential in the practice of counseling and psychotherapy in India. Awareness of the multiple cultural expectations and belief systems of clients and an active engagement with them are essential for effective practice in India. Training of counselors and psychotherapists must therefore consider these as essential competencies.

QUESTIONS

1. How do collectivistic patriarchal cultures address issues of female infertility and associated depression?
2. What are the roles and responsibilities of women in collectivistic patriarchal cultures, and how can these act as a double-edged sword?
3. How did Radha's moving to India at an early age and learning to function within a pluralistic society marked by higher levels of tolerance, socialization, and religious coping affect the onset of her difficulties and facilitate her counseling and recovery?
4. How could emotion-focused therapy help Radha and her husband understand their emotions arising out of infertility and change their attachment bonds?
5. Evaluate how acceptance and alternatives to infertility can be addressed in a collectivistic patriarchal society using culturally approved meanings and social support networks.

REFERENCES

Barua, A., Apte, H., Pande, R., & Walia, S. (2013). Infertility concerns among young couples in rural India. In H. K. Bhat, P. C. Joshi, & B. R. Vijayendra (Eds.), *Explorations in Indian medical anthropology: Vol. 2. Disease, health and culture* (pp. 93–108). New Delhi, India: Concept.

George, T. S., & Pothan, P. (2013). Counseling and psychotherapy in India: Professionalism amidst changing times. In R. Moodley, U. P. Gielen, & R. Wu (Eds.), *Handbook of counseling and psychotherapy in an international context* (pp. 193–203). New York, NY: Routledge.

Jejeebhoy, S. J. (1998). Infertility in India—Levels, patterns and consequences: Priorities for social science research. *Journal of Family Welfare, 44,* 15–24.

Kumar, U. (1991). Life stages in the development of the Hindu woman in India. In L. L. Alder (Ed.), *Women in cross-cultural perspective* (pp. 142–158). Westport, CT: Praeger.

Mental Health Atlas. (2011). *World Health Organization—India.* Retrieved from http://www.who.int/mental_health/evidence/atlas/profiles/ind_mh_profile.pdf

Roland, A. (2005). Commentary on building multicultural counseling bridges. *Counseling Psychology Quarterly, 18,* 283–285.

Sudha, G., Reddy, K. S. N., Reddy, K. N., & Reddy, B. K. C. (2011). Emotional distress in infertile couples: A cross-cultural study. *Asia Pacific Journal of Social Sciences, 3,* 90–101.

Times of India. (2012). *Infertility hits mental health.* Retrieved from http://timesofindia.indiatimes.com/life-style/health-fitness/health/Infertility-hits-mental-health/articleshow/15358716.cms

Chapter 11

COUNSELING AND PSYCHOTHERAPY IN JAPAN: MASAKO'S STORY

Shigeru Iwakabe and Carol Zerbe Enns

INTRODUCTION

Japan is a highly industrialized country and internationally known not only for its contribution to global economy but also for its traditional and modern culture. In the current Japanese society, traditional collectivist values are intertwined with more modern consumerist values that have emerged from the economic development of the last 50 years. Some of the psychological problems experienced in Japan are attributed to the clash between traditional and modern values.

Japanese psychotherapies are characterized by diverse approaches that include indigenous counseling, adaptations of Western psychotherapies, as well as the integration of Western and indigenous approaches (Iwakabe & Enns, 2012). Psychodynamic and humanistic therapies are among the psychotherapies with Western origins that are most widely practiced in Japan. More recently, cognitive behavior therapy has also gained recognition as a short-term practical approach for managing work-related stress and depression in the workplace. In general, an eclectic theoretical approach is most frequently endorsed by Japanese psychologists (Iwakabe, 2008).

The approach featured in this case study focuses on issues embedded in family systems and involves therapy with a child and a mother. This type of therapy, mother–child parallel therapy, is often initiated by a mother who is seeking help about a troubled child. The mother typically sees one therapist for individual sessions, whereas the child receives play therapy from another therapist in the same clinical setting. This format reflects current social circumstances and clinical realities in which fathers are often unavailable to attend therapy sessions because of their work hours, and parenting is often left to mothers, especially in the family in which the mother is a full-time housewife. The mother's therapy usually has two foci: (a) psychoeducational counseling involving direct guidance and information about parenting skills as well as advice about how to deal with the child's teacher and school, and (b) an exploratory focus on personal issues that play out in the woman's struggles dealing with family and parenting issues. The child's therapy often emphasizes expressive activities that deal indirectly with the child's issues.

In this chapter, we discuss the case of Masako and Kota, with a main focus on the process of Masako's therapy. We explore how some of the current cultural, social, and economic issues in Japan are played out in her dilemma. In particular, this chapter discusses Masako's experience of being a working mother after separation from her husband and her effort to define her life apart from social expectations that placed a lot of pressure in her parenting.

The Client

Masako is a 39-year-old working mother who came to the university counseling center for consultation about her 6-year-old son, Kota, whose aggressive behavior at the private school he had recently begun attending had become the subject of parent–teacher association meetings. Kota had repeatedly been getting into physical fights with his classmates and had even stabbed his female classmate in the leg with a pencil.

Presenting Issues and Challenges

As with many mothers who visit counseling services in Japan, Masako did not present a chief complaint of her own but sought concrete professional advice to deal with her son, Kota. Masako felt totally out of control with her son's trouble at school. Kota had frequent fights with his classmates that typically had ended with Kota beating up other kids. One of the students testified that Kota did not initiate the fights but reacted strongly to being teased about his ptosis, or drooping eyelid. After Kota used a pencil to stab his classmate's leg, resulting in a minor injury, shocked and outraged parents of Kota's classmates fiercely protested that he should be expelled. Masako felt cornered, and the school principal urged her to consult with the school counselor. Distrustful of the school, Masako sought help from a university counseling center that she found on the Internet.

Case History and Developmental Background

Masako grew up in a family of four. Her father worked for a local government and often complained that his salary was lower than other workers simply because he did not hold a university degree. He strongly believed in the importance of education for his two children, and Masako was sent to cram school (*juku*) from an early age. However, she did not get into the best university, and she blamed her parents' economic status for not making it possible for her to attend a prestigious private elementary or junior high school, which would have automatically guaranteed her entrance to a highly ranked university. Masako's pressure to excel was exacerbated by her brother's truancy and social withdrawal (*hikikomori*). He was bullied in junior high school and confined himself in his bedroom for several years, leading Masako to feel that she might need to support her extended family financially after her father's retirement. Her father blamed her brother for being weak-willed and avoiding school, which often resulted in physical fights between the two. Masako and her mother helplessly yelled and screamed as they tried to stop these fights, revealing that the whole family was caught in this conflict. Her brother eventually attended high school and maintained a full-time job, but he has never married and continues to lead a secluded life. These family events provided an additional impetus for Masako's strong career orientation.

Masako works in a major corporation that has promoted women's career paths and continuing employment while raising their families. She has maintained her job for 15 years, since graduating from a university. Masako and her spouse were introduced to each other by her boss, who judged her husband—an employee of a major bank—to be good husband material for Masako. After a very short and rather formal courtship period, they married.

Although their marriage appeared ideal from the outside, as both appeared to be "elites" who worked in stable major corporations, their marriage started to break down soon after they started to live together and Kota was born. They bought a house within walking distance of Masako's parents' house so that Masako's mother could spend time with Kota in the early evening before Masako came home from work. Her mother often completed chores such as cleaning and laundry. Her husband agreed with Masako about maintaining her career after they got married, but he expected her to quit her job after childbirth.

Masako's husband left home shortly before Kota started attending his new school. Masako felt an enormous sense of guilt that Kota was separated from his father. Her shame about having failed in marriage kept her from mentioning this living arrangement to anyone outside her family. She deplored the apparent negative effects his father's absence and temper had on Kota, yet she did not recognize her own contribution and had limited awareness of her own difficulties.

THE THERAPY

Masako initially came to therapy alone. The therapist (the first author, Shigeru Iwakabe) is a male psychologist similar to the client in age; he brings a humanistic integrative orientation to psychotherapy (Iwakabe, 2008). Masako typically brought a notebook and often asked for advice about how to deal with Kota's school teachers and other parents who formed an alliance to have him expelled from school. Initially, Masako seemed to want quick answers and directives that would involve delegating difficult decisions to the therapist, but soon she understood the therapist's explanation that they needed more time before identifying solutions. Masako experienced great comfort from being able to talk about her feelings, such as an enormous sense of societal shame about her failed marriage and the troubling family and school situation, which she was not able to mention to her friends and coworkers.

As a part of parallel therapy, Kota worked with a female trainee therapist in play therapy. As his school performance was not an issue, no formal cognitive assessment was conducted. It is not unusual for Japanese psychotherapists to skip a formal assessment to protect the child from feeling that his or her privacy has been invaded and exposed when the possibility of learning disorder is excluded. It was clear to the therapist that Kota was a very physical, energetic, and active boy, and that it was very stressful for him to commute to his school every day on a crowded train without having time to play after school. It also became apparent that he was self-conscious and hesitant to express himself other than through physical activities.

Kota participated in *hakoniwa* [sandplay therapy; see Enns & Kasai, 2003]. At the beginning, he constructed a series of similar landscape designs in which fierce animals were attacking tame animals. In one particularly striking scene, a baby was surrounded by fierce animals, while adults simply observed the scene from a distance. The therapist understood that Kota expressed his internal struggle with helplessness and fear. In later sessions, although Kota continued to create fighting scenes, themes related to cooperation and harmony started to emerge: Tame animals and people fought back and cooperated in building castles and villages and in solving their problems. He also made landscapes in which no animate objects were placed, which the therapist recognized as the expression of internal loneliness. When these observations were communicated to Masako, she felt that she was starting to understand how Kota felt, which in turn appeased her frustration with him and also helped her regain affection toward him. As the therapy progressed, Kota became more expressive both in hakoniwa and other play activities.

Individual sessions with Masako focused on exploring her sense of failure as a mother and wife as well as providing her with specific advice to establish a postdivorce family relationship. The therapist helped her express and accept her negative feelings toward Kota, which Masako experienced as socially unacceptable. Masako apologetically admitted feeling fearful and even disgusted that Kota behaved like his father. The therapist normalized her feelings toward Kota as a part of the long-strained marital relationship.

The therapist explained how Kota's aggressive behaviors might be related to recent changes in the living arrangement, and that Kota's feeling of abandonment and loss needed to be recognized and communicated with her. The therapist also explained the importance of Kota's connection with his father and proposed a few weekend plans for father and son to spend time together. Although Masako was reluctant at first, worrying that this would only aggravate Kota's feelings, she agreed to try it out. Masako was also encouraged to talk with Kota about her feelings of sadness and disappointment about the family's inability to be together. Although Kota did not respond verbally, he soon related to her more affectionately without resisting, thus acting on his own need for closeness and nurturing.

The therapist helped Masako explore her anxiety about Kota's education. At first, she had no doubt that her decision to send Kota to a private school was necessary. She soon noticed how much anxiety she had built up around schooling and education, stemming from her feeling of inferiority for failing to get into the best school and her brother's truancy. After 3 months of therapy, Masako decided to send Kota to a local school so that he would have more time to play after school. Kota adjusted well to this change. He also joined a local soccer team and made several close friends. Although her excessive concern about Kota's future academic achievement continued to overwhelm her at times, she was able to understand the link between the academic pressure she placed on him and his defiant and oppositional behaviors. Biweekly therapy continued for 1 year for both the mother and the child. Masako chose not to deal with her marital situation, as this was more difficult to deal with, and she preferred to maintain the equilibrium achieved in therapy.

DISCUSSION AND ANALYSIS

Japanese culture is an important aspect of diversity that is relevant to this case study. Researchers indicate that compared with most cultures, Japan's ranking on "masculinity" and "uncertainty avoidance" are especially high (Hofstede, Hofstede, & Minkov, 2010) and are manifested by more gender-differentiated roles than are seen in most countries (masculinity). In addition, Japan's culture has complex social rules that apply to life tasks from cradle to grave, which gives greater predictability to life (uncertainty avoidance). Japan also receives moderate scores on both collectivism, which emphasizes embeddedness in social contexts, and power distance, which involves sensitivity to social ranking. Each of these dimensions appears relevant to the concerns and issues faced by the members of this family.

Whereas this case study reflects many challenges faced in typical contemporary Japanese families, family members' lives reflect diversities that interact with and contribute to the complexity of their circumstances. With regard to gender, Masako is an adult woman who is choosing a nontraditional path within a society in which women are often expected to exit the workforce and devote all their energies to parenting, at least for the first 3 years after childbirth (Tokuhiro, 2010). Although a labor equity opportunity law was implemented in the mid-1980s, hidden barriers remain (e.g., limited enforcement and promotion opportunities, beliefs about "women's work") and contribute to Japan's low gender-equality rankings (101st out of 135 nations in 2012). Masako's husband, who was socialized to assume that his wife would conform to traditional women's roles, is also likely to have experienced struggles as he lived within a family unit that did not match his expectations and social ideals.

Masako's strength, tenacity, and nontraditional attitudes are revealed in her genuine enjoyment of her work and strong career motivation. Nevertheless, cultural attitudes contributed to her self-consciousness about her femininity, her lack of trust in her own judgment, her need to follow socially sanctioned standards, and her anxiety about not adhering to expected gender roles. Masako's determination to put Kota in a good school was partially caused by her need to prove that she was a good mother and to show that Kota's life was not compromised because of her career or failure to provide a stable family environment. Psychotherapy helped her clarify her own values as well as the importance of her emotional support of Kota.

The challenges experienced by Masako and family members were complicated by social class comparisons that are common in Japan, including the tendency to be especially attentive to one's relative placement vis-à-vis hierarchies related to work, status, and education. Masako was highly concerned about status and appearances related to *seken-tei*, which often involves social comparisons as well as social shame or feeling "frowned upon" for deviating from powerful but invisible community standards within a relatively mono-ethnic and collectivist society (Sugimoto, 2010). Masako's anxieties were shown in her worries about the reputation of her son's school and her own university education, and these anxieties reflected her internalization of Japanese middle-class values. These values often include a preference for expensive goods and, by extension, an expensive brand-name education.

Masako's choice of a husband was also based on his social status rather than his personal character, also revealing Masako's difficulty differentiating her own values from those of the larger society. The likelihood of divorce posed another diversity challenge in that divorce is somewhat less common in Japan than many industrialized countries and may result in social penalties and stigma in some contexts (Sugimoto, 2010; Tokuhiro, 2010), leading some partners to remain in unsatisfying relationships.

Another related diversity is represented by Kota's mild physical difference (drooping eyelid), which resulted in his "standing out" in a social structure and school setting in which similarity and "standing in" are highly valued (Weisz, Rothbaum, & Blackburn, 1984). This reality may increase Kota's vulnerability to bullying (*ijime*), a potential consequence that is consistent with the Japanese proverb that "the nail that stands out gets pounded in." Masako also worried excessively about Kota's eyelid and the possibility that any visible abnormality or difference would evoke a sense of inferiority in Kota or result in major social disadvantage.

Individual dynamics as well as extended family system features are relevant to this case. Masako's strong career orientation was influenced by her family values and her brother's social withdrawal (*hikikomori*), which has been identified as a Japanese problem that tends to affect young men who are faced with the high expectations placed on men in Japan. Masako's personal and family conflicts were sometimes projected on Kota as when she expressed resentment about the past and replayed her father's unfinished business of feeling inferior because of educational limitations. Despite these personal and family issues, which are sometimes referred to as *enmeshment* in Western theories, current transgenerational caregiving relationships and closeness can be framed positively as aspects of *amae* (Doi, 1973), which is defined as a form of healthy dependency, mutual attachment, and unconditional acceptance that provide sustenance and meaning to family members. Despite the presence of ongoing difficulties and unresolved issues, the changes experienced by mother and son and the positive transgenerational assistance provided by Masako's parents are likely to lead to greater flexibility and additional positive changes in this family.

Finally, the mother–child parallel therapy is probably the most common form of therapy involving a child and family in trouble. It is practical and reasonable because it reflects a sociocultural reality in Japan in which mothers play a primary role in parenting, whereas fathers are usually not available for psychotherapy sessions because of extensive work expectations. However, it also inadvertently reinforces both a prevalent gender-role stereotype in Japan and the potential dysfunctional family structure by discouraging fathers to get involved in parenting and leaving unexamined the father–child relationship that might have contributed to the child's problem. The mother–child parallel therapy may also be a preferred form of therapy because it allows mothers to "save face." Mothers often feel like failures as mothers when their children have psychological problems. As a result, requesting a father to join therapy can feel very shaming to them; therefore, Japanese therapists may choose to keep the confidential relationship with the mother to build a better working alliance. Saving face is also one of the reasons for not conducting a formal assessment in which children may feel scrutinized for their defects. Shame played a major role with the therapeutic work with Masako and Kota.

CONCLUSION

This case study illustrates parent–child parallel therapy in which the parent experienced culturally sensitive humanistic integrative therapy, which involved working through painful emotions as well as experiencing confidence building and greater health. The child received play therapy and *hakoniwa*, an indigenous approach that integrates assumptions based in Jungian psychology and Buddhism. In contrast to many Western therapies, hakoniwa offers a holistic approach that allows for nonverbal and high-context communication as well as mind–body integration. Together, the approaches used in this case demonstrate some of the breadth and diversity of psychological practice in Japan.

QUESTIONS

1. How does Masako's sense of gender role contribute to the occurrence and maintenance of the problem she and her son were experiencing?
2. How do the components of the diversity matrix (gender, race, sexuality, class, disability, religion, etc.) contribute to Masako's vulnerabilities and difficulties?
3. What are the components of diversity matrix that contribute to Masako's resilience and strengths?
4. What are some of the weaknesses and potential problems of the approach that was used in this case study?
5. How would you treat this client in your own approach?

REFERENCES

Doi, T. (1973). *The anatomy of dependence.* New York, NY: Kodansha International.

Enns, C. Z., & Kasai, M. (2003). Hakoniwa: Japanese sandplay therapy. *The Counseling Psychologist, 31,* 93–112.

Hofstede, G. H., Hofstede, G. J., & Minkov, M. (2010). *Culture's consequences: Software of the mind* (3rd ed.). New York, NY: McGraw Hill Professional.

Iwakabe, S. (2008). Psychotherapy integration in Japan. *Journal of Psychotherapy Integration, 18,* 103–125.

Iwakabe, S., & Enns, C. Z. (2012). Counseling and psychotherapy in Japan. In R. Moodley, U. P. Gielen, & R. Wu (Eds.), *Handbook of counseling and psychotherapy in an international context* (pp. 204–214). New York, NY: Routledge.

Sugimoto, Y. (2010). *An introduction to Japanese society* (3rd ed.). New York, NY: Cambridge University Press.

Tokuhiro, Y. (2010). *Marriage in contemporary Japan.* New York, NY: Routledge.

Weisz, J. R., Rothbaum, F. M., & Blackburn, T. C. (1984). Standing out and standing in: The psychology of control in America and Japan. *American Psychologist, 39,* 955–969.

Chapter 12

COUNSELING AND PSYCHOTHERAPY IN MALAYSIA: AARON'S STORY

See Ching Mey

INTRODUCTION

Malaysia is a multiracial nation with a population of diverse ethnicity and a multitude of faiths. Malaysian population consists of ethnic groups such as Malays (67.4%), Chinese (24.6%), Indians (7.3%), and others (0.7%). Islam is the official and most widely professed religion in Malaysia, practiced by 61.3% of the population; however, other religions that are embraced are Buddhism (19.8%), Christianity (9.2%), and Hinduism (6.3%).

Because of the religious and ethnic diversity in Malaysia, the development of a Malaysian counseling approach is still being pioneered (see, for discussion, Ng, 2013). The guidance and counseling movement reached Malaysia through the work and leadership of the U.S. counseling profession. The Malaysian Ministry of Education first accepted the importance of school guidance in its schools in 1963. School guidance became a fundamental part of education to foster the ability of the youths to make decisions independently. In the 1980s, the drug problem among youths in Malaysia deteriorated. Hence, the Ministry of Education announced the need for guidance and counseling teachers in the schools and implemented the position of full-time school counselors in 1996. By 2000, every secondary school had at least one full-time counselor. In spite of this presence at secondary schools, there is no counselor placed in primary schools in Malaysia. Thus, there are inadequate counseling services provided. Furthermore, there are no counseling services for children with special needs.

Computer-assisted learning is a proven tool in the educational process of learning to process vocabulary knowledge, language, speech and communication, and mathematics (Hall, 2000) and is also effective for use with individuals who have special needs (Moore & Calvert, 2000). The advantage of using computer-based application for learning and training is the ability to simultaneously present multiple sources of information, such as text, pictures, animations, and sounds. Children with autism are more likely to show greater response and improved memory with computer-assisted learning programs because the information is being presented in a multisensory format and because the environment is controlled and structured (Hetzroni & Tannous, 2004). Hodgdon (1995) described that fewer behavioral problems and improved compliance were displayed by children with autism when visual supports were used as a tool to communicate expectations.

A multimedia program that includes multisensory stimuli such as voice, video, and animation was developed by Heimann, Nelson, Tjus, and Gillberg (1995) to facilitate language learning in children with autism. The children demonstrated improvement in reading, phonological awareness, and vocabulary. Through these computer-assisted interventions, the children with autism were able to transition the skills learned to real-life social contexts. Such findings raise the possibility that a computer-based auditory and visual aid for understanding the thought patterns of an autistic child might enable teachers, parents, and caregivers to intervene and redirect thinking to manage the child's behavior and remove rigid thinking and behavior. Hence, I developed a multimedia cognitive aid as a tool to counsel autistic children in this study; these children's responses were then observed. For the purpose of this chapter, I focus on analyzing the therapy process and the drawings created by one child from the moderate-functioning group. This child underwent therapy with a psychologist who observed and gauged the autistic children's behavior and progress.

THE CLIENT

Aaron is a 5-year-old Malaysian Chinese boy and the eldest son in the family; he has a brother who is 2 years younger than him. Aaron was delivered as a 6-pound baby using induced delivery method and had jaundice after birth. He had a prolonged crawling period and only started to walk after 18 months. Aaron's parents had graduated from high school. His mother works as a clerk and his father as a sales representative. There is no family history of mental illness or intellectual disability.

PRESENTING ISSUES AND CHALLENGES

Aaron was diagnosed with moderate to severe autism when he was 3 years old. He displayed hyperactivity, temper tantrums, and destructive behaviors such as biting, pinching, grabbing, beating, and kicking. He also displayed obsession with arranging things in horizontal and vertical arrays, held his hands in an odd posture, was obsessed with alphabets and cartoon movies, loved jumping up and down, and flapped his hands when happy. He often hit his head or hand against the wall. He liked to swing himself and spin objects, resisted wearing new clothing, had unusual cravings for porridge, chewed and swallowed nonfood objects, and got very upset when he was interrupted. He had unclear repetitive speech and could say about three to four words independently. He took an adult's hand to do things, disliked people touching him, and did not socialize with other children.

CASE HISTORY AND DEVELOPMENTAL BACKGROUND

Aaron was selective about people touching him, and he was very attached to his mother. He could imitate to wave goodbye and give flying kisses to people when he was 1 year old. He started to say first words such as "mama," "mum mum," and "papa" after 13–15 months but stopped when he was 17 months. His speech started to improve tremendously after undergoing intensive training at the Resource and Education for Autistic Children Centre when he was 3 years old.

He was fascinated by advertisements showed on television and was able to sit quietly and watch television for long periods of time. Aaron acted as deaf sometimes as he did not react to loud sounds. He also had peculiar habits; for example, he disliked people using a plate or glass to eat or drink, and he tended to tear papers or books. He showed indifference to being liked as he was happier when left alone.

Aaron was sensitive to criticism but not affectionate. He was aloof, indifferent, self-contented, and remote; he was also unaware of fearsome objects but scared of some television advertisements, such as a dragon or lion dance. He would ignore, grunt, or wave his arms to show that he did not want to do anything and had difficulty acting or responding appropriately in social situations. Aaron needed verbal reminders from time to time to stay focused on a task. When he had a task to do, he became very anxious and fidgety, played with his fingers, and paced up and down.

THE THERAPY

During the therapy, I, his psychologist, noted that Aaron had poor eye contact and would look past a person during a conversation. He only responded when his name was called and would follow simple instructions generally. He did not initiate a conversation and had difficulty sustaining a conversation.

Because autistic children have limited or delayed language and speech, I mainly used drawing in the therapy. Aaron was not able to express his opinion well or talk about the topics. Hence, to fully understand and analyze his drawings, I also interviewed his parents and teachers to obtain information on his behaviors and life events to connect with his drawings. A triangulation analysis was used; that is, I used more than two methods to analyze the same set of data for validation purposes.

A computer-based multimedia cognitive aid in the form of multimedia presentation was specially developed as a tool to understand the thought patterns of an autistic child so that therapy could be given to manage the child's behavior and remove rigid thinking and behavior. This tool is a product of a Malaysian Research University grant awarded to me, See Ching Mey. It has been validated and used on more than 100 children with autism. The tool is not commercially available but can be obtained by e-mailing me at cmsee@usm.my.

The visual images in the presentations are accompanied with soft and pleasant music. The visuals in the multimedia cognitive aid are organized into the following five themes:

1. *Color:* A series of 174 slides of paintings and illustrations are selected where colors clearly form the defining elements to stimulate the children and gauge their thought patterns with regard to aesthetic values and their ability to see colors as differentiating characteristics in nature. Contrast is introduced with slides that use shades, tone, and colors. Slides also progress from simple line to more complicated forms of abstract art. Many of the slides display primary colors blending into other colors in many designs.

2. *Light:* There are 44 slides in this collection compiled from paintings of nature and activities. The paintings are mostly selected for their association with weather, the seasons, and sceneries. There are obvious related sequences: six initial slides with black and white sketches of activities; six others illustrating weather; 17 slides with paintings of sceneries; two slides of lighting at the window; and 11 slides of seasons, day, and night. Two other slides of art pieces that are not related to the collection are inserted randomly.

3. *Visual perception:* There are 69 slides in this collection, all of which are visual illusions formed from dots, lines, and space elements. Tone and different shades complement the visual elements. There are slides with dots that eventually coalesce into patterns, objects, and abstract art. The abstract art pictures were selected for their colorfulness. There are also slides with line drawing that form patterns and abstract art, and there are illustrations that use combinations of lines, dots, and space.

4. *Cartoon:* The cartoon collection is made up of two separate sequences. There are 71 slides in Cartoon I, which consists of illustrations with colorful backgrounds and emphasized expressions such as happiness, sadness, shock, friendship, and love; in addition, they depict activities such as flying, drawing, reading, eating, being outdoors, and playing together. Cartoon I is expected to stimulate logical and illogical reasoning in the child. The child is expected to see, imagine, and relate the incident behind each slide to his daily routine. Cartoon II is composed of 74 slides with various sizes of cartoon characters from television and film. The cartoon characters display different facial expressions. They are simple, precise, attractive, and usually colorful. All of the slides have a simple plain background. The child needs to imagine a story from a selection of slides and then describe it (verbally or in drawing).

5. *Character:* There are 207 slides in this collection, which consist of portraits by well-known artists, with many selected for distinct facial expressions of feelings. They are of individuals, couples, and groups. There are also abstract paintings. The intention of this collection is to examine a child's ability to distinguish between the different faces and to describe or predict the feeling and thoughts behind each facial expression.

A 45-minute session was provided three times a week for Aaron for 6 months. A video recording of each therapy session was made for later analysis of the child's behavior and response after each session. After Aaron had viewed the multimedia presentation, he was asked to draw and/or describe, if possible, what he had seen and connect it to his day-to-day experiences. His drawings or descriptions were then analyzed to understand his thought patterns, and conclusions were made to provide therapy to modify his thinking or behavior.

DISCUSSION AND ANALYSIS

At regular intervals ("periods") scheduled every 2 months, I performed a qualitative analysis of Aaron's collected drawings, writings, behaviors, and verbal expressions. Conclusions were drawn from the analysis to form the basis of suggestions for teachers, psychologists, social workers, caregivers, and parents to use in training Aaron. The analyses focused on Aaron's behavior and speech, interpretation, synthesizing and generalization abilities, and creativity.

Furth's (2002) three principles in analyzing drawings were applied in the analyses of the drawing and descriptions of the child. The first principle is to note the child's initial impression of a picture that describes his initial feeling. The second principle is to systematically comb through the picture objectively for several elements or characteristics, such as odd representation, missing elements, and focal points such as size, shape distortion, repeated objects, perspective, representation of self in the drawing, use of shading and edging, comparison with the surrounding world, encapsulation, extension, words in drawing, line drawing, movement, use of abstract elements, and space filling. The final principle involves a synthesis of the observations gathered into a report as a whole.

During the first period, Aaron repeatedly drew lines and circular strokes. His emotion was not stable in this period, which was apparent from his use of a lot of red and black. The color red signals surging emotions, problems, or danger. The color black denotes negative thinking and fear. However, he also used a lot of purple color, and the purple color implies that Aaron has control. In many of his drawings in this period, a drawing of a flower can be found at the bottom part of the drawing papers. However, the flower had no connection to what he saw from the multimedia presentation. This representation points out that Aaron might not have been aware that there was no flower in the multimedia presentation—it existed only in his own thoughts. As such, I described the content of the multimedia presentation to Aaron and encouraged him to draw what he saw from the slide, rather than what he had in his mind. I also encouraged Aaron to use more colors in his drawing.

During the second period, Aaron still did not draw what he saw from the multimedia presentation, but he was able to name the objects or pictures he saw during the multimedia presentation slides. Aaron still drew what came to mind, but he did not draw a flower anymore. Instead, he kept drawing what he remembered from weeks or months ago or past experiences. His drawings reflected what he was thinking, not what he saw. Nevertheless, after consistent encouragement, Aaron showed improvement as he started to use more colors later in this period. This increasing use of color correlated to the observation that his emotions became more stable during this time.

During the third period, improvement was apparent as Aaron started to be able to draw what he saw in the slides. He started to make sense of what he saw, such as figures and shapes, and transferred that into drawing. Aaron developed the concept/sense of space in his drawing (such as animals standing on the field, clouds or rainbow in the sky, etc.). He drew what he saw in the slide and also added his own ideas and imaginations. In the later period, he added colors to the background of his drawing. Aaron became more aware of his surroundings. He also started to talk about the character and the actions or activities while viewing the multimedia presentation. In one of his drawings, he displayed the emotion of happiness through drawing a sun with a smiling face. He displayed more energy and more stable emotion as his drawings had multicolored objects and backgrounds.

Aaron became more observant and calmer and was more willing to talk about what he saw from the multimedia presentation. He showed improvement in terms of the use of more vocabulary in expressing his opinions or describing his drawings. His drawings became more concrete and congruent with what he saw in the multimedia presentation. By the third period, Aaron filled the drawing papers with his drawings, in contrast with his drawings during the first and second periods. Aaron's emotion was more stable as shown in his use of more colors in his drawings, and he had become more energetic, responsive, and interactive.

CONCLUSION

Generally, the child with autism in this case study responded positively to the use of multimedia cognitive aid, which is easy to develop and can be tailored to the specific needs of the child. It can be used as a tool to train children with autism to be responsive, focused, compliant, cooperative, and aware of their surroundings. Drawings made by children with autism show the mental and physical processes of self-expression, imagination, and creativity. The use of colors and space in their drawings are related to their emotional and awareness state. Thus, counselors or psychologists working with children with autism can use multimedia cognitive aids as a tool to provide therapy and help modify thinking and behavior without using too much language.

QUESTIONS

1. Can the therapy techniques used in this case also apply to other populations with disabilities?
2. What are the symptoms of autism, and how can therapy deal with these symptoms?
3. How do the families that have a child with autism cope with their special-needs child?
4. What other therapy approaches can be used with children with autism to help them reach their full potential and be included in society?
5. Outline the limitations and strengths of the behavioral approach to psychopathology throughout this case.

REFERENCES

Furth, G. M. (2002). *The secret world of drawings: A Jungian approach to healing through art.* Toronto, Ontario, Canada: Inner City Books.

Hall, T. (2000). Computer assisted instruction in reading for students with learning disabilities: A research synthesis. *Education and Treatment of Children, 23,* 173–193.

Heimann, M., Nelson, K. E., Tjus, T., & Gillberg, C. (1995). Increasing reading and communication skills in children with autism through an interactive multimedia computer program. *Journal of Autism and Developmental Disorders, 25,* 459–480.

Hetzroni, O., & Tannous, J. (2004). Effects of a computer-based intervention program on the communicative functions of children with autism. *Journal of Autism and Developmental Disorders, 34,* 95–113.

Hodgdon, L. Q. (1995). Solving social behavioral problems through the use of visually supported communication. In K. A. Quill (Ed.), *Teaching children with autism: Strategies to enhance communication and socialization* (pp. 265–286). New York, NY: Delmar.

Moore, M., & Calvert, S. (2000). Brief report: Vocabulary acquisition for children with autism: Teacher or computer instruction. *Journal of Autism Developmental Disorders, 30,* 359–362.

Ng, W. S. (2013). Counseling and psychotherapy in Malaysia: The joys and pain of (continuous) pioneering work. In R. Moodley, U. Gielen, & R. Wu (Eds.), *Handbook of counseling and psychotherapy in an international context* (pp. 215–225). New York, NY: Routledge.

Chapter 13

COUNSELING AND PSYCHOTHERAPY IN PAKISTAN: ZOHRA'S STORY

Humair Yusuf

INTRODUCTION

Pakistani society consists of a number of distinct ethnic groups; most are Muslim, religious, patriarchal, collectivist, and family-oriented, with high levels of income disparity and a primarily urban elite dominating political and economic activity (Federal Bureau of Statistics, 2013). Although the state pursued a nationalist agenda aimed at eliminating the humiliations of colonization, rapid urbanization resulted in superficial modernization that distorted the traditional culture without providing a viable replacement. Conservative forces responded by depicting this upheaval in a religious context, resulting in a resurgence of Islam, which, influenced by the Wahabi movement in Saudi Arabia, led to the tolerant, Sufi-inspired faith traditionally practiced in Pakistan being supplanted by an unforgiving and puritanical version hostile to Western culture.

Although many Islamic healing techniques are comparable to contemporary practices in psychotherapy, the colonial legacy of parallel systems of treatment—a Western one for the country's Anglicized population and an indigenous one for the rest—restricted the use of psychotherapy to affluent residents of Pakistan's major cities. Traditional values of relying on elders to solve problems instead of turning to outsiders further contributed to psychotherapy's low utilization rates. Moreover, because Pakistani counselors and psychotherapists assumed that clients expected concrete solutions from psychotherapy rather than insight or opportunities to share emotions, they tended to use cognitive and behavioral approaches (Suhail, 2004). Although these approaches, for the most part, failed to resonate with clients, a shift toward humanistic approaches such as emotion-focused and client-centered therapy during the last decade has facilitated the incorporation of Islamic values into psychotherapy to make it more culturally relevant and compatible with Pakistani worldviews; consequently, there has been an increase in the number of Pakistanis seeking psychotherapy (see, for discussion, Yusuf, Sarfraz, & Askari, 2013).

Emotion-focused therapy (EFT), the primary approach used in this case, is based on a view of human functioning in which emotional experience occurs independently of conscious thought. Focusing on emotions, therefore, is more likely to facilitate enduring change in individuals than interventions that are based purely on cognition or behavior (Greenberg, 2012). EFT assumes a dialectical–constructivist process in which individuals make sense of their experiences by articulating them in language, and personal meaning emerges through the explication and organization of emotional experiences. EFT, therefore, aims to help individuals express, understand, and ultimately transform their emotions. This process entails accessing maladaptive emotions such as shame or hopelessness and replacing them by adaptive emotions such as sadness at what was denied or anger at being treated badly.

This chapter discusses the therapy of Zohra, who presented with feelings of despair and guilt, to illustrate how an individual's social and cultural identities can result in oppression and distress. By discussing Zohra's therapy and its outcome, this chapter explores how EFT can facilitate the transformation of social and cultural identities from a source of oppression to a source of self-affirmation and resilience.

THE CLIENT

Zohra is a 43-year-old heterosexual woman who does not consider herself disabled. She has been married for 22 years to a successful businessman, and the two of them are a prominent and socially active couple. Her sons are attending university in the United States and expect to join the family business after graduating. Although her first language is Urdu, Zohra's school and college education was in English, and she is equally fluent in both languages. Zohra identifies as a Pakistani but has traveled extensively in North America and Europe and is comfortable with Western culture and values. Although she dresses in traditional Pakistani clothing, she does not wear a *niqab* (veil) or *hijab* (headscarf). She is an observant Muslim who attempts to fulfill religious obligations, such as praying, fasting, and abstaining from alcohol.

PRESENTING ISSUES AND CHALLENGES

Zohra's presenting issues were persistent low mood and depression accompanied by intense despair and guilt. She was in a strained relationship with her husband, whom she described as being indifferent and uncaring toward her. Although their marriage lacked intimacy and was characterized by conflict, she did not consider divorce an option because although divorce is permissible in Islam, she was unwilling to face the ensuing stigma. She also believed she was too old to find someone with whom she could enjoy a fulfilling relationship. Zohra had, however, just ended an extramarital relationship with a married man, which she considered sinful and consequently believed that her suffering was punishment for her immorality. Therefore, the challenges posed by Zohra's therapy were attending to her distress and developing alternative emotional responses along with a narrative that did not evoke feelings of guilt and despair while keeping her marriage intact.

CASE HISTORY AND DEVELOPMENTAL BACKGROUND

Zohra's parents belong to the first generation of Pakistanis born after the independence from Britain and possess the conservative values shaped by the heightened religiosity prevalent in Pakistani society. Zohra was subjected to traditional gender roles and, as the eldest of three children and the only daughter, faced considerable pressure to conform to them. For example, academics were not a priority, but she spent a considerable amount of time helping her mother look after her brothers.

Zohra was educated at an all-girls convent school, and despite receiving a bachelor's degree from a women's college, there was no question of her working or embarking on a career. During her education she had negligible access to boys, and her activities were closely monitored and supervised. As a result, Zohra did not have any relationships with men until her marriage at the age of 21, which was arranged, with her consent, by her parents. Her husband came from a similar social and cultural background, and his family was known to Zohra's parents.

Zohra belongs to an elite and privileged social class, isolated and distinct from the general population, with its own expectations and rules of behavior. For example, women rarely work but are expected to manage large households, entertain lavishly, and sustain active social lives. Although social events are not segregated and men and women can mix freely, friendships between them are strictly proscribed. In a similar manner, although women have considerable independence regarding their households and their children's upbringing, deference to their husbands, elders, and the extended family is expected. As part of this privileged class, Zohra lives a highly visible existence in which its members constantly scrutinize each other; thus, she quickly internalized its customs and conventions and learned to fear the consequences—ridicule, criticism, ostracism, or even expulsion—of deviating from them.

The centrality of Islam to Pakistani society means that Zohra is expected to fulfill religious obligations such as reading the Quran, praying, and fasting. The unforgiving and punitive interpretation of Islam to which Zohra has been exposed, however, emphasizes ritual and obedience and was devoid of personal resonance and spirituality for her. Thus, the religiosity of Zohra's environment coupled with her own superficial faith resulted in Islam being a source of rules accompanied by the fear of punishment for not adhering to them.

Ultimately, Zohra's diverse identities as a woman, a Pakistani, a member of a privileged class, and a Muslim converged to represent a burden of expectations, obligations, and oppressions. They fostered a sense of conditional approval and acceptance along with increased vulnerability to self-criticism and feelings of inadequacy and defectiveness.

THE THERAPY

Zohra's treatment consisted of 26 hour-long weekly sessions over 8 months. Initially Zohra's sessions focused on accessing and exploring her emotional experiences. Zohra was encouraged to examine and articulate how she felt about her husband, his indifference toward her, the state of their marriage, the previous lack of physical and emotional intimacy in her life, her relationship with the other man, her faith, and herself as a woman who had been unfaithful to her husband. By resonating with her experiences and helping her to reflect on and elaborate them, as well as affirming and validating her emerging emotions, I, her therapist, enabled her to deconstruct her experience into the underlying emotions that constituted it. Around her 12th session Zohra was able to understand and organize her emotional experience primarily in terms of feelings of worthlessness because of her husband's treatment of her, failure because her marital difficulties, hopelessness because she felt trapped in her marriage, and guilt and shame because she had engaged in an extramarital relationship.

The focus of Zohra's therapy then shifted to transforming these emotions and developing alternate healthy responses along with new narratives that assimilated her experiences. During her next eight sessions, Zohra's needs to be respected, desired, and loved were emphasized, and rather than feeling worthless because her husband did not fulfill these needs or feeling like a failure for the state of her marriage, she was encouraged to feel angry at being treated badly and sad for what had been missing in her life. In a similar manner, the shame and guilt that Zohra felt for being in a relationship with another man were reframed in terms of her asserting herself and seeking to fulfill her needs for respect, love, and emotional and physical intimacy, to which she was entitled but had been denied by her husband.

In order to facilitate the transformation of Zohra's emotional responses, empty-chair dialogue was attempted in her 20th session to deepen her anger toward her husband and hold him accountable for his treatment of her. Zohra responded positively to the empty-chair dialogue over the next three sessions and was able to evoke the presence of her husband, express and assert her unmet needs, and hold him accountable for his neglect and emotional abuse. Empathic affirmation was provided for these needs, and Zohra described a shift in her representation of her husband from someone whose neglect had made her feel worthless and inadequate to someone who had let her down, mistreated her, and failed to fulfill his responsibilities as a husband and companion. However, Zohra was unable to fully affirm herself or experience the desired resolution and relief. Instead, the intervention highlighted a conflict between her need for validation and love—regarding which she reported enhanced awareness, legitimacy, and entitlement and was appropriately angry at being denied—and her shame and guilt at embarking on a relationship with another man to fulfill her unmet physical and emotional needs.

Empty-chair dialogue thus provided a segue into a two-chair dialogue. During her 23rd and 24th sessions, Zohra was encouraged to identify and differentiate the two aspects of herself that were in conflict with each other, namely, the neglected aspect that desired validation and love—and sought it through an extramarital relationship—and the critical aspect that considered such a relationship to be immoral, sinful, and a source of shame and guilt. Two-chair dialogue between these two aspects of Zohra's self aimed to allow the neglected aspect to assert itself with the critical aspect, with the critical aspect being understanding and compassion toward the neglected aspect. The ultimate goal was to eliminate or at least mitigate Zohra's shame and guilt. Like the previous intervention, this one did not provide complete or even partial resolution, but it did allow Zohra an opportunity to identify and differentiate the antagonistic aspects of herself and access the feelings underlying each along with their respective needs.

In her 25th session, Zohra reported an improved ability to tolerate her distress and manage her emotions, and she expressed her desire to terminate therapy. During Zohra's last session, we reviewed her progress over the last 8 months and reiterated the importance of her being aware of her multiple emotions and accepting and attending to them despite them being in conflict with each other.

DISCUSSION AND ANALYSIS

Exploring and deconstructing Zohra's emotions over the course of her therapy suggested that underlying her distress were feelings of worthlessness, hopelessness, failure, guilt, and shame. Zohra felt worthless because of her husband's mistreatment of her, and her troubled marriage—with its implications for her role as a wife—resulted in a sense of failure. Meanwhile her hopelessness stemmed from her perception that she was too old and that the expectations and constraints of her social class would prevent her from leaving her husband and seeking another relationship. It was the guilt and shame of her extramarital relationship, however, that weighed most on her. Zohra's distress can thus be conceptualized in terms of her multiple and intersecting sociocultural identities as a woman, a 43-year-old, and a Muslim who belongs to a privileged but highly visible, demanding, and unforgiving strata of Pakistani society.

Discussions of sociocultural identities in counseling and psychotherapy have typically focused on oppression and marginalization attributable to "difference" and "otherness" (e.g., Pedersen, Crethar, & Carlson, 2008). Yet, as a healthy, able-bodied, heterosexual Pakistani Muslim adult in her 40s, who was also member of her country's social and economic elite, Zohra belonged to a dominant and possibly hegemonic majority. It was only as a woman living in a patriarchal society that she could be considered part of an oppressed group; the gender roles, obligations, and constraints that applied to Zohra were certainly oppressive. For the most part, however, the oppression that she experienced as a result of her sociocultural identities was based on the privileges afforded by her multiple identities and the fear of losing those privileges, because by failing to conform and meet the expectations of her gender, ethnicity, age, class, and religion by having an extramarital affair, she risked being stigmatized and marginalized. Zohra's distress, therefore, illustrates how despite occupying a place of privilege as a result of the convergence of their sociocultural identities, the fear of being "different" or relegated to "the other" can also be a source of oppression for individuals.

When Zohra entered therapy her distress could be framed in terms of the oppressions implicit in her intersecting sociocultural identities of class, age, ethnicity, religion, and gender. During the course of her therapy, she gradually began to see herself as deserving of respect, validation, and physical and emotional intimacy; if her husband was unable or unwilling to fulfill these needs, she felt entitled to seek fulfillment through a relationship with another man. Moreover, because this man was part of the same social class to which Zohra belonged, he could fulfill her needs while remaining mindful of the constraints imposed by Zohra's membership of it. Thus, by identifying, validating, and affirming the needs of her identities of age, gender, and class those needs were transformed into a source of resilience for Zohra.

In contrast, Zohra's identity as a Muslim continued to be distressing because of her sense of betraying her husband and behaving in a sinful manner. This distress is an example of how the oppressive structures embedded in religion can engender feelings of guilt and shame (Smith & Richards, 2005). Although Zohra made an effort to fulfill her religious obligations, her religion provided no relief and instead exacerbated her suffering by highlighting her immorality and lack of repentance.

Ultimately religion, specifically the unforgiving and puritanical version of Islam prevalent in Pakistan that lacked any meaning for Zohra, remained a source of oppression for her. Moreover, it was in conflict with her transformed identities of gender, age, and class, which provided Zohra with the resilience she required to cope. The convergence of Zohra's sociocultural identities of gender, age, and class therefore provided a safe "holding environment" in the Winnicottian sense (Moodley, 2005) that enabled her to negotiate and contain the oppression and distress that emanated from her religious identity.

CONCLUSION

This case illustrates how an individual's sociocultural identities can be a source of resilience as well as oppression, and distress can result not just from oppression caused by otherness and marginalization but also from privilege and the fear of marginalization. It also describes how religious beliefs, which can alleviate suffering in devout individuals, can exacerbate it in those without the same conviction. Thus, it highlights the need for a greater understanding of the role of religion for individuals who have a complex and problematic relationship with their faith, along with the implications for counseling.

Zohra's therapy also suggests that EFT is particularly suitable for deconstructing the convergence and intersections of an individual's sociocultural identities and then affirming, validating, and attending the needs of each identity, despite possible conflicts and contradictions between them. This process can facilitate self-affirmation and transformation from oppression to resilience. In instances where such transformation is not possible or conflicts cannot be resolved because of the inherent and entrenched values associated with the multiple identities, the process can also enable improved regulation of emotional experiences.

QUESTIONS

1. Zohra's distress was understood in terms of the oppressions implicit in her class, age, ethnicity, religion, and gender. In what other ways could her distress be conceptualized?
2. How might the conflict been Zohra's sociocultural identities have been resolved?
3. Were the goals of Zohra's therapy appropriate to her presenting issues? What alternative goals might have been more effective in providing relief?
4. What other approaches (e.g., cognitive, behavioral, narrative, traditional healing) could have been incorporated into Zohra's therapy?
5. How could Zohra's distress caused by her religious beliefs have been addressed in a sensitive and relevant manner?

REFERENCES

Federal Bureau of Statistics. (2013). *Statistical yearbook 2013*. Islamabad, Pakistan: Author.

Greenberg, L. S. (2012). Emotions, the great captains of our lives: Their role in the process of change in psychotherapy. *American Psychologist, 67*, 697–707.

Moodley, R. (2005). Outside race, inside gender: A good enough "holding environment" in counseling and psychotherapy. *Counseling Psychology Quarterly, 18*, 319–328.

Pedersen, P., Crethar, H., & Carlson, J. (2008). *Inclusive cultural empathy.* Thousand Oaks, CA: Sage.

Smith, T., & Richards, S. (2005). The integration of spiritual and religious issues in racial–cultural psychology and counseling. In R. Carter (Ed.), *Handbook of racial–cultural psychology and counseling* (pp. 132–163). Hoboken, NJ: Wiley.

Suhail, K. (2004). Psychology in Pakistan. *The Psychologist, 7,* 632–634.

Yusuf, H., Sarfraz, S., & Askari, L. (2013). Counseling and psychotherapy in Pakistan: Colonial legacies and Islamic influences. In R. Moodley, U. Gielen, & R. Wu (Eds.), *Handbook of counseling and psychotherapy in an international context* (pp. 226–236). New York, NY: Routledge.

Chapter 14

COUNSELING AND PSYCHOTHERAPY IN THE PHILIPPINES: JOJO'S STORY

Maria Isabel E. Melgar and Roberto E. Javier

INTRODUCTION

Known in the world for its finest island provinces and beautiful beaches, the Philippine Archipelago is strategically located in Southeast Asia. It is home to approximately 100 million Filipinos, about 2 million of whom work overseas and contribute 10% to the gross national product (Philippines Statistics Authority, National Statistics Office, 2012). The two main languages spoken are Filipino and English. The biggest influence on the counseling and psychotherapy practice in the Philippines is the United States because the Philippines was colonized by the United States for 50 years. The degree programs in psychology and counseling offered by local universities were patterned after the U.S. system. Filipino practitioners use a variety of Western techniques and often combine some of these models in their practice. These techniques include behavioral, client-centered therapy, and cognitive behavior models. Recently, the trend has been toward the use of mindfulness therapy and trauma recovery techniques for survivors of natural calamities, sexual abuse, war, and other traumatizing events.

A recent development in the field of counseling and therapy in the Philippines is the professionalization of the practice through government licensure and private certification (Melgar, 2013). There is a slow but growing public demand for psychological services, such as psychological assessment and therapy for children with special needs; therapy for young people with presenting problems such as depression, suicide, trauma, or addiction; and therapy for couples as well as families.

In this chapter, we discuss the therapy of Jojo, who presented with general life dissatisfaction and depression and felt stigmatized. The chapter describes the role of solution-focused story sharing in enabling him to take small steps in doing something about the predicament he is in and in adopting a more positive attitude about his future.

THE CLIENT

Jojo is a 54-year-old male who lives with a younger male partner, Ronnie, who is 8 years his junior. Jojo sees himself as bisexual. He is the second youngest child of a family of eight children. He comes from Cavite, a progressive province close to the capital of the Philippines. He is estranged from his wife and son. His father was half Spanish and a Christian born-again pastor. Jojo obtained a college degree in a Catholic university in Manila. He receives financial support from his siblings and his current partner.

PRESENTING ISSUES AND CHALLENGES

Jojo presented with general life dissatisfaction and depression and felt stigmatized. He was also diagnosed with having HIV. This diagnosis totally devastated him because it meant he could no longer work in the Middle East as most employers in this region reject job applicants or contractual employees who test positive for HIV. Contract workers applying for overseas jobs typically undergo HIV testing along with the other blood tests as part of the standard screening protocol. Jojo did not pursue looking for jobs in other countries such as the United States because his qualifications and experience do not match most government postings. Job openings are mostly in the paramedical field, such as nursing, speech therapy, or occupational therapy. Immigration to the United States is also a long and complicated process. Since his HIV diagnosis 10 years ago, Jojo has not been able to get an overseas job but was able to land temporary jobs in Manila. His wife eventually left him and decided to migrate to Australia. At this point he felt abandoned, jobless, and hopeless. Jojo attempted suicide a few times. Jojo hid his HIV condition from his family, partner, and friends. (Note, in the Philippines, there is no mandatory reporting law for people who test HIV positive.)

CASE HISTORY AND DEVELOPMENTAL BACKGROUND

Jojo married his grade-school classmate soon after finishing college. His wife bore him an only son, but before his child could walk, Jojo left the Philippines to work as a housekeeping manager in Qatar. Several years later, upon his return, he discovered that his son had married at an early age and had addiction problems while his wife was wasting the money he had regularly been sending home.

To earn some income, he rented out a portion of his small house to a ministore, but it soon closed for economic reasons. Ronnie, one of the occupants of the ministore, asked him if he could stay and pay for a bed space. Eventually, Ronnie became Jojo's live-in sexual partner and breadwinner of the household.

Jojo still longs for a well-paying job in the Middle East. His family owns a vast coconut plantation, but being a farmer was not part of his personal plans. "The place is too far," he said, "and there are no people there." He was urged to look for local openings, but he did not seem interested in them because of the low pay.

THE THERAPY

We first met Jojo when he joined a small group sharing I (Maria Isabel E. Melgar) organized among clients with HIV. He was noticeably quiet and was not as cheerful as the rest of the group. He shared a little about himself, though not enough to know him. Some who knew him well observed that he was a depressive and anxious person.

Following this group sharing we offered to have an individual session with him as he admitted to being severely depressed. He came a few weeks later. I followed up on his personal and family background using a clinical interview procedure. He said that he does not have a supportive family and the only sibling who would have sympathy for him is his sister living abroad. None of the family knew he had HIV. I asked him to come again for another session to explore employment opportunities and what he could do with his idle time. He was eager for these appointments and appeared more hopeful each time I saw him. Luckily, a part-time job at a nongovernmental AIDS organization was offered to him. This job required him to commute anywhere from 2 to 3 hours a day from his house to the place of work. He did not complain. He said it kept him away from depression.

During the next session, I heard Jojo repeatedly narrate his past lifestyle and his own family. He said that while he was in the Middle East he had plenty of money and led a happy bachelor's life. His life then was a polar opposite to what it is now. On one occasion, he was invited by my cotherapist for a casual conversation outside the clinic. Man to man, he poured out his emotional pain about what had happened to his wife and son.

To establish better rapport and understand the context of a client like Jojo, *kuwentuhan* [story sharing] was used during the private talk with him. In story sharing, the counselor engages the client in a kind of informal interaction that defies structure and logic. The conversation starts from wherever the client chooses to begin his or her story. The counselor reciprocates this dialogue by sharing his or her stories.

Through the narratives of this story-sharing strategy, we were able to identify Jojo's negative thinking and negative self statements as well as to detect the positive spin on his experience. Occasionally, we diverted our conversations to what he could do about the issues that perpetuated his beliefs about coping with HIV. The themes in Jojo's stories were memories of his youth and his marriage, what it was like to be an overseas worker, his current relationship, and his life aspirations.

In the last session, I shared stories how, for instance, a man with HIV was able to get past the shame of disclosing his HIV status and his real sexual orientation to his parents by enlisting the support of his friends. I asked him how he could slowly get out of a self-imposed stigma. He felt he needed help disclosing his HIV status to his lover. We explored with him ways in which he could approach his partner to do this. He found it difficult to understand why his partner continued to reject his suggestions to be tested for HIV.

The solution-focused approach in Jojo's therapy helped ground our counseling goals to address the immediate cause of his depression. Although there were past issues that he had difficulty in resolving, the pragmatic approach of "what can we do from here" helped him focus on concrete steps and be less overwhelmed by the hopelessness of the big picture. We reviewed with him the possible resources he could access while looking for a more stable job. He was able to reconsider attending skills-training programs offered by the government. He joined a massage training seminar and subsequently provided private services. He also went to different hotels to submit job applications forms, but he has not gotten any positive responses so far. While going through these steps, he called me to let me know how he was doing. He was happy to say that he had accepted a position as an auditor of a support group for people living with HIV.

Finally, through the narratives, the memories that were constructed and expressed by Jojo helped change the content through a process known as reconstruction. Regarding the strong attachment to his past life in the Middle East and to the conceptualized self as a physically healthy, financially stable, and fun-loving man, we listened to his story without diminishing its importance. However, we were conscious in weakening his attachment to the never-ending story of the past that could paralyze him rather than inspiring him to move on.

DISCUSSION AND ANALYSIS

Our analysis revealed the following findings about the client: (a) He experienced stigma and survival issues related to living with HIV; and (b) he experienced problems with emotional adjustment rooted in unresolved family issues having to do with siblings, marital life, and parental responsibility.

Jojo is a former migrant worker who was diagnosed with HIV but refused to disclose this matter with anyone, including his closest family relatives and current partner. He had adopted an identity that hid this fact. Like any typical HIV-infected person, he thought a part of him died after the multiple losses he had experienced in life (Nord, 1997). Consequently, this masked identity affected the way he experienced his social world, his environment, and the things he could do after receiving the HIV diagnosis.

He holds strongly to an identity of someone who is physically healthy, fun loving, and financially stable while being distressed by the life events that threaten all of these. He is fiercely attached to this reconceptualized self. His memory of this glorious past helped him restore a self-image that was once alive and highly motivated. However, it is also this maladaptation to the circumstances that prolongs his grieving and guilt. He stays at home all the time, never interacting with neighbors and hardly has any contact with his siblings. Hayes, Strosahl, and Wilson (2012) identified experiential avoidance as one of the keys to the cycle of suffering. They posited that if most distressing content is not subject to behavioral regulation, the client is left with one strategy: emotional and behavioral avoidance. Hayes et al. further stated that "the long term result is that the person's life space begins to shrink, avoided situations multiply and fester, avoided thoughts and feelings become more overwhelming, and the ability to enter into the present moment and enjoy life gradually withers" (p. 22). Unless Jojo is able to fully accept who he is, an escape only reinforces a sense of loneliness and a disconnect with the world. People who loved him were not aware of his medical and emotional condition, and therefore no support was there when he needed it.

Jojo described himself as a parent who failed his son. He was imprisoned in this cognition that there is a "right" or "wrong" way of performing this parenting role. In Philippine society, parents continue to provide for the material needs of their children even when they are of mature age. Filipinos are family oriented, and parents are child centered (Javier, 2005). Jojo was nurtured well by his father while finishing college, getting married, and landing a job that secured his adult life. Sadly, he did not experience this role as a parent when it was his turn, which is another part of himself that he continues to criticize and finds it hard to accept.

It seems that while Jojo believes that he is a victim of HIV, he does not realize that he is victimizing other people by refusing to disclose his HIV status. The issue of disclosure remains to be resolved as it provokes feelings of anxiety. It is extremely difficult for him to commit to an action of disclosure as the very act poses a direct challenge to his mental and emotional health.

Taking good care of his partner helps reconstruct Jojo's own story as he tries to be a be a good and loyal partner to Ronnie. He never experienced loving this way in his previous life. As Arden and Linford (2009) explained, this reconstruction builds new neural connections every time stories are told. The changes could reflect new perspectives or insights about the self through the passage of time.

How does this new private identity (e.g., a person with HIV and living with a male partner) affect his social connectivity in the local community? As mentioned, Jojo remained anonymous to the community because he had imposed a form of self-isolation and was living in the confines of his bungalow. In Philippine culture, aloofness is typically avoided because a more communal self is much preferred. Although persons living with HIV frequently do not disclose their medical condition in the community, they thereby fail to gain the strength that comes with enjoying a certain esprit de corps. Thus, it is not uncommon to find a friend worthy of trust and emotional intimacy in this culture that fosters *pakikipagkapwa* [literally, to share the self with others]. Pakikipagkapwa is a cultural process where persons go through multiple levels of entering meaningful relationships ranging from simple civility and building mutual regard to a more complex level of oneness with the other. It is more adaptive, therefore, to share sentiments with someone in whom you can place high confidence so that both of you can enjoy complete trust.

The therapy with Jojo centered on cognitively reframing the meaning of a "good and happy life." This reframing means embracing the risks of personal changes and accepting potential outcomes such as failures. Broadening his perspectives about the value of imperfections for self-growth and the value of slowly building new relationships and friendships that are less utilitarian might help Jojo find more depth and real meaning in his present life. Understanding the limits of what money can do and a more open realization about how relationships with other people are based on trust could serve as the key to a more satisfying view about life, no matter how imperfect it might be. Helping Jojo develop healthy coping skills to move on as a person living with HIV and soliciting important social support to survive in spite of HIV should be considered as an intermediary goal. Counseling interventions should help empower him to choose his battles while experiencing small successes and pains along the way.

CONCLUSION

This chapter discusses the therapy of Jojo, who has HIV. It charts the tumultuous journey of an overseas contract worker who was betrayed by his wife, has a son who battles drug addiction, and eventually fell for a male lover. Through his narratives, we had a better grasp of his coping mechanisms and discovered his patterns of avoidance and his inability to accept the realities of his current circumstances. The specific counseling strategy we used aimed to help the client deal with the losses he experienced after HIV and gain more confidence in reconstructing his future. Our approach specifically identified a solution-focused approach, but we adapted the method to the nuances of a local culture and combined it with a story-sharing approach known as kuwentuhan. The therapy ended with an analysis of the client by looking at his post-HIV identity and how his coping reactions such as emotional and behavioral avoidance could further push him to chronic depression. The rapport built by the counselors and the open attitude of the client to listen and learn from the interactions helped him see the light and get on with being alive.

QUESTIONS

1. How can a client work on resolving his or her life issues in the here and now while living with the challenges of HIV?
2. Consider the personal history and social background of the client. Explain how these factors could predispose him to depression and suicidal tendencies.
3. What are the major stressors associated with living with HIV that are perceived by the client as personally challenging? What are the client's coping strategies that are helping him deal with these major stressors?
4. How else can we engage our client in sharing his life story by using a more culturally familiar technique of elicitation?
5. What is the essential element in a solution-focused story sharing that helped the client deal with his presenting problems? What are its limitations?

REFERENCES

Arden, J. B., & Linford, L. (2009). *Brain-based therapy*. Hoboken, NJ: Wiley.

Hayes, S. C., Strosahl, K. D., & Wilson, K. G. (2012). *Acceptance and commitment therapy* (2nd ed.). New York, NY: Guilford Press.

Javier, R. E., Jr. (2005). *Pampamamaraang kaangkinan ng pakikipagkuwentuhan* [Methodological properties of story-sharing]. Quezon City, Philippines: BINHI.

Melgar, I. E. (2013). Counseling and psychotherapy in the Philippines: A discipline in transition. In R. Moodley, U. Gielen, & R. Wu (Eds.), *Handbook of counseling and psychotherapy in an international context* (pp. 237–246). New York, NY: Routlege.

Nord, D. (1997). *Multiple AIDS-related loss: A handbook for understanding and surviving a perpetual fall*. New York, NY: Taylor & Francis.

Philippines Statistics Authority, National Statistics Office. (2012). *Statistical tables on overseas Filipino workers (OFW): 2012*. Retrieved from http://web0.psa.gov.ph/content/statistical-tables-overseas-filipino-workers-ofw-2012-0

Chapter 15

COUNSELING AND PSYCHOTHERAPY IN SOUTH KOREA: MISUN'S STORY

Eunsun Joo

INTRODUCTION

Although Korea has a long history of more than 5,000 years, little is known about Korea internationally. Throughout its long history, the country has developed a unique culture and characteristics. Historically, Koreans had to stand together in groups based on family lineage as well as educational and geographical backgrounds. This phenomenon naturally led Koreans to form a collectivistic society. Traditionally, Korean culture emphasized hierarchy and a collective emotional state. Individual needs were often sacrificed for group needs, especially by people who were younger, female, and from a lower social class. As a result of this, psychologically suppressed Koreans were found to accumulate (repress) anger.

The concept of Western counseling and psychotherapy was first practiced in the 1950s, and because of an increasing public demand for mental health practitioners, counseling and psychotherapy are actively practiced in Korea. Various approaches, such as psychodynamic, person-centered, gestalt, cognitive behavior, and systematic therapies, are practiced in Korea by different professionals, such as psychiatrists, clinical psychologists, counseling psychologists, counselors, social workers, art therapists, and pastoral counselors (Joo, 2012).

Among other approaches, focusing-oriented therapy provides a mind–body integration approach. Focusing-oriented therapy encourages the client to "focus" on the vague sensation inside of one's body, giving it attention and respect, so that the inner experience becomes clearer and a space is opened up for new insights and unexpected possibilities. The "felt sense" of the situation changes, and the shift in bodily-felt experience often leads to changes in behavior (Gendlin, 1996).

In this chapter, I discuss the case of Misun, who presented with feelings of anxiety and somatic pains such as heaviness in her chest. She was having difficulty with marriage and relationship problems. I discuss her therapy and explore how a focusing-oriented approach was used to treat her *Hwa-byung* [a Korean somatization disorder]. I discuss Misun's presenting issues and challenges as well as the history and developmental background associated with her case. Furthermore, I discuss the potential applicability in Korea of the focusing approach, which is based on a mind and body integration.

The Client

The client, Misun, is a 50-year old Korean woman who married a Japanese man 25 years ago and immigrated to Japan. She has two sons, a 23-year-old college dropout and a 20-year-old who is currently a college student. She is a Christian.

Presenting Issues and Challenges

Misun came into counseling because of problems she was having in her marriage and with her children. In addition, she also complained of somatic symptoms of neck pains, blurred vision in her left eye, and a feeling of anxiety with a blockage in her chest. Misun had seen an ophthalmologist for approximately 6 months before she came into counseling and had received two family counseling sessions in Japan with her family, but the family counseling was discontinued because of her husband's hesitation to participate. The client was diagnosed as having *Hwa-byung*, a Korean somatization disorder that literally translates as an "illness of fire" (Min, 2009) and is similar to *Khyal cap* (Khyal attacks) described in the *Diagnostic and Statistical Manual of Mental Disorders* (5th ed.; American Psychiatric Association, 2013). Khyal cap is a cultural syndrome found among Cambodians who live in the United States and Cambodia. Khyal cap usually meet panic attack criteria and may shape the experience of other anxiety, trauma, and stressor-related disorders (American Psychiatric Association, 2013).

According to the client, married life in Japan was not easy, and she struggled to fit into Japanese society. Communication with her husband was not very open, and she developed few friendships. The situation did not improve with the arrival of two sons; in fact, it deteriorated further. Misun especially had a poor relationship with her eldest son, who was ashamed of having a Korean mother and blamed her for the teasing and discrimination he faced from his peers. Slowly, Misun's marriage and family relationships had broken down, and she was under a trial separation when she came to Korea.

Case History and Development Background

Misun grew up in a very patriarchal family in Korea, even by average Korean standards at the time. As the first born of three siblings, despite being smart and clever, she received little support or encouragement from her parents. Her parents' attention was focused on Misun's younger male sibling because sons were favored over daughters at that time in Korea. As she explained, she felt she was treated as a second-class citizen in her own family. In fact, when she received good grades in school, her parents actually disapproved, saying that her strong energy (Korean concept of *chi*) was taking away her brother's confidence.

One of the most hurtful experiences for Misun was when she was accepted to a prestigious university, but her parents refused to let her attend. Despite the fact that the family was sufficiently well to do, Misun's parents were against Misun getting advanced education. Rather, she was told to forget college and look to getting married instead. Misun very much wanted to go to college, so she left home and worked for 2 years to save money for college. Those years were very difficult as Misun worked several part-time jobs to earn tuition at a time when society did not provide many opportunities for or look kindly upon a single woman living by herself. Misun mentioned that she resented the fact that her parents always discriminated against her for being a female. During college, Misun met a Japanese exchange student and fell in love. Marrying a foreigner is forbidden according to traditional Korean culture because it is considered to contaminate the pureblood. Though her parents objected vehemently, she flew to Japan with him and got married. It can be interpreted that over the years, Misun developed *Hwa*, which is repressed anger toward her parents, brother, and society. As a result, the chronic Hwa-byung from the repetition of the Hwa and *Wul* (which means stuffy and stifling) conditions causes the feelings of futility, isolation, depression, alienation, and nothingness, which in turn give rise to a critical situation of existential emptiness.

THE THERAPY

Ten sessions comprised the therapy, and those sessions could be categorized into three stages. Sessions 1 through 3 were categorized as the initial stage, Sessions 4 through 7 as the working stage, and Sessions 8 through 10 as the wrap-up stage (Joo, 2011). During the initial stage, Misun put effort into the first step of focusing—clearing space—and revealed a broad spectrum of issues. She started with her childhood, when she experienced severe discrimination as a daughter, and moved forward to the frustration and isolation of living in Japan. Her narrative revealed that much of Misun's self-confidence and self-esteem had been lost over time. She had struggled to prove her self-worth first to her parents and later to her husband and children. As she spoke of her experiences, Misun looked uncomfortable, with a tense facial expression and rigid posture. She described loss of energy, a constant feeling of frustration, and a sense of being lost. Although these sessions were meant to bring out broad issues without delving into analysis, Misun pointed to being a female as the main cause of the problems. In this stage, the client let out accumulated thoughts and feelings so that she was ready to get in touch with her felt sense.

In the working stage, Misun was asked to choose the problem that she felt was the worst at the moment and relate that to the kinds of bodily feelings it evoked. Her marriage problems evoked a strong bodily sense, which she felt was related to the blurred vision in her left eye. Most strongly, it brought a feeling of blockage in her chest. To make this blockage more concrete and tangible, words, phrases, and images were explored until one emerged that fit the best. After several thoughts and feelings were bounced around, the client arrived at the image of being in a dark, foggy tunnel with a feeling of heaviness. The felt sense of being in the dark tunnel was further explored to refine and enhance the relationship between the felt sense and imagery. Through the process of resonating, Misun was able to gain a clearer picture of why the imagery of being in the tunnel bothered her so much. She mentioned that the felt sense of driving very fast on a foggy road was frustrating because she was not able to see. She felt that as the driver she should be in control; however, she felt out of control and was angry about it. The next step involved getting to know the felt sense. Misun explained that what made her most uncomfortable was the feeling that she was a victim of her own decisions. She had chosen to live a life that she hoped would be better, but it turned out to disappoint her. Initially, Misun blamed external factors: being a woman and a foreigner in Japan. However, when she further explored the problem, she began to realize the source of these feelings was created internally, rather than externally. Finally, when Misun began to look within herself for the answers and received feedback from her felt sense, she started to look at her situation from a different perspective. She mentioned that despite things not turning out as she had imagined, she was proud, even astonished, looking back at the fact that she had lived her life to the fullest under such difficult circumstances.

In the wrap-up stage, Misun was able to gain self-strength and decided to take control of her own life. What focusing did for her was to help her listen to her own inner self by paying attention to her felt sense, which in this case was heaviness and blockage in her chest.

DISCUSSION AND ANALYSIS

Misun grew up in a very patriarchal family in Korea that, combined with her passive personality, prevented her from fully expressing her wants and needs. Her strong belief in Christianity served as both a source of strength and as a crutch. Misun explained that her belief in God had helped her endure her difficult life, and because of her religion she did not feel so lonely. However, religion also served to reinforce her passive nature as she tended to accept her lot in life, believing that God had something planned for her. But even her faith could not overcome the accumulation of a long and difficult life and era. As Misun entered middle age, both her psyche and her body began to give signs of needing help. Finally, when Misun turned 50 years old, it forced her to examine her life and make the determination to seek professional help. During therapy, I did not tell her to be more in charge of her life. However, the focusing process helped the client to be the master of her life. In other words, Misun chose to be her own self and live her life according to her decisions. Both the focusing approach, which is based on mind–body integration, and the client-centered approach enabled the client to deal with her anger by focusing on her felt sense of bodily experience. Furthermore, it enabled her to gain trust in herself and opened up the possibility of using this approach in the Korean counseling setting.

According to Kirschner (2004), focusing can help people step back from the cultural stereotypes and pause to find the felt meaning in the body: "This allows a person to live from their felt experience, even when it contradicts outside expectations" (p. 8). This articulation of human potential to make felt meaning a direct referent reveals a new evolutionary development that comes after culture, language, and emotion, which enables us to further differentiate experience. Also, according to Ikemi (2001), many Japanese found that through engaging in a focusing process, they valued aspects of their own traditions that have been rejected by modernity (Ikemi, 2001). By checking the felt sense, cultural meanings are also selectively valued according to this bodily resonance, and so a new form of cultural expression becomes possible. The characteristics of focusing may enable us to incorporate other forms of traditional healing, such as the *Han-bang* approach (which combines medicinal herbs and minerals to treat illness).

Finally, this case study points toward the development of the focusing approach in Korea. Research that is based on the scientist–practitioner model should be conducted on the use of the focusing approach in Korea; this research may be in the form of case studies and the development of focusing-related scales.

CONCLUSION

As mentioned earlier, many disciplines of counseling were imported from the West to Korea within the last 20 years (Joo, 2012). Because of rapidly growing demands for counseling, practitioners were eager to apply many Western approaches of counseling without much verification of the efficacy. Furthermore, it is not easy to find an appropriate approach that considers the unique characteristics of Korean female clients. The case that was presented in this chapter features a typical Korean female client. This client chose to repress her emotions rather than to express them, showed psychosomatic symptoms, and was not able to live an independent life. It is recommended that focusing-oriented therapy, with its holistic view, will be well adopted in Korea. Furthermore, it is also suggested that a counseling model appropriate to the Korean cultural context and based on a solid foundation of research will be developed in the future.

QUESTIONS

1. In your own perspective, how do you think age, gender, and religion affected Misun's emotional and somatic pains?
2. What role do you think age, gender, and religion played in Misun's Hwa-byung?
3. Have you ever treated a client with psychosomatic difficulties? How was he or she similar and different from Misun?
4. Do you think a focusing-oriented approach was appropriate for the case? What do you think were helpful and not so helpful components?
5. If you were to treat Misun, what counseling approach would you use, and what would the procedure be like?

REFERENCES

American Psychiatric Association. (2013). *Diagnostic and statistical manual of mental disorders* (5th ed.). Washington, DC: Author.

Gendlin, E. (1996). *Focusing-oriented psychotherapy*. New York, NY: Guilford Press.

Ikemi, A. (2001). Presence, existence and space: Key concepts in focusing-oriented psychotherapy. *The Focusing Connection, 18*, 1–4.

Joo, E. (2011). Application of focusing-oriented psychotherapy in dealing with issues of Asian immigrants: A single-case study of a Korean immigrant in Japan. *Japanese Psychological Research, 53*, 97–102.

Joo, E. (2012). Counseling and psychotherapy in South Korea. In R. Moodley, U. Gielen, & R. Wu (Eds.), *Handbook of counseling and psychotherapy in an international context* (pp. 247–257). New York, NY: Routledge.

Kirschner, E. (2004, October). Focus on: Atsmaout Perlstein. *Staying in Focus: The Focusing Institute Newsletter, 6*, 8.

Min, S. K. (2009). Hwa-byung in Korea: Culture and dynamic analysis. *World Cultural Psychiatric Research Review, 4*, 12–21.

Part Four

COUNSELING AND PSYCHOTHERAPY IN CENTRAL, NORTH, AND SOUTH AMERICA

Chapter 16

COUNSELING AND PSYCHOTHERAPY IN ARGENTINA: MICHAEL'S STORY

Diego Benegas Loyo

INTRODUCTION

Argentina has a well-established and developed tradition in counseling, clinical psychology, and psychoanalysis. Despite its persecution by the last dictatorship (1976–1983), the profession has been expanding both in numbers and in perspectives, including psychodynamic, systemic, and cognitive approaches as the most prevalent outside of psychoanalysis, which is the most predominant. Many therapists use eclectic and integrative approaches for group, family, and community interventions. The rich tradition that has been called Argentine School of Psychoanalysis follows the path of various theorists and practitioners who share a regard for social, economic, and political influences, together with an ethical mandate to push theory to respond to emerging complex clinical challenges (for discussion, see Muller & Palavezzatti, 2013).

For many psychoanalysts, the ethical core of the approach is to listen to clients in their singularity, putting theory under discussion in each encounter. Conceiving the unconscious as "structured as a language" entails acknowledging the centrality of desire in shaping symptoms and a regard for enjoyment, or *jouissance*, that point where the subject actively participates in maintaining his or her own suffering. As the individual is an emergent product of a social network, we understand the body as an erogenous reality, a surface of pain and pleasure that bears the marks of a person's history with social discourses and practices in constant struggle (Bleichmar, 2002; Davoine & Gaudillière, 2004; Kordon, Edelman, Lagos, & Kesner, 2005; Pichon-Rivière, 1985). Socioeconomic determinants situate individuals in a diversity matrix, as the crossing of multiple systems of oppression allows for different degrees of agency. This diversity is crucially relevant when working with populations historically traumatized but also with communities who have advanced political struggles to acquire a sense of dignity and pride (Benegas Loyo, 2011; Muñoz, 2009; Pellegrini, 1997).

This chapter discusses the case of Michael, who sought therapy when a physical condition made him face the need to undertake an important lifestyle-changing process.

125

THE CLIENT

Michael is a 66-year-old male, gay, retired, Anglo Saxon, English speaker, and Catholic who lived for most of his life in the United States. Michael has been HIV positive for the last 30 years and takes medication every day; he is also a cancer survivor. For several years, he has been spending the summer in Argentina, returning to the United States to spend the northern summer there. He is single, and in the United States he lives alone, next door to his 80-year-old parents. There, he has two siblings around 10 years younger who live with their partners in a town 2 hours south.

PRESENTING ISSUES AND CHALLENGES

Michael presented with stress, anxiety, and depression. During a recent U.S. stay, he was diagnosed with having cirrhosis, a condition requiring special care and some lifestyle changes. As an HIV positive individual and cancer survivor, he has lived for decades with challenging conditions, so this last discovery not only implied the need for important emotional and volitional investment but it also meant imposing more restrictions in his already much restricted life. Denying suicidal ideation, he consulted because he was not sure he had the will to undertake yet one more challenge in order to stay alive. At the time he presented, he had plans to leave the city 6 weeks later; he also asked if the therapist worked with "sexual diversity," but beyond declaring he is gay, he did not refer in the first interview to discrimination, sexuality, or even a love conflict. This contradiction is especially puzzling and would become a central aspect of this case.

CASE HISTORY AND DEVELOPMENTAL BACKGROUND

Living near his parents is very stressful for Michael. His mother complains about everything; she is very aggressive, criticizes his friends, or says things she knows will hurt others. His father, however, is independent, has many friends, and goes out in town all the time. Michael has not disclosed his recent diagnosis to anybody. Ten years ago, he had a cancer surgery that took him 1 year to recover and that still required special care. Michael is a proactive person, quite independent, yet very social and connected to different networks. Defining himself "a news junky," he is up to date with world developments and sports and takes much interest in culture. Michael has several friends in different places and especially two in the city, with whom he meets regularly. He is also an active participant in two local organizations, one with foreigners and one with gay men.

THE THERAPY

After Michael talked at length about his physical conditions and his family conflict, I asked him what he thought therapy could do for him. He talked about the life changes he needed to make in order to face cirrhosis: adhere to a strict diet, undergo specific treatment, quit smoking, and quit drinking alcohol. He said,

> To keep being alive I have to make a lot of changes . . . I know I can do it. I have done it twice before, 30 years ago, and again 10 years ago . . . What I don't know is if I want to keep being alive . . . I don't really have a reason to live.

I asked about suicidal ideation; he denies that but explained,

> I don't need to do anything like that in order to die . . . you know, a couple drinks could kill me, not taking my pills could kill me . . . if I don't do all these things I would die pretty soon . . . just being alive is a lot of work.

As a conclusion of this interview, I reformulated for him his demand as "In therapy you want to find a reason to live . . . and all of that in 6 weeks." I proposed to him to begin by addressing his family situation as a way to see how this was affecting his will; he would also continue his medical and nutritional treatments for his physical condition; as for the reason to live, we would start working on that, but that search would not finish in such short time. He agreed, and with this contract, we scheduled all future sessions.

He brought up spontaneously the problematic relationship with his mother. He seemed anxious yet somehow comfortable with that topic. However, he hinted from the start a definition of himself as "dysfunctional," which he later developed. In different senses of that term, he mentioned coming from a "dysfunctional" family, his relationships failed, and he failed to fall in love. He also said he felt sexually "dysfunctional" because of his multiple conditions; a big part of it came from a highly invasive surgery 10 years before that affected greatly his sense of attractiveness. An important goal of therapy was to question these negative definitions of his body (dysfunctional), aiming to let him see how the game of life could continue, because beyond having a different body from a decade ago, his desire and will to live were still strong. This will to live made him a passionate person, indeed, a very interesting one.

I noticed that explaining his surgery was unpleasant for him but not as difficult as talking about love. Only when asked would he talk about his last breakup. He would refer to his former partner as "John, the last one." This nickname is significant because after the separation, Michael decided not to have partners anymore. It was at that time that the cancer appeared, and it is after this that he began to feel "dysfunctional."

In talking about this relationship, which elicited great anxiety and affective pain, Michael began to confront a situation that was different in nature, as it was an affective, romantic issue rather than a virus, a physical condition, or surgery. This relationship was weighing on his mind greatly, perhaps as the background of his anxiety for the current diagnosis. After feeling "used and discarded," he never again considered himself desirable, and he took a sort of leave from the world of love, sex, and emotional attachments. After all that, he had a new body, a new life, and a new identity, and he had not come to terms with that.

Within this topic, he mentioned he had never known love, perhaps because in his upbringing there was none. According to Michael, his parents married young because his mother was pregnant. They were around 17 years old, and when Michael was a child, they had many fights. He described the following childhood memory:

> One time, when I was eight, Dad said he was leaving, and Mom started crying, and I saw her crying, and I went after him at the door and took him and asked him "Dad, don't go." He did not go, and they remain together until this day.

In this childhood memory, he is in the middle, uniting this couple. His parents are together *because* of him. Though distant, this memory seems truly present. In fact, the fear of his mother crying appears in each decision he takes: He would not contradict her, he would call her, and his career choices would be made based on whether or not they would make Mother cry. As this maternal cry plays a central role in configuring his life, this childhood memory revealed itself as dramatically current. In this structure lies a critical source of Michael's anxiety and the reason why the trip home had made him sad to the point of questioning his will to live. This scene works as an important metaphor for his life today, because still now he feels responsible for his parents being together: He is still in the middle, being the one who begs Father not to leave so Mother would not cry. Furthermore, this sense of responsibility means that in times of marital discord between his parents, he would be failing at his role as mediator and his mission of maintaining their marital bond. He was "dysfunctional" foremost when he could not bring happiness to their relationship.

DISCUSSION AND ANALYSIS

This case presented some challenging characteristics as well as some important strengths. The client's age, the multiple conditions, and the short time we had made it difficult to propose a goal of personality restructuring or a deeper revision of long-established behavioral and affective patterns. Furthermore, the client did not ask for that, and it was not strictly necessary for the situation at hand.

Michael had also several distinct strengths: strong self-control and a developed ability for rationalization and sublimation, indicating a personality on the obsessive side. He was nonetheless histrionic, funny, and even seductive, showing a balanced and rich defense repertoire and making him quite resourceful. Michael's ego functioning was strong and healthy. He also communicated frequently with his family in the United States and with some of his ex-partners, and he maintained lifelong friendships. He was actively involved in different community organizations, and he had a variety of interests and activities and a rich social network. Michael was a survivor of the first AIDS epidemic; had been involved in organizing actions with ACT-UP, Pride Marches, and Gay Games; and had also survived an important surgery a decade ago, keeping himself in fairly good health at the present. Nobody accomplishes all of that without a strong ego defense structure and solid affective bonds.

I work with interventions at different levels in different moments, according to what the client brings. The Lacanian concept of "enjoyment" highlights the subject's role in his own suffering and the kinds of intensities produced. Michael said he neither has nor searches for sex and that he does not need it, portraying himself as beyond these passions. Here, my intent was not to depict him as a socially correct elderly person, retired from sex. Instead, later I mentioned the "passion" of the scenes where his mother humiliated him. These seemingly paradoxical interventions do not aim for reason, because he would not understand rationally his persistence in seeking the intensity of these painful fights. These comments mark points and set up questions that might resonate later. It is like planting seeds for eventual self-reflection.

Rational interventions go a different direction. We explored alternatives in the arguments with his mother. I signaled all-or-nothing ways of thinking and gave him a training program for saying "no" and establishing boundaries. We also worked on differentiating issues within his power from those beyond his control. These interventions aimed to provide him with concrete tasks and skills development that might prove to be beneficial for him. However, if the interventions directed toward enjoyment went too far for this short treatment, interventions aimed at rational thinking would fall too short. For instance, conflict resolution skills could help ease his daily stress, but they would not solve the deeper existential crisis.

The critical work in this case lies in the dialogues on love, desire, romance, and his history with partners. These questions allowed him to talk about previous relationships in which he had felt "used" to such a degree that he had decided to avoid having any other partner in the future. Later, meeting John, he allowed himself one extra chance but thought that it would be *the last one*; hence, John was, from the beginning, "the last one." This history of romance, in turn, revealed his "dysfunction" as a defensive position engrained in lifelong structures and existential decisions rather than just a biologically determined fact. This revelation was the most productive part of the treatment. Those instances where we discussed this issue were characterized by a relaxed and sometimes witty mood of gossipy chit-chat on love and relations. In those moments, Michael could emerge as a loving person; a person who desired, who made decisions, who felt and hurt; a person who tried and fell. In a sense, we had stopped talking about his liver and started talking about his heart.

In the last sessions, Michael expressed that he was feeling better, "back to [his] usual self." Although this result is always important, and nice for the therapist to hear, we need to find in his productions the indications of a subjective movement that even if minimal would let us have an idea about his prognosis. We find it in a very different scene. In one of the last sessions, he mentioned almost randomly that he had gone to the theater:

> I arrived early as usual and had a coffee in a nearby café. I see a man, a young boy, probably in his forties. He does not look at me . . . but I thought, "He is so good looking, *it would be nice*, as in other times, to go and talk to him." Later, at the door of the theater, he comes, and we recognize each other from the café . . . you know one of those looks like, "Aha! I knew you were coming here too" . . . you know, this play is kind of very glamorous . . . we later talk about it.

This is a minimal scene but quite different from "being beyond mundane needs" as he presented in the beginning. First, his body is involved differently, for there is a pleasurable game of looking and being looked at, where Michael's body is an object of attraction and not of medical intervention. However, the essential part is that he is in a desiring position. Desire is again present and at play, but above all, his expression "it would be nice" opens to a possible future as it enunciates a will hinting toward the "will to live" that he was looking for. Michael's body appears here involved in a desiring situation that gives the feeling that he is back into the game of life.

In therapy, it is of vital importance to respect the client's demand and to validate his unique approach to life. We often find this in the first formulations of transference, what the therapist is imagined to know. Michael's problem was a lack of reason to sustain a body that only gave him pains and restrictions; he consulted somebody whom he felt knew about "sexual diversity." His demand communicated that he suffered because he could not imagine himself as a sexual person anymore. I find him a fascinating person who has a lot to teach us. His own answer at the end opens the possibility for a future, an expectation for potential encounters with persons who will see in that body much more than a biological organism. In the theater scene, there is complicity, there is community, and there is play, but most of all, there is longing, which is a not-so-distant cousin of hope.

CONCLUSION

It is important to keep in mind the various identities and multiple systems of oppression that a person faces. While listening to a man who talks about giving up desire and life, a therapist should not lose track of the different social discourses that portray elderly people as disposable, out of the economy, and out of sexual life. One should not forget discourses that tell gay people that their affective bonds are less valid and their families are not real families. With this in mind, it was critical to meet this client where he was, for Michael did not come to discuss politics, but his words would not make sense in a void because he did not live in an ideal world but in one crisscrossed by power inequalities. The economy of unconscious desire only emerges from social discourses, which are the threads with which subjects weave their lives.

Despite the prevalence of psychoanalysis in Argentine psychology, there is no unifying perspective in psychotherapy. Nevertheless, it is a widely recognized fact that therapists need to understand clients in their uniqueness, including accounting for age, religion, sexuality, gender, nationality, and even language. Although these can be barriers, because difference makes expressing and understanding more challenging, they are also potential sources of much growth. I believe this respect and attention for the complexities of a client's sociocultural identity, always determined by multiple factors, has been shown in this case.

QUESTIONS

1. What aspects of the encounter of Argentine and U.S. cultures do you think are shaping both the presentation of the client's symptoms and also his possibility to seek help?
2. What aspects of the particular configuration of identities of this client—that is, sexuality, age, nationality, religion—might be triggering or accentuating his symptoms?
3. How do you think the particular configuration of identities—that is, sexuality, age, nationality, religion—of the client, and perhaps of the therapist as well, might have helped the client resolve this particular existential crisis?
4. What do you think are the strengths and weaknesses of the way Michael's case was handled?
5. How would you engage Michael's case from your own therapeutic viewpoint or approach?

REFERENCES

Benegas Loyo, D. (2011). "If there's no justice . . .": Trauma and identity in post dictatorship Argentina. *Performance Research, 16,* 20–30.

Bleichmar, S. (2002). *La fundación de lo inconciente: Destinos de pulsión, destinos del sujeto* [The foundation of the unconscious: Destinies of the drive, destinies of the subject]. Buenos Aires, Argentina: Amorrortu.

Davoine, F., & Gaudillière, J. M. (2004). *History beyond trauma: Whereof one cannot speak, thereof one cannot stay silent.* New York, NY: Other Press.

Kordon, D., Edelman L., Lagos, D., & Kesner, D. (2005). *Efectos psicológicos y psicosociales de la represión política y la impunidad: De la dictadura a la actualidad* [Psychological and psychosocial effects of political repression and impunity: From dictatorship to the present]. Buenos Aires, Argentina: Madres de Plaza de Mayo.

Muller, F., & Palavezzatti, M. C. (2013). Counseling and psychotherapy in Argentina. In R. Moodley, U. Gielen, & R. Wu (Eds.), *Handbook of counseling and psychotherapy in an international context* (pp. 85–94). New York, NY: Routledge.

Muñoz, J. E. (2009). *Cruising utopia: The then and there of queer futurity.* New York, NY: New York University Press.

Pellegrini, A. (1997). *Performance anxieties: Staging psychoanalysis, staging race.* New York, NY: Routledge.

Pichon-Rivière, E. (1985). *Teoría del vínculo* [Theory of the bond]. Buenos Aires, Argentina: Paidós.

Chapter 17

COUNSELING AND PSYCHOTHERAPY IN BRAZIL: SR. K'S STORY

William B. Gomes, Vânia Maria Domingues, and Maria Adélia Minghelli Pieta

INTRODUCTION

Brazilian physicians and educators have been following with interest the development of psychological treatments in Europe and the United States since the early decades of the 20th century. Psychoanalysis caught the attention of psychiatrists in Rio de Janeiro and São Paulo in the 1920s, with some professionals maintaining correspondence with Freud. Adler's ideas and U.S. counseling theories circulated among educators, who had already offered this service in schools since the 1940s. However, psychoanalysis and its variations have gained primacy, first in psychiatry and then in psychology. There were animated study groups and clinical services in virtually every therapeutic approach that moved the Brazilian psychological scene in the 1970s and 1980s. Approaches such as person-centered therapy, gestalt therapy, transactional analysis, psychodrama, and behavior modification received attention and attracted loyal followers and still have some moderate influence (see, for discussion, Hutz & Gomes, 2013).

In recent decades, Brazil has witnessed a strong growth of cognitive behavior psychotherapies and community psychological services, with psychoanalytic tradition declining among psychiatrists but maintaining predominance among psychologists. In Brazil, there is no clear distinction between *counseling* and *psychotherapy*, the latter being the most commonly used term. Alternative treatments based on African or Eastern practices and combination of flavors, colors, and medicinal plants are offered by psychologists, but they are not recognized by the Federal Council of Psychology.

In this chapter, we discuss an 83-year-old White man ("Sr. K") in therapy with a 63-year-old White female psychologist ("Dr. B") who has 35 years of experience conducting individual and group psychotherapy. The therapist used a psychodynamic approach, which may be considered typical in southern Brazil, but was open to influences from interpersonal and cognitive approaches. She delivered 12 weekly sessions of a flexible brief psychotherapy that were based on some Freudian concepts such as unconscious, free association, dream interpretation, humor, and parapraxis to understand the patient's unconscious conflicts. Despite the use of transference and countertransference patterns in understanding the patient, the treatment differed from classical psychoanalysis by not using the couch, by having a lower frequency of sessions (only one to two sessions instead of three to five sessions per week), and by the use of extratransferential interpretations in place of transferential. The counselor, or psychotherapist, also used empathic understanding and cognitive confrontations to challenge believes and habits.

THE CLIENT

The client was a single, heterosexual, Catholic 83-year-old White man who was a retired accountant of lower-middle-class socioeconomic status. He sought treatment because he was afraid of death and dying. Sr. K came from a very poor family. He lost his father when he was 6 years old. He had two sisters; one had died of cancer, and her orphaned daughter chose to live with him. The other sister, following her divorce, also moved into his house. Therefore, even though he was not married, he had a nuclear family composed of his divorced sister and a niece. Sr. K had always been studious, even when he was an accountant, and he is currently a graduate student in philosophy.

PRESENTING ISSUES AND CHALLENGES

The client sought therapy for anxiety caused by serious health problems. He had undergone several surgeries and was waiting to undergo more, but the diagnosis was not good. Therefore, he felt insecure and anxious in the face of an uncertain future, of death and the process of dying, or of survival with many limitations (thus being dependent on the care of others). Sr. K was very concerned about the schedule for surgery; he was also trying to better understand his physical conditions, the details about the medical intervention, and what would be his real chances of surviving. When talking about death, he remembered his sister who had died of cancer after 2 years of suffering and his stepfather who also died of cancer a year after receiving his diagnosis.

CASE HISTORY AND DEVELOPMENTAL BACKGROUND

Stricken with tuberculosis at the age of 15 years, Sr. K was subjected to an experimental method of drying out one lung to save his life. For this process, he was admitted to a tuberculosis hospital for 2 years. Removed from society and family, he devoted himself to reading. He described the hospital as if it was out of a scene from Dante's Inferno. Paradoxically, he was proud to have worked at a hospital in an administrative position for 32 years out of his 56 years of professional life.

Sr. K believed that his life had developed along two axes: (a) the consequences of tuberculosis, which damaged his chances of interpersonal relationships with family, work, and women; and (b) the effort to overcome the disease, which took him on a solitary life, although he was productive in professional aspects.

Three years ago he was diagnosed with a bilateral abdominal hernia by the medical staff of a hospital to which he makes regular visits. Eighteen months before seeking psychological help, he underwent surgery to treat one of his abdominal hernias. The surgery was successful, and he was discharged after 24 hours. It was recommended that he stay home for 90 days. Another surgery to fix the other hernia would be scheduled soon. Given the fear he had concerning the risks of the second surgery, he was admitted to the hospital twice for cardiac arrhythmias. That was when he heard about a lecture by the Medical Association on "good death." He attended the lecture and learned about medical and psychological aspects involved in dealing with dying clients or irreversible disabling diseases, including issues relating to euthanasia and orthothanasia. At that time, his biggest concern was a possible postsurgical vegetative life, which would be a burden to his family.

A tuberculosis infection and its treatment strongly influenced the earlier development of Sr. K's personality. He felt rejected and discriminated against and was discouraged by friends from seeking prestigious jobs, because he would be unable to pass the required medical examinations. He recalled that after leaving the hospital, he was not welcomed home by relatives because they feared contagion. He was only received in his fourth try with relatives. He was prevented from dating a young girl because of his illness, which brought him much grief and a pronounced sense of humiliation.

THE THERAPY

In the first session, Sr. K introduced himself politely but with few glances to the therapist. His concern was to know how he should proceed. After understanding that he could speak freely, he began recounting his history. During his conversation he kept his head down, was attentive, and concentrated. With a certain amount of sadness, Dr. B listened to Sr. K's life history. Sr. K had sought psychotherapy for concerns about death and dying or the possibility of being near death. He was anxious about this impending death or the possibility of surviving in a vegetative state. So he wanted to talk about orthothanasia, and he stubbornly pursued that idea. He also seemed to enjoy the opportunity to share his concerns with an expert in the field of psychotherapy.

On the basis of the cathartic function of verbalizing anxiety, Dr. B began to listen attentively to the client's free associations and to the veracity of his related condition. In the early sessions, the evaluation of internal and external reality was an important issue for driving the process. It was necessary to know whether the client had chances of surviving a second surgery and what kind of therapeutic approach to adopt. According to Sr. K, his chances of survival were 50%.

Sr. K could be described as a person who relied on rationality, avoided unnecessary risks, and made good use of time. Therefore, he tried to exert some control over the therapist. His personality presented strong obsessional traits, surrounding himself with defense mechanisms for streamlining and insulating in order to keep his fears under control and avoid unbearable sufferings. He said he often felt like closing the apartment and throwing the keys away or forgetting the many losses in his life. This description was a way for him to communicate his hopelessness, irritation, and dissatisfaction with the world and with people. As an example, he mentioned his niece's stubbornness and the authoritarianism of some professors in the philosophy program. He could not stand professors who presented themselves as keepers of the law and order in the classroom.

Gradually, the intense emotional life of Sr. K began to unfold, revealing happy moments and great suffering, especially in adolescence. Throughout his life, he regarded rationality as his main strategy to deal with feelings of fear, rejection, and disappointment. In the sequence of sessions, he became more open about his life, bringing up very personal and confidential matters, which suggested an increased trust toward the therapist. At times the therapist resorted to confrontation, questions, immediacy, and some interpretations applicable in the context of a brief psychotherapy.

Trying to understand what was going on, Dr. B asked herself, "What could Sr. K have done but hadn't? How is his day-to-day routine? What's he really like?" The therapist then began to explore aspects of Sr. K's affective and emotional life, something that seemed buried but was still latent. The real challenge would be for Sr. K to have the same success with his second surgery as his first. The task was to explore what Sr. K could do with the remaining time of his life.

The last five sessions were devoted to exploring secret aspects of Sr. K's life history as they related to an aborted engagement with his girlfriend. He had said that prejudices related to his disease and low social status were a heavy disadvantage for him. Hence, the task now for the therapist was to know if some recovery was possible, if it would be desired, and if it was worth investing in. Meanwhile, Sr. K seemed to continue with his plans to enroll in a philosophy program.

In the ninth session, Dr. B asked Sr. K about the notes he used to bring to the sessions. The idea was to know the role they played in the therapeutic process. A possible interpretation would be that Sr. K would need some order and certitude in his matters. He was a methodical person, appearing to be very keen and efficient with his time. Affection was always present in his speech because he did not recite what he read; there was emotion in his voice, although controlled. His notes consisted of comments, explanations, and memories. He even said that he was recovering memories from 40 years ago. A strong indication of his motivation and involvement with the treatment was the fact that even during the winter, despite his age and respiratory limitations, he did not miss the sessions; in addition, he always showed up on time.

At the 11th session Sr. K came up with a list of benefits he had received from psychotherapy, titled "What I will take from here." He said that he had absorbed 40% of what was spoken, that he ruminated about 30%, but that he rejected 30%. He was surprised to see Dr. B listening in silence, but after a brief moment she asked him what he wanted out of life:

> *Dr. B*: It seems to me that you have within yourself a rebellious side that was contained. Have you thought about bringing out this rebel?
> *Sr. K*: But how can you do that without facing the consequences of a hypocritical society, [that is] false and oppressive?

The therapist felt that such issues would be too complex for brief psychotherapy. In his last sessions he brought a written list of personal improvements comparing the time before and after therapy. He mentioned that he had a file containing his benefactors and that Dr. B was among them.

DISCUSSION AND ANALYSIS

Sr. K sought treatment because of death fears and anxiety. Death fears seem to increase with an awareness that one is approaching the end of life, whether by growing old or by experiencing a serious illness. Especially among mid-old-age individuals

(75–84 years of age), fear of the dying process and fear of the unknown can be very strong (Cicirelli, 2006). As their health declines, there is a desire to live longer than expected, and there is increased fear. The experience of being close to death can make mid-old-age individuals feel that they will not be able to fulfill life goals.

Sr. K's death fears can be interpreted as related to his old age as well as to the series of surgeries he had undergone and the surgery he was due to undergo with serious health risks. The anxiety Sr. K presented is also a common disorder in older adults (Blay & Marinho, 2012) that is typically underdiagnosed and in need of a specific treatment (Lenze & Wetherell, 2011).

In the absence of evidence on how to best treat Sr. K's anxiety, Dr. B tried to shift his expectations on how to prepare for a good death by getting him to acknowledge his own free will. From a psychodynamic point of view, Sr. K's obsessive trait might have prevented him from getting in touch with his desire and from living according to it. Instead, Sr. K seemed to have conformed to what he thought others expected from him. His behavior is understandable if we take into account Sr. K's stigma of tuberculosis, reinforced by his family and acquaintances who ended up dictating the rules of his living (e.g., he could not date). Also, it is not difficult to understand the barriers faced by Sr. K in living his own life when he accepted the role imposed by his family of being a male provider. To that point, Dr. B believed that Sr. K had been living his whole life within the realm of "shoulds," and now it was time for him, even though so close to the end, to consider living his life the way he really wanted to. Living a fulfilling life could have a positive impact on Sr. K's anxiety and death fears, especially if taking into account that death fears may be intense when one feels he or she will not be able to fulfill life goals. Above all, preparing Sr. K for a good life means also ultimately preparing him for a good death.

Sr. K's adherence to treatment, observed by his attendance to sessions, as well as his openness to talk about his problems and his active participation in treatment could be attributed to the quality of the therapeutic relationship established with Dr. B. Treatment effectiveness has been strongly associated with the quality of interpersonal relationship between the therapist and the client, regardless of the theoretical approach being used (Horvath, Del Re, Flückiger, & Symonds, 2011; Horvath & Greenberg, 1989). The therapeutic relationship is characterized by the way that the therapist and the client express the mutuality of feelings and attitudes between them. Other terms also used with the same meaning are therapeutic alliance and working alliance.

The case of Sr. K could be considered as a typical illustration of psychotherapy practice in Brazil, with accentuated influence of psychoanalytic and psychotherapeutic theories. Details of the therapy highlight the exchange between the narrative flows linking two kinds of dialogues: therapist with client and therapist with himself. The distinction between these two dialogic modalities is instructive for understanding the intervention procedures and the effectiveness evaluation. The interpersonal dialogues brought objective aspects from the sessions as did discussions about medical examinations, use of notes by the client, existential impasses, therapist's questions and confrontations, and descriptions of feelings and behaviors expressed by the client, for example, "What could Sr. K have done but hadn't? How is his day-to-day routine? What's he really like?" The intrapersonal dialogues brought the dilemmas of the therapist's feelings about the progress of the sessions and therapeutic approaches to be explored into focus.

CONCLUSION

In this chapter Sr. K, who is facing risky medical procedures, fears, anxiety, and death, was helped by the therapist to search for a good life in order to have a good death. By listening empathetically to Sr. K's feelings of rejection caused by tuberculosis's stigma since adolescence and by his lower-class family's conservative values, Dr. B interpreted and questioned the positions Sr. K had taken in life. Despite Sr. K being intellective, reflexive, attentive, and critical, he had prevented himself from carrying forward his interpersonal development. Being a single male who is methodical and rational is an unusual pattern in Brazilian culture, even though Brazil is a vast and multicultural country, with huge variations within and between states.

Sr. K had the misfortune to become an adult in a period when psychotherapy was almost unknown in Brazil. Had Sr. K lived in a later time he might have had access to psychological treatment during his development, addressing important issues in an encouraging dialogue with a professional. Psychotherapy, in its innumerable well-known approaches, is a growing and accessible practice in Brazil, reaching different regions and social status and drawing many young people to psychology courses. The offer of psychological treatment by different means throughout the country is fully promoted by public policies, bringing quality of life to those individuals who strive for longevity. Even though Sr. K did not benefit from psychological treatment when it would have been best, there was still much to be done for him. Sr. K is a happy case of an old man finding hope even at the end of his life.

QUESTIONS

1. Would it be a common concern to prepare for death in older adults? How do we respond to such a demand in therapy?
2. Would a preoccupation with death be an inevitable element of human life to be discussed in the sessions, let alone for older adults?
3. One of the goals of a psychodynamic treatment with obsessive clients is to allow contact with one's desire. Thus, learning to desire can be the same as preparing for life. Is preparing for life ultimately preparing for death? Would those who have a good life have a good death?
4. Could we consider the concern to prepare for the death of Sr. K a manifestation of an obsessive trait?
5. The obsessive is very self-critical. Would too much self-criticism and stigma adversely affect self-esteem, so that an attention on this issue should be addressed?

REFERENCES

Blay, S. L., & Marinho, V. (2012). Anxiety disorders in old age. *Current Opinion in Psychiatry, 25,* 462–467. doi:10.1097/YCO.0b013e3283578cdd

Cicirelli, V. G. (2006). Fear of death in mid-old age. *Journal of Gerontology: Series B. Psychological Sciences and Social Sciences, 61B,* P75–P81.

Horvath, A. O., Del Re, A. C., Flückiger, C., & Symonds, D. (2011). Alliance in individual psychotherapy. *Psychotherapy: Theory, Research, Practice, Training, 48,* 9–16.

Horvath, A. O., & Greenberg, L. (1989). Development and validation of the Working Alliance Inventory. *Journal of Counseling Psychology, 41,* 438–448.

Hutz, C. S., & Gomes, W. B. (2013). Counseling and psychotherapy in Brazil: From private practice to community services. In R. Moodley, U. P. Gielen, & R. Wu (Eds.), *Handbook of counseling and psychotherapy in an international context* (pp. 95–105). New York, NY: Routledge.

Lenze, E. J., & Wetherell, J. L. (2011). Anxiety disorders: New developments in old age. *American Journal of Geriatric Psychiatry, 19,* 301–304. doi:10.1097/JGP.0b013e31820db34f

Chapter 18

COUNSELING AND PSYCHOTHERAPY IN CANADA: KAMALPREET'S STORY

Robinder P. Bedi and José F. Domene

INTRODUCTION

Canada is a country of substantial cultural diversity, with one of the largest per-capita immigration rates in the world and ample government policies that support the retention of traditional ethnic practices (Domene & Bedi, 2012). Despite shared expertise, counselors and psychotherapists tend to be a highly diverse group in terms of educational level, licensure/certification, and discipline. According to Domene and Bedi (2012), many Canadian practitioners are integrative or eclectic in their therapeutic orientation and draw on both long-established (e.g., cognitive behavior, humanistic/existential) and newer (e.g., feminist, narrative) theories.

Solution-focused counseling (SFC) is one of many approaches widely practiced in Canada. In SFC, the presenting problem is often reframed as the ineffectual strategies currently used to deal with the problem and the disempowering way in which the client discusses the problem. Bedi (2009) summarized the core principles of SFC as follows: (a) focusing on the client's mental health rather than psychological disorders; (b) incorporating the client's customs, values, and other idiosyncrasies into counseling; (c) focusing on the concrete present and future instead of assuming that there is a historical, underlying cause for psychological symptoms; (d) expecting that small changes will snowball into bigger changes; and (e) cooperating fully with clients on their expressed goals within legal and ethical constraints. Bedi also reiterated the importance of avoiding labeling something as a problem if the client does not and of persisting in trying different things, because this persistence will eventually lead to the discovery of a functional resolution.

In this chapter, we present a case where SFC was used with a Canadian-born woman of Punjabi Asian Indian descent, who presented with academic difficulties. We describe the client, Kamalpreet, focusing on her background, salient aspects of her developmental history, and the issues that led her to seek counseling with an English-speaking Canadian male counselor of European descent. We then sequence and discuss her counseling process and outcomes. The chapter is concluded by highlighting key aspects of the case and the therapeutic process.

THE CLIENT

Kamalpreet is a 22-year-old woman. She is a heterosexual, unmarried South Asian Punjabi woman who has no visible disabilities. Kamalpreet is Canadian-born, and her first language is English. She usually dresses in North American clothing, and most of her friends are not South Asian. In terms of her ethnic identity, Kamalpreet refers to herself as "Sikh" or "Indo-Canadian." However, Kamalpreet is not very familiar with the Sikh Holy Scriptures and rarely attends *Gurdwara* [the Sikh temple]. She has never had a boyfriend because of perceived cultural and parental sanctions. Kamalpreet currently attends university full time, where she is completing a bachelor's degree in criminology.

PRESENTING ISSUES AND CHALLENGES

As she entered her senior year, Kamalpreet became anxious about schoolwork and experienced difficulty with concentration and attention. She started ruminating about her future in a haphazard, intrusive, and distracting way. As her grades began to fall, Kamalpreet felt depressed and experienced tension headaches, sleep disturbances, and restlessness. Her family and friends started complaining that she was very irritable, which led her to reduce contact with them.

CASE HISTORY AND DEVELOPMENTAL BACKGROUND

Kamalpreet is the eldest daughter of Punjabi Sikh parents who emigrated from India 23 years ago. Her parents were raised in neighboring agricultural communities, and their marriage was arranged by village elders. Her father now manages a farming supply store, where her mother also works. Kamalpreet has an 18-year-old brother who does not work or attend college. Her paternal grandparents and her father's widowed sister also reside with them.

Kamalpreet lives in the city of Surrey. According to Statistics Canada (2003), Surrey has the highest percentage of South Asians in Canada. This presence of South Asians has afforded the opportunity for Kamalpreet's family to readily practice their religion, socialize with other Punjabi Sikhs, and retain many of their traditional ethnic customs. Consequently, her parents live similarly to how they lived in India. For example, they maintain a strong patriarchal family structure with a traditional gender-based division of home labor, regularly attend and volunteer at Gurdwara, socialize primarily with other Sikh families, and celebrate all major holidays and festivals of their country of origin and religion.

THE THERAPY

Kamalpreet went to the university counseling center, citing academic difficulty as her presenting concern. She was assigned to Rick, a 43-year-old English-speaking Canadian man of European descent who practices primarily from an SFC orientation.

During the intake session, Rick learned that Kamalpreet had adopted many English Canadian values, and that certain elements of Sikh Punjabi culture played an integral role in her sense of self. Kamalpreet also reported that, although she was not highly religious in her day-to-day activities, she had a very strong belief in God. Rick asked Kamalpreet whether she wanted to involve traditional healers or advisors (e.g., her Sikh priest) in counseling, and she declined. Kamalpreet expressed concern about the embarrassment that would be brought upon her family if her problems became public knowledge within her community. She also stated that she was more comfortable with Western counseling methods because they are "more scientific." Kamalpreet further declined an invitation to have her parents attend a session, citing the dismay her father would experience knowing she shared family information with an outsider.

It soon became evident to Rick that Kamalpreet's symptoms began when her parents started to plan for her marriage; they had identified several eligible men and were eager to arrange meetings to see whether she felt a match. Despite aspiring to become a lawyer when she started university, she agreed to limit herself to a bachelor's degree so that she could, in the words of her father, "devote herself to marriage." However, Kamalpreet started to reconsider this decision after enjoying her criminology courses so much and began questioning if she could truly be happy if she were not a lawyer. She felt guilty about the possibility of reneging on her arrangement with her family and letting them down.

During the first session, Kamalpreet disclosed that maintaining family cohesion was very important and that she felt selfish for even considering focusing on her own needs rather than what seemed best for her family. Rick noted the disempowering ways in which Kamalpreet described herself and the situation and addressed this by highlighting concealed resources, suggesting hidden areas in which she did have agency and choice, and genuinely complimenting her strengths. For example, he noted her thoughtfulness and commented that she clearly valued her family because she was trying to find a solution that would be beneficial for all, rather than only for herself. Rick also asked Kamalpreet about her sources of strength that allowed her to endure the stress of having to carry the expectations of so many people for so long before becoming overwhelmed.

In the second session, Rick asked Kamalpreet what would need to happen for her to see that session as valuable. She responded, "Knowing what to tell my parents. They won't agree to law school and will be embarrassed about how old I'll be before I marry—I'm worried how others will judge them." Kamalpreet then elaborated, "Actually, I just need to know how to convince my parents to take my side for a change." After agreeing to this goal and through use of exception questions, they identified times when Kamalpreet's parents were more accommodating to her wishes, for example, when she was taking Punjabi language classes at the Sikh temple and when she attended a Sikh youth summer camp. Kamalpreet realized that, as she engaged in these behaviors less frequently, her parents became less willing to accommodate her wishes. Rick asked if repeating these types of behaviors would make life easier for her and her family, and she agreed it would. The second session ended with Kamalpreet committing to a small, concrete goal: to volunteer at the temple on the coming Sunday.

The next session, Kamalpreet reported that her parents and relatives were happy that she volunteered at the Gurdwara. Rick also discovered that Kamalpreet's aunt was married and in medical school. He wondered if consulting with the aunt would be beneficial. Kamalpreet agreed and decided to continue volunteering at Gurdwara so she could continue to casually confer with her aunt. As a second goal, Kamalpreet agreed to brainstorm how to minimize her family's embarrassment and loss of social standing if she did not marry soon.

Over the next two sessions, Kamalpreet and Rick continued to brainstorm and evaluate options, using information provided by her aunt and other elder women from the Gurdwara. Eventually, Kamalpreet concluded that it was only realistic to expect a compromise, in which her parents would tolerate—rather than outright support—her decision to pursue law school in exchange for other desirable behaviors. Between the fifth and sixth session, Kamalpreet approached her parents and, after several tense conversations, they realized how serious she was about law school. Kamalpreet learned that her parents' greatest fear was that she would reject her culture and ultimately shame the family by not marrying. After reassuring them that this was not the case, she discussed with them how to minimize the impact of her career decision on her family, including helping them "save face" in the larger community.

In the sixth counseling session, Kamalpreet informed Rick that she agreed to volunteer at the Gurdwara every Sunday and to let her parents make introductions to find a suitable marriage match. However, her parents understood that she would only accept a spouse who supported her career plans. In addition, she had the idea of volunteering with a prominent and well-respected local Punjabi lawyer, which would likely result in making a positive impression in the local Punjabi community, something very highly valued by her family and prized within Punjabi culture. When asked about her symptoms, Kamalpreet sheepishly admitted that she was so caught up in the events of the past week that she had not noticed them. When asked about how well, on a scale of 1 to 10, things were, Kamalpreet responded that the situation with her parents was a 7, but that she was satisfied with this, and she rated her overall well-being as 10. She further offered that, at the outset of counseling, her ratings were 4 and 5, respectively. Kamalpreet chose to end counseling at that point, saying, "Seven out of 10 is good enough for now."

DISCUSSION AND ANALYSIS

The SFC approach has been mentioned as an approach consistent with the predominant worldviews of many Asian cultures, including South Asian Indian clients (Shariff, 2009). Throughout the counseling, Rick attempted to remain true to the SFC principles and underlying guidelines. For example, he kept the focus on the present and future and emphasized areas of agency and the small successes that Kamalpreet achieved along the way.

Berry's (2002) model of acculturation can be used to understand some of Kamalpreet's circumstances. It appears that her parents have adopted more of a separation approach to residing in Canada, where they have primarily maintained the values and practices of Northern India and interact mainly with other Punjabi Sikhs, despite having immigrated to Canada more than two decades ago. In contrast, Kamalpreet appears to have adopted more of an integration approach to acculturation, seeking to find a balance between the traditional culture of her family and the dominant English Canadian culture in which she was raised. Furthermore, although her worldview as a well-acculturated, Canadian-born woman includes the belief that it is a legitimate choice for women to value a career, Kamalpreet was aware that her family did not share this perspective. Indeed, a major focus of the counseling was finding a compromise to the conflicting directions in which her two ethnic cultures were leading her.

Rick's exploration of Kamalpreet's cultural identity is consistent with the SFC framework, which emphasizes accepting and working within the client's individual customs and values. Moreover, his decision to accept Kamalpreet's assertion about Western counseling as more "scientific" at face value (instead of exploring whether this statement reflects an underlying self-stigmatization or overidentification with the majority culture) is consistent with SFC's emphasis on avoiding labeling something as a problem if the client does not. Furthermore, Rick's willingness to accept and cooperate with Kamalpreet's expressed counseling goals (rather than judge and challenge them) demonstrated a clear respect for her personal worldview and the unique manner in which she has constructed her cultural identity with both Canadian and Punjabi Sikh elements.

Following the lead of Kamalpreet's concern with how her family would be perceived by others, Rick recognized and honored the powerful cultural norm of saving face, which is very common for those of South Asian descent but much less common in more individualistic cultures (Berg & Miller, 1992; Nayar & Sandhu, 2006). In line with this, the issue of saving face remained central to Kamalpreet's solution seeking, and her distress substantially reduced once she figured out how to pursue her career goals in a way that allowed her family to maintain their standing within their community.

As is common in India, Indo-Canadians often discuss concerns in multigenerational but gender-similar groups using a more impersonal and existential context, rather than direct inquiry (Sandhu, 2004). This cultural practice was evident in Kamalpreet's decision to casually consult with her aunt and other female elders at the Gurdwara. This casual consultation was suggested by the counselor and serves as a successful example of both incorporating a client's cultural customs into suggested counseling interventions and highlighting concealed resources. Kamalpreet's ongoing attendance at Gurdwara also illustrated her complex relationship with Sikhism. Although she did not describe herself as devout, she recognized the importance of the religion to her cultural identity, her family, and her community. This recognition allowed her to realize the connection between attending Gurdwara and alleviating her parents' fears that she was turning her back on her culture. As with many Canadian young adults from cultural minorities, religion was fully intertwined with issues of identity, culture, and community for Kamalpreet.

Finally, interventions and a relational stance that carefully considered gender-role expectations proved to be very effective in this case, where a male European Canadian counselor was providing counseling to an Indo-Canadian woman. In the beginning, Kamalpreet was expecting to be more comfortable with a female counselor, though she did not realize she could request one. If she were to be questioned about the issue, Kamalpreet would have cited the fact that she expected a male counselor to be overly directive and somewhat insensitive to her experiences as a woman, consistent with her experience of living in a traditional, strongly patriarchal family structure. Nonetheless, Rick's collaborative SFC approach of letting the client define the goals and direction of counseling, as well as his choice to defer to Kamalpreet's own solutions, helped to alleviate Kamalpreet's discomfort with the gender dynamic and facilitated a strong working alliance.

Conclusion

Canada is a country with many immigrants and in which immigration remains a major catalyst for continued population growth; thus, the case of Kamalpreet provides a snapshot into the diverse Canadian social landscape. Nevertheless, it must be recognized that there is no prototypical manner of conducting counseling and psychotherapy in Canada. A plethora of theoretical orientations are commonplace. Counseling services are provided not only in universities but in a wide range of publically and privately funded settings; although clients are sometimes seen for six sessions, this is often not the case. One commonality that permeates across the country, and is promoted in the ethics codes of all professions that provide counseling and psychotherapy in Canada, is the explicitly expressed expectation that practitioners will tailor their services to reflect their clients' gender, ethnicity, sexual orientation, social class, disability status, age, religion, and other diversity variables. We believe that this respect for a client's sociocultural identity has been evident throughout the counseling work that Rick and Kamalpreet did together.

Questions

1. To what degree are Kamalpreet's presenting issues a result of her culture, gender, and social class?
2. What are the possible limitations of applying SFC interventions to cases such as Kamalpreet's?
3. Drawing on your own theoretical perspective, what would you consider to be the most urgent priorities for working with Kamalpreet, and why?
4. How might the experience be different for Kamalpreet's brother, if he chooses to delay marriage, attend and prolong his university studies, and pick a culturally nontraditional career?
5. What potential resiliency assets and coping challenges can you identify related to the traditional Punjabi Sikh culture?

References

Bedi, R. P. (2009). Solution-focused therapy. In G. F. Fisher & N. A. Roget (Eds.), *Encyclopedia of substance abuse prevention, treatment, and recovery* (pp. 843–845). Thousand Oaks, CA: Sage.

Berg, I. K., & Miller, S. D. (1992). Working with Asian American clients: One person at a time. *Families in Society: The Journal of Contemporary Human Services, 73,* 356–363.

Berry, J. W. (2002). Conceptual approaches to acculturation. In K. M. Chun, P. B. Organista, & G. Marin (Eds.), *Acculturation: Advances in theory, measurement, and applied research* (pp. 17–37). Washington, DC: American Psychological Association.

Domene, J. D., & Bedi, R. P. (2012). Counseling and psychotherapy in Canada: Diversity and growth. In R. Moodley, U. P. Gielen, & R. Wu (Eds.), *Handbook of counseling and psychotherapy in an international context* (pp. 106–115). New York, NY: Routledge.

Nayar, K. E., & Sandhu, J. S. (2006). Intergenerational communication in immigrant Punjabi families: Implications for helping professionals. *International Journal for the Advancement of Counselling, 28,* 139–152.

Sandhu, J. S. (2004). The Sikh model of the person, suffering, and healing: Implications for counselors. *International Journal for the Advancement of Counselling, 26,* 33–46.

Shariff, A. (2009). Ethnic identity and parenting stress in South Asian families: Implications for culturally sensitive counselling. *Canadian Journal of Counselling, 43,* 35–45.

Statistics Canada. (2003). *Religion and visible minority groups for population, for Canada, provinces, territories, census metropolitan areas, and census agglomerations, 2001 census.* Retrieved from http://www5.statcan.gc.ca/bsolc/olc-cel/olc-cel?lang=eng&catno=91-541-X

Chapter 19

COUNSELING AND PSYCHOTHERAPY IN THE CARIBBEAN (TRINIDAD AND TOBAGO): OLIVIA'S STORY

Gerard Hutchinson

INTRODUCTION

The Republic of Trinidad and Tobago is a rapidly developing country in the English-speaking Caribbean. It has a highly diverse multiethnic population of 1.3 million people. Having experienced British colonialism and sustaining strong ties with the United States, this country maintains an active syncretism between Western cultural influences and traditional Indian and African cultures as well as many other cultures that make up the cultural mosaic of the country, including Chinese, Syrian–Lebanese, Portuguese, Spanish, and French. This diversity sometimes generates tensions, but in general the country's culture has evolved and continues to evolve into an all-encompassing nature. However, issues with relationships, child abuse, and, more recently, violent crimes have challenged this view (Kirton, Anatol, & Brathwaite, 2010) and affected many individuals' ability to control the unpredictable and unseen forces that shape their worldviews.

The most common psychotherapeutic approaches used in the country are cognitive behavior therapy and, for some practitioners, rational emotive behavior therapy and psychodynamic therapy. There is also growing interest in newer therapies, such as neurofeedback and neurolinguistic programming and regression therapy. Group, family, and marital therapy are also widely practiced. Rational emotive behavior therapy is useful because it addresses long-standing problems that may have caused a client to become dysfunctional and irrational in his or her interpretation of social and behavioral stimuli. Systematic psychotherapy is becoming more common in the treatment field as the number of psychologists grows. With this increasing number of trained mental health professionals, these problems can be framed in a more direct psychotherapeutic context. Cognitive behavior therapy is the most commonly used form of psychotherapy in Trinidad and Tobago. In previous years, the focus of mental health treatment was predominantly psychiatric, with psychotherapy and counseling serving as more of an additional form of support for the psychiatric interventions. Counseling in spiritual and religious contexts has also been traditionally sought (Hutchinson & Sutherland, 2013).

In the case study presented in this chapter, the overarching approach was to challenge belief systems about the self that undermine personal and social well-being. In postcolonial societies, individuals often struggle with these issues of agency, control, self-worth, and efficacy, creating self-defeating and psychologically undermining self-concepts (Fanon, 1961; Hickling & Hutchinson, 2000). These issues sometimes express themselves as a lack of confidence and self-esteem but may also be represented as a cavalier overconfidence that turns into destructive narcissism, consequently leading to poor decision making. It is the feeling that decisions are made about you without your input and that they may not reflect your identity, interests, or desires.

In this chapter, I discuss the case of Olivia, who presented with suicidal behavior in the context of depressive and anxiety symptoms. I describe our therapeutic interaction and the use of rational emotive behavior therapy in the negotiation of her psychological distress and in our attempt to help her regain a sense of psychological well-being and eliminate suicidal ideation.

THE CLIENT

Olivia is a 28-year-old single woman of mixed descent (Indian and African). She currently lives in the rural area despite having a university degree and working as a public servant in a government office in the Port of Spain, the capital city 50 kilometers from her home. She has no known disability and places herself and her family in the lower-middle-class category. Her mother is a nurse, and her father is a laborer with whom she has had limited contact. She has a stepfather who is now estranged from her mother. She has no strong religious affiliation but identifies herself as Roman Catholic and goes to church intermittently. She identifies herself as heterosexual and has never had any inclination toward same-sex relationships.

PRESENTING ISSUES AND CHALLENGES

Olivia was hospitalized after overdosing on her mother's pain killers. She complained of marked depressive and anxiety symptoms and recurrent, sometimes intense, suicidal ideation. She was discharged after a week with a diagnosis of major depression, but she did not want to take prescribed medication except for the one that helped her to sleep. She requested psychotherapy as her preferred treatment regimen. Although it was her first attempt at suicide, she admitted that she had had suicidal ideation for several years, and this attempt was only triggered after breaking up with a man who had cheated on her.

Olivia held a series of irrational beliefs about herself, such as deeming herself to be unworthy of any relationship or thinking that people do not like her. She always felt that people were looking at her and judging her negatively, although she had never obtained any substantive evidence to support these beliefs. This perception led to feelings of being alienated and disadvantaged in every environment.

CASE HISTORY AND DEVELOPMENTAL BACKGROUND

Olivia's sense of rejection had its origins in her childhood, when at the age of 6 her mother married her stepfather and had three children of their own. Olivia's stepfather abused her both physically and emotionally in a manner that bordered on sexual, and she felt that her mother did not provide any support during these times. When she was younger, her stepfather always said she was ugly, which she eventually internalized. By the time she presented for treatment, she was at the point where she could not accept compliments about her looks as she believed she was irredeemably ugly and so felt that anyone who complimented her looks was trying to fool her. In addition, she had an all-or-nothing belief that she was completely unlovable because there was something irrevocably wrong with her. In her household, she was constantly being told she was oversensitive and was blamed for all problems that occurred. As a result, she felt she could not complain or protest when experiencing negative treatment from her work colleagues or in social situations. She learned to undervalue her feelings and seek external validation for her experiences. She found it extremely difficult to maintain friendships as she put too much pressure on her friends to be faithful and responsive to her.

She described a depressive incident when she was studying for her bachelor's degree in the United States, but she never sought treatment and eventually recovered on her own. While fighting against these depressive symptoms, she managed to successfully obtain a degree in business management in the United States. She constantly feared she was not intelligent enough to complete her degree. When she returned to Trinidad she easily found a job, and she continues to work in the same position today. She continues to live with her mother despite their poor relationship. Olivia constantly struggled between wanting to achieve her independence and feeling unable to function effectively on her own.

Her antenatal and childhood history were normal, and she achieved all of her developmental milestones appropriately. She performed consistently well in school and, after passing her 11 plus examinations, went to live with an aunt who resided closer to her secondary school. She was relatively happy there, feeling she had escaped from her stepfather, but when her aunt migrated to the United States, Olivia felt abandoned once again and had no choice but to return home to the same abusive environment. By this time, her mother and stepfather's relationship was deteriorating, and she felt guilty for their eventual breakup. Each of these events continued to build upon the overwhelming sense that there was something innately wrong with her and that nothing would ever work out.

She developed a relationship with a young man who lived in her area, but her low sense of self-worth and fear of rejection created an atmosphere of tension and distrust. It did not help that he reinforced many of her fears when they argued, calling her names and comparing her unfavorably with his previous girlfriends. This turbulent relationship inevitably ended, prompting her to overdose on the pain killers.

THE THERAPY

We embarked on a year-long therapeutic relationship with weekly sessions and e-mail communication. We identified and agreed that the problems stemmed from low to absent self-worth, feelings of loneliness, and a sense of complete helplessness to change her circumstances. When asked to find one word that explained or described her condition, she replied with "helpless." During therapy, we talked about the relational and transference issues regarding my gender and ethnicity. Her stepfather was Afro-Trinidadian as I am, and she acknowledged that she saw her stepfather in most men. We agreed that her many negative beliefs about herself were

151

compromising her ability to lead a healthy, productive life. She needed successful academic, occupational, and social functioning in order to feel fulfilled. In addition to the weekly sessions in the first 3 months, we communicated frequently via e-mail to promptly address any questions or uncomfortable feelings she had. The sessions decreased from weekly meetings to once every 2 weeks over the next 3 months and then to once every month over the last 6 months. However, we kept up with our daily e-mail correspondence. She required constant reassurance that someone was there for her because of her lack of confidence in society and in males.

According to our e-mail agreement, she could e-mail me whenever she felt like but had to allow a 24-hour period for a response. During the initial phase of our therapeutic relationship, she sent as many as six e-mails per day. I think it helped to develop a faster therapeutic alliance and gave her the opportunity to clarify her homework assignments and the issues we discussed in therapy.

The first step in building a therapeutic alliance incorporated relaxation training in order to reduce the general level of anxiety whenever she felt things would turn out negatively. There was some initial resistance to this, but through frequent e-mail correspondence, she gave me the benefit of the doubt and trusted me to support her unconditionally. Once the therapeutic alliance was formed, the capacity to challenge the dysfunctional beliefs became more achievable.

We worked through the challenges of living in Trinidad as a single woman, fearing the possibility of becoming a victim of crime, and her feelings that she is always noticed and negatively judged. We used real-life examples to demonstrate this was not the case and to encourage her to think logically and rely on reasonable evidence before assuming other people's motives toward her.

She wanted to resume the relationship with her ex-boyfriend even if he continued to emotionally abuse her. She felt he was all she had and could ever hope to get, even if it meant being his second choice while he established other relationships with different women. The emotional turmoil derived from comparing herself to his other female friends and lovers eventually became too overwhelming, and she was able to break away from this relationship. She admitted that this action had a positive impact on her sense of self-worth.

After evaluating options to establish more independence, we agreed that she should buy a car; this worked well. She went out more socially and developed more confidence as an independent woman. However, she would still often feel overwhelmed, anxious, nervous, confused, and depressed at work. Although she performed well at work, her self-consciousness hindered her from forming successful relationships. She felt people could sense her nervousness during the times when she had to confront tough situations, and her mind would then cave in. She would hide in a private space and cry, but she could not switch off the feelings of inadequacy long after the situation had been resolved. We devised role-play and mirror activities to overcome these thoughts. She wanted to act independently and assertively and to overcome her sense of helplessness and hopelessness. We also practiced speaking up and assertively broaching issues whenever she received bad service in public places, and she learned to overcome her fear of being laughed at or feeling embarrassed.

Through these means we were able to work through her helplessness and hopelessness. We sought to establish control over her environment, and she was also able to confront the conflicting relationship she had with her mother. She found that her mother had also endured a traumatic childhood, and by participating in nonthreatening activities together such as walking, cooking, and going out for meals, they were able to forge a more mutually supportive relationship. She also made peace with her siblings, whom she felt had displaced her from her mother's affections. She saw that they also had emotional difficulties from her stepfather's abuse, so she was not alone in that regard.

DISCUSSION AND ANALYSIS

This case reveals several common consequences of dysfunctional developmental experiences. Olivia's feelings of helplessness and hopelessness reflect a wider sense of being rejected by the people around her: her father, who left the family; her mother when she remarried; her stepfather, who never accepted her; and her aunt when she left the country. In a semirural setting in Trinidad, beliefs about women's place and their role in homemaking counter the developmental trajectory of women seeking career development and further education. The experience of studying abroad and working full-time on her return has given Olivia some power to oppose the oppressive memories of her upbringing. Religion has been useful as a mediator demonstrating to the family that in spite of her desire for more and better, she retains the commitment to religious observation (the family is staunchly Roman Catholic) and maintains family bonds in spite of the various hurts and disappointments.

Olivia took assertiveness training and learned to always challenge her lack of control. She was encouraged to forgive her stepfather and move past her anger and suspicion of all men. We tackled her fear of failure and her attempts to minimize the risk of going out in order to prevent her theories from coming true. Assertiveness training bolstered her self-confidence and encouraged her to confront her fears in social situations, helping her reach a level of unconditional self-acceptance that would allow her to accept her flaws without being defined by them. She would have the strength to challenge these issues and overcome them. I used her experience of attending a university in the United States as an example of her resilience in overcoming her challenges; she had successfully completed her bachelor's degree.

As a young woman, she had concerns about her lack of a long-term relationship and the lack of possibilities for becoming pregnant; however, we emphasized that parenting as a single working woman is challenging and that she should be cautious in finding a partner who could facilitate the fulfillment of these maternal needs.

Suicidal behavior is one of the major health issues in Trinidad and Tobago. Relationship problems—between parents and children or romantic partners—are usually identified as the reasons associated with this behavior (Hutchinson, Bruce, & Simmons, 2008). In past years during colonial times, this region struggled with color and class divisions (Brereton, 1979) as well as power distribution, issues that induced in the people a sense of inadequacy because they come from a small island and have a tendency to doubt their own capacity to achieve life efficacy on their own terms. As a result, problems such as sexual child abuse and intimate partner violence (Arias, 2004), both of which many young people in Trinidad are exposed to, create a platform of vulnerability and hinder individuals' ability to properly engage in the greater community.

The models of influence have evolved over the years, but they constantly reflect a sense of powerlessness and helplessness. These issues appear frequently in this case study and came to my attention after the client attempted suicide. Certain beliefs can negatively interfere with one's efforts to achieve life satisfaction and a sense of well-being, especially beliefs that reinforce the sense of helplessness in effecting change in oneself or the environment and beliefs that there is something innately wrong with one's being.

Although Olivia has not completely resolved these negative feelings, she manages to exert greater control over her emotions and, by extension, the way she lives her life while accepting the realities of her living circumstances. Psychotherapy and counseling in this context must also take into account that the overlap of living in one kind of environment and—because of education and employment—being exposed to different social norms requires ongoing negotiation. The use of technology was also relevant and illustrated the growing need to engage clients in multiple ways as the distance she had to travel to get home made scheduling sessions sometimes difficult; our e-mail correspondence certainly enhanced the therapeutic alliance.

CONCLUSION

This case represents the use of rational emotive behavior therapy to overcome deep-seated beliefs about inadequacy and low self-worth that consequently impaired the client's interpersonal relationships and social skills. The consequences were a depressive illness that included moderate to severe depressive symptoms, suicidal ideations and attempts, and the inability to fully optimize personal growth consistent with the client's intellectual capacity and opportunity. The year-long therapeutic process addressed these issues through building a strong therapeutic alliance and assisting the client to work toward greater independence, higher assertiveness, better social skills, and unconditional self-acceptance.

QUESTIONS

1. Do the client's age and religious background (Roman Catholic) pose additional stressors with regard to the societal expectation of marriage and motherhood?
2. Individuals who identify themselves as mixed ethnicity can have identity problems as they may be torn between allegiances to the differing ethnicities of their parents. Can these identity problems be a predisposing factor for the development of psychopathology?
3. How can religion be useful as a means of coping with adverse life experiences?
4. Major depression can be treated using a variety of psychotherapeutic techniques. What alternative approaches could have been used in this case?
5. What are the limitations of the therapeutic intervention that was used in this case? Should outcomes be more clearly defined?

REFERENCES

Arias, I. (2004). The legacy of child maltreatment: Long-term health consequences. *Journal of Women's Health, 13,* 468–473.

Brereton, B. (1979). *Race relations in colonial Trinidad.* New York, NY: Cambridge University Press.

Fanon, F. (1961). *The wretched of the earth.* New York, NY: Grove Press.

Hickling, F. W., & Hutchinson, G. (2000). Post colonialism and mental health. *Psychiatric Bulletin, 24,* 94–95.

Hutchinson, G., Bruce, C., & Simmons, V. (2008). Increasing incidence of deliberate self-harm in Trinidad. *West Indian Medical Journal, 57,* 346–351.

Hutchinson, G., & Sutherland, P. (2013). Counseling and psychotherapy in the (English-speaking) Caribbean. In R. Moodley, U. P. Gielen, & R. Wu (Eds.), *Handbook of counseling and psychotherapy in an international context* (pp. 117–127). New York, NY: Routledge.

Kirton, R. M., Anatol, M., & Brathwaite, N. (2010). *The political culture of democracy in Trinidad and Tobago: 2010.* Retrieved from http://www.vanderbilt.edu/lapop/trinidad-tobago/2010-political-culture.pdf

Chapter 20

COUNSELING AND PSYCHOTHERAPY IN MEXICO: MRS. FABIOLA'S STORY

María Fregoso-Vera, Samuel Jurado Cárdenas,
and Angélica Riveros Rosas

INTRODUCTION

In Mexico, health services in general span a wide variety of interventions, some of which include mystic beliefs related to loss of health and a notion that allopathic medicine can lead to some kind of damage. These beliefs impose, especially in uneducated populations, a burden characterized by a lack of confidence in health services, family pressure, and reproach, particularly related to the caring of children (Hamui, Fuentes, Aguirre, & Ramírez, 2013).

A common perception among Mexicans is that psychotherapy is more a luxury than a needed service, unless there is a conspicuous condition. Psychotherapy is delivered in both public health institutions and private practice. The main therapeutic approaches in Mexico are related to psychodynamic (Freudian, Frommian, etc.) or humanistic (Rogerian) traditions. Because the cognitive behavior approach has been progressively recognized as more evidence-based, its use is growing at a relatively fast rate. Other approaches, such as the systemic tradition, are mainly aimed at treating family interaction problems. In this context, people expect specifically trained professionals such as psychologists and psychiatrists to treat severe mental health conditions. Mexico has a long history related to counseling that has been achieved with the support and within the range of the activities sponsored by the Universidad Iberoamericana (Lara, Tena, & Hinkle, 2010).

However, there are many other groups claiming they practice counseling, but they are not doing it professionally. As these people practice it, counseling is an undefined or blurry activity that could be practiced by anyone who gives useful advice; it tends to focus on brief, problem-specific interventions. Counseling is usually provided in schools, sports or religious organizations, and other community-based facilities. Counseling is sometimes carried out by trained psychologists but also by social workers, pedagogues, philosophers, priests, and nurses, among many others. In Mexico, a relatively widespread lack of systematic follow-up on the effects of counseling has made it difficult to reach social clarity regarding its professional identity, scope, and limitations (Riveros, Cortazar-Palapa, Alcazar, & Sánchez-Sosa, 2005; Sanchez-Sosa & Riveros, 2013).

This chapter outlines the use of a single-session and brief counseling with an asthmatic child's mother. Single-session therapy is different from traditional counseling in that the latter involves an ongoing process where trust develops over time between the client and the therapist. In the Mexican culture, there are prevalent beliefs favoring forms of abuse around the female role and motherhood because of notions of retribution and the male role of discipline (i.e., machismo). The social demands concerning women's family responsibilities in Mexico are likely to be maintained by the woman's husband, his family, and her own family (Agoff, Rajsbaum, & Herrera, 2006). Thus, there are cultural issues about the maternal role and criteria that proscribe when a mother—or other female caretaker of children—is considered to be a failure at this role. Such issues come into play in the case study discussed in this chapter concerning a mother whose child has asthma. In addition, we also consider the personal attention demanded by the disease as well as the economic conditions that are relevant with asthma.

THE CLIENT

The client, Mrs. Fabiola, is a 32-year-old married woman of mixed ethnicity (as are most populations in Latin America). She has a 9-year-old child diagnosed with moderate persistent asthma. Mrs. Fabiola has a higher than average level of education, graduated as a nurse, and works in a veterinary clinic. Between her and her husband, the family's monthly income is approximately $1,500 (U.S. dollars), which surprisingly corresponds to upper middle class by Mexican standards. She has been married for 10 years, her declared religion is Catholic, and she and her husband come from conservative and traditionalist families.

PRESENTING ISSUES AND CHALLENGES

Mrs. Fabiola presented in therapy with anxiety, stress, and depression. The allergy and immunology department at a specialty hospital in Mexico City recommended that she learn about stress management for caregivers of children with asthma. Mrs. Fabiola said she felt a lot of *nervios* [nerves]—a culturally bound syndrome occurring mostly in Latin America—and that she was very sad because her husband and her family were continually telling her that she was responsible for her child's sickness. Social pressure from her husband and extended family led her to feel helpless to deal with her son's illness, and according to her, the situation was too much to cope with—she was not sure what to do. She reported feelings of sadness, hopelessness, and incompetence.

CASE HISTORY AND DEVELOPMENTAL BACKGROUND

Mrs. Fabiola felt responsible for her son's asthma, which was diagnosed at birth. Mrs. Fabiola's husband, her mother, and her mother-in-law held her responsible for the child's illness. Her husband told her that she was making her child ill by being overprotective, but her mother and her mother-in-law told her that she was not caring enough. This situation generated a lot of conflict, because apparently she could do nothing right.

Following the diagnosis of her child, Mrs. Fabiola tried to prevent him from becoming ill by becoming obsessive in the daily cleaning of her home: She cleansed it thoroughly every day, with substances that often caused her son's dyspnea. She stopped exposing her child to the cold and temperature changes, and when he had to go out she would cover him with layers of sweaters and jackets. She stopped taking him to the park, enrolled him in an afternoon school, avoided participation in children's parties, and discouraged him from interacting with other children so as to prevent possible infections.

She quit her job to dedicate herself to her sick child and to house cleaning, a task she invested a considerable amount of time in. This lifestyle did not allow her to go anywhere with her child.

THE THERAPY

According to Mrs. Fabiola's belief system, the purpose of her life is to free her child from the disease. A recurring theme during the therapy was that she must keep absolute cleanliness in the place where the child stays because "ultimately that is the role of women, while the role of men, such as that of [her husband], is to work and maintain the household"; in her speech it was clear that she believed everything her husband said was true. This belief led to suffering because of her inability to make decisions, guilt for not preventing her son's sickness, and feelings of worthlessness toward everything that represents personal failings. In this case, her child's disease was attributed to her inability to care for him and preserve cleanliness.

Mrs. Fabiola was interviewed on the health of her child and what it meant to her and her husband, as parents, to care for their child. Then the investigator explained the purpose of the intervention, which would be a single psychotherapy session that would take place at the Service for Allergy and Immunology. The intervention was designed to present information on asthma and allergies, including the feelings and emotions commonly experienced by those who have a child with a chronic illness. Mrs. Fabiola recognized that her problems were related to the acceptance of her child's illness and her role as primary caregiver, which evoked nervios and sadness.

Before the single psychotherapy session, Mrs. Fabiola signed an informed consent form and completed several different measures, including the following: a sociodemographic data questionnaire (nine items); the Beck—II Depression Inventory (Beck, Steer, & Brown, 1996); the Beck Anxiety Inventory (Beck & Steer, 1993); a behavioral record of manifestations of asthma symptoms and other manifestations, including parental psychological responses; a self-recording card on adherence behaviors; and the asthma parental report module of a Quality of Life Inventory (Frisch, Cornell, Villanueva, & Retzlaff, 1992).

During the next appointment, Mrs. Fabiola was given the general results from the inventories and questionnaires. Two days later, the single-session intervention was presented via a laptop (Moneo, Oliván, Forés, & Lambán, 2009). The intervention consisted of a presentation of 57 PowerPoint slides, which provided psychoeducation around allergic diseases, asthma, anxiety, depression, the ABC model, strategies for crisis support, diaphragmatic breathing, and deep muscle relaxation. Finally, six videos on asthma were presented, with a total duration of 9 minutes and 33 seconds.

Mrs. Fabiola was always attentive, informing the therapist that she was unaware of all this information and was beginning to realize what she could do for her child and how to change what was not desirable, such as cleaning too much. She also stated that she realized that many of the substances she was using were not beneficial to her child. The therapist noted Mrs. Fabiola's comments, particularly concerning her conceptions and beliefs before the intervention versus after. For example, after the intervention, she realized that neither her husband nor her family had enough information about the illness of her son. She also better understood the role of her emotional state in weariness, sadness, and nervios as well as in her well-being and her ability to care for her child. In addition, she better understood the aspects that she could control and those that would require the support of health personnel and her family. Each time Mrs. Fabiola expressed doubt, the presentation was stopped and clarifications were made.

Mrs. Fabiola received a booklet containing the same information that had been presented visually via the laptop. The information provided in the brochure had previously been approved by 10 experts in health psychology. Participants also received a compact disc containing the verbal instructions of diaphragmatic breathing and deep progressive muscle relaxation. The training instructions and guide had previously been successfully used to treat clients with panic disorder.

Over the course of the next 7 days, Mrs. Fabiola was instructed to record the symptoms of her son's asthma and her psychological responses to his illness, and a telephone contact was scheduled to discuss her responses. Mrs. Fabiola was asked about any problems that had arisen during record collection, and the therapist reviewed the homework assigned to her (practicing relaxation, identifying and challenging irrational cognitions and emotions, and reading the booklet when necessary). Finally, the remaining session was devoted to reviewing the assigned homework for the child, which was similar to that assigned to the mother. Special attention was placed on the practice of muscle relaxation.

The intervention described in the present chapter was aimed at examining the effects of a brief therapeutic intervention on the primary caregiver of a child with allergic asthma. The results revealed that psychoeducation on asthma combined with cognitive strategies for use in emergencies, diaphragmatic breathing training, and deep progressive muscle relaxation training were effective in reducing depressive and anxious symptoms experienced by Mrs. Fabiola. Her depression and anxiety symptoms decreased significantly from pretest results and continued to be lower at the 2-month follow-up, 6-month follow-up, and at the time of termination.

DISCUSSION AND ANALYSIS

Mrs. Fabiola's decision to seek therapy was motivated primarily by her desperate desire to find an alternative way to solve her problem. Mexican culture plays a critical role in the shaping of beliefs and stereotypes about women. In Mrs. Fabiola's opinion, the value of a woman's role falls predominantly on characteristics of selflessness, submission, and self-sacrifice in order to be the person who cares for and protects her children and husband. From her perspective, if she had done well enough, her son would have been healthy. Mrs. Fabiola expressed a strong interest in participating in the program in light of her statement, "I cannot stand my son's disease. It is a burden, and my husband and my extended family think that I'm worsening my child's sickness."

Cognitive behavior interventions are also permeated with the positions of gender and equality. During the development of the psychotherapy session, it was noted that Mrs. Fabiola's beliefs were derived from cultural stereotypes about her maternal role, in which the interaction with her husband and her family was characterized by criticism and judgment and by her assuming guilt for her child's illness. In Mexico, it is common for husbands to blame their wives for what they see as flaws in family functioning, as the management of the home is her sole responsibility (Agoff et al., 2006). This attribution of blame was justified by Mrs. Fabiola's family because she did not work and was not the main supplier of money needed for the household.

Catastrophic thoughts with respiratory symptoms were exacerbated by traditional beliefs in Mexican culture about a possible "cure" of the disease if home remedies were used (Berenzon & Saavedra, 2002). For example, some believe that putting a paper vest and a red rag on the child would remove the "cold" that causes the disease; indeed, Mrs. Fabiola initially came to therapy with these items.

During the process, the therapist was constantly empowering Mrs. Fabiola in order to elucidate that her beliefs and catastrophic thoughts would not help the sick child, and positive responses to the disease were generated through successive approximations (i.e., "baby steps"). During the follow-up sessions, Mrs. Fabiola continued showing adaptive responses that highlighted her ability to manage her child's asthma. At the last follow-up, Mrs. Fabiola said that she provided the drug as prescribed and kept the house clean without being obsessive as she once was. She felt much better without the criticism of her husband, mother-in-law, and mother. She had more time to spend with her son, more space to relax, and more opportunities to enjoy family walks with her son and husband.

Family (and cultural) processes have a powerful influence on health and pediatric asthma control and are strongly associated with healthy family functioning, because in the family, the role of the caregiver and the caregiver–child interactions influence the manifestations of pediatric asthma (Méndez, Castro, & Durán, 2009). The changing perception of respiratory symptoms is critical in the management of pediatric asthma, and it is the primary caregiver, usually the mother, who can realize the changes that occur in young children with asthmatic symptoms. Thus, it is necessary to change mothers' often-catastrophic perceptions that frequently trigger or exacerbate asthma attacks and related anxious symptoms. Also, high rates of depression have been reported in caregivers of children with asthma (Celano et al., 2008; Yorke, Fleming, & Shuldham, 2007).

Regarding stress experienced by primary caregivers of children with asthma, results of a study by Wright, Cohen, Carey, Weiss, and Gold (2002) revealed that primary-caregiver stress predicts wheezing in asthmatic children. The influence of psychological factors on asthma attacks and visits to the hospital emergency room have also been associated with insufficient knowledge of disease prevention and poor adherence to treatment by clients. It is thus important that interventions focus not only on crisis management but also on education about the disease, crisis prevention, and disease control.

Counseling and psychotherapy in Mexico face several challenges, such as a lack of social acceptance of useful professional services. This lack of acceptance occurs in a context where children's health generally and mental health particularly are seen as a natural realm of mothers' expertise. This belief leads to real difficulties when dealing with chronic diseases. For example, in Mrs. Fabiola's family, she was blamed her for her child's asthma. Consequently, she became obsessive with her cleaning routines, which, in turn, increased her anxiety regarding her child's symptoms. She was incapable of enjoying herself as a mother, a wife, and a professional. Paradoxically, this anxiety-laden state, in addition to time pressure, made it very difficult for her to seek and obtain counseling services, which made it harder to deal with his son's condition. Thus, a one-session counseling treatment provided her the opportunity to receive psychoeducation and training within these constraints and to learn emotional regulation abilities that allowed her to cope differently with her role as a mother and to live a more pleasant and self-controlled life.

CONCLUSION

Psychotherapy in Mexico, particularly in an institutionalized environment, may need to be very short; users generally have very little time and face challenges when accessing psychological care, so people who require care are often left without necessary support. For informal primary caregivers—usually women—it is difficult to enter a psychotherapeutic process, because they do not consider having a child with a chronic illness a problem that requires professional attention. The prevailing gender attitudes in Mexico dictate that women with family problems need to be very strong, bear up, and be submissive, rather than seeking professional support.

Women like Mrs. Fabiola need to develop and strengthen their ability to make decisions in managing their child's illness. In addition, they need to develop their ability to assess family criticism in terms of its usefulness, without compromising their beliefs about their value as mothers and caretakers for their children and homes.

QUESTIONS

1. How do some biases or cultural characteristics in Mexico seem to affect the development of health problems with psychosomatic components?
2. What aspects of Mexican culture are likely to promote resilience in cases like the one described in the chapter?
3. Please describe the strengths and weaknesses of the way Mrs. Fabiola's case was handled.
4. How would you engage Mrs. Fabiola's case from your own therapeutic viewpoint or approach?
5. How would your own ethnic and cultural identity influence Mrs. Fabiola's therapeutic process?

REFERENCES

Agoff, C., Rajsbaum, A., & Herrera, C. (2006). Perspectivas de las mujeres maltratadas sobre la violencia de pareja en México [Perspectives of abused women about intimate partner violence in Mexico]. *Salud Pública de México, 48,* S307–S314.

Beck, A. T., & Steer, R. A. (1993). *Beck Anxiety Inventory manual.* San Antonio, TX: Psychological Corporation.

Beck, A. T., Steer, R. A., & Brown, G. K. (1996). *Beck Depression Inventory manual* (2nd ed.). San Antonio, TX: Psychological Corporation.

Berenzon, S., & Saavedra, N. (2002). Presencia de la herbolaria en el tratamiento de los problemas emocionales: Entrevista a los curanderos urbanos [Presence of herbs in treating emotional problems: Interview with urban healers]. *Salud Mental, 25,* 55–66.

Celano, M., Bakeman, R., Gaytan, O., Smith, C., Koci, A., & Henderson, S. (2008). Caregiver depressive symptoms and observed family interaction in low-income children with persistent asthma. *Family Process, 47,* 7–20.

Frisch, M. B., Cornell, J., Villanueva, M., & Retzlaff, P. J. (1992). Clinical validation of the Quality of Life Inventory: A measure of life satisfaction for use in treatment planning and outcome assessment. *Psychological Assessment, 4,* 92–101.

Hamui, L., Fuentes, R., Aguirre, R., & Ramírez, O. (2013). *Expectativas y experiencias de los usuarios del Sistema de Salud en México: Un estudio de satisfacción con la atención médica* [Expectations and experiences of users of the Health System in Mexico: A study of satisfaction with medical care]. Mexico City, Mexico: Facultad de Medicina, Universidad Nacional Autónoma de México.

Lara, E., Tena, A., & Hinkle, S. (2010). Counseling in Mexico: History, current identity, and future trends. *Journal of Counseling & Development, 88,* 33–37.

Méndez, A., Castro, I., & Durán, E. (2009, April–June). Posibilidades educadoras de los campamentos jornaleros agrícolas migrantes [Educational possibilities of migrant agriculture camps]. *Revista Educación y Desarrollo, 10,* 57–65.

Moneo, I., Oliván, M., Forés, M., & Lambán, E. (2009). Tools in the education of the asthmatic child. *Revista de Pediatría Atención Primaria, 11,* 415–422.

Riveros, A., Cortazar-Palapa, J., Alcazar, F., & Sánchez-Sosa, J. J. (2005). Efectos de una intervención cognitivo-conductual en la calidad de vida, ansiedad, depresión y condición médica de pacientes diabéticos e hipertensos esenciales [Effects of a cognitive behavioral intervention on quality of life, anxiety, depression, and health condition of diabetic patients with essential hypertension]. *International Journal of Clinical and Health Psychology, 5,* 445–462.

Sanchez-Sosa, J. J., & Riveros, A. (2013). Counseling and psychotherapy in Mexico: Moving towards a Latin American perspective. In R. Moodley, U. Gielen, & R. Wu (Eds.), *Handbook of counseling and psychotherapy in an international context* (pp. 139–150). New York, NY: Routledge.

Wright, R., Cohen, S., Carey, V., Weiss, S., & Gold, D. (2002). Parental stress as a predictor of wheezing in infancy. *American Journal of Respiratory and Critical Care Medicine, 165,* 358–365.

Yorke, J., Fleming, S., & Shuldham, C. (2007). Psychological interventions for adults with asthma: A systematic review. *Respiratory Medicine, 101,* 1–14. doi:10.1016/j.rmed.2006.04.003

Chapter 21

COUNSELING AND PSYCHOTHERAPY IN THE UNITED STATES: ROLANDO'S STORY

Gargi Roysircar and Vincent Pignatiello

INTRODUCTION

The United States is a multicultural country with more than 315 million people representing a plethora of ethnic groups and religious affiliations, and it ranks 26th in the world in terms of net migration. As such, the U.S. citizenry is composed of an array of different cultures and subcultures. One in five speaks a language other than English (Central Intelligence Agency, 2012). Moreover, nearly one third of U.S. adults are considered obese. In general, the United States possesses an individualistic and liberty-oriented worldview, yet there is a long history of oppression and discrimination against minority individuals.

There are many counseling approaches available to clinicians in the United States (see, for discussion, Roysicar & Hodges, 2013). Gurman and Messer (2003) outlined the use of psychoanalytic, humanistic, cognitive, behavior, brief, and family/marital therapies as well as integrative approaches to psychotherapy. Many of these therapies take a directive or pathologizing stance toward human existence. Existentialism, conversely, with its focus on one's subjective existence and being alive, provides the counselor with a nondirective, meaning-making approach to treatment. Rigid adherence to particular techniques is authoritarian, obscures a counselor's understanding of a client, undermines authenticity, and leads to short-lived rather than enduring outcomes. Moreover, the existential counseling process accommodates a culturally adapted model (Roysircar & Mayo, 2012).

American existentialist Yalom (1980) described anxiety as the apprehension that arises because of the givens of existence: death, freedom, isolation, and meaninglessness. According to May (1969), people experience anxiety whether they live a life of freedom and relationships or whether they face death, isolation, and/ or meaninglessness. In addition, each person has a core, a self that is deeper and truer than an identity defined by others. To be specific, Vontress (1985), an African American existentialist, stated that people who are living authentically, that is, being their true selves, are comfortable and accepting of elements such as their "likes and dislikes or strengths and weaknesses" (p. 208). The realization that one is not living up to his or her full potential results in existential guilt and suicidal ideation. Awareness of this guilt is possible through self-reflection, a means of taking responsibility for oneself (Yalom, 1980).

In this chapter, we discuss the case of Rolando, a second-generation Caribbean American. Rolando underwent therapy with Gargi Roysircar (the first author of this chapter). Rolando presented with existential guilt and suicidal ideation. We outline in this chapter the treatment he undertook and discuss his case.

THE CLIENT

Rolando is a 22-year-old Dominican male who grew up in a working-class neighborhood in New Jersey with his mother and older sister. He identifies himself spiritually as a Catholic. Although he has not had a girlfriend, Rolando identifies himself as heterosexual. Currently, Rolando lives at home with his mother and works as a substitute teacher at his local high school.

PRESENTING ISSUES AND CHALLENGES

Rolando presented with existential guilt and suicidal ideation. He was not living authentically because he had not fully embraced his unique identity that is made up of his heritage, spirituality, life goals, and family culture. His anxiety, family curse, and lack of a true self had left him paralyzed in his relationships and career. Rolando was in search of meaning.

A common theme throughout Rolando's life revolved around what it means to be Dominican. The role of Dominican males is well defined within Rolando's culture: They are macho, powerful, and sexually experienced. Rolando has very dark skin, is extremely overweight, and has never had a girlfriend. He is still a virgin. Although girls in school and college saw him as a good platonic friend, they refused to become romantically involved with him.

Rolando had also been criticized by his few male school friends, mother, uncle, sister, and even strangers for his color and weight, his role-playing and Internet game hobbies, not being "Dominican enough," his use of classical English vocabulary, and his unevidenced sexual prowess. Rolando's belief that he did not meet everyone's expectations had left him feeling hopeless and inadequate all his childhood and young adulthood.

CASE HISTORY AND DEVELOPMENTAL BACKGROUND

Rolando's mother is a tough immigrant survivor who—having had much experience in love relationships in her past—is frustrated with Rolando's lack of sex appeal. She shows Rolando little affection, but Rolando's sister is supportive and caring, and often looks out for him. Rolando never knew his father and, consequently, grew up without a male model. An uncle, his mother's brother, lives with them and tries to encourage Rolando, but this uncle is in and out of jail and brings home new unsavory women every night. Rolando's mother supports her family by keeping boarders, most of whom are illegal immigrants, and these guests bring more and more undocumented people into the house. Throughout his childhood, Rolando spent most of his summers in the Dominican Republic visiting family members and experiencing his heritage.

Rolando considers himself a "nerd" and enjoys writing fantasy stories. On a related note, Rolando often finds himself dwelling on the reality of the *fuku*, a curse that is placed upon individuals who defied the Dominican ruler El Jefe. Although this curse was placed on Rolando's family three generations ago (starting with his grandfather), the fuku is believed to affect one's entire family intergenerationally. His mother's torture and near-death experience in a cane field was attributed to the fuku curse, and her escape was credited to the divine intervention of a magical mongoose. The idea that he is ultimately doomed incessantly haunts Rolando.

THE THERAPY

Rolando came to counseling because of increasingly depressive symptoms since his recent suicide attempt. Although he still contemplated suicide, he had not attempted for fear of the impact it would have on his sister. He felt socially isolated, had no male friends, and had no girlfriend either, but he expressed the desire to fall in love and be sexually intimate. He had minimal interactions in the workplace and knew that his students made fun of him and that other teachers ignored him. Rolando stated that his greatest struggle was finding his personal identity and place in the world.

I (Gargi Roysircar) modified existential counseling to allow Rolando to accept supernatural powers. We discussed how he could counteract the evil of fuku with a spiritual counterspell, which Rolando called *zafa*. I asked Rolando to create a myth that counteracted the fuku. Rolando told the story of a mongoose with golden lion eyes and absolute black felt that appeared just before he was going to throw himself from a bridge and guided him with songs away from death. We concluded that the magical mongoose was Rolando's zafa, and the creation of the myth was a source of regaining control of his life.

As an existential counselor, though, I had to be aware that my self-insertion as a counselor would relieve Rolando from his responsibility for finding meaning in his suffering. In order to maintain the treatment's fidelity in reference to his oppression as a minority, I told Rolando, "The one thing the oppressor can't take away from you is the way you choose to respond to what the oppressor does to you. The last of one's freedom is to choose one's attitude in any given circumstance," and "You cannot control what happens to you, but you can control your attitude to what happens to you, and in that you will be mastering change rather than allowing it to master you." I encouraged Rolando to take responsibility for the freedom to act upon this capability. For instance, Rolando and I determined that he is able (i.e., possesses the freedom) to walk to the doors of a gym one day following a counseling session. Whether Rolando chose to go or not to go was less important; what was important was that he felt the sense that he had some control over his actions and in his life.

I also encouraged Rolando to tell me his experiences and share his emotions. This process was painful for Rolando, but sharing emotional experiences allowed him to make his feelings external rather than keeping them internal. In addition, he named his emotions, a feat that normalized them and allowed them to more easily be mastered. Rolando had kept many of his painful emotions inside because of his fear of stigmatization of mental health concerns in Latino communities.

In addition, I encouraged Rolando to write about his experiences and explore his identities through his words. I did not provide Rolando any specific guidelines for writing but rather increased his freedom by allowing him to find his own. Through this writing he learned to accept the idea that he can be both Dominican and a writer of Spanglish diaspora literature, and that neither defined the other. Furthermore, writing helped Rolando to accept previously unacceptable parts of himself and provided greater meaning in life.

By termination, Rolando's depression and suicidal ideation had subsided. Three months later, I received Rolando's manuscript—his biography narrated by him in the third person and uniquely in the second person by his sister and his college roommate. Code switching between English and Spanish was central to the narrative as Rolando switched back and forth between his Dominican identity and American identity.

DISCUSSION AND ANALYSIS

Existentialism is not without its limitations for work with multicultural clients. For instance, Rolando may not want to relinquish his beliefs in supernatural curses or in predestination, such as the fuku, a view of destiny that is in stark contrast to May's (1983) view of creating one's destiny and the concepts of freedom and self-determinism. Finding a way to honor spiritualism within counseling may help to develop Rolando's inner self, whereas trying to have him simply forego *espiritismo* may impede his bicultural identity. Emphasis on the latter would reveal a counseling bias in favor of assimilation to the European American culture.

In addition, Hispanics are more likely to rely on and value social support of the family and their Latino neighborhood. Rolando's presenting problem was that he was not good at social interactions, which to him was his culture-specific deficit. This goal for connections made him resist the existential notion that a human being, being ultimately alone in the world, seeks autonomy. Rolando, although unique in many respects, had trouble discussing self-determination when he lived in the context of in-group hierarchies, natural support systems, and strict gender roles, however limiting these societal mores may be. The interaction of abusive microsystems in Rolando's life (family, the prejudiced Dominican ethnic group, the prejudiced dominant White group, peers, emasculation by Dominican women) made for a life of persecution.

In a similar manner, immigrants of color are a part of the larger U.S. society, which has discriminated against them for their ethnicity, nationality, color, low social class, culture, language, and gender-role behaviors. Whereas others in the dominant culture may have the freedom to make particular choices, some minorities may not. What may result from oppression is *internalized marginalization*—an individual's acceptance of societal discriminatory attitudes that convey that one is subhuman, inferior, or incapable, which can have an insidious effect on one's motivation and self-esteem (Roysircar, 2008; Roysircar & Mayo, 2012). Yalom (1980) would not consider internalized marginalization to be a genuine constraint on an individual's freedom. Instead he would believe that individuals are responsible for their psychological response to adversity. However, this clinical judgment is like blaming the victim.

Such a clinical judgment, which could further the process of internalized marginalization, places it in direct contradiction to the knowledge, skills, and attitudes that are recommended for training and education (Roysircar, Dobbins, & Malloy, 2009).

Thus, for Rolando, freedom from the barrier of hopelessness, as well as the actualization of freedom through recognition of the external source of oppression, was a *goal* of counseling, not a personal responsibility. Assuming responsibility for internalized marginalization would only be empowering if one actually had the resources to overcome the imposed constraints. Roysircar and Mayo (2012) suggested that tenets of multicultural practice can be woven into existential work to address the oppressive societal practices that result in internalized marginalization.

Although Rolando is fairly self-aware, his compulsive fantasy world and *machismo* insecurities have left him out of control of his own destiny. Perhaps his use of the fuku is a means of avoiding his freedom by attributing responsibility to an external source that is beyond his control. In addition, Rolando is struggling with his personal, cultural, occupational, and recreational identities, hindering him from living authentically and causing existential guilt. He suffers from meaninglessness as he is unclear about his purpose in life. Last, Rolando's anxiety to live as well as to die has immobilized him. His overruling fear of dying at the whim of the fuku is not allowing him to live in the present, and he escapes into the game of Dungeons and Dragons. The task of therapy was to first help him clarify the upper limits of what he is actually capable of doing at present. When free will is considered in this light, as a relative goal based on both external *and* internal resources, existential counseling seems less at odds with multiculturalism and is a hopeful and empowering therapy.

Furthermore, therapy helped Rolando to appreciate his unique bicultural life as a Dominican American and to define his own identity rather than rely on others to do it for him, which helped him live more authentically. He found meaning and purpose in life as a science fiction writer and as a teacher and harnessed his anxiety as a heterosexual male so that it was useful rather than immobilizing. Rolando recognized that women, including his sister, liked to talk to him because he was a respectful listener, trustworthy, and insightful. In that sense he was superior to his Dominican male peers who focused on sexual mastery. Rolando became comfortable with his eventual death—perhaps caused by the untimely interference of the fuku—in order to live a more productive life and optimize his development in the here and now and not to precipitate meaninglessness and despair and have suicidal thoughts.

Rolando's issues of identity and meaninglessness were addressed by relying on the four principles of an intervention put forth by Walsh and Lantz (2007): holding, telling, mastering, and honoring. This intervention is a process of self-reflection that raises self-awareness. Rolando was conflicted because he allowed others to define his identities for him (too American, not man enough, too dark, fat, unique hobbies) rather than defining these for himself, causing him to live inauthentically. Much of Rolando's self-esteem and beliefs about himself were based on the opinions of others. The first stage of the intervention required Rolando to "hold" the experience, that is, to hold "up the problem experience so that it may be seen, remembered, and reexperienced" (Walsh & Lantz, 2007, p. 28). Rolando had many memories of being discriminated against for not fitting stereotypical ideals for Dominican males, including times when others' judgments gave him inauthentic identities. Holding these experiences was difficult for Rolando as they dealt with painful emotions. Thus, as an existential counselor, I had to show "empathic availability" toward Rolando (Walsh & Lantz, 2007, p. 35)—be present and compassionate.

Essentially, Rolando's depression and suicidal ideation were wrought from others defining—often in negative, demeaning, or oppressive ways—who he was. The mastering stage involved Rolando creating and accepting his own definition of his Dominican, American, Catholic, "geek," and writer identities. Rolando acknowledged the fact that he is alone in the world and, as such, he needs to search for definitions of self from within rather than relying on others to define him. He began to question the validity of the beliefs, values, and assumptions he had previously made about himself and to challenge the idea that his identities needed to be based on the expectations of others. He worked to integrate and accept the parts of himself that he had chosen. He was able to appreciate and celebrate his various intersecting identities: a Dominican American, a spiritual being, a Catholic who revered saints, a computer geek, a teacher, a writer, a son, a brother, a nephew, a faithful friend, an overweight person, and a lover of women of all ages with diverse roles and experiences. At the core of these intersections was his unique being.

The final stage involved honoring Rolando's pain. Once Rolando found greater understanding and acceptance of his true self of multiple identities, he appreciated the opportunities provided by the pain of identity conflicts. He had a greater awareness of the pain others have experienced, for instance, his mother's trauma and persecution in the old country as well as her difficult immigration to the United States. Rolando felt sorrow for his mother and grew closer to her as he finally persuaded her to tell him her immigration journey. Through his mother's story, he learned who his father was. Rolando's writing was used as a means of reaching out, relating to other individuals, and helping them overcome their pain. Rolando can now draw on his true self as a source of resilience. For instance, rather than dismissing his Dominican and immigrant identities, Rolando can embrace them as sources of persistence and strength to overcome future obstacles. In a similar manner, Rolando can use his identity as a writer to make meaning out of pain rather than create suffering. In essence, Rolando can develop his own voice rather than echoing the voice of the internalized oppressor who marginalizes from within.

The telling of Rolando's story acted as the zafa to his family's fuku. Fuku and zafa may mean the burdens and blessings that every family carries. Characters of their own, especially in the immigrant experience, they relate to the themes of encountering new worlds and the limits of the past world.

CONCLUSION

In delivering counseling services to multicultural clients, a counselor should demonstrate multicultural competence in self- and other-awareness, knowledge, and skills (Roysircar et al., 2009). It is crucial for the counselor to be aware of personal values, biases, and assumptions about a culturally different client and to tailor counseling interventions to a client's worldview in order to increase their effectiveness and to do no harm. Existential counseling acts as an efficient cross-cultural modality for providing counseling to individuals such as Rolando, a second-generation Dominican American male, as it focuses on the experience of being human within multicultural settings rather than on specific interventions that may be European American biased. Although existentialism may work well for diverse clients, it was accommodated with cultural modifications for work with Rolando, the client presented in this chapter.

QUESTIONS

1. Consider that the existential interventions used in this chapter have analogs to other theories. How might the therapy have looked different had one of these other approaches been used? (Such analogs may include Rolando's different identities being viewed as different self-states in interpersonal theory, the creation of myths being similar to thickening in narrative therapy, his distorted beliefs about himself in cognitive behavior therapy, and Rolando's experience of guilt and attack on himself from a psychodynamic perspective.)
2. Think about your own cultural identities. Where do your identities coincide with Rolando's? How might this overlap of your identities with your client serve to both facilitate and obstruct the therapeutic process?
3. Consider Rolando's depressive symptoms (e.g., escapism and retreat into fantasy). How might these have served as a "solution" to an earlier problem (i.e., transgenerational trauma from immigration, lack of affection from his mother, or the curse of the fuku inherited from his original culture)? How might this "solution" have developed into what eventually became the problem?
4. In what ways could the focus on choice in existentialism exacerbate symptoms? How do you view the aspect of choice within your own theoretical orientation?
5. What other barriers might Rolando come up against aside from the barriers discussed in the chapter? How would you apply existentialism to helping Rolando free himself from these barriers?

REFERENCES

Central Intelligence Agency (2012). *World Factbook: United States*. Retrieved from https://www.cia.gov/library/publications/the-world-factbook/geos/us.html

Gurman, A. S., & Messer, S. B. (Eds.). (2003). *Essential psychotherapies* (2nd ed.). New York, NY: Guilford Press.

May, R. (1969). *Love and will*. New York, NY: Norton.

May, R. (1983). *The discovery of being*. New York, NY: Norton.

Roysircar, G. (2008). Social privilege: Counselors' competence with systemically determined inequalities. *Journal for Specialists in Group Work, 33*, 377–384.

Roysircar, G., Dobbins, J. E., & Malloy, K. (2009). Diversity competence in training and clinical practice. In M. Kenkel & R. Peterson (Eds.), *Competency-based education for professional psychology* (pp. 179–197). Washington, DC: American Psychological Association.

Roysicar, G., & Hodges, S. (2013). Counseling and psychotherapy in the United States: Multicultural competence, evidence-based, and measurable outcomes. In R. Moodley, U. Gielen, & R. Wu (Eds.), *Handbook of counseling and psychotherapy in an international context* (pp. 151–168). New York, NY: Routledge.

Roysircar, G., & Mayo, J. (2012). Individual identity, psychosocial conditions, and existential anxiety: Vontress in the context of the U.S.A. In R. Moodley, L. Epp, & H. Yusuf (Eds.), *Counseling across the cultural divide: The Clemmont Vontress reader* (pp. 332–347). Ross-On-Wye, United Kingdom: PCCS Books.

Vontress, C. E. (1985). Existentialism as a cross-cultural counseling modality. In P. Pederson (Ed.), *Handbook of cross-cultural counseling and therapy* (pp. 207–212). Westport, CT: Greenwood.

Walsh, J., & Lantz, J. (2007). *Short-term existential intervention in clinical practice.* Chicago, IL: Lyceum.

Yalom, I. D. (1980). *Existential psychotherapy.* New York, NY: Basic Books.

Part Five

COUNSELING AND PSYCHOTHERAPY IN EUROPE

Chapter 22

COUNSELING AND PSYCHOTHERAPY IN DENMARK: MARIANNE'S STORY

Nanja H. Hansen and Andrea L. Dixon

INTRODUCTION

In Denmark there are multiple theories within the fields of counseling and psychotherapy. The most common ones are psychodynamic, cognitive behavior, existential–humanistic, gestalt, narrative, and systemic therapies. There are also more integrative approaches, such as dialectical behavioral therapy (DBT), mindfulness-based cognitive therapy, and acceptance and commitment therapy (Dixon & Hansen, 2010; Hansen & Dixon, 2013).

DBT was developed as a way to work therapeutically with individuals who were diagnosed with borderline personality disorder (BPD; Rathus & Miller, 2002). As evidence for the efficacy of this therapeutic model grew, it was implemented in varying Danish populations and showed promising results (Miller, Wyman, Huppert, Glassman, & Rathus, 2000; Rathus & Miller, 2002). One of these populations consisted of individuals diagnosed with eating disorders. Empirical evidence suggests that DBT helps individuals who have a comorbid diagnosis of BPD and disordered eating (Chen, Matthews, Allen, Kuo, & Linehan, 2008).

The case study presented in this chapter summarizes counseling and psychotherapy with Marianne Nielsen (not her real name), who was given a comorbid diagnosis of BPD and disordered eating behaviors (binge eating disorder). The treatment modality was DBT. The client has received 1 hour of individual therapy weekly, 2 hours of group therapy weekly, and access to the psychologist via telephone when a self-harming or suicidal crisis emerges. The psychologist receives group consultation from her team of trained DBT psychologists and supervision from a seasoned DBT psychologist (Linehan et al., 2006). In addition, the client sees a physician, a dietician, and a social worker at the Anorexic Clinic in Copenhagen, Denmark, in order to treat her disordered eating. The therapist meets with the treatment team at the Anorexic Clinic once a week.

THE CLIENT

Marianne is a 24-year-old Danish woman with no disability. Marianne was born without any physical or mental complications. She was well taken care of and loved by her parents. Her mother was a stay-at-home mother, and her father had a well-paying and powerful position in an architecture firm. Both parents are Caucasian and Danish of ethnicity. They are not religious and do not attend church besides on the traditional holidays such as Christmas and Easter. Marianne was baptized and confirmed into the Danish Folk Church, which is a Lutheran denomination. Though she does not attend church regularly, she believes in God and is spiritual. She grew up in the upper-middle class of a Copenhagen suburb. She lives with her boyfriend of 3 years in an apartment in the aforementioned suburb. She is studying to become a veterinarian at the Copenhagen Veterinarian School. She enrolled in the school 5 years ago, and though the degree is limited to 5 years, Marianne has been given extra time by the Ministry of Education because of periods of absence caused by illness. Though she earns some pocket money working with horses, her main source of income is the Danish government, as is the case with her boyfriend. Because they are both pursuing an education, they are each entitled to receive approximately 5,000 kroner (approximately €740, or $820) a month tax-free.

Presenting Issues and Challenges

When Marianne entered into the DBT treatment program, she was self-harming by biting herself, slapping her cheeks, scratching her arms, and banging her head into walls. She was overeating every day and was overweight, which put her at risk for type 2 diabetes. She was struggling with ovarian cysts, and her menstrual cycle was very irregular. Marianne was extremely anxious and fearful every time she came in for individual and group therapy and often self-harmed right before a session started. This self-harm made it very difficult for Marianne to practice her mindfulness skills. In addition, she preferred to talk about the latest crisis than practice any DBT skills. She used the crisis phone in excess, calling the psychologist multiple times a day asking for advice on issues ranging from a fight she had with her boyfriend to an individual in a grocery store who made a comment she did not like. Finally, Marianne began using cocaine a year into her treatment and sometimes did not show up for sessions.

Case History and Developmental Background

When Marianne was 3 years old her mother gave birth to her brother and suffered from undiagnosed, untreated postpartum depression. Her mother began drinking, and Marianne took care of her mother. She often felt ashamed and guilty and desperately wanted her mother's love and affection. As she grew older, her father used her as a confidant. She had to give daily updates on her mother's behavior and her "illness." If Marianne did not behave, her father would get very angry, and Marianne was often frightened of him. Her father also stated that pretty women were skinny women, and so Marianne began running track at the age of 13. By age 14, she was very underweight and was diagnosed with the eating disorder anorexia nervosa. She received no treatment at that time.

When she was 15 and began attending high school, she struggled. She had many sick days and great difficulty maintaining friendships. Often she felt very lonely and would resort to a fantasy world where people loved her unconditionally. She began drinking, partying, and having brief relationships with young men. At parties, Marianne engaged in risky sexual behavior, seeking the approval of her friends. She finished high school a year later than her classmates.

At the age of 18, Marianne attempted suicide and was committed to one of the main hospitals in Copenhagen for a psychiatric assessment. The doctor overseeing the case diagnosed her with BPD using the International Classification of Diseases—10th Edition (ICD–10) diagnostic system (World Health Organization, 1992, 2009). She was given antidepressants and an unlimited number of hours with a psychologist. The psychologist in charge of Marianne's treatment worked from a psychodynamic framework. Marianne attended individual sessions (she refused group sessions) for approximately 6 months before she stopped attending the sessions and stopped taking the antidepressants because she did not care for the side effects.

Six years after Marianne's suicide attempt, her primary care physician referred her for a visit with one of the primary physicians of the anorexic clinic at a main hospital in Copenhagen. The physician diagnosed her with an eating disorder not otherwise specified using the ICD–10 diagnostic system. The doctor decided that Marianne would receive treatment from a dietician and a psychologist; the method of treatment would be DBT.

THE THERAPY

Marianne came for individual and group counseling every week for 2.5 years. Each individual counseling session followed the DBT model, going over her weekly goal sheet and conducting a chain analysis when it had been too difficult for her to follow through on practicing her DBT skills. We would practice mindfulness and crisis skills whenever Marianne became dysregulated within a session (*dysregulation* is a term used in DBT, meaning that the person has great difficulty with emotion regulation).

Marianne had great difficulty within her interpersonal relationships. These difficulties in interpersonal relationships showed up in the relationship between Marianne and myself (first author, Nanja H. Hansen) continuously. She was oftentimes very dependent on her relationship with me, interpreting things that I said in ways that disturbed the counseling process. For example, if I asked Marianne to wait in the waiting area because she was early, she would interpret this to mean that I was angry with her. This in turn would cause her to become highly dysregulated (i.e., she experienced strong feelings of fear, sadness, and shame). At times this behavior was very frustrating for me because I felt like I had to be extra careful in how I would phrase things when speaking to Marianne, which took away from the authenticity of the relationship (which is a principle in DBT). Moreover, Marianne always stated that I was a "crystalized" person, meaning that everything in me was pure and good. I often struggled with, on the one hand deflating this notion, and on the other hand keeping a professional distance.

Marianne often dissociated, going into a kind of fantasy world, which made it difficult for her to work on improving acceptance of reality (a DBT skill). As an example, she wanted to start studying theology because she believed that if she was in a close relationship with God then she would be "cleansed" and perfect and people around her (i.e., her mother and father) would be able to love her again. At these times, I encouraged Marianne to use her belief in God to help and guide her when she felt empty or lonely.

177

Other ways that Marianne would enter into these fantasy states is when she would purchase a new coat, purse, or jewelry or go to the mall and have her make-up done. The overspending (she was in great debt) was always an attempt to look pretty so that people (again, her mother and father) would like her. Her debt was a source of stress for her, and reducing her overspending was one of her DBT goals. Even though the overspending was part of Marianne's treatment goals, I was keenly aware of the fact that the overspending also gave Marianne a moment of reprieve from her suffering; although it was not beneficial to her from a long-term standpoint, she used the spending as a way to stay resilient toward her anxiety, depression, and shame. Validation of Marianne's wish to have and receive unconditional love from her parents became very important at these times, and I found it easy to provide this validation as her pain was always very visible.

Marianne also continued to enter into so-called friendships with people whom she did not know, and then would proceed to end these friendships very abruptly. The friendships added to her dysregulation as they caused much drama and chaos in her life. One result of this was that a year into treatment Marianne began using cocaine. Time was spent on changing this behavior so that Marianne could continue working on her original treatment goals.

Another issue that arose in the treatment of Marianne was her level of anxiety, fear, depression, anger, and shame. Her fears of always being in trouble with me, her fear that I was tired of her, her depressive thoughts and anger toward her parents, her yearning for love and acceptance, and her persistent sense of emptiness all made it difficult to engage in a relationship with Marianne. When she was regulated, she was quite insightful and was able to state and understand that her behavior, when dysregulated, was not helpful to her, yet it took very little to put her right back into a state of dysregulation. I encouraged Marianne to write stories, as she greatly enjoyed both writing and telling them. The stories became Marianne's outlet for expressing things that were difficult for her to say in the counseling sessions (when dysregulated by shame or fear) and allowed her to be mindful and stay present.

Discussion and Analysis

Marianne was in many ways a "normal" Danish woman, who received many benefits from the Danish government so as to help her maintain a certain standard of living and to try to circumvent her marginalization from society. To this end she received unlimited access to mental and physical health care; she received funds to continue to pursue her education and funds to live in a nice apartment.

In attempting to view the case of Marianne through the lenses of social economic class and ethnicity, a few obstacles present themselves or are culturally "nonexistent." Denmark's emphasis on egalitarian objectives and social welfare (Lundberg, 2001) is ingrained in the Danish culture in the idea that all are equal, or the same, and have equal/same rights. The high taxes in Denmark help maintain this view as Danes may have access to the same opportunities (i.e., access to universities, jobs, housing, and physical and mental health services). The government provides help to those in the Danish society who are unable to care for themselves. Though Marianne came from an upper-middle-class family, she would not feel more or less entitled to the help from the government than someone who came from a lower socioeconomic status. Therefore, Marianne's socioeconomic class did not contribute to her understanding of her presenting issues. Instead she struggled to understand or make sense of why she was not loved unconditionally. She did not understand what it was about her that made her unlovable. The psychologist would often offer Marianne an alternative way of viewing her childhood: One of her two parents was not emotionally equipped to raise children in a loving and understanding manner, and her mother's own untreated mental health issues created many difficulties that were compounded by her father's emotional unavailability. This alternate view usually created only short-term solace for Marianne.

As mentioned, Marianne did believe in God and was spiritual. Her belief in something higher than herself helped her in times of great sadness and pain. She desperately wanted to study theology and had to struggle with the acceptance that she needed to finish her veterinarian degree and that studying theology would not give her the love and acceptance from her parents that she so desperately yearned for. Although Marianne did show improvements in her DBT treatment, her deep-rooted psychological issues made it difficult for her to change her behavior and difficult for the psychologist to work with her at times.

Marianne's was a particularly difficult case, as she had many longstanding psychological issues. After 2.5 years of treatment, Marianne reduced some of her symptoms as revealed by scores on pre- and posttests, such as the Beck Depression Inventory (BDI; Beck & Steer, 1993), a questionnaire measuring self-reported levels of depression; the Symptom Checklist 90 (SCL-90), a self-assessment instrument that aims at rating the severity of symptoms on nine dimensions reflecting different types of psychopathology; and the Eating Disorder Examination—12th Edition (EDE–12; Fairburn & Cooper, 1993), which is an investigator-based interview aimed at gathering information about the client's eating-disordered behavior and frequency. Marianne's score on the BDI changed from severe to moderate; her scores on the SCL-90 decreased on the dimensions of Depression, Anxiety, Hostility, and Psychoticism; and her scores on the EDE–12 subscales of Eating Concern, Shape Concern, and Weight Concern decreased. Her body mass index was 25, indicating that she is less at risk for type 2 diabetes and other health issues that are associated with being overweight. In addition, her weekly goal worksheets also showed reduced symptoms. She decreased her self-harming behavior, though she occasionally slaps herself, and she no longer uses cocaine. She is attending school on a regular basis and has improved her emotion-regulation skills, allowing her to better handle feelings of sadness, shame, or anger. She is working to create a positive social network and will finish school within 6 months.

CONCLUSION

As Denmark is a country with socialized medicine, Marianne continues to have access to the primary physician at the Anorexic Clinic, she still has a caseworker, and she continues to receive financial support from the government. Even though she finished her DBT treatment, at any time that the primary physician deems it necessary, Marianne would be offered more mental health treatment to help her at no cost to her. Marianne may need more therapy in the future as her psychological issues are longstanding; however, it was with great joy that the psychologist sent Marianne "out into the world" to live her life using her new skill set, hoping that Marianne could prove to herself that she was capable of creating a life worth living.

As stated before, DBT is a well-documented treatment model for working with people diagnosed with BPD and disordered eating (Chen et al., 2008). DBT is at times a trying approach as it requires the psychologist to continue to monitor the regulation or dysregulation within the client–psychologist relationship, and the psychologist must adhere to the principles of DBT in order for the therapy to be effective. With that said, this psychologist thoroughly enjoyed working with this therapy approach as it not only had positive results for Marianne but also is a compassionate mode of therapy. Although the case of Marianne is not representative of all mental health therapy in Denmark, counseling and psychotherapy here continue to grow and evolve.

QUESTIONS

1. What ways does a country such as Denmark that has implemented socialized medicine help or hinder the mental health of individuals such as Marianne?
2. As part of Marianne's personality disorder, she often idealized her therapist. Would transference and countertransference issues be similar or different had the gender of Marianne's psychologist been male?
3. Would Paul Gilbert's compassion-focused therapy benefit individuals diagnosed with an eating disorder and BPD, as the focus in this mode of treatment is on developing skills to regulate high levels of self-criticism and shame?
4. How might Marianne's gender, race, sexuality, and/or class aid in her potential for coping and resilience in her life despite her past experiences and current diagnoses?
5. Describe the strengths and limitations of the approach(es) used with Marianne in therapy on the basis of her identities and diagnoses.

REFERENCES

Beck, A. T., & Steer, R. A. (1993). *BDI: Beck Depression Inventory.* New York, NY: Psychological Corporation.

Chen, E. Y., Matthews, L., Allen, C., Kuo, J. R., & Linehan, M. (2008). Dialectical behavior therapy for clients with binge-eating or bulimia nervosa and borderline personality disorder. *International Journal of Eating Disorders, 41,* 505–512.

Dixon, A. L., & Hansen, N. H. (2010). Fortid, nutid, fremtid (Past, present, future): Professional counseling in Denmark. *Journal of Counseling & Development, 88,* 38–42.

Fairburn, C. G., & Cooper, Z. (1993). The Eating Disorder Examination (12th ed.). In C. G. Fairburn & G. T Wilson (eds.), *Binge eating: Nature, assessment, and treatment* (pp. 317–360). New York, NY: Guilford Press.

Hansen, N. H., & Dixon, A. L. (2013). Counseling and psychotherapy in Denmark: Counseling the "happiest people on Earth." In R. Moodley, U. Gielen, & R. Wu (Eds.), *Handbook of counseling and psychotherapy in an international context* (pp. 271–281). New York, NY: Routledge.

Linehan, M., Comtois, K. A., Murray, A. M., Brown, M. Z., Gallop, R. J., Heard, H. L., ... Lindenboim, N. (2006). Two-year randomized controlled trial and follow-up of dialectical behavior therapy vs. therapy for experts for suicidal behaviors and borderline personality disorder. *Archives of General Psychiatry, 63,* 757–766.

Lundberg, I. (2001). Zeitgeist, Ortgeaist, and personalities in the development of Scandinavian psychology. *International Journal of Counseling Psychology, 36*, 356–362.

Miller, A. L., Wyman, S. E., Huppert, J. D., Glassman, S., & Rathus, J. H. (2000). Analysis of behavioral skills utilized by suicidal adolescents receiving dialectical behavior therapy. *Cognitive and Behavioral Practice, 7*, 183–187.

Rathus, J. H., & Miller A. L. (2002). Dialectical behavior therapy adapted for suicidal adolescents. *Suicide and Life-Threatening Behavior, 32*, 146–157.

World Health Organization. (1992). *International classification of diseases* (10th ed.). Geneva, Switzerland: Author.

World Health Organization. (2009). *Psykiske lidelser og adfærdsmæssige forstyrrelser. Klassifikation og diagnostiske kriterier* [Mental disorders and behavioral disorders. Classification and diagnostic criteria]. København, Denmark: Munksgaard.

Chapter 23

COUNSELING AND PSYCHOTHERAPY IN FRANCE: ALICE'S STORY

Jacques Pouyaud and Nicole Baudouin

INTRODUCTION

Traditionally, a distinction is made in France between psychotherapy and counseling. This distinction is mainly based on a marked difference between caring professions and counseling and guidance occupations (e.g., career counseling). The historical roots of these two fields of practice and research explain this distinction. Career counseling emerged in the beginning of the 20th century from educational and economical issues, whereas psychotherapy has found its legitimacy within the field of medicine. Nowadays counseling is rarely considered psychological practice, and the general field of psychology is mainly associated with the notion of disease. Therefore, in France, there are no professionals who are both therapist and advisor. However, these two professions share similar theoretical foundations. In France, psychotherapy is influenced by psychoanalytic, cognitive, and behavioral approaches as well as Rogers's (1942) work. These latest humanist approaches also have a dominant position in many consulting practices as well as in the field of differential psychology and psychotechnical methods (see, for discussion, Cohen-Scali, Pouyaud, Baudouin, & Vignoli, 2013).

The way mental health is managed is essential to understanding the professional issues of consultants/counselors and the practices they implement. Medical care is a line that counselors and therapists would never cross, as if normality and pathology fell under two different states and not under a continuum. However, in many cases, it is important to understand individuals and their specific issues in a comprehensive and holistic way.

The Group of Seven identities model certainly enables us to think about a more comprehensive approach and way to consider the client. However, the seven identities may not be equally relevant across the country's specific cultures and contexts. In France, for instance, the concept of race or ethnic origin is not part of the way in which a therapist thinks about the client. In a similar manner, religious or sexual orientation issues are never addressed directly with the client, unless he or she refers to them during the discussions.

How can the therapist ensure in practice that he or she is addressing issues relating to career or family counseling? How can the career counselor be careful enough in his or her guidance to the dimension of care?

The practice of counseling presented in this chapter refers to clinical psychology and uses concepts from the humanistic (Rogers, 1942) and the psychoanalytic (Winnicott, 1971) approaches. This case focuses on a young woman, Alice, who was in a state of depression. The institutional context here was not in a clinical care center but a center for school and career guidance and counseling. Her case reveals how career counseling may have therapeutic effects that had not been initially anticipated.

Our client, Alice, booked an appointment with a career guidance counselor to consider her future career direction after she had completed her studies but before she had undertaken any professional activity. It was essential for the counselor first to clarify the client's interests and assess her level of motivation and engagement to explore the solutions to her problem, even if the request could be interpreted as a problem that might require therapy.

THE CLIENT

Alice is a 25-year-old French woman living in Paris; she comes from a privileged social background. We do not know anything about her sexual orientation or religion, which in theory, are not questions asked in France. During the interview, these components may be addressed to the extent that they have an impact on the academic and vocational interests considered by the client. Alice had always excelled academically, graduating from a renowned high school and successfully obtaining her bachelor's degree in philosophy at the university. Since graduating 2 years earlier, Alice had been unemployed except for occasional work as a babysitter.

PRESENTING ISSUES AND CHALLENGES

Alice came to the career counseling center and met with a school and career counselor who works with young adults. Alice voiced her concern about the future and wanted to collect information about occupations and training programs. This was not an unusual request, but the way in which Alice expressed her needs clearly indicated that she struggled with depression. In French society, the education and vocational field is explicitly separated from the caring professions. Career counselors are not seen as professionals who can conduct psychotherapy or handle psychological care problems. In cases such as Alice's, the counselor often tries to take into account the first request in order to refer the client to a psychotherapist if necessary.

CASE HISTORY AND DEVELOPMENTAL BACKGROUND

Alice came from a wealthy family. She lived alone in a small apartment that her grandparents owned, and her parents lived nearby in the same district. They gave her enough monthly allowance to meet her daily needs. Although neither her parents nor grandparents expected her to provide any monetary contributions, Alice still occasionally worked as a babysitter out of pleasure rather than financial necessity. Despite being 25 years old, Alice was completely dependent on her family, just as a teenager would be. Her parents and grandparents did not force her to find a job. It seemed they were not ready to initiate the necessary separation that would help her become an adult. She did not express any conflicts with them. Nothing was expected from her. Therefore, she felt abandoned and neglected by her family.

THE THERAPY

We chose to begin by concentrating on her primary demand (the explicit one) regarding employment. If Alice were eventually to consider more profound issues, we had to first focus on what her initial needs were. This approach resembled an archaeological excavation, gradually removing the surface layers in order to reach the deeper ones. If Alice were to engage in real therapy, the most important condition was to avoid the brutality of invading her space; our goal was to analyze and interpret her story with her consent. The real challenge was to progressively guide Alice onto a new path, starting with her career concerns and then helping her overcome the lethargy in which she seemed to be immersed. It was only after this challenge was met that we could refer her to a health center.

Alice attempted to hide her depression, but her disclosure betrayed her feelings of sadness and discouragement. She described her situation as "frozen." What were the reasons that led her to meet a career counselor? Was she tired of being in this discouraged idleness? What could the counselor do to help her? A therapeutic treatment at the career counseling center was impossible as counselors in France are not licensed therapists. The framework in which counselors work is incompatible with providing therapy. Moreover, Alice's request pertained to career counseling, not mental health problems. Alice had the tendency to hide her discouragement with anger. The counselor's work, therefore, consisted of offering to help Alice with her career direction (as Alice requested) while taking care of her psychological state and helping her to put into words what prevented her from undertaking a training program or pursuing an occupation. This process meant lifting the barriers that prevented her from acting.

There were several options to help Alice with her vocational issues. Behind her request for career guidance, we suspected some depressive symptoms. As the counseling interviews went along, this situation became more complicated than simple career guidance. Alice's anxiety about the future resembled some existentialist preoccupation. Indeed, the initial request referred to something that was never expressed in the beginning of the interview. In addition, the real demand is not always the first one. Alice had no outlets other than asking for career advice in order to find someone who would listen to her lack of recognition, her hesitations, and her embarrassments.

The counselor could use two main methodologies: One way involves using adapted tests. Some practitioners may focus on making a clear diagnostic examination in order to offer advice. This perspective emphasizes the expert role of the counselor, who knows and thinks in place of the client. Other practitioners may choose to "listen" to the client. This is a more holistic approach: By listening to how the individual is adjusting in his or her own dynamic manner, practitioners attempt to discover how the individual is positioned in the context and in the situation. At the same time that the counselor is listening to this singularity, both client and counselor are coconstructing solutions in order to solve the client's problems. The counselor must actively listen instead of asking questions; the most important concept to remember is what the client has to say and how it is said, *not* the counselor's own framework. In Alice's case, the career counselor opted for the second approach. It was important to accompany her on her explorative journey and not act as an expert, especially given that Alice in fact knew what career she would like to choose. Her problem was not in finding a career but in starting it and making it happen within the context of her familial situation.

In the interview with the counselor, Alice expressed a strong interest in juvenile literature, which she knew quite well. She read extensively during her babysitting hours. Could this interest have stemmed from the long hours she spent reading during her childhood? The publishing sector appeared as a potential profession that she could explore. Because she was not completely confident in her decision, she planned on looking into internships to explore this possibility. Nevertheless, Alice continued to express negative statements that indicated a lack of confidence in her own self to reach this goal. She believed she had no chance of finding an internship because she was no longer a student, was too old, and had no particular skills in the publishing sector. Her discouraging attitude showed that she had not truly convinced herself to commit to this path.

These self-defeating reasons prevented her from active engagement and trapped her in a hopeless situation. All the career suggestions appeared difficult in light of her discouragement and negativism. Alice would display this symptomatic behavior during the entire duration of these interviews. What was hiding behind the seemingly rational discourse between the counselor and Alice? What was she trying to avoid? Did she really want to change her situation? She said she wanted to, but at the same time she always pronounced that nothing could change. We sought to test her desire to change with the help of a professional. Someone needed to stand in front of her, someone who could confront her with reality and whom she could not resist; she needed someone who could take on the role that her parents never played. Hidden behind her vocational demand, Alice was seeking something else, but what was it?

The interviews did not succeed in broadening her career choices. It quickly became obvious that what she wanted was to tell us precisely what she did not want or could not do. She could not escape the material comfort that her family provided. She listed out the various career paths that she could plausibly adopt immediately. However, she would eventually reject all these paths in a triumphant tone that nevertheless resembled defeat. It was a manner of expressing her revolt and her despair.

Several months later, out of this "nothing," something did indeed emerge. Alice needed to be lying fallow for a while in order to be able to imagine a professional project. Lying fallow here meant being in a transitory state where time seemed to stand still and where nothing seemed to occur. In farming, to let a land remain fallow meant letting it rest so as to preserve or promote its fertility.

For Alice, this time of seeming idleness turned out to be a time of maturation (she had not engaged in any activity for 2 years and would not do anything for another 3 months). While appearing to be empty on the surface, this fallow time actually revealed itself to be as rich as the harbinger of a new potential future. After 3 months of silence, she e-mailed the counseling service, telling them of an internship that she found and liked a lot. She was committing herself to a librarian training program. Alice thanked us for the help and support she had found through the counseling interviews.

The counselor's position, which consisted of letting Alice take time to express this "nothing," allowed her in some degree to reconcile with herself and the social reality. She was emerging from her feeling of loneliness. Maybe she succeeded a bit in pushing away the depressive feelings she had probably experienced for a long time.

DISCUSSION AND ANALYSIS

At the risk of destroying Alice's career and development, the counselor opted to listen and support her on the path that she wanted to take. From a certain point of view, this process involved resisting Alice's attacks, being patient, and helping her engage in a constructive process. The counselor allowed her to express her difficulties and develop a plan rooted in her history—a plan that made sense in her eyes. For the counselor, it was more important to create a counseling situation that would allow Alice to find her own answers. In counseling or in psychotherapy, "It is the patient and only the patient who has the answers" (Winnicott, 1971, pp. 87–88).

Then, it was important to wait, listen, and allow Alice to bring herself out of the tunnel by allowing her to express her plea for recognition of a woman whom she felt "doesn't make," "doesn't want," and "is not able to." Another way of doing might have been to use an "armed clinic" (Lagache, 1949), which relies on tests, instruments, and manuals to do clinical work. It consists then more of making a "study of a case" rather than being careful of the individual's own dynamism. The psychologist considered the possibility that there was a risk in making hasty decisions. Letting Alice express her distress was important to avoid the damages of a deadlocked counseling situation. "The child who asks is searching for the recognition of himself through others, more than the satisfaction of his needs" (Guyomard, 1992, p. 23).

The few initial interviews that the counselor had with Alice ended without any change of attitude. Alice's situation did not change, except that she had been able to place a bit of suffering (suffering she hardly accepted) in an outside space. She finally left saying, "I want nothing more, I shall make nothing, it is finished!" leaving the counselor with a feeling of failure and wondering, "What will she do?" Wasn't this "nothing" a necessary digression? Did that mean that there was no solution in sight? Some months later, out of this nothing, something was to be born, as if having been in fallow had finally allowed Alice to commit herself to a project. "Lying fallow" is a term borrowed from Masud Khan (1990) in an article to pay tribute to Winnicott.

In Alice's case, what would have been the point to explore consistently the components of identity to guide her? On the one hand, in France, some dimensions of diversity such as race, religion, and sexual orientation remain within the sphere of individual privacy and in theory cannot be subjected to systematic questioning. On the other hand, for Alice, it was clearly essential to create an area of freedom that would allow her to address her own issue. The aim was to encourage her thoughts at her own pace rather than adopting a questioning approach that would have provoked resistance.

CONCLUSION

The counselor had to be patient, giving up the position of an expert. This approach requires that the counselor suppress the urge to find all the answers. Sometimes, the counselor is not able to do more than try to understand the stakes that the client has to deal with and let the client express herself or himself, even if the decisions arrived at are unconvincing. Despite being confronted with this helplessness, the counselor can keep his or her door open and let the client make choices of her or his own will. Finally, the issue is not to give good advice—the counselor here had been given only limited information—but to be a good listener. The counselor must be able to let the client say what is being pent up inside. Once this condition is fulfilled a new path can be created.

In this sense, counseling can have a therapeutic component as long as the psychologist gives up the expert position of the one who knows best and instead adopts a clinician's role. It is obviously important for a counselor to pay attention to the complexity of the person, his or her situation, and diversity issues. In that sense, a multifaceted model of diversity such as the Group of Seven underlines the importance of taking into account the different key determinants at stake in the client's issue, provided that they are used in a flexible manner, that is to say with respect for the individuals and their sociocultural contexts. The counselor will therefore have to avoid any stereotypes and give priority to the client's own questions.

QUESTIONS

1. What links can be made between Alice's difficulty entering the professional world and the fact of being a woman coming from a wealthy social class?
2. How can the social, cultural, and psychological characteristics of Alice be resources? Which ones did she especially mobilize? Which ones could have she exploited more?
3. What questions could have been examined with a behavioral approach that is not reported here?
4. What are the limits and positive points of the practice presented in Alice's case?
5. What do you think of the fact that Alice did not finally find any clear solution? What other attitude could have the counselor taken?

REFERENCES

Cohen-Scali, V., Pouyaud, J., Baudouin, N., & Vignoli, E. (2013). Counseling and psychotherapy in France: An evolving heterogeneous field. In R. Moodley, U. Gielen, & R. Wu (Eds.), *Handbook of counseling and psychotherapy in an international context* (pp. 282–291). New York, NY: Routledge.

Guyomard, P. (1992). *La jouissance du tragique* [The enjoyment of tragedy]. Paris, France: Aubier.

Khan, M. (1990). L'être en jachère [To lie fallow]. *L'Arc, 69*, 52–57.

Lagache, D. (1949). Psychologie clinique et méthode clinique [Clinical psychology and clinical method]. *L'évolution psychiatrique, 2*, 155–174.

Rogers, C. (1942). *Counseling and psychotherapy*. Boston, MA: Houghton-Mifflin.

Winnicott, D. W. (1971). *Playing and reality*. London, England: Tavistock.

Chapter 24

COUNSELING AND PSYCHOTHERAPY IN GERMANY: DAVID'S STORY[1]

Karen Krause and Silvia Schneider

INTRODUCTION

The statutory health insurance system in Germany generally takes over the cost of psychotherapeutic treatments that have been empirically—through scientific studies—proven effective, that is, analytical, psychodynamic psychotherapy, and cognitive behavior therapy (CBT). Basically, treatment is conducted by psychotherapists, child and adolescent psychiatrists, as well as medical psychotherapists, who work in office-based practices or in health care facilities. Psychosocial counseling facilities funded by cities, counties, churches, and charities provide short-term consultation and support in a crisis situation. Child and adolescent psychotherapists in private practice provide overall the largest share of psychotherapeutic care. Clients for whom outpatient and day-care treatment measures are not sufficient are treated in clinics. As the consequences of mental disorders also affect the family as a whole and because family and other caregivers (teachers, educators, etc.) constitute an important role in familial protective and risk factors, therapy sessions with caregivers are usually included in the therapy process (see, for discussion, Warschburger, 2013).

A framework for child and adolescent psychotherapy in Germany is well developed. The German Health Interview and Examination Survey of Children and Adolescents (Holling, Kurth, Rothenberg, Becker, & Schlack, 2008) collected data from a representative sample of German children and adolescents on their symptoms of emotional health and behavior and existing specific diagnoses. On the basis of parents' judgment, a total of 18.5% of the boys and girls were classified as borderline or abnormal regarding their mental problems (Holling et al., 2008).

Every year approximately 300,000 accidents in Germany involve head injuries, and almost half lead to severe and long-lasting damage. More than half of the clients with traumatic brain injury (TBI) are younger than 25 years (Heubrock & Petermann, 2000). In general, neurological clients are transferred from neurological acute care to inpatient extended care in a neurosurgical rehabilitation clinic for interdis-

---

[1]Parts of this case study have already been published in Krause (2011). The publisher has granted permission for the use of the case study in this book.

ciplinary therapeutic treatment. In addition to neuropsychological assessment and therapy, the main treatment component is CBT for stress crises, brain organic mental disorders, and personality changes as well as premorbid existing mental illnesses.

In this chapter, we discuss David's therapy and outcomes. The case illustrates the interdisciplinary diagnostic and therapeutic approach of clinical child neuro-psychology and CBT in a German neurosurgical rehabilitation clinic.

THE CLIENT

David, a 17-year-old Caucasian male, lives at home with his parents and older brother. Both parents work in their medium-sized family craft business. The family has a middle-class background with Christian orientation, although religion seems to have no impact in the family's daily life.

PRESENTING ISSUES AND CHALLENGES

David was diagnosed with a severe TBI. He was aggressive, and his ability to assess his illness was hindered (diagnosis according to the International Classification of Diseases—10th Edition [World Health Organization, 1992] was "F 07.2 Organic brain syndrome after TBI"). In comparison with his reference age group, the client showed below-average performance in all examined areas and generally a below-average cognitive performance level. The client was severely impaired in attention performance. David showed an impulsive cognitive style characterized by volatility and working too fast. In the areas of logical abstract thinking and action planning ability, David's achievements fell far short of age-appropriate needs. His impulse control ability was reduced, and his self-evaluation was negative.

CASE HISTORY AND DEVELOPMENTAL BACKGROUND

David was (as a passenger) involved in a traffic accident with unclear circumstances and was diagnosed with a severe TBI. At the time of admission, he was significantly lethargic, could not use a wheelchair, and was greatly slowed down in his attention span. David had difficulties with orientation, memory, and understanding. He appeared grumpy, aggressive, and uncooperative. His ability to critically assess his illness and his own abilities was hindered. However, David could read, he recognized his parents, and he was oriented in first encounters. His parents described David as being a good student in the ninth grade. He had successfully engaged in completing his vocational school placements (metal crafts, cooking). Family atmosphere was warm and supportive, especially after David's accident.

THE THERAPY

The initial goal of the therapy was to improve David's focus, drive, and attention during individual therapy sessions. David was unable to occupy himself because of his neuropsychological limitations. Through daily, short therapy sessions that were tailored to his very limited attention span, incentives and opportunities were first created to increase his activity level. The consistent structure of therapy aimed to convey a sense of security and trust: David should recognize activities that were "familiar" and "recurring." Gradually, David succeeded in adapting the therapist's positive evaluations of his slowly improving performance and in praising himself for his own success. His motivation improved, and he clearly enjoyed the opportunity to socially interact and communicate. Because of David's improved endurance, his therapeutic goals were then extended. The therapeutic range was expanded by offerings of the clinic school; his cognitive impairment was taken into consideration in the school program.

In Phase 2, David was in a wheelchair and could get involved in age-appropriate activities on the ward. The gradual increase of cognitive load and development of improved impulse control were now in the foreground of therapy. Positive self-reinforcement aimed to further promote David's success motivation and positive self-concept. David's integration into the daily clinic routine along with other clients of the same age proved difficult: Interactions were filled with conflicts. A significantly decreased frustration tolerance and impaired impulse control with aggressive behavior outbursts prevented further therapeutic advances. Therefore, the following interventions were developed: A small-step, resource-oriented approach across all therapies was agreed on. Tangible achievements aimed to mediate a sense of self-efficacy and maintain therapy motivation and to work generally toward building a positive self-image. "Success Book" was introduced first in psychological therapy then across all therapies.

After each treatment session, David's good therapy cooperation was recorded as a success; if David was not motivated, there would be no entry. In the further course of treatment, the parents were also involved in the therapeutic principle of the Success Book. In regular meetings, David's parents were informed about the content, progress, and problems of therapy. Furthermore, they got help for their own problems in interactions with David, especially in stressful situations on weekends at home. In addition to receiving psychoeducation on TBI, parents are integrated in the operant principles of therapy (positive reinforcement, time-out). Success of these methods is reflected and transmitted into various domestic problem areas, such as going to the toilet and dressing independently. In addition, unwanted reinforcement processes of problem behavior are identified, and alternative strategies are discussed with parents.

In regard to David's reduced impulse control, a concept of self-control was carried out. His uncontrollable urge to talk was identified as a behavior problem, and thus stopping the urge to talk was jointly formulated as a target behavior. Quiet work time was measured using a stopwatch and was, in the course of therapy, visualized. In a further step, its use was extended to clinic school and other therapies. Transferring this progress of individual therapy into a group setting was defined as an additional therapeutic goal.

David was integrated into a psychological therapy group (PLOP group) with the goal to promote planning, logical thinking, organizing, and problem solving. In the PLOP group, desired behavior is mediated by the principle of "learning on the model." Compared with individual therapy, a major advantage of group therapy for David was the feedback on an "equal" client level. David integrated well into the group. Group integration led to new objectives: In order for David to be punctual at the PLOP group, he needed to be time-efficient in his morning routine. Also, during the morning care routine David interrupted the individual courses of action. In therapy, an action plan with different morning bathroom activities was developed to provide David orientation, drive, and motivation support. The familiar stopwatch method provided feedback on the time spent. Thus, in further course of therapy, the target behavior of "getting ready independently in the morning" was built up gradually. Assistance by the caregiver was gradually decreased (shaping), and goal achievement ("be on time for therapy") was rewarded by positive reinforcement from the caregiver.

By the time of his discharge, David had made good progress with these steps toward target behavior. The reached steps and necessary interventions for transfer to the home environment were discussed with the parents. After 40 weeks of inpatient treatment, David was discharged home. He will have to live with his parents and attend a special school for the disabled.

In therapy the client's attention span and general resilience significantly improved. David is able to work up to 60 minutes on simple cognitive tasks. He is still not able to consistently provide positive self-assessment of individual success. To manage complex tasks, David needs encouragement and verbal support. Impulse control is still affected, but at the time of discharge David was able to suspend his needs and change the perspective in a group setting; in addition, he showed mostly socially appropriate behavior.

DISCUSSION AND ANALYSIS

In a phone follow-up assessment half a year after discharge, both the client's father and David, himself, continued to report individual progress: David successfully attends a school for the physically handicapped and has integrated well into the classroom community; he is self-sufficient in the morning and is still very motivated in outpatient therapies. He has good social contacts, which he attends to by himself. However, outpatient psychological therapy still provides important support, even 2 years after the accident. Meta-analyses and long-term studies show that after even mild TBI, long-lasting neuropsychological impairments are common, and the impact of cognitive deficits extends into adulthood (Ritz, 1993). A TBI is not only a unique critical event but is also an important factor influencing the child's brain development as well as psychomental development as a whole; it requires intensive neuropsychological and psychotherapeutic treatment (Benz & Ritz, 1996).

A small-step, resource-oriented therapeutic approach in an interdisciplinary team was required to successfully improve David's basic cognitive limitations and their impact on his daily competencies. The early start of the intensive therapy after the accident, the inpatient setting, and the age of the client provided the needed framework: In close consultation and neuropsychological coordination, various professional groups jointly developed and pursued common therapeutic goals, and they discussed achievement and adjustment of therapy in regular case conferences, while working with high-frequency, short sessions with the client.

The highly structured therapy sessions with familiar and recurring elements supported David when he felt insecure and his self-esteem was low. The middle-class familial background with highly motivated and supportive parents and the warm and supportive atmosphere within the family provided valuable backing for David. As the consequences of the severe TBI greatly affected the family as a whole and his family functioned as an important protective factor, sessions with parents were very beneficial for David's positive outcome.

Operant methods could be developed in the therapeutic setting and then successfully transferred to everyday problems in the family. The parents also supported David in engaging in inpatient therapy. The family experienced their close-knit involvement, psychoeducation, and supportive crisis sessions as necessary and helpful. The work within the group therapy was also an important aspect in David's therapeutic success. Model learning, operant methods, and feedback on the client level helped David to improve his ability to assess his illness and the changes in his abilities. For David and his parents, counseling and psychotherapy support were vital factors in counterbalancing the profound, multifaceted, and long-lasting consequences (e.g., handicap, change in school and further work life) of his accident.

CONCLUSION

David's case illustrates the importance of basal operant methods for the therapeutic approach at the interface between clinical child neuropsychology and CBT in early neurosurgical rehabilitation. Operant principles, such as positive reinforcement, time out, model learning, response cost methods, prompting, shaping, and so forth, are sufficient and successful in early neuropsychological therapy. Such principles have been used to establish advances in the therapeutic setting and then successfully transferred to everyday problems in the family. The counselor's role was to coordinate and monitor the transfer of operant methods into the daily routine during inpatient care and in family life. The following example illustrates how basal operant methods were incorporated into counseling. David wandered repeatedly into conversations or would engage in a monologue in therapy and everyday situations as well during school tasks. Therefore, stopping the urge to talk was jointly formulated as target behavior. Lengthening the periods of silence was formulated as a positive goal. Quiet work time was measured using a stopwatch and in the course of therapy was visualized with a system of coordinates that was comprehensible for David. Quiet work time was included in the self-observation protocol and Success Book. Ultimately David controlled the stopwatch himself, and in a further step its use was extended to two other therapy situations (occupational therapy and clinic school). In the further course of treatment, the duration of quiet work time was extended up to 25 minutes.

Inclusion of the family, especially the parents as primary caregivers, is essential at this stage to secure therapeutic outcomes for the clients and to transfer those outcomes permanently to everyday family life. In addition to the supportive conversations needed by parents in order to deal with irretrievable losses after injury, psychoeducation and parents' involvement as cotherapists are central building blocks of successful therapy. The long-term course and telephone anamneses showed the serious long-term consequences of TBI; children and adolescents with TBI require permanent therapeutic support to achieve best possible daily competencies and to regain as far as possible their pretraumatic development potential. Intensive inpatient therapy and subsequent outpatient care are essential. Affected parents and families need competent support over a subsequent period of time to compensate for the profound, multifaceted, and long-lasting consequences of the injury. The corresponding health care structures need to be further expanded in Germany.

QUESTIONS

1. How does the age of the patient influence the central problems of his diagnosis at the beginning of therapy (severe TBI with circumscribed brain contusions bifrontal)?
2. Which factors of the diversity matrix (gender, race, sexuality, class, disability, etc.) influence the patient's psychopathology after the TBI?
3. How does the diversity matrix (gender, race, sexuality, class, disability, etc.) influence the therapy outcome of the patient after the TBI?
4. Why is the CBT approach in this case appropriate and effective? How does the psychopathology of the patient limit the use of other treatment approaches?
5. How could the therapy process described above be improved? Which aspects could have been regarded more carefully to improve the therapy outcome?
6. How does the counselor's role in coordinating with other medical professionals affect treatment and treatment outcome?

REFERENCES

Benz, B., & Ritz, A. (1996). Verlauf neuropsychologischer Störungen nach Schädel-Hirn-Trauma im Kindesalter [Course of neuropsychological disorders after traumatic brain injury in childhood]. *Kindheit und Entwicklung, 5*, 201–208.

Heubrock, D., & Petermann, F. (2000). *Lehrbuch der Klinischen Kinderneuropsychologie* [Textbook of clinical child neuropsychology]. Göttingen, Germany: Hogrefe.

Holling, H., Kurth, B.-M., Rothenberg, A., Becker, A., & Schlack, R. (2008). Assessing psychopathological problems of children and adolescents from 3 to 17 years in a nationwide representative sample: Results of the German Health Interview and Examination Survey for Children and Adolescents (KiGGS) [Supplement 1]. *European Child & Adolescent Psychiatry, 17*, 34–41.

Krause, K. (2011). Klinische Kinderneuropsychologie—Einblick und Fallbericht [Clinical child neuropsychology—Insight and case study]. *Verhaltenstherapie mit Kindern & Jugendlichen–Zeitschrift für psychosoziale Praxis, 7*, 97–106.

Ritz, A. (1993). Neurologische Rehabilitation von Kindern und Jugendlichen nach sekundär erworbenen Hirnschädigungen. In K. R. H. von Wild (Ed.), *Spektrum der Neurorehabilitation* (pp. 208–217). Munich, Germany: Zuckschwerdt.

Warschburger, P. (2013). Counseling and psychotherapy in Germany: Common past but different present. In R. Moodley, U. Gielen, & R. Wu (Eds.), *Handbook of counseling and psychotherapy in an international context* (pp. 292–309). New York, NY: Routledge.

World Health Organization. (1992). *International classification of diseases* (10th ed.). Geneva, Switzerland: Author.

Chapter 25

COUNSELING AND PSYCHOTHERAPY IN ITALY: MIRIAM'S STORY

Thierry Bonfanti

INTRODUCTION

Although there is much counseling training taking place in Italy, there are very few counselors actually working. Counseling is not a regulated activity, and its legitimacy is contested by some psychologists who accuse counselors of the illegal practice of psychology. Counseling training programs are extremely varied, with the person-centered approach, psychosynthesis, Gestalt therapy, neurolinguistic programming, and transactional analysis being the most popular ones. However, counseling in Italy is mostly practiced by psychologists or implicitly by other professionals, such as social workers (for discussion, see Gemignani & Giliberto, 2013).

The theoretical model of counseling and psychotherapy pursued in the following case study is the nondirective intervention (NDI), which was created by Michel Lobrot (1989, 2009). This approach evolved out of person-centered theory, but it is different from Carl Rogers's person-centered approach. For Carl Rogers (1980), "Individuals have within themselves vast resources for self-understanding and for altering their self concepts, basic attitudes and self directed behavior" (p. 115). NDI goes farther, emphasizing the importance of the environment in personal growth. That means more interventions, but these interventions are centered on the client's desire in order to influence his or her growth. For NDI, the desire is a driving force with which the counselor has to compromise. The counselor cannot do anything without taking into account this force. Moreover, influence is different than directivity. NDIs are not directive, though they can influence the person. For some people, influence is often associated with power, authority, and pressure, but real influence—the one that changes people—is nondirective. Pressure can superficially and temporarily modify the behavior but is inefficient in rendering personal changes. Rather, it often generates reactance (Brehm, 1966). If personal change is an inner process, then it also needs environmental feedback and inputs. Nonetheless, not every kind of environmental intervention is beneficial for the person. It must agree with the client's dynamism, be based on an understanding of the client, and fit the client's desires. From an NDI perspective, only the client knows what is best for him or her. On the methodological front, this perspective means that the counselor's interventions must be directed toward the client's desires or at least take them into account. Possible interventions include questioning, hypothesizing, rephrasing, and proposing.

This chapter discusses the therapy of Miriam. The diversity issues explored in this chapter have to do with gender and religion. Being Catholic and female in an Italian environment was significant and exerted a profound influence on Miriam. Within this cultural context, the role of being a woman relates above all to one's husband, family, and children. Miriam was not a practicing Catholic, but Catholic culture permeates Italian society even in an anticlerical environment.

THE CLIENT

Miriam is a 37-year-old Catholic Italian woman from a middle-class background. She is heterosexual and does not have any disability. Miriam has two children, 8-year-old Paolo and 3-year-old Silvano. She lost her father when she was 1 year old, and her younger brother, who was 1 year her junior, passed away when she was 29 years old. She used to work as a cataloger.

PRESENTING ISSUES AND CHALLENGES

Miriam's presenting issues had to do with anger and anxiety. Miriam complained of her aggressive reactions toward her children. She had no activity outside of the caretaking role. She admitted feeling oppressed by her children and feeling inadequate, and she complained of panic attacks. One day as she was driving to work, she started to feel very afraid and had to turn back home. She admitted being afraid of men—feeling inhibited and shy around them. She talked about her sexuality. Overall she reported a lack of experiences and positive drives in her life.

CASE HISTORY AND DEVELOPMENTAL BACKGROUND

Before her marriage, Miriam grew up in a mostly all-female environment. She never developed a close relationship with her brother. When they were young, she refused to play with him because he was always crying, and so Miriam played alone. She said she was "pissed off" with him. Her mother was reserved and spent most of her time with her brother and her job as a cook. Miriam always felt alone. She used to be left with her grandmother. She was upset that her mother did not take care of her or stimulate her. She bore a grudge against her mother for not remarrying, as she would have liked to have had a father.

There was nobody in her childhood. She did not go out because she never felt at ease with anybody. She was afraid to be rejected by others. She used to live in her own inner world and passed the time by reading. Her best childhood memory was a solitary one about reading on the balcony. She said she still lived in that inner world, and she described herself as a very sad child. She wanted her children to have a completely different childhood.

Miriam grew up in a Catholic environment that extolled chastity. As a teenager, she felt disgusted by men's lust for her. She was often courted, and as a result, she felt the need to protect herself. She wondered whether she was interesting apart from her physique. In the catechesis class she learned that the perfect child attended mass and was helpful, studious, and virtuous. She remembered viewing lust as a deadly sin, and this image deeply affected her.

She did not have a great desire to become a mother, but when she got married, she thought she needed to build the ideal life in accordance with her Catholic cultural upbringing. Having children was part of that ideal life.

Three years after Miriam got married, she gave birth to Paolo, who was born with craniostenosis. He underwent surgery, and Miriam feared that others would think he was retarded. She expected her son to prove that he was not.

Breastfeeding was painful, and she developed rashes on her nipples. Although her mother and husband implored her to stop, she was stubborn and continued breastfeeding. It matched her personality, but she was unable to say why. She still felt inadequate as a mother. Her Catholic education taught her that sacrifice was praiseworthy and it should be model behavior to be followed at home. She tried to give her children what she had never received as a child, especially in terms of help and care. However, her desires clashed with her children's wants, particularly in regard to school, and she got angry at her children when things did not work out as she wanted. Paolo and Silvano's father did not help her take care of them, so much of her time was divided between her children and her job. She liked that her son Paolo was sociable. She valued sociability and relationships, although she felt better staying at home.

THE THERAPY

Before coming to therapy, Miriam had been in counseling with an educational counselor. She had been given a book by Thomas Gordon but had trouble applying his theory into practice. She felt she would not be herself if she followed Gordon's prescription. Moreover, she did not believe she would succeed anyway. She had an authoritarian personality, but paradoxically she was attracted by a nondirective approach in education.

In the beginning of counseling, sessions were mainly focused on educational matters. Miriam often talked about rules in education. In this context, we talked about functional and self-protective rules for the parent in order to help her clarify her motivations to be so authoritarian. However, treatment was more focused on Miriam as a person than on educational matters. These interventions were part of a strategy geared to spur Miriam to find her own interests in order to live her own life.

Although she felt she always had difficulty talking about herself and was afraid she would be unable to talk about certain things, she was able to talk to me about her life without much hesitation. She progressively focused on herself. She admitted being too absorbed with her children rather than making time for herself or any hobbies.

Moving from educational matters to her relationship with her children, she admitted having little freedom. I tried to explore with her what dreams or desires she might have for her future. She seemed to have no idea what her life could be like outside her children. Rearing her children was her priority because she had no other wishes. Yet, this was her greatest challenge, which caused her to be angry and aggressive with them.

As she loved reading, I recommended some books to enrich her imagination. She read *On Personal Power* by Carl Rogers (1977) and appreciated the concepts of acceptance, empathy, and congruence.

During the counseling process, she also realized she had difficulties not only with her children but also with her husband. She explained that she and her husband were not in love anymore. After the second session and just before heading out of her house, she told her husband she was consulting a counselor. She made fun of the fact that she had not told him everything. In addition, she realized she could do a lot of things without telling her husband; this fact seemed to give her much pleasure.

In the last several sessions I used some focusing exercises so that Miriam could begin to imagine things, events, places, and possibilities for herself. Our final sessions centered on these exercises. My hypothesis was that if she had personal gratifications, she would be more serene with her children.

Miriam ended the counseling having gained a better relationship with her children. She learned to listen to her children and to have a constructive dialogue with them. She said she loved her children, and she felt serene toward them. Her relationship with them has become more conducive for her well-being and for their development. Although she has decided to stay with her husband for the children's sake, she feels more content that she can also live her own life and has more power over the decisions she can take regarding her future. She found a *modus vivendi* in her relationship with her husband. This is the compromise she could reach taking into account her need for security and the Catholic influence on her.

DISCUSSION AND ANALYSIS

The result of the counseling was Miriam's awareness about the relationship between her aggressiveness toward her children and her unhappiness with her husband. Coming to the sessions improved her relationship with the children, as she implemented some of the strategies that we talked about. Talking about herself and her lack of freedom made her feel better disposed toward them. However, in the beginning, the effect faded quickly. Realizing that she had problems with her husband was a case of questioning her choices, her life. She was not assertive enough with him.

Miriam had difficulty developing relationships with men because of her lack of experience growing up. Her current situation contrasted with her upbringing when she was a child. Raised in a predominantly female environment, she was now surrounded by her two sons and husband. Her struggle to get closer with men was aggravated by her Catholic background. She felt frightened, especially because she was being constantly "courted because of her beauty." Miriam's difficulties are a question of gender diversity. The lack of knowledge of the other sex or gender culture is one of the reasons why many marriages fail, as Zola (1893) maintained back in the 19th century.

Being a woman in an Italian and Catholic environment made Miriam feel that she was unable to discuss some aspects of her life, given the gender roles in this particular culture. Her husband took no responsibility for the caretaking of the children, and she had to put up with this. In Italy, the cultural conditioning through religion and masculinity makes it possible for men to earn more money than women; women's roles are often defined as being housewives, mothers, and cultural keepers. Even if women work, they are expected to come home and cook dinner, take care of their children, and do many other home chores. This economic dependency made Miriam feel oppressed and stuck.

Moreover, her loneliness was linked to the lack of stimulation she experienced as a child. Her parents did not allow her to develop any interests and ambitions, which—in addition to her issues with men—was the source of her fixation on her children. Her lack of motivation explained her insecurity and the reluctance to change her life even though she no longer loved her husband. He offered her security and financial support. To separate from her husband meant having to deal with the tough consequences from a material and moral standpoint. In Italy, as in many other countries around the world, men have the economic power such that separation forces women to lose their financial stability. In addition, divorce is morally condemned in a predominantly Catholic country such as Italy; in fact, divorce has only been legal in Italy since 1970. The divorce rate is one of the lowest in Europe.

Religion influenced Miriam's personality also by leading her to sacrifice her life for her children. It was difficult for her to even question this sacrifice; her personal growth would have required her to change attitudes. She was aware of her frustrations, but she felt that sacrificing herself was her duty. She considered it a part of her personality. In particular, she would never have separated from her husband, because she thought staying married was for the children's good. The holy family is a model for many Italians. One can see the power of religion and the church over the lives of many women in Italian culture.

But sacrifice for children is also a phenomenon linked to female gender role in a masculine culture even if many speak of "maternal instinct." This position has been criticized by Elisabeth Badinter (1980), who affirmed that love for children has not been a constant throughout history.

The combination of religious and gender influences seemed to have strengthened Miriam's sense of duty. There is no doubt that being a woman in a very Catholic country such as Italy is different from being a woman in England, for instance.

Another hypothesis was that she was afraid of people and that positive relationships might have helped her. In the beginning of counseling, Miriam said she needed a clever and nonjudgmental person to whom she could disclose her feelings. In reality, by expressing her feelings to me, she started learning to communicate and be less afraid of disclosing her inner feelings about her children, husband, and her environment. Through this process she was experiencing something that was positive for her.

It was interesting to see how a supportive relationship with a counselor could be a new experience for a client. In Miriam's case, the opportunity to experience a positive relationship with the therapist in a nonjudgmental way made her feel understood and accepted. The experience of challenging the frameworks of the historical, cultural, and religious conditioning have represented an important step in Miriam's emotional evolution and in the development in her womanhood. This process seems to demonstrate Carl Rogers's (1967) words, "The therapeutic relationship is only a special instance of interpersonal relationships in general" (p. 39).

CONCLUSION

In Italy, people seldom consult a counselor when they have a problem. They prefer to see a psychologist, even if in the end the methodology does not differ very much. This situation is probably linked to the lack of regulation of counseling. Thus, the counseling profession is not well known. Many counselors tend to refer the client to a psychologist as soon as the case seems a little bit serious, even though counselors in Italy are often very competent and the frontier between counseling and psychotherapy is not always very clear. Nonetheless, counselors' legitimacy is constantly undermined by the guild of psychologists, who consider counseling practice as illegal practice of psychotherapy. In this country, corporatism has a long history, beginning in the Middle Ages, and is an anthropological fact.

Counselors are mainly trained by psychologists. The training is organized by various schools generally accredited by counseling associations. However, the practice of counseling is free; that is, it is not restricted, controlled, or limited. On January 14, 2013, a law was passed on the nonregulated intellectual professions (*Gazzetta Ufficiale*, 2013). Counseling can be considered an intellectual profession, and this law is a step toward that acknowledgment. It stipulates that the professional associations can issue their members with a certificate of quality.

Counselors trained in Italy receive at least 950 hours of training, including 450 hours of a qualifying period and 50 hours of personal training according to European standards of the European Association for Counseling.

NDI originated in France. Michel Lobrot said that it is an educational conception of psychotherapy and a psychotherapeutic conception of education. Hence, counselors and psychotherapists may have the same skills. NDI was introduced in Italy in 1991, but the first training took place in 2007. Since that date, Michel Lobrot, Nicole Habrias, and I have been training counselors in this approach, contributing to a growth in its application. In addition to counseling, NDI is obviously the methodological background of psychotherapy but also of many social practices, such as mediation, debate leading, training, and coaching as well as new practices at an experimental level, such as language teaching, conference organization, and art exhibition openings. NDI is a multicultural approach for two reasons: first, because it is an empathic and nonanalytical approach and, second, because counselor interventions match the client desires.

In 1994, 1995, 1997, and 2007, Michel Lobrot, Nicole Habrias, and I organized the annual international meeting of NDI in Italy. The International Federation of NDI was born in Italy as the preparatory works were held in Trento in 2011 and 2012. Many Italians also participated in the annual international meetings of NDI in France between 1998 and 2006. Italy and Greece are the two European countries in which NDI has had even greater success. In addition, it is represented in many other countries, such as Mexico, Argentina, and Canada.

QUESTIONS

1. How does the client's Catholic background affect her family life?
2. What kinds of choices might the client have had if she had been a man?
3. How do cultural variables such as religion or gender affect one's freedom to experience—and, consequently, affect one's resilience?
4. What interventions would not have been done in the person-centered approach?
5. What could have been done to help Miriam build herself a new life separate from her husband?

REFERENCES

Badinter, E. (1980). *L'amour en plus* [Love in addition]. Paris, France: Flammarion.

Brehm, J. W. (1966). *A theory of psychological reactance.* New York, NY: Academic Press.

Gazzetta Ufficiale, serie generale, No. 22 del 26/1/2013, about law 14 January 2013.

Gemignani, M., & Giliberto, M. (2013). Counseling and psychotherapy in Italy: Historical, cultural and indigenous perspectives. In R. Moodley, U. Gielen, & R. Wu (Eds.), *Handbook of counseling and psychotherapy in an international context* (pp. 303–314). New York, NY: Routledge.

Lobrot, M. (1989). *L'écoute du désir* [Listening desire]. Paris, France: Retz.

Lobrot, M. (2009). *The non-directive influence.* Retrieved from http://lobrot.ndi.fr/?wiki=the_non-directive_influence

Rogers, C. R. (1967). *On becoming a person.* London, England: Constable.

Rogers, C. R. (1977). *On personal power: Inner strength and its revolutionary impact.* New York, NY: Delacore Press.

Rogers, C. R. (1980). *A way of being.* New York, NY: Houghton Mifflin.

Zola, E. (1893). *Comment on se marie* [How one gets married]. Paris, France: Flammarion.

Chapter 26

COUNSELING AND PSYCHOTHERAPY IN THE NETHERLANDS: TOM'S STORY

Giel Hutschemaekers, Caroline Vossen, Wubbo Scholte,
and Wiede Vissers

INTRODUCTION

In the Netherlands, the practice of psychotherapy is regulated by the law known as BIG (which translates as Professions in Individual Health Care). The law does not regulate different therapies as such, but the professionals who could provide therapy adhere to formally recognized high qualitative standards. The law describes psychotherapy as belonging to the expertise of solely three academic professions: the psychiatrist, the psychotherapist, and the clinical psychologist. These professions conduct psychotherapy according to three different traditions (Hutschemaekers & Oosterhuis, 2004). The oldest tradition is the person-oriented approach. It is called person-oriented because therapy focuses on structural aspects of behavior, or habits, that exist for years. This form of psychotherapy uses the traditional psychodynamic, client-centered, and systemic frames of reference. Therapy in this approach is usually frequent, is of long duration, has fundamental goals, and is mainly used for the treatment of clients with a personality disorder. Examples are dialectical behavioral therapy, schema-focused therapy, mentalization-based treatment, and short-term psychodynamic treatment.

A second more contemporary tradition is the symptom-oriented approach, with cognitive behavior therapy (CBT) as its main therapy. The CBT approach advocates an integration of behavioral therapy and cognitive therapy and is dominant within academic clinical psychology as well as within the community mental health centers that have organized their care according to multidisciplinary evidence-based guidelines. This approach fits into the medical psychiatric paradigm, in which disorders are seen as diseases, as well as the dominant research paradigm (Hutschemaekers & Dijk, 2012).

In recent years a third more pragmatic model has become more dominant: In a small number of sessions, treatment is provided to clients who have less invalidating and more circumscriptive disorders according to the *Diagnostic and Statistical Manual of Mental Disorders* (5th ed.; *DSM–5*; American Psychiatric Association, 2013). In literature this approach is described within the tradition of solution-focused therapy (Shazer, 1994). Within the Dutch context this approach is called *problem-oriented psychotherapy*. It focuses on the explanatory contexts in which the complaints have come about and consists of helping the client create a different interpretation of the onset of the complaints in reaction to changing circumstances, such as events, stress, and life stages. Much attention is paid to strengthening competencies and developing solutions (Rijnders & Heene, 2010).

Although in the literature the differences between these psychotherapeutic traditions have traditionally been stressed, nowadays their common factors also receive attention. This new attention has led to two new frameworks in which existing approaches were rearranged: the integrative approach (Trijsburg, Colijn, Collumbier, & Lietaer, 2005) and the stepped-care model. In the integrative approach the effective components of the different traditions are put together in one integrative framework. Ideally, treatment is tailored to the specific demands of the client and is theoretically and empirically based. The stepped-care approach, however, does not use a tailor-made mixture of different traditions but fully recognizes and maintains the distinction between the different therapeutic approaches. In stepped care, treatment starts with the least intensive and least invasive but still effective intervention (Bower & Gilbody, 2005; Donavan & Marlatt, 1993). Although it is difficult to give an exact definition of least intensive and least invasive, it is generally acknowledged that the amount of treatment time, the amount of care offered by specialized professionals, as well as the goal of treatment and the intensiveness of the interventions used should be taken into account. In this definition the goal of dealing with urgent work-related problems is seen as less invasive than symptom reduction, which in turn is less invasive than attempting to realize structural personality change.

The stepped-care approach fits almost perfectly with the new Dutch mental health care system (reformed in 2014), in which three settings of mental health care are distinguished: the primary care setting, the basic mental health care setting, and the specialized mental health care setting. In the primary care setting, a practice assistant—often a nurse or a social worker—provides problem-oriented psychotherapy (up to five sessions). In the basic mental health care setting, the primary care psychologist offers symptom-oriented psychotherapy (up to 12 sessions). Finally, in specialized mental health care, more structural and person-oriented forms of therapy are offered by the clinical psychologist, the psychotherapist, and the psychiatrist.

In the following case history, we discuss the story of Tom and the stepped-care process. The previously described psychotherapeutic approaches are viewed as different and consecutive steps of care. The starting point is the problem-oriented approach, which is considered the least invasive. The second and third steps are the symptom-oriented approach and the person-oriented approach. These steps are increasingly invasive and intensive, and they are applied when the previous step has insufficient effect. It is shown that each step has its own diagnostic features, a unique way of understanding psychological problems, as well as specific interventions.

THE CLIENT

Tom is an information technology specialist in his 40s. He is divorced; 4 years ago his wife left him for another man. Since that time he has had little contact with his 15-year-old daughter, who lives with her mother and her new partner. Tom is living alone and has few social contacts. He spends a lot of time on the Internet or watching TV.

Presenting Issues and Challenges

Tom had been suffering from mood-related problems for several years. The situation had gotten worse in the months before he presented for treatment. He complained of suffering from depressive mood, lack of energy, inertness, insomnia, anger, and abuse of alcohol. Tom was withdrawing from social activities and was having difficulty functioning at work.

Case History and Developmental Background

Tom was a shy boy who grew up in a small village as a son of a farming family in a strictly religious community. The relationship between Tom and his parents was strongly hierarchical. Tom was often criticized, and independence was not encouraged. Tom's mother had periods of depression during his youth and was often lying in bed when he came home. His father was an alcoholic who was aggressive when he was drunk. Tom took care of his mother while she was depressed and did a lot of household chores. In high school Tom had difficulty finding friends and felt lonely. When Tom started university in a large city, he had difficulty living on his own and maintaining social contacts. At the age of 20 he had his first depressive episode, related to the break-up with his first girlfriend.

The Therapy

Step 1: Problem-Oriented Approach

Because antidepressants prescribed by his general practitioner did not have much effect, Tom was referred to a psychologist in a primary care context. In the first session, Tom started telling about his awful weekend. He had received two tickets for a tennis tournament from his boss and, proud of this, invited his daughter to join him. The daughter agreed, but Toms' ex-wife immediately forbade her to go with him. Tom fell back into depression and agony.

The psychologist intervened by questioning whether his bad weekend could be seen as a reaction to his ex-wife. Tom realized his depressive feelings were reactive to what had happened. Next, the psychologist put forward another hypothesis: It was not a depression that put him down but the "terrible conduct" of his ex-wife preventing him from having a nice weekend with his daughter. Tom agreed that it was not his depression that had to be treated but, rather, his impressionability, that is, the influence of his ex-wife on his current life. The problem definition now became that Tom was "too sensitive for an insensitive ex-wife." The goal of treatment was finding ways to keep more distance from his ex-wife and gaining more autonomy to withstand her psychological attacks. Next the "miracle question" was introduced (What is the first thing you would remark if because of a miracle the problem was entirely solved overnight?). His first reaction was "I am not thinking all the time of her," and his second reaction was "I have room for other people." Then Tom realized that he overcame his first depression by looking for people to talk with. Why not search the Internet for colleagues in this misfortune?

One week later, when Tom came back, the situation had already changed. On the Internet he had found a chat group of "victims" of misfortune in marriage. He got a lot of sympathy and understanding. Also he developed interest in a woman, who was also divorced. The psychologist reinforced Tom's behavior, and after four sessions his complaints apparently had disappeared completely.

STEP 2: SYMPTOMS AND CBT

Six months later, Tom was again seen by the psychologist. Three months after finishing the first treatment, symptoms started to worsen again: Tom had lost his appetite for chatting and had withdrawn from social life completely. He even resigned from work. Psychological tests were done to assess the severity of Tom's symptoms in general, and he was diagnosed as having a moderate unipolar depressive episode in accordance with the *DSM–5*. The assessment showed Tom's preferred coping style to be highly passive and palliative and insufficiently active.

In accordance with the multidisciplinary guideline for depression, CBT was offered. The approved protocol that was used started with the explanation that depressive symptoms were maintained by social withdrawal and inactivity. Therefore, a normal activity level needed to be restored, and also Tom needed to become socially active again. Tom was told that increasing his activity level would be difficult at the onset but would eventually result in renewed experience of pleasure that was currently lacking in his life. The subsequent sessions were used to discuss what activities Tom could undertake in the following week. Furthermore, he was asked to monitor depressive symptoms and the amount of difficulty and pleasure experienced while becoming active. As a result of being more active, Tom's mood enhanced. Subsequently, negative cognitions were targeted in treatment. In the sessions, examples from Tom's daily life were used to help him distinguish situations, thoughts, and feelings. By delving deeper into the thoughts reported by Tom, the psychologist found that Tom had an underlying scheme of feeling worthless, which originated from his youth and adolescence. Tom linked this feeling to the criticism that he had so often received from his stern father. By systematically performing activities designed to change this type of idea about himself, Tom gradually gained more self-confidence, which in turn helped him to improve his social functioning. After 15 sessions, treatment could be successfully terminated.

STEP 3: PERSONALITY AND MENTALIZATION-BASED TREATMENT

However, feelings of depression and powerlessness kept coming up each time something upsetting happened to Tom. Also, his social functioning remained at times problematic. A psychotherapist Tom was referred to described the symptoms as affective unstableness, the pattern of switching between idealization and deprecation in intimate relations, impulsivity, and his chronic feeling of emptiness and weariness. The therapist developed the hypothesis that the symptoms were attributable to a personality disorder. With a clinical interview Tom's attachment history and traumas were reconstructed to investigate whether the relapses of Tom's problems could be understood from the perspective of failures in his mentalization ability during activation of his attachment system. The conclusion was that Tom had learned to take care of his mother and to ignore his own feelings of emptiness and loneliness. Tom had developed a false self as a helping and empathic partner for depressive feelings. He was also traumatized by his father's aggressive drunkenness. As a result, feelings of aggression seemed to be split off by Tom and were expressed in his extreme feelings of devaluation to his ex-wife and others. This explanation could account for the switches between different modes or states and the decrease of Tom's capacity to mentalize about his own and others' feelings and motives.

Given this diagnosis, an intensive group mentalization-based treatment was recommended for 3 full days a week to continue for at least half a year. Mentalization-based treatment assumes that a lack of capabilities to mentalize behavior causes the inability to fully recognize the motives and underlying intentions of behavior. Mentalization, which is learned during early childhood by the encounter of oneself through the eyes of a warm and caring other, creates a distance between the internal world and external reality. If this process is not completed in a healthy way, it may lead to the emergence of a false self that protects the child against abandonment and aggression. Therapy is aimed at restoring a stable feeling of self and at enhancing the capability of mentalization, focusing on the here and now and on affect.

During the first months Tom appeared to be a rather silent, timid client who kept his distance. The therapist confronted him by asking whether he recognized this. Tom first denied it and made a more or less aggressive statement. Another client reacted by remarking, "Last time you made such a statement, it came out that you were angry." Tom agreed by saying he was feeling some irritation, not knowing why. Then the therapist asked at what moment it started. Tom answered, "This morning, at the parking place when I did not see your car. I thought you were having some appointment elsewhere again." The therapist acknowledged this by saying, "You're right, the last weeks, I was absent too often." Then for the first time, Tom was able to articulate his feeling of loneliness and helplessness. This moment was the start of his becoming more a member of the group, which also frightened Tom at first. But gradually, he expressed his feelings of anger and pain more often and could also talk about the trauma of his father's aggression. As a result of this process, Tom's feelings of depression diminished, and he developed a more coherent sense of his self and was more able to reflect on his feelings during periods of stress.

DISCUSSION AND ANALYSIS

In Dutch mental health care, the number of clients with problems like Tom's has increased over the last few years. Psychological help has become much more acceptable, even among men, and general practitioners have become more willing to refer their clients to mental health care; in addition, health insurances are paying for treatment.

In this case story, we showed some of the presenting pictures that could be drawn from Tom and his problems. In the problem-oriented approach, Tom was described as a more or less normal functioning man facing the refusal of his former wife. With a few encouragements from his therapists, he was able to activate more healthy coping mechanisms and to pick up his former life. In the second approach, Tom suffered from a well-described medical condition, a recurrent depression that needed more specialized mental health care. Within the third approach, Tom was not only suffering from depression but was also diagnosed with a comorbid personality disorder. This Tom was far less capable of living a healthy life on his own. In the stepped-care approach, Tom presented with all these pictures, which brings us to our first conclusion: It is probably not the client (the case) but the way he is described (case construction) that provides us with the best illustration of a country and its mental health institutions.

At the same time, we have constructed the case study in a way that entails all three steps. Although figures are absent, it is expected that about half of the clients referred to psychological help in the Netherlands are treated only within the first step. A smaller second half is probably helped within the second step. Only a minority needs help within the third step. Is it because Tom needed all three steps that the first and second interpretations of Tom's problems were too simple? Not necessarily. We do not know whether the third approach itself would result in a complete cure, but—and this is more important—there is no indication that starting with the third approach would have been more effective in this case or, indeed, in most cases. Because, on the one hand, starting with the most invasive treatment, with no growing into it by less invasive forms of treatment, the risks for dropout may be higher. On the other hand, the more invasive a treatment, the higher the risk of serious side effects, such as growing dependency and loss of autonomy. Moreover, therapists who have knowledge of their clients' comorbid personality disorder are in general less effective in their treatment of anxiety or depressive symptoms (Dreessen & Arntz, 1998). It is not without reason that the stepped-care approach starts with the less invasive approach. Jumping over the first steps is only justifiable when there are clearly defined contraindications.

CONCLUSION

In this chapter, we described the stepped-care approach as a model in which different psychotherapeutic traditions are brought together without putting all evidence-based pieces of the different approaches together in one new meta-approach. The identity of, and probably the evidence for, the original approaches is not lost in the mix. On the contrary, the different approaches may only cohabitate together under the condition of strict distinction. Each step has its own approach, and each approach proposes a unique diagnostic picture of the client, unique working hypotheses on what is going on, as well as unique treatment goals and unique interventions. Finally, stepped care not only implies a strict hierarchy between steps in interventions (from less to more invasive) but it also asks for a strict hierarchy in the way the client and his or her problems are described or are even being understood.

With its stepped-care approach, psychological care in the Netherlands combines traditional unique treatment approaches in a way that is as invasive and expensive as necessary and as short and cheap as possible, with retention of the scientific evidence of the treatments.

QUESTIONS

1. To what degree are Tom's presenting issues influenced by the culture in mental health care in the Netherlands?
2. What are possible limitations of applying solution-focused interventions, CBT, and mentalization-based therapy in a stepped-care approach to cases such as Tom's?
3. Drawing on your own theoretical perspective, what would you consider to be the most urgent priorities for working with Tom, and why?

4. How might the experience of Tom be different if Tom had chosen to visit specialized mental health care first?
5. Please elaborate on the following proposition: The three therapeutic approaches affect resiliency assets and coping challenges differently.

REFERENCES

American Psychiatric Association. (2013). *Diagnostic and statistical manual of mental disorders* (5th ed.). Washington, DC: Author.

Bower, P., & Gilbody, S. (2005). Stepped care in psychological therapies: Access, effectiveness and efficiency. *British Journal of Psychiatry, 186,* 11–17.

Donavan, D., & Marlatt, G. (1993). Recent developments in alcoholism: Behavioral treatment. *Recent Developments in Alcoholism, 1,* 379–411.

Dreessen, L., & Arntz, A. (1998). The impact of personality disorders on treatment outcome of anxiety disorders: Best-evidence synthesis. *Behaviour Research and Therapy, 36,* 483–504.

Hutschemaekers, G., & Dijk, F. V. (2012). Psychotherapy and clinical psychology in the Netherlands: Settlement of five distinctive psy-professions. In R. Moodley, U. Gielen, & R. W. Lin (Eds.), *Handbook of psychotherapy and clinical psychology in an international context* (pp. 315–325)., New York, NY: Routledge.

Hutschemaekers, G., & Oosterhuis, H. (2004). Psychotherapy in the Netherlands after the Second World War. *Medical History, 48,* 429–448.

Rijnders, P., & Heene, E. (Eds.). (2010). *Kortdurende interventies voor de eerste lijn* [Brief interventions for primary care]. Amsterdam, the Netherlands: Boom.

Shazer, S. D. (1994). *Words were originally magic.* New York, NY: Norton.

Trijsburg, R. W., Colijn, S., Collumbier, F., & Lietaer, G. (2005). *Handboek Integratieve Psychotherapie* [A handbook of integrative psychotherapy]. Amsterdam, the Netherlands: De Tijdstroom.

Chapter 27

COUNSELING AND PSYCHOTHERAPY IN SPAIN: ANDRES'S STORY[1]

Carolina Marín-Martín and José M. Prieto

INTRODUCTION

The history of psychotherapy began in the 20th century in Spain under the influence of psychoanalysis in the 1920s, phenomenological psychology and psychiatry in the 1950s, the person-centered approach in the late 1970s, transactional analysis or gestalt therapy in the 1980s, and schools such as neurolinguistic programming or what is known as cognitive and behavioral therapy around the turn of the century (García-Vera, Sanz, & Prieto, 2013). *Counseling psychology* is an expression rarely used and never translated into Spanish. Thus, counseling is not a professional branch of psychology, and in the 21st century it has not yet been integrated into educational standards, at least in a university setting. Indeed, this term is conspicuously absent as a regular course in any syllabus.

Registered psychologists in the professional association—the Spanish Council of Psychologists (known as Colegio)—may gain their expertise via private seminars, workshops, and summer schools as well as supervised practice in the country, in the United States, or in the United Kingdom.

Coaching is another term that does not yet have a Spanish translation, but it can be found as a course in a university campus syllabus. It is the epithet that, in the 2010s, has become popular for use in referring to those applied psychologists who are sympathetic to this kind of know-how in what concerns their qualified action and intervention. Traditionally, it involves sport and organizational psychology and is au courant among some clinical psychologists.

In the case study presented in this chapter, spousal abuse is the underlying problem. This type of abuse is a surreptitious problem rooted for centuries in many societies around the world, and Spain is no exception. Two components are involved: power and violence. Power and control are held by the abuser, and fear, helplessness, intimidation, and humiliation are suffered by the victim. One partner seeks to dominate over the other, and financial control becomes a priority because (a) the family patrimony must be partitioned and (b) the ambition is to gain (or not lose) territory. One spouse takes the initiative to promote and strengthen

---

[1]We would like to thank Carmen M. D., who was the main counselor in this case. (We use the counselor's initials instead of her full name to maintain her anonymity.)

factors that drive success. This is the heart of the matter under scrutiny in the current case study: The wife abruptly initiated the judicial proceeding to legal separation and divorce.

Territorial dominance as understood in ethology is the capacity of individuals to dominate interpersonal interactions (at home, in this case). The territory is a sociogeographical area that an animal consistently defends against members of the same species, and spouses are sometimes natural and legitimate allies; however, spouses can also be antagonists if they do not share priorities or prerogatives in what concerns their breeding and living quarters. Comparative psychologists and animal psychopathologists have performed case studies with mammals and nonmammals in the zoo, in the circus, or in the wild and natural environment to explore individual and group behavior as well as two mated animals' life affairs (Brüne, Brüne-Cohrs, McGrew, & Preuschoff, 2006; Hediger, 1954/1955).

Spousal abuse is examined in the current case study as an example of territorial dominance: A wife and husband may use different game plans to defend their mating and nesting territory, and each may converge or diverge while aging together or when, unforeseen, one decides "so far and not further." It entails a psychobiological viewpoint, especially with respect to female versus male brain functioning, as summarized by Brizendine (2007, 2011), to understand the influence of hormones in mood disorders and anxiety problems when one spouse catches the other by surprise. Finally, transactional analysis terminology is used to articulate observations and findings on dyadic interactions and the treatment process in this case study.

Six Characters in Search of an Author, a well-known play by Luigi Pirandello (1867–1936), contains an appropriate metaphor. Within both the case study family and the fictional family in the play, there are similar characters in conflict— a father, a mother, two sons, and one daughter, all maneuvering and settling accounts throughout phases of confusion (Act 1), separation (Act 2), and divorce (Act 3). The leitmotiv in the plot, which deals with spousal abuse, revolves around the question, Who controls who?

THE CLIENT

The client was Andres, a 45-year-old man married to 50-year-old Amparo. Both are heterosexual, White, Mediterranean, Catholic, highly conservative, and wealthy university graduates in social sciences. They have two sons (16 and 14 years old) and a daughter (11 years old). They have no disabilities or major illnesses recorded in their medical histories. Andres contacted a counselor when he learned of Amparo's decision to seek a divorce, pleading "mistreatment and maltreatment." (She never made a formal accusation, and the little information she added to the psychologist was the allegation of Andres being an absent father, silent and aloof, who paid little heed to comments and suggestions.) He denied the recrimination and was shocked by his wife's handling of this faultfinding because there were no warnings of a tension-building phase. On a deeper level, it involved a direct assault on his self-esteem among relatives and acquaintances. The shame was more bitter than the embarrassment, he said. It was something that discredited him. He did learn to heal in private at home; however, his wife's claims in the divorce proceedings resulted in rumors spreading.

Presenting Issues and Challenges

Andres presented with feelings of total helplessness and depression. The shame was crushing. His concern was survival. The first challenge Andres faced was the argument used by his wife to end their marital life. It was the first time that he was forced to cope with a combat-oriented, face-to-face situation, and he was not used to dealing with sudden grief emotions. Although he might have expected poor affective communication between Amparo and himself, he would never have anticipated such an unforeseen and disgusting rivalry. The second challenge was that Andres not only needed to deal with the normal emotions triggered by a divorce but also with the possibility of losing everything, even being rejected by relatives and others because of Amparo's accusation. Another challenge he had to face was how to reestablish his emotional life without any psychological after-effects of being labeled forever as a batterer in his personal and professional surroundings. His main concern was to prove to his children that the situation had nothing to do with them and the love he felt for them would continue. Both his difficulty in expressing affection at home and perhaps the acrimony he conveyed in delicate moments were the consequence of his traditional gender-role expectations. Feelings of inarticulate guilt emerged at times.

Our main challenge once Andres and Amparo started to live in different apartments was to determine whether there was, in fact, a case of spousal abuse and recurring victimization. The psychologist contacted Amparo, who agreed to at least one monographic session, but she avoided further therapeutic involvement. She was not interested in clarifying certain aspects of their past shared life.

The psychologist performed a clinical assessment of Andres and held two sessions with the three teenagers to analyze the situation. The information gleaned from those assessments, combined with the fact that Amparo never carried out a legal accusation of domestic violence and the elusive information she provided in the first two meetings (she said that yes, there was abuse, but she was very sparing with her words), enabled the psychologist to appraise that it was not a case of intimate partner violence.

Case History and Developmental Background

Andres is the fourth of five brothers; he had one older sister. He grew up in a wealthy Catholic family. Throughout his childhood and into his adulthood, his memory of his parents was one of silence, absent mindedness, and self-importance. He pointed out,

> My father was always absent, even when he was at home, and Mum was ever a hieratical woman, aloof in manners and deadpan. She was only concerned about Catholic traditions like going to the church, household shrines coming and going, and other spiritual activities . . . such as fasting and not playing at all in Lent.

After finishing high school, Andres studied economics and management at a private Catholic university because his grades were not good enough to enroll in a public university. He met Amparo in his second year there while she was in her last year of a degree in psychology. She also had a traditional and Catholic education; thus, it was effortless to agree on many things. In relation to his previous emotional experience, he stated that he never had a real and passionate romantic relationship when he was a teenager. Amparo was the first and only woman of his life.

THE THERAPY

Following a formal clinical assessment, Andres was diagnosed with major depressive disorder and attended one session per week for a span of 18 months. The intervention involved three main goals: identifying his role within the family, establishing new bonds, and establishing a new system of behavior.

1. Identifying his role within the family: Andres attended the first session showing some anxiety symptoms and distress, stating that he felt lost and confused. "My wife is deranged and also needs help," he said. At that time the main goal was to help Andres clarify the role and function he performed within the family. During the therapy, it became clear that he played a passive and reactive role, in contrast to his wife's function within the family, which was more active, being in turmoil in all kind of family matters. The intended aim of treatment was to change his mind-set, helping him forget his portrayal as a rejected father and emerge again as an adult with greater autonomy and camaraderie with his children. A few months later, with an understanding that Amparo was immovable in her decision to file for a divorce, the psychologist informed him that the only suitable way to continue was to accept and move forward with the divorce. Presenting with depressive symptoms, sadness, apathy, and finally helplessness, Andres decided to move into his sister's apartment.

2. Establishing new bonds: Once Andres accepted Amparo's decision, it was necessary to work on establishing new bonds with his children, which he tried to do by devising activities to spend time with them and to enjoy being together. Another approach followed, focusing on the quality of the relationship rather than on the amount of time spent together. During this time frame, the children would refuse to cooperate and spend time with their father, and all kinds of excuses would surface, reaching the critical point when his 14-year-old son went to the police station to denounce him after having an argument. According to Andres, his son did this on his mother's instructions. Andres came to the session downhearted and confused because the children were ostensibly giving him a hard time whenever possible. Some of the children's comments and behaviors led the counselor and Andres to believe that Amparo was slandering him, which may have been a means of empowering herself as a mother. Through therapy Andres was able to understand the conflict with his son and to reestablish the climate of a respectful relationship. It helped him identify the transactions among them before and after the separation. However, after several sessions, Andres's feelings of helplessness and other depressive symptoms increased, prompting the initiation of pharmacological treatment (Prozac). He refused to take sick leave, hoping to get better with the pharmacological treatment combined with therapy. According to transactional analysis terminology, Andres was again a child while living with his sister and a child with his children when they met somewhere else. They were strong, and he was weak. He increased discretionally the monthly stipend for their private use.

3. Establishing a new system of behavior: A year later, Andres began to behave again as an adult and was able to take care of himself. Journal diary entries allowed him to register and pick up on manipulations in his intermittent transactions with each child. His handwriting reflected increased self-confidence and a more positive self-perception. Instructional self-talk, inner speech, and positive thinking coalesced during this phase.

Several sessions were devoted to helping Andres engage in social networking. He started to make new friends and to access and harbor social support with co-equals. He learned to empathize with persons in similar situations. He started to feel self-confident, and a new love (Laura) appeared in his life. They eventually moved in together and were generally welcoming toward Andres's children. Andres and Laura's relationship was characterized by an adult transaction at the outset of their relationship. There were no feelings of guilt, even though their living together goes against Catholic morality. Somehow he was immunized by the therapy.

DISCUSSION AND ANALYSIS

Reliable data surveying attitudes of children toward parents has been traced back to 1894 by Stogdill (1937), but it was in 1985 when Richard A. Gardner launched his hypothesis on the parental alienation syndrome (PAS), which was based on information gathered throughout years of private practice as a psychiatrist with children of divorcing parents. In 1985 Gardner defined the symptoms of the PAS, and the complete definition was entrenched in 2001 and published in the *Academy Forum* as follows:

> The Parental Alienation Syndrome is a disorder that arises primarily in the context of child-custody disputes. Its primary manifestation is the child's campaign of denigration against the parent, a campaign that has no justification. The disorder results from the combination of indoctrinations by the alienating parent and the child's own contributions to the vilification of the alienated parent. (Gardner, 2001, p. 10)

Clinical experience has led to this syndrome being renamed parental alienation complex or awareness or game. The characterizing category (syndrome) is controversial but so too is the label *parental alienation* as used in the court because its diagnosis, course, and treatment are vaguely enigmatic (Warshak, 2001). Because it was not included in the *Diagnostic and Statistical Manual of Mental Disorders* (5th ed.; American Psychiatric Association, 2013), it may be relegated to the level of being only an assumption or theory. Is it a question of empowerment or brainwashing, as Gardner initially asserted? Is it a question of money with sexist connotations? Some aspects of the current case study can be analyzed within ethological and psychobiological frameworks; in addition, some aspects can be analyzed using transactional analysis, which categorizes family responses.

Why did Andres not anticipate Amparo's decision to file for divorce? Considering the traditional Catholic notions of paternal roles, the father's functions are more focused on material needs and making the family feel secure by guaranteeing financial support (i.e., patrimony), and he therefore delegates family issues to the mother. This pattern of family dynamics involves a more passive role of the father within the family and consequently a more active function of the mother.

Within this perspective, Andres was successful in fulfilling his role. Saint Joseph is a father who is not a father. It is the prototype Andres knows.

When viewed from a transactional analysis perspective, Andres behaved as an assertive adult aware of professional matters and quality-of-life standards in the family but bypassing the nurturing parent role. In therapy it was necessary to work with Andres on identifying his role within the family and the need to change it. At first this approach led to a hope to save his family; however, it soon became clear that this was the first step of his grieving process.

Andres was reared in a matriarchal household where the Holy Virgin's (Mother Mary's) image presided over several rooms. She is the reference model used while bringing up children regarding what is right or wrong. Andres described his mother as hieratic, inscrutable, and expressionless in public. He was reared in a coldhearted family atmosphere devoid of any parental model of affective communication.

Andres could not isolate a crucial event, a pivotal concern that marked the turning point in his parents' marital relationship, only some antagonism at the beginning and slamming the door at the end. Likewise, he had no idea about what inspired Amparo to end their marriage. Amparo's decision was consistent with Brizendine's (2011) finding that about 65% of the divorces launched by women in their late 40s and early 50s are a direct consequence of decisions they make by themselves. The prefrontal cortex seems to be involved when they conclude that their marriage is finished; decreases of oxytocin levels, in charge of emotional communication, lead to a decrease of empathy, making it easier to leave a relationship that is no longer considered good enough. Behaving as an absent father with little family involvement, Andres demonstrated negligence according to psychological standards but not according to the standards of his cohort of Catholics.

Ethologically, Andres's behavior may be explained as a question of territoriality and protection: He became an outsider in the family by fleeing to a shelter. His wife embraced the alpha position in the litter. He is not the nurturing parent, and a direct consequence of his confrontation with the oldest son is that he is not viewed as the main adult. Shots of testosterone between them transformed the son into prosecutor (high dose), the father into a scared victim (low dose), and the psychologist (through therapy) into the rescuer. The son became the young adult at home, looking after the house and guarding it from intruders. His younger brother started to spend more time outside than inside, playing outdoor sports.

Some behaviors displayed under traumatic situations involve hormones to elucidate who is in charge and in command of the territory (Honess & Marin, 2006). If the children are controlled by the mother, then the father must survive by establishing a new territory—that is, a new family. It has been so for centuries, and it generated the distinction between legitimate and illegitimate descendants among aristocrats, kings, and emperors.

CONCLUSION

Psychobiology, ethology, and psychological frameworks can lead us to understand plots and strategic game plans in a broken family. Although it is not possible to generalize from Andres's story, it offers therapists a glimpse into the dynamics of a client's life experiences. Spousal abuse is a notion but also a strategy in the court and a play that requires at least three main characters: perpetrator, victim, and rescuer—plus children as support actors.

The National Institute of Statistics publishes, by mid-May, a report on domestic and gender violence. Regarding Spanish data on domestic violence, there was a 5.8% decrease in the number of cases reported in 2012 and a 3.3% decrease in 2013. The basic unit is a report with interim measures in the court. This register is held at the Ministry of Justice. Regarding domestic violence, 4,425 women and 2,635 men were reported to be the victims. Of perpetrators, 3,790 were men, and 1,247 were women. Of those who were both victim and perpetrator, 129 were men, and 65 were women. Amparo never reported Andres to the authorities for domestic violence. It was just the argument she used for the divorce procedure.

In 2003 the Spanish government created a register at the Woman Institute for tracking women murdered by their partners. Over the last 10 years, the outcome has been 649 cases; of those cases, 80% of victims were female, and 75% of perpetrators were male. From January to August 2014, 39 women were murdered by their partner; for 2013, the number was 59. The highest rate, 76, was in 2008, and the lowest, 49, was in 2012. There is not such a register of men murdered, but at the Ministry of Justice it is reported indirectly: There were two cases in 2007 (lowest figure) and 13 cases (highest) in 2013.

QUESTIONS

1. If the basic unit of analysis is the family, that is, the litter, how can we decipher PAS in ethological terms? In fact, it is an exemplary challenge, an archetype; who is the custodian, the angel at home? A direct consequence of a divorce is that the alpha (female or male) is not in a congenial pair anymore. The alpha succeeds and is the insider, the hero, and a great person. As long as the loser is the outsider, then she or he has almost no rights at all, only assignments.

2. In relation to the physical and psychological mistreatment that men and woman might display, are there hormonal levels that could explain these behaviors, especially testosterone and oxytocin levels? Could PAS be considered a type of spousal abuse characterized by psychological mistreatment, maltreatment, and humiliation—either directly or indirectly through the children—and biologically defined by low levels of testosterone and decreases of oxytocin levels, which lead to a decrease of empathy? If so, this definition would contrast with the socially well-known definition of mistreatment that is legally punished and that is mainly characterized by physical aggression and intimidation and high levels of testosterone.

3. The distinction between matrimony and patrimony is not neutral. In etymological terms *matrimony* means duties, actions, and conditions under the control of the mother; *patrimony* is the matter of a father, and so it alludes to inheritance, properties, and wealth. Who provides what in the case of a divorce? PAS may be examined by taking into consideration (a) what entails the idea of family patrimony, understood as shared capital and household; and (b) what brings about the notion of matrimony, understood as caretaker, babysitter, and maintenance person but not shared household if a divorce is forced and is sanctioned.

217

4. Victims of spousal abuse might be defined by a specific personality trait, such as low self-esteem and a tendency to display more behaviors related to inward aggression. In contrast, the personality traits that define an abuser may be the tendency toward physical attack and psychological offense—that is, general outward aggression. Looking at statistics when PAS has been identified, physical aggression accusation usually has not been proved from either spouse. Could PAS be a type of psychological outward aggression?

5. Looking at the ethological point of view, females with infants display a high percentage of behaviors designed to protect their infant and her territory from the male; this behavior occurs more frequently when other females are trying to seek attention from the male. Could it be that PAS is a female strategy to protect the children (that is, heirs) against the father when another woman is around?

References

American Psychiatric Association. (2013). *Diagnostic and statistical manual of mental disorders* (5th ed.). Washington, DC: Author.

Brizendine, L. (2007). *The female brain*. New York, NY: Three Rivers.

Brizendine, L. (2011). *The male brain*. New York, NY: Three Rivers.

Brüne, M., Brüne-Cohrs, U., McGrew, W. C., & Preuschoff, S. (2006). Psychopathology in great apes: Concepts, treatment options and possible homologies to human psychiatric disorders. *Neuroscience Biobehavioral Reviews, 30,* 1246–1259.

García-Vera, M. P., Sanz, J., & Prieto, J. M. (2013). Psychotherapy in Spain: Rapid growth and the vicissitudes of clinical psychology. In R. Moodley, W. Gielen, & R. Wu (Eds.), *Handbook of counseling and psychotherapy in an international context* (pp. 326–336). New York, NY: Routledge.

Gardner, R. A. (2001). Parental alienation syndrome (PAS): Sixteen years later. *Academy Forum, 45,* 10–12.

Hediger, H. (1955). *Studies of the psychology and behaviour of captive animals in zoos and circuses.* London, England: Butterworths Scientific Publications. (Original work [in German] published 1954)

Honess, P. E., & Marin, C. (2006). Behavioural and physiological aspects of stress and aggression in nonhuman primates. *Neuroscience and Biobehavioral Review, 30,* 390–412.

Stogdill, R. M. (1937). Survey of experiments on children's attitudes toward parents: 1894–1936. *Journal of Genetic Psychology, 51,* 293–303.

Warshak, R. A. (2001). Current controversies regarding parental alienation syndrome. *American Journal of Forensic Psychology, 19,* 29–59.

ONLINE DATABASES

National Institute of Statistics website contains information on domestic and gender violence in Spain: http://www.ine.es/jaxi/menu.do?type=pcaxis&path=/t18/p468&file=inebase

Woman Institute website contains information on murdered women in Spain: http://www.inmujer.gob.es/estadisticas/consulta.do?area=10

Chapter 28

COUNSELING AND PSYCHOTHERAPY IN RUSSIA: CLIENT A'S STORY

Alla Kholmogorova and Svetlana Volikova

INTRODUCTION

Many psychotherapeutic approaches exist and have been developed in contemporary Russian society, including psychoanalysis, psychodrama, gestalt therapy, the humanistic approach, existential analysis, family systems psychotherapy, and cognitive behavior therapy (CBT; see, for discussion, Kholmogorova, Garanian, & Krasnov, 2013).

One of the most important trends in modern psychological counseling and psychotherapy in Russia is the creation of original integrative models combining Russian and foreign concepts. For example, personal reconstructive psychotherapy integrates the developments of Myasishchev's relationship theory and group psychodynamic psychotherapy; coexperiencing psychotherapy, developed by Vasilyuk, integrates the developments of Leontiev's activity theory and humanistic psychotherapy; and the reflexive activity approach to psychological and pedagogical counseling integrates the developments of Vygotsky's cultural–historical concept, Leontiev's activity theory, and Galperin's theory of intellectual activity formation (Zaretsky, 2010).

In this case study, we discuss integrative psychotherapy, which was used in therapy with the client being discussed. This approach integrates the developments of Beck's cognitive psychotherapy, family systems psychotherapy, social psychoanalysis, and Vygotsky's cultural–historical concept (Kholmogorova, 2001). The original multifactorial psychosocial model of affective spectrum disorders (Kholmogorova, 2011; Kholmogorova & Garanian, 1998; Volikova & Kholmogorova, 2001) consists of four levels: macrosocial, familial, personal, and interpersonal. Each level includes different factors that become the targets of interventions in the process of psychotherapy. The effectiveness of this integrative approach has been demonstrated in a long-term naturalistic study carried out with the support of the Russian Foundation for Basic Research (Kholmogorova et al., 2010).

In the chapter we discuss the therapy of Client A, a Russian ex-serviceman who undertook individual CBT combined with family consultations using the family systems approach.

The Client

Client A is a 52-year-old Russian heterosexual male who is a retired serviceman. He has no religious affiliation and is married with a daughter who is a student. At the start of psychotherapy, he was unemployed and was receiving treatment in a psychiatric clinic.

Presenting Issues and Challenges

The client was diagnosed with obsessive-compulsive disorder (OCD) and dependent personality disorder. A number of compulsions were presented that were expressed as rituals, such as the following: he would scrutinize himself (hour-long examinations of skin appearance), he would do a great deal of uniform physical exercises to the point of exhaustion (the number of exercises should have been divisible by 30), and he would scan numbers on the cell phone. The above activities were done repeatedly, and once started he was unable to stop or control the desire to do such activities. Only his wife was able to interrupt these activities. These compulsions resulted in depressive symptoms. The client abandoned his job.

Case History and Developmental Background

The client comes from a family of rural country residents who live in a typical Russian village far from any big cities. His father has been suffering from alcoholism for a long time. His mother is a very dominant tyrant who makes scenes, constantly criticizes family members, and treats them as subordinates. His parents were like this the entire course of his life. It is not customary in the family to pay attention to the emotional state of other family members or complain about bad health. Any signs of feelings are seen as weaknesses, which is not atypical in rural Russia. Wars and repressions during the entire 20th century resulted in men dying or becoming alcoholics and passing away prematurely. The women who had to live through these traumatic experiences also had to take on the burden of responsibility for the family and became more rigid, became closed up, became dominant, and constantly experienced pressure.

Widespread methods of relieving stress both for men and women were conflicts and alcohol. This familial scenario secured its place in the following generations: Families could cultivate the dominant characteristics in women and dependent characteristics in men. Another important value that is also based in the historical past is seen in the familial rule or belief that "life is hard"—it has no place for rest or relaxation. This value led to the strengthening of a monotonous and secluded family lifestyle, which in turn promoted fixations on negative events and symptoms.

Client A's obsessions and compulsions first appeared 15 years ago after the death of a relative to cancer. The client was hospitalized and received medication. His obsessions did not disappear entirely, but the intensity reduced considerably. He was able to control his obsessions and return to ordinary life. For many years he suffered from alcohol abuse. A few years ago his wife talked him into undergoing aversive therapy to treat his alcoholism. The client gave up drinking; however, the obsessions became so strong that he had to leave his job. He was referred to a psychiatrist, which initially helped, but later the symptoms worsened again. He was admitted to a hospital and was referred for psychotherapy by an attendant physician psychiatrist after 2 months of ineffective pharmacological treatment.

THE THERAPY

The client was prescribed combined therapy: a course of medication and psychotherapy. Psychotherapy was both individual CBT and family systems therapy. The client described his symptoms as follows:

> I brood over small things. I look at birthmarks, small lines, or small scars. I look in the mirror and can't stop scrutinizing myself until someone drags me away. I do exercises. For example, I have to do sit ups or have to touch my nose with my knees . . . I don't know why I do all these things. They have a pull on me. I can't stop doing them . . . I have a lot of superstitions: I have to do things 15 times or 30 or 60 or 90 times . . . I do this so nothing bad will happen (my parents won't die, my wife and daughter won't get run over by a car . . . I won't die).

In line with the multifactorial model of affective spectrum disorders in addition to symptoms, the psychotherapist also identified therapeutic targets at each of the four levels of the model.

At the macrosocial level, the environment in which Client A and his family lived reinforced and formed a number of dysfunctional familial rules: seclusion of family, focus on material gains at the expense of the emotional life of family members, and hierarchical dysfunctions (control and tyranny in the family). Dysfunctions of the family structure could be seen both in the client's family of origin and in his own nuclear family. These dysfunctions reflect the typical cultural context; thus, they are seen as natural and are treated like they do not need to be discussed or changed. As a result, the dysfunctions are resistant to modification, which makes it very important to separate them into the macrosocial level as a target of special attention from the psychotherapist.

At the family level, Client A's family life is centered on controlling OCD symptoms (the wife and the daughter monitor him to ensure he avoids rituals; they track his mood and constantly control his emotional state). The wife's mood entirely depends on the intensity of Client A's obsessions: The more obsessions there are, the more irritated she gets. A monotonous and depressive lifestyle is clearly seen: For instance, he and his wife have never gone out, he has read practically no books, and his everyday life lacks positive impressions. In fact, the client's illness is the only communicative content between him and his wife. The following is his description of his day-to-day life at home when he first began psychotherapy:

> I don't work. I sit at home. I clean the apartment. Every day. But my wife is often mad. I don't clean very well. I also wash the windows. Very often. And the garage. It is necessary to sort and clean things in there, take something home. The car must be warmed up. I go there at least once a week. All the other time I lie on the couch and watch TV.

There was a high level of criticism from his wife (e.g., if he washed the floor, the wife would criticize him that it was not clean enough). It appeared as though she was positioned at a high level in the familial hierarchy, whereas the client was positioned at an extremely low level. The client's opinion about his wife was expressed in the following statement: "She is—wow! I can't say she is a tyrant. But she does scold me! And never mind me—I'll get over it. I'll huff and puff for a while but then get calm," or "I always avoid heated relationships. I don't like conflicts. It is better to stay quiet and keep silent."

At the personal level, the client shared the following dysfunctional personal traits and behavioral patterns:

> I must have everything in perfect order. Even the smallest things. Take a look [showed the psychotherapist his wallet]. The money is sorted, like in a bank. I have always been that way. I don't remember this in my childhood. But when I was a cadet I remember that I organized my bag in the evening and everything there was in order: my notebooks separately, books in another compartment. In perfect order.

Perfectionism was expressed as extreme meticulousness and accuracy (the slightest mess caused discomfort, unrest, and emotional tension, thus increasing the symptoms). For example, the client paid close attention to the condition of his clothes and shoes. Once he noticed a thread on his jacket during the session and was ill at ease until he took it off.

At the interpersonal level, the client lacked a social network outside the family. He said,

> There are no friends. Neither my wife nor I have any friends. We never go to anyone's houses. There are things to be done. My wife is tired when she comes home from work. She would like to rest. She often finishes work at home if she didn't have time to do it in the office. There is no time for guests or entertainment. She is home. And I am by her side.

For the therapy, the following were established as the sequence of psychotherapeutic objectives:

1. Establish contact and discuss the role of psychological factors in the illness. In addition, form a biopsychosocial aspect of disease with the client; he saw his illness as being merely biological and did not believe in the possibility of psychological control of his conditions (i.e., identification of situations that increase anxiety, implication of a ritual, and development of skills to resist the craving for rituals).
2. Make progress in emotional self-regulation skills (e.g., enrichment of the emotional vocabulary and development of skills to help him understand and observe his own emotional state).
3. Handle the OCD symptoms. A coping card proved to be a great help for the client. It read, "If I start a compulsive action, this will make me unable to stop. I won't be able to stop and will want to do this again and again. This is the way back, back to the illness, rather than forward to health. Therefore, I'd better not start doing it."
4. Reduce family involvement in controlling the client's OCD symptoms.
5. Overcome the depressive lifestyle of the client and his family (through reading, film viewing, etc.).
6. Develop autonomy (framing of independent attitudes to various events and situations, developing his own opinion and mode of action, and promoting tolerance to disagreements and conflicts with his wife).
7. Expand his social network.

The client received individual psychotherapy. In addition, he and his wife were invited to family counseling, as they had dysfunctional relationships that reinforced his symptoms. Two psychotherapists conducted family counseling in a systems approach of Bowen. The goals of the family counseling mostly coincided with the goals of individual consultations. They are stated earlier (Items 4–7). It was highly important to motivate the wife to change communication style and family living style and involve her in cooperation. Each consultations took 1.5 hours. After each consultation, the family was given homework. After 35 individual and two family consultations, there was considerable decrease in the intensity of compulsive ideas, and the client's cravings for physical exercises disappeared. He still had a desire to scrutinize his skin appearance and monitor the cell phone, but the intensity of these desires apparently decreased. His moods normalized because the intensity of compulsive ideas decreased. The client understood that he could control and manage compulsive actions by himself. Now he had time to work or to see new things. He made progress in managing the discomfort caused by household vicissitudes or petty troubles with the car, developed more tolerance toward the condition of clothes, and became less obsessed with household orderliness. His lifestyle changed: He started to read fiction and get pleasure from reading, and he started to go to the movies with his wife. They decided to go on a holiday abroad for the first time. He resumed working and was promoted to another job. He started to socialize more with his coworkers. The wife continued to try to control her husband's obsessions and involve the daughter in this control, but the client became more able to resist these attempts.

The client's resources and countertherapeutic factors that slowed down the process of healing were identified during therapy. Therapy was complicated by low cultural and intellectual levels, alexithymia, inertia of psychological processes, and long-term illness. As a result, positive changes in the client's condition were extremely slow and vague. In addition, family therapy sessions revealed the wife's clear opposition to a number of recommendations that aimed at increasing her husband's autonomy. All of this often led to the psychotherapist (Svetlana Volikova) experiencing feelings of hopelessness and uncertainty in the chosen work method and in the adequacy of professional qualifications in order to help such a difficult client. The course of work with this client was regularly discussed with colleagues and the supervisor (Alla Kholmogorova). Supervisions helped guide the direction of work and discover the resources the client had, which in turn promoted the professional confidence of the psychotherapist.

At the beginning of psychotherapy, Client A was receiving treatment in a psychiatric clinic and received medical drugs. For last 4 weeks he had been receiving 150 milligrams of Zoloft (Sertraline) per day and 600 milligrams of Seroquel (Quetiapine) per day. However, his state did not improve. Before that his psychiatrist had twice changed the drugs that the patient received, depending on this state; however, there was no positive effect. As a result of the combination of pharmacological treatment and individual and family therapy, the intensity of rituals declined, the client started to work, he and his wife became more active, and the life of their family became less monotonous.

DISCUSSION AND ANALYSIS

When formulating the sequence of therapeutic tasks that needed to be solved, the psychotherapist used the central concept of the cultural–historical theory of psychological development by Vygotsky—*zone of proximal development* (Kholmogorova & Zaretsky, 2010; Zaretsky, 2007). This concept was developed by Vygotsky when he was working with children who had developmental disorders. It proved to be especially valuable when working with difficult clients who have limited resources and chronic long-term problems. It focuses the therapist's work on finding the current capabilities of the client and creating situations of success, because this is very important to promote the client's motivation over the course of the long and difficult joint work to overcome painful symptoms and life problems. Overstepping the boundaries of the proximal development zone into the zone of "the unreachable" may lead the client to feel that the barrier is invincible, which may cause him or her to discontinue therapy. According to Vygotsky, work within the zone of proximal development assumes the identification of the initial level of the child's psychological development and development of a sequence of steps that need to be taken in order to expand his or her *psychological toolkit* (i.e., psychological means of self-regulation and self-organization; Zaretsky, 2010). In addition, an important principle of psychological help is the stabilization of the *social situation* of the child's development, which is defined by the closest social surroundings.

These are the concepts and principles that were used in the process of psychotherapy in this case study. To establish contact and collect primary data, it was extremely important to question the value of a happy facade, because it did not allow the client to talk about real problems in his family or his life and it made him concentrate exclusively on his symptoms. The next task was to gradually overcome the alexithymia barrier by expanding his emotional vocabulary, developing his ability to understand and express feelings, and increasing his ability to differentiate stimuli that influenced his emotional state. On the basis of this work, it became possible to develop a step-by-step plan for enhancing his ability to overcome and control OCD symptoms. In order to accomplish this task, it was necessary to engage the family in the therapeutic process, because the wife's interference and elevated level of control impeded the client's attempts to begin controlling his symptoms on his own. After some positive shifts and a decrease in the level of symptoms, it became possible to gradually expand the sphere of interests and overcome the monotonous and repetitive lifestyle of the client and his family. During family consultations a common activity for the family members was planned. A separate and very important target was to reinforce Client A's autonomy—his belief in his capability to make independent decisions, carry out his own activities (job searching, performing functional exercises, etc.), plan to begin working again, and participate in activities that were pleasurable.

Countertherapeutic factors that hindered the course of the treatment, as well as the client's resources, were identified during therapy. The most crucial countertherapeutic factor was a high level of alexithymia. Previously, the client hardly ever thought of or spoke about his psychological life; he found it difficult to monitor his feelings and failed to answer questions about how he felt or what was going on with him. This alexithymia complicated his ability to monitor his moods and anxiety reactions, to register situations that caused adverse mood changes, and to identify negative automatic ideas, all of which are very important for CBT. Unfortunately, the client failed to learn how to associate anxiety-provoking situations with rituals as dysfunctional methods of anxiety reduction.

The analysis of the sources of Client A's symptoms, the high level of inclusion of his symptoms into the life of the family, the high level of the family's participation in regulating his symptoms, and his dependence on his wife all led the therapist to believe that it was necessary to include family consultations in his treatment. The following goals were addressed during family consultations: increasing the family's awareness of the causes of OCD, changing the family's reactions and strategy toward Client A's visible symptoms (ceasing to control how rituals are performed or attempting to stop them), decreasing the levels of criticism and control in the family, discussing the role of a depressive lifestyle in the development of issues in the emotional sphere, and motivating the family and the client to change.

During individual consultations CBT methods were used to discuss and work through problems of the personal, familial, and interpersonal levels that are described earlier. The consideration of countertherapeutic factors and resources during individual and family consultations allowed the therapist to lower the intensity of the OCD symptoms.

CONCLUSION

The multifactorial psychosocial model of affective-spectrum disorders offers the possibility of identifying a system of factors that influences the development of various types of disorders, including OCD. It also makes it possible to identify directions of therapeutic help for this group of clients. On the basis of the multifactorial model, we identified ways to help the client at the macrosocial level, familial level, personal level, and interpersonal level. The client's treatment included drug therapy, individual CBT, and family consultations using the family systems approach. As a result of this comprehensive approach, the intensity of the client's OCD symptoms declined.

QUESTIONS

1. What personality traits of the client could have increased the symptoms of his illness?
2. What dysfunctional characteristics of the client's family of origin could have influenced the client's disorder?
3. What stressful events in the client's life could have provoked the symptoms of his illness?
4. Why is it necessary to combine individual psychotherapy, family consultations, and drug therapy in the treatment of this particular client?
5. What psychotherapeutic approaches and methods can you recommend for this client?

REFERENCES

Kholmogorova, A. B. (2001). Kognitivnaia psihoterapia i perspektivy ejo razvitia v Rossii [Cognitive psychotherapy and Russian psychology of thinking]. *Moscow Psychotherapy Journal, 4,* 165–181.

Kholmogorova, A. B. (2011). *Integrativnaia psihoterapia rasstrojstv affektivnogo spektra* [Integrative psychotherapy of affective spectrum disorders]. Moscow, Russia: Medpractice.

Kholmogorova, A. B., & Garanian, N. G. (1998). Mnogofaktornaia model' depressivnyh, trevozhnyh i somatoformnyh rasstrojstv [Multi-factorial model of depressive, anxious, and somatoform disorders as a basis for their integrative psychotherapy]. *Social and Clinical Psychiatry, 1*, 94–102.

Kholmogorova, A. B., Garanian, N. G., & Krasnov, V. N. (2013). Counseling and psychotherapy in Russia: Reunion with the international science community. In R. Moodley, U. Gielen, & R. Wu (Eds.), *Handbook of counseling and psychotherapy in an international context* (pp. 337–347). New York, NY: Routledge.

Kholmogorova, A. B., Pugovkina, O. D., Garanyan, N. G., Dovzhenko, T. V., Volikova, S. V., Petrova, G. A., & Yudeeva, T. U. (2010). Factors of effectiveness of the integrative psychotherapy of affective spectrum disorders. *Journal of Counseling Psychology and Psychotherapy, 2*, 77–109.

Kholmogorova, A. B., & Zaretsky, V. K. (2010). *Mozhet li byt' polezna rossijskaia psihologia v reshenii problem sovremennoj psihoterapii: razmyshlenia posle HH kongressa internacional'noi federacii psihoterapii (IFP)* [Whether the Russian psychology can be useful for the solving of actual problems of modern psychotherapy: Reflection after 4th Congress of International Federation of Psychotherapy (IFP)]. Retrieved from http://www.medpsy.ru/mprj/archiv_global/2010_4_5/nomer/nomer09.php

Volikova, S. V., & Kholmogorova, A. B. (2001). Semejnye istochniki negativnoi kognitivnoi shemy pri jemocional'nyh rasstrojstvah na primere trevozhnyh, depressivnyh i somatoformnyh rasstrojstv [Familial sources of negative cognitive schemas in affective spectrum disorders]. *Moscow Psychotherapy Journal, 4*, 49–60.

Zaretsky, V. K. (2007). Zona blizhajshego razvitia: o chem ne uspel napisat' Vygotskii [Zone of proximal development: What Vygotsky had not time to write about]. *Cultural–Historical Psychology, 3*, 96–104.

Zaretsky, V. (2010, June). *Zone of proximal development as the basis for psychological help to children with learning problems.* Paper presented at the FMPP Annual Congress of Psychiatry and Psychotherapy and the 20th IFP World Congress of Psychotherapy, KKl, Luzerne, Switzerland.

Chapter 29

COUNSELING AND PSYCHOTHERAPY IN THE UNITED KINGDOM: WINSTON'S STORY

Del Loewenthal

INTRODUCTION

Integrative counseling is one of the most popular and diverse therapeutic approaches in the United Kingdom (Palmer & Woolfe, 2000). This type of counseling often incorporates humanistic, cognitive, and psychodynamic approaches. For the United Kingdom, Freud's arrival in London in 1938 and his presence there, together with that of Anna Freud and Melanie Klein, greatly assisted the development of a British tradition in psychoanalysis. This tradition included Bion, Bowlby, Winnicott, and, more controversially, R. D. Laing. Since that time there have been further developments in psychoanalysis, alongside the development of U.K. traditions in humanistic, existential, and behavioral therapies.

Historically the trends in counseling and psychotherapy that have been favored in the United Kingdom have been psychodynamic and humanistic approaches. The United Kingdom continues to be influenced by developments in North America and perhaps to a lesser extent by those in continental Europe. Within psychoanalysis there is increasing interest in relational psychoanalysis (with this interest being mirrored in psychotherapy in general) and mentalization-based treatment. Within humanism, both the person-centered approach and particularly integrative approaches have come more to the forefront. In the last 20 years following the rise of cognitive behavior therapy (CBT), the trend within the United Kingdom is currently toward what are regarded as evidence-based practices. With regard to CBT there has been a growing interest in broadening its definition, including what has been termed *third-wave approaches*. Critiques have highlighted, however, that the overall standard of what is taken as evidence in randomized control trials is highly questionable. However, many universities in the United Kingdom are increasingly involved with providing CBT training, whereas previously they were involved in more psychoanalytic and humanistic modalities (see Loewenthal, 2013a).

The integrative approach presented here is based on phenomenology, existentialism, and the therapeutic use of photographs. *Talking pictures therapy* (Loewenthal, 2013b, 2013c) is an approach to brief therapy in which photographs are used to help clients explore presenting issues. The therapy presented in this chapter sits within postexistential perspectives in which an attempt is made to offer a space where we might think about how alienated we are through valuing existential notions such as experience and meaning. Thus, identity is seen as a fluid rather than fixed category. Theoretically, it is hoped that postexistentialism provides greater possibilities for accepting, rather than escaping, the identities we form (Loewenthal, 2011).

Photographs can be a route to the unconscious mind, via the meaning clients attach to them. They may act as a tool, helping the client to become aware of his or her interpretation of the world. When incorporated into therapy, photographs may facilitate improvements with impulse control, social skills, and self-esteem. This technique is particularly effective with children who struggle to articulate themselves emotionally but respond powerfully to visual images (Loewenthal, 2013b). In particular, research around the use of photographs with children has reported that the use of photographs facilitates enhancement of self-concept and improvements in mindstate and emotional management (Cosden & Reynolds, 1982). Talking pictures therapy is introduced as a method for promoting well-being in children and can be carried out by psychotherapists (Loewenthal, 2011).

In considering therapy in the United Kingdom with reference to the Group of Seven identities (gender, ethnicity [race], disability, class, age, sexual orientation, religion), we should highlight the ethical trend in therapeutic intervention with diverse groups toward considering any identity as a fluid and not a fixed category (Hollway, Lucey, & Phoenix, 2007). U.K.-based perspectives on gender, ethnicity, class, age, sexual orientation, disabilities (both "seen" and "unseen"), and religion tend to approach identity in ways that accept that identities are continually in flux and transitions are often context dependent. This approach is preferred in terms of conceptualizing difference and avoiding discrimination (Wheeler, 2006). In reconsidering this case, ethnicity, disability, class, gender, and age were regarded as the most pertinent of the seven identities. This chapter presents therapy with Winston, who had recently arrived in the United Kingdom and experienced racism.

THE CLIENT

Winston is a 13-year-old African boy who arrived in the United Kingdom just months before undergoing therapy; as such, Winston's cultural identity was in transition, or flux. The class identity of Winston's family was also in a state of flux because of their recent arrival in the country. Moreover, Winston appeared to be what might be termed colloquially as mute (though there was no knowledge of any medical record regarding this).

PRESENTING ISSUES AND CHALLENGES

Winston was almost mute; though obedient in class, he barely whispered if he spoke at all. Indeed, Winston did present this way to me, the therapist, at the initial meeting. When Winston did talk, it was in such a whisper that I had to put my ear in front of Winston's mouth to hear him. Winston's mutism brought issues in terms of potentially categorizing him as disabled, though this presenting problem did indeed disable him. In working with such clients it is important to attend to the politics of discourse in categorizing people as disabled because all disability experience is context dependent. I learned during our time together that Winston had experienced racism and abuse from other children, and his integration was not easy. Winston was adjusting to his family's recent arrival in the United Kingdom, and he was experiencing racism from other children.

CASE HISTORY AND DEVELOPMENTAL BACKGROUND

Winston was new to the country and may have been struggling culturally with enforced changes in his environment. Because of this, there were no official records concerning Winston's development before his arrival in the United Kingdom— something that can be an issue when working therapeutically with migrant populations. It was unclear to the school as to when Winston had become mute, and at the time of assessment there was no record of this on file. However, despite his difficulties in communicating in English because he came from a non-English-speaking African country, Winston appeared to be bright. This appearance was confirmed during our time together by his obvious abilities in the word game Scrabble. It seems that Winston was well-educated and may have come from a wealthy African family background.

THE THERAPY

Winston was obedient in our first meeting but did not want to speak. When Winston did talk, it was in a very quiet whisper. The first photograph he chose was of a Ferris Wheel at a fairground, which he said reminded him of when he went to a fair with his parents and two sisters last summer. It appeared that he sometimes played at home with his sisters but not his parents.

At the next meeting, Winston was asked to choose another photograph that called to him. This time he chose one with noughts and crosses (tic tac toe), which he said, whispering, that he enjoyed playing with his sisters. Winston and I played noughts and crosses together for about 20 minutes. I then asked him if he would like to play another game called Connect 4. Winston was very interested in this game and soon became proficient at it. While playing Connect 4, I told him I had noticed that when he was asked the pretherapy evaluation questions, he had chosen the response "sometimes" for the statement "over the past week, I have made plans to end my life," and I wondered what had made him say that. Winston confessed in a whisper that another child told him she did not like him because of the color of his skin, and that she hit him and insulted him and his family, saying "Your mother and father . . ." and accompanying the insult with an obscene gesture. I offered Winston to speak to the staff about this. He nodded vigorously in agreement.

At the start of the next session, Winston wanted to play Connect 4 again. When asked whether the other student had stopped bullying him, Winston nodded with a happy smile on his face and whispered "yes." After two more games, I asked him whether he had always spoken quietly. "No," he said faintly to my ear. When I asked when it began, he replied, "I was five," and resumed the game.

At the following session, Winston appeared more relaxed and was engaging more. He chose to play a game I had introduced to him in one of the sessions: Scrabble. While we were playing, I said to him that I had wondered what happened to him at the age of 5 as he had said that was when he stopped talking.

Winston seemed unable to even whisper, so I said, if he wanted to, he could write it down. He wrote, "My mother tell me to stop talking too much and I stopped talking." I asked him whether he would like to talk more, and when he nodded I wondered aloud how we could help him.

In the penultimate session, I asked Winston whether he would like to choose another photograph that called to him, and he chose one depicting playing cards. When asked why he chose that card, Winston replied, "My mother used to play cards in Africa before we came here a year ago." He told me that he no longer played with his mother, who also does not speak very much. I then asked whether it was common for women his mother's age not to talk very much in his African country. Winston looked at me, amused and smiling, then shook his head as if I was a bit stupid; then he made me understand that he wished to carry on playing Scrabble.

At the start of the sixth and last session, I asked Winston whether he wanted to play games or to talk, and surprisingly, his response was "talk." Then, hesitantly and quietly, he said that he had been thinking that while his mother does not talk, this was not the same for his mother's sister. He also told me in the course of the same session that he played tennis with his mother after telling her that he wanted to become a tennis player. Smiling, he also told me that he had a friend now with whom he plays at school.

Winston scored 5 on the PHQ-9 scale measuring depression at the start of therapy, and 7 at the end of his last session, the primary change being that he now felt he had trouble concentrating. This score indicated mild to moderate depression. On the GAD-7 scores, which measure anxiety, he scored 0 both pre- and posttherapy. Regarding the CORE-10, his initial score was 8, and his final score was 14. Changes included an increase in "feeling depressed or unhappy," though he did now feel that he had "someone to turn to for support." It could be that the increase in CORE-10 scores was a result of the new ability to voice what was of concern to him.

In the course of the six sessions, Winston seemed to have changed from being described by his teachers as "an elective mute" to a young boy who was now able, according to staff, to look at people.

DISCUSSION AND ANALYSIS

I reflected on my own position here as a White psychotherapist and had concerns that Winston may have found exploring topics difficult with someone whom he might not trust. I had also wondered whether Winston may have preferred to see a female therapist, as he gradually revealed strong ties to female family members, and it appeared he was perhaps more familiar and comfortable with female company.

As there was little on record about Winston's development, the onset of his mutism, or his language abilities, much of my work with him was tentative and exploratory. These type of issues can present significant challenges for therapists working in the United Kingdom with children from migrant families, and it poses significant challenges in terms of assessing and meeting needs.

The talking pictures therapy approach appeared to engage Winston; overall, it seemed to provide a useful way of opening up a therapeutic encounter. By being able to get quickly to the client's concerns, it also provided a way that the actual looking at photographs enabled Winston to manage his own therapy. In turn, the findings may suggest that talking pictures therapy enables clients to quickly bring to mind and explore that which is troubling them; this type of therapy is in contrast to the current dominance of CBT in the United Kingdom, which focuses more on taking a client's mind off the problem in question.

Because of Winston's cultural difference and abilities, his presentation required an alternative approach to intervention as he was lacking both the English language and the ability to speak, which are essential factors in therapy as exemplified initially in Freud's conceptualization of the "talking cure." In this respect the talking pictures therapy approach appeared to better meet Winston's cultural and (dis)ability needs. Some of the pictures used, in retrospect, may have been culturally biased toward Westernized presentations of the world. However, many were universal as Westernized images and representations of the world are dominant in many cultures. This approach may also have helped to bridge some of the cultural differences between Winston and myself as we shared some representations of the world in imagery if we could not do so in language. Furthermore, Winston appeared far more confident in selecting images of possibly shared representations than words that were from a language he was neither accustomed to nor competent in using. Moreover, the asking of questions can produce an expectation that the therapist is then going to solve the problem, as in, for example, a medical model, which therefore only suits a particular type of therapy.

The use of images also has another function in client work with children like Winston in schools: It can afford more power to the younger clients as they give meaning to their selected image through their own interpretations and experiences rather than those of the therapist as in traditional therapy. Thus, this type of therapy can help the therapist at least recognize, though not remove, the power relations in such work with children. Furthermore, the practice of talking about one's problems is not always welcomed in all cultures, though talking about how one feels about a picture or an image may be more comfortable for people of some ethnic backgrounds.

I remained convinced that Winston may have preferred a female therapist, as he did seem to have more of a connection with women on an emotional level, which may have also been a cultural factor; however, this did not seem to affect the therapeutic outcome unduly. I also still wonder what the outcomes might have been for Winston had his therapist been Black or African, though assumed similarity to clients can bring about as many issues as obvious differences can.

CONCLUSION

With regard to the theory of the Group of Seven identities, Britain is still a predominantly White society, with 87% of its population forming the White majority (Office for National Statistics, 2012). This demographic is changing, however, with a rapidly increasing diversity of ethnic groups and cultures. The fastest growing group is Black African—the group from which Winston came—which more than doubled from 1991 to 2001 (Lupton & Power, 2004). This client's age also saw him at a disadvantage in terms of the power relations within the therapeutic context. How issues of diversity were worked through with Winston, with particular reference to racial prejudice and age difference, are described next.

Working with Winston in a way that was respectful of his identities as he transitioned from African to British national, or from "disabled" to "enabled" (in terms of communication difficulties), required an integrative approach that was able to accommodate the state of flux that his identities were in at the time of therapy. Such a state of flux and transition appeared to be well-accommodated by the talking pictures therapy approach. This approach allowed Winston freedom to explore aspects of his life in a somewhat less culturally biased framework for therapy that is not reliant on the need for words and language or the ability to speak and communicate directly with the therapist. In this respect, the diverse approaches to therapy in the United Kingdom today, such as talking pictures therapy, are at last helping to provide an alternative therapy that better reflects and meets the needs of the multicultural society the United Kingdom has become. Thus, if we were to work toward an ethically just and inclusive therapy without borders in the United Kingdom, with reference to Winston's case, we might have to reconsider the cultural diversity issues that may arise from our traditional assumptions concerning therapy as a predominantly talking cure.

QUESTIONS

1. Winston's "disability" appeared to be a protective factor for him. He did not want to speak. How might viewing this as a disability rather than a protective factor affect your approach?
2. There are always unavoidable power relations in work with clients. These are particularly salient in psychotherapy with children and adolescents. To what extent should one attempt to assuage or engage with these in work with Winston?
3. Talking pictures therapy appeared to be a productive approach to working with Winston, who could not speak. With regard to your own orientation, how might you engage a client who was unable speak?
4. Where, if at all, might you need to think reflexively about your own identity in your practice with someone like Winston? Where might possible tensions arise here for you personally and for the client?
5. If you were working with a child whose family would fall into the category of migrants, how might this highlight issues with therapy in general as a Westernized cultural practice?

REFERENCES

Cosden, C., & Reynolds, D. (1982). Photography as therapy. *Arts in Psychotherapy, 9*, 19–23. doi:10.1016/0197-4556(82)90023-5

Hollway, W., Lucey, H., & Phoenix, A. (2007). *Social psychology matters*. Milton-Keynes, England: The Open University Press.

Loewenthal, D. (2011). *Post-existentialism and the psychological therapies*. London, England: Karnac.

Loewenthal, D. (2013a). Counseling and psychotherapy in the United Kingdom: Future of talking therapies. In R. Moodley, U. Gielen, & R. Wu (Eds.), *Handbook of counseling and psychotherapy in an international context* (pp. 348–358). New York, NY: Routledge.

Loewenthal, D. (2013b). *Phototherapy and therapeutic photography in a digital age*. London, England: Routledge.

Loewenthal, D. (2013c). Talking pictures therapy as brief therapy in a school setting. *Journal of Creativity in Mental Health, 8*, 21–34.

Lupton, R., & Power, A. (2004). *Minority ethnic groups in Britain*. Washington, DC: Center for Analysis of Social Exclusion.

Office for National Statistics. (2012). *Ethnicity and national identity in England and Wales 2011*. Retrieved from http://www.ons.gov.uk/ons/dcp171776_290558.pdf

Palmer, S., & Woolfe, R. (2000). *Integrative and eclectic counselling and psychotherapy*. London, England: Sage.

Wheeler, S. (2006). *Difference and diversity in counselling: Contemporary psychodynamic approaches*. Hampshire, England: Palgrave Macmillan.

Part Six

COUNSELING AND PSYCHOTHERAPY
IN THE MIDDLE EAST

Chapter 30

COUNSELING AND
PSYCHOTHERAPY IN IRAN:
JAVAD'S STORY

Behrooz Birashk

INTRODUCTION

Iran is located in the Middle East, bordering the Gulf of Oman and the Persian Gulf in the south and the Caspian Sea in the north, with a population of more than 77 million (Central Intelligence Agency, 2011). A large majority of Iranians are Shiite Moslems.

Modern psychiatry, psychology, psychotherapy, and counseling were introduced to Iran in the 20th century at the newly established medical schools and universities. Following the worldwide adoption of modern theories and approaches to counseling and psychotherapy by academic institutions, universities in Iran started developing similar curricula and introduced this discipline into their regular training programs. Thus, many kinds of new and practical psychotherapies such as acceptance and commitment therapy, schema therapy, and dialectical behavior therapy are applied to counseling Iranian clients. Recent developments in training and practice of counseling and psychotherapy are responses to increasing demand for such services across Iranian society (Birashk, 2013).

The application of behavioral therapy or modern behavioral therapy as a systematic approach has a 35-year history in Iran (Birashk, 2005). Contemporary cognitive behavior therapy (CBT) underscores the importance of the culture-specific variables in the treatment of psychological problems. The strengths and the flexibility of CBT provide an excellent opportunity to build a cultural model of CBT based on the clinical, theoretical knowledge of the practitioners and researchers working in different cultural settings (Ghassemzadeh, 2007). Since the late 1980s, CBT has been the main approach to psychotherapy at many universities and psychotherapy centers. Research in many areas shows numerous good reasons to believe that CBT therapists are well-suited to providing culturally sensitive services to Iranian society (Birashk, 2012, 2013).

This chapter discusses the therapy of Javad, a youth who experienced a marginal social class status and who presented with anger, depression, and anxiety. In this case presentation a psychoeducational approach within the broad method of CBT was adopted with specific consideration of the client's cultural context— for example, his beliefs and value system. Moreover, modifications had to be made to the techniques and language used in order to accommodate the client's low literacy.

The Client

Javad is a single young male who is 17 years old and lives with his family: his mother, a sister, and one brother. They are Shiite Moslem and come from a low-income background in the northern region of Iran. Javad is quite behind in his schooling and is currently in the elementary level.

Presenting Issues and Challenges

Javad's initial reason for consulting with a therapist was related to his asthmatic problems, which he associated with his nasal condition, a deviated septum caused by an accident he had 10 years ago. He wanted to have plastic surgery as a solution for his problem. Javad's presenting problems also included anxiety and depression. He would frequently lose control and had shocking behavior. His difficulties with anger management had led to problematic interpersonal relationships. As a youth, Javad had not developed an optimum self-confidence and hence had a low level of self-respect. This young man often experienced a high degree of stress and went through the states of hopelessness and despair. His spiraling challenges stemmed from passive confrontational approaches when dealing with life problems. Javad said his chief complaint was asthmatic problems associated with his nasal deviation. His formulation of his problem was based on the belief that his difficulties (i.e., psychological issues) stemmed from his nose problem and that the surgical alteration of his nose was the ultimate solution for his aforementioned behavioral problems.

Javad initially visited a surgeon for nasal deviation problems, with a demanding request for a nose surgery. He had been dealing with his deviated septum for 10 years; the deviation was caused by an accident back in his town in the northern part of the country. When examined by the site's psychologist, it became evident that this young client suffered from a severe level of anxiety and depression and displayed psychological symptoms such as rage, anger, and low self-confidence, among other issues. Javad's excessive level of stress and anxiety could be associated with the tough responsibility of having to take care of his family since his father, a drug addict, was being held in a rehabilitation camp. This responsibility involved having to work for long hours, struggling to pay the rent, and not having enough money to pay for his surgery. Adding to the family misery, Javad and his family had to live with the fact that his father had recently stolen the money that had been put aside for buying a computer. The harsh living conditions had put a tremendous amount of pressure on this youth, was a cause of his various psychological problems, and played a role in exacerbating the asthma he had been suffering from. The continuation of this complicated condition caused Javad to feel helpless, as though he had little control over his life. He seemed to be incapable of explaining and analyzing his life situation. The feeling of helplessness and the impression of having no control over the problems greatly contributed to the anxiety and depression he was experiencing. At the time of his referral to the outpatient clinic at the hospital, Javad had not received any psychotherapy, and he also had not received any psychosocial support. He reported no substance or alcohol abuse, and he did not smoke. An interview with Javad yielded no evidence of any particular developmental or behavioral disorders during his childhood and/or adolescence.

CASE HISTORY AND DEVELOPMENTAL BACKGROUND

Javad completed sixth grade with an average academic performance. He left school because his family moved from the northern part of the country to a small town near Tehran, the capital city. He wants to continue his education but has to work for up to 14 hours a day. His interpersonal skills are limited, but he has managed to have a few friends.

The father is 43-year-old drug addict. He has quit substances a few times and is currently residing in a substance use rehabilitation facility. Javad's mother is a 36-year-old housewife with no articulated problem. The client is the first child of the family. His brother is 14, is in the eighth grade, and has shown no particular problem. His sister is 12, is in the fourth grade, and has no identified problem. Javad's relationship with his siblings was not good because of stress, excessive work, and lack of adequate rest.

Javad quit studying while in elementary school when his father was imprisoned for theft. The father was recently indicted for drug dealing and was sent to a rehabilitation camp. Consequently, Javad had to leave school and work 14 hours per day in very difficult and complicated conditions in order to support his mother, sister, and younger brother.

THE THERAPY

Because Javad had initially stated nasal deviation as his main problem, he believed that a plastic surgery would solve it. He was examined by a plastic surgeon and was told that he did not need a surgery. The surgeon, however, introduced him to a psychologist to continue his treatment for depression, anxiety, and rage.

To me, the therapist, Javad appeared depressed, hopeless, angry, and anxious, and he had low self-confidence. Javad is preoccupied by his deformed nose and struggles with the idea of having his nose deviation problem fixed through a surgical operation. With Javad I adopted a CBT technique, approaching the work using an individualized format in the case formulation; this approach was mainly done to help the client manage his excessive level of stress and to effectively cope with his debilitating depression and anxiety.

The therapy with Javad consisted of a series of 45- to 50-minute sessions for several weeks. Treatment began with cognitive and behavioral methods, focusing on enhancing the client's understanding of asthma and its potential association with the client's nose deviation/deformation. Focus was also on Javad's living circumstances and his psychological responses to his socioeconomic status.

The therapy plan also included the following: participating in an anger management program; planning for various life activities; rebuilding cognitive processes; discussing the relationship between thoughts and emotions; changing his thinking pattern and mindset, along with learning stress- and anxiety-management techniques; learning effective and competent confrontation skills; training in life skills; and building/providing social support. Other components of the therapeutic approach involved the following: enhancing self-confidence and developing an improved self-competency, organizing for daily chores and activities, improving interpersonal relationships, and developing effective methods for dealing with sleep disturbances.

At the interview session, the focus was on establishing rapport with the client. An introduction to cognitive errors in a simplified manner, consistent with the client's intellectual capacity, was offered along with the appropriate homework. In the following sessions I reviewed the homework that had been given in previous weeks. Furthermore, Javad learned a relaxation method to help him cope with his stresses and anxiety. His low self-confidence was addressed by adopting the following steps: desiring or having a motivation, gaining self-recognition through making a list of personal positive and negative points, challenging self-images, and changing his way of thinking. I taught Javad various anger management techniques, such as relaxation exercises. The treatment was based on cognitive reconstruction in order to better manage the anger. The plan was to slow down the automatic anger process that was scripted and ingrained in his personality.

In subsequent sessions I undertook a full review and assessment of Javad's anger control experiences and discussed steps for improved anger management. Javad provided feedback on the helpfulness of the relaxation method. Throughout therapy he was encouraged to continue and work hard at doing the relaxation exercises. The feedback from Javad was that he was able to better manage his anger toward his brother and sister and also to deal more desirably with conflicting issues at his work. Javad was encouraged to continue to keep these strategies as part of his ongoing homework.

During one of his therapy sessions Javad stated his desire to undergo nose surgery. I discussed Javad's impractical view of the nose surgery and challenged those views when appropriate. I explained to Javad that I had consulted with the plastic surgeon, who did not believe Javad's nasal deviation was in a critical stage and added that because Javad's body was still developing, it was not justifiable for the medical staff to perform an operation on his nose. These issues were discussed in detail with Javad. After several sessions, Javad's view on the nose surgery changed. For the last session, Javad was asked to bring his mother to the session.

In the last session Javad's mother was present. I explored with her ways in which the home environment could be made more desirable and conducive to support Javad in his relationships with his siblings. Javad was advised to carry on relaxation exercises and anger management techniques.

Regarding follow-up, Javad was seen after 4 months, and he reported experiencing a good level of psychological well-being and coping relatively well with his life challenges, including his work stresses. He also reported having an improved relationship with his family members. Javad no longer seemed to be preoccupied with his nose and hence did not feel the need to have surgery. He also expressed his willingness to continue his treatment when and if necessary.

DISCUSSION AND ANALYSIS

As a result of the family situation, a great deal of pressure was put on 17-year-old Javad. The family's low-income social class status appeared to be the trigger and the root cause of his challenges. He suffered from a severe level of anxiety, depression, helplessness, and extreme dissatisfaction with his appearance because of his nasal deviation. He was unable to have any control over his mental state. His presenting issues were a result of this intense experience, and his preoccupation to undergo nasal surgery provided him with an outlet for this pressure that was overwhelming him. The following CBT methods were adopted from Persons and Davidson (2010), and they suited the client's presenting issues: anger management program, formulation of a plan for various life activities, transformation of the cognitive process relating to thoughts and emotions and an alteration of the thinking pattern and mental aspects, stress- and anxiety-management techniques, and effective confrontational techniques and life-skills training.

These techniques not only enhanced Javad's self-confidence but also improved his relationship with his family, his ability to organize daily chores and activities, and his interpersonal relationships. He also developed effective techniques in life skills, and he no longer blamed his physical problems and his nose deviation for all his predicaments. He became interested in continuing his education and engaging in other activities that he liked. The involvement of family members such as Javad's mother was critical as it provided the basis for integrating his family into his social support network. It also meant that there was some sort of continuity in the work that therapy had started. Now Javad's mother is better informed of his therapy and will encourage him to do his relaxation exercises. She will also make an effort to establish a more harmonious home setting. Engaging the family is also an important part of the intervention when considering the multicultural facets of working with clients in the Middle East.

CONCLUSION

This case emphasizes that contemporary CBT underscores the importance of the culture-specific variables in the treatment of psychological problems. The flexibility and ability of CBT that is based on empirical and theoretical grounds and on the research and studies done in cultural backgrounds show the suitability and efficiency of this therapeutic method in the Iranian context. As in the case of Javad, the efficacy of this therapeutic method is evident when working with people who are not highly educated and who come from lower socioeconomic backgrounds.

QUESTIONS

1. If a hypothetical client was under similar psychosocial stresses as experienced by Javad but was from a Western family, how might his or her chief complaint be different from Javad's?
2. What specific parameters could you identify in this case report as to the focus of the therapy and as indications for the therapy being customized for Javad, bearing in mind the client's specific demographic background?
3. Considering Javad's age and religious belief system, in what manner do you think his coping style is influenced by his cultural upbringing?
4. What different approach or techniques would you adopt to help an alternative client presenting with the same symptoms as Javad but living in a well-off family environment and having higher academic performance?

5. Read the article again, trying to be as critical as possible, and determine the following: How could you best have compiled this case presentation? What alternative method of breakdown would you have adopted? How differently would you have conducted the discussion? What additional level of scrutiny could you have adopted to strengthen the argument and to offer a more robust analysis to the readers?

REFERENCES

Birashk, B. (2005, September). *Cognitive behavior therapy in Iran*. Paper presented at the 5th International Congress of Cognitive Behavior Therapy, Thessaloniki, Greece.

Birashk, B. (2012, February). CBT in Iran. *Advances in Cognitive Therapy, Newsletter, 13*(1), 6–8.

Birashk, B. (2013). Counseling and psychotherapy in Iran. In R. Moodley, U. Gielen, & R. Wu (Eds.), *Handbook of counseling and psychotherapy in an international context* (pp. 361–370). New York, NY: Routledge.

Central Intelligence Agency. (2011). *The World Facebook: Iran*. Retrieved from https://www.cia.gov/library/publications/resources/the-world-factbook/geos/ir.html

Ghassemzadeh, H. (2007). Practice of cognitive–behavior therapy in Roozbeh Hospital: Some cultural and clinical implications of psychological treatment in Iran. *American Journal of Psychotherapy, 1*, 53–69.

Persons, J. B., & Davidson, J. (2010). Cognitive–behavioral case formulation. In K. S. Dobson (Ed.), *Handbook of cognitive–behavioral therapies* (pp. 172–196). London, England: Guilford Press.

Chapter 31

COUNSELING AND PSYCHOTHERAPY IN ISRAEL: LEE'S STORY

Sharon Ziv Beiman

INTRODUCTION

The field of psychotherapy and counseling has undergone a massive change over the past 15 years in Israel. After many years in which the psychodynamic approach predominated, a variety of cognitive behavior therapy (CBT) models have recently began to flourish—in parallel with a rise in tension between clinical psychologists in the public mental health services and academia. This trend is encouraged by the interest the local professional community has exhibited in innovative approaches; an increased demand for mental health services; and the greater attentiveness of clients, practitioners, and policy makers to the efficacy of diverse psychotherapeutic approaches. These processes pave the way for an acknowledgment of the crucial contribution psychotherapy integration is making to the development of the field (see, for discussion, Jacoby, 2013).

The core psychotherapeutic method adopted in the presented case study was the relational psychoanalytic approach (Mitchell, 1993). Cognitive behavior techniques were also adopted (Stricker & Gold, 2005) in order to foster cyclic change between the symptoms, the client's experiences of herself, and her relational world (Wachtel, 1997). The case demonstrates how multifaceted personal and collective transgenerational trauma severely and unconsciously affects the client's mental life by creating unformulated mental zones dissociated from consciousness and inaccessible to mental processing (Faimberg, 2005). The trauma is consequently expressed through the repeated reenactment of traumatic states, accompanied by depressive symptoms, high distress, experiences of worthlessness, and social withdrawal. The case study demonstrates how a relational-oriented psychoanalytic psychotherapeutic process augmented by CBT interventions sought to alleviate the client's symptoms, expand her acceptance and awareness of herself and others, and enable her to open up herself to a variety of personal and interpersonal experiences and configurations. The case study presented here seeks to demonstrate the decisive and long-term impact of transgenerational trauma on Israeli society in general and psychotherapy and counseling in Israel in particular.

The Client

Lee is a single, White, 31-year-old major in the Israeli military intelligence whose stressful job is characterized by long hours and a large measure of responsibility. She is slender to the point of virtual transparency (a diagnosis of an eating disorder was ruled out), her meticulous grooming and appearance producing an impression of artificiality.

Presenting Issues and Challenges

Lee entered therapy for help coping with her painful romantic relationship with Udi (41 years old, divorced, with one child). Beginning as an intermittent romance, the relationship grew more serious over time and is now in its 5th year. The couple broke up 3 years ago, but they have been getting back together and separating again repeatedly since then. Although the sexual intimacy between the two is intense, Udi can disappear for weeks, and Lee has learned that initiating contact is fruitless because he will not respond. When he returns, her life revolves around him. She comes alive or wilts again according to his proximity or distance. She suffers from frequent waves of depressive mood; finds it very difficult to stay alone; gets upset very easily; frequently becomes enraged; is intensively accusative toward her family and colleagues; and avoids social, intellectual, or leisure activities as well as interpersonal engagements.

Case History and Developmental Background

Lee is her parents' eldest child, her brother being 3 years younger than she. Her mother is a bookkeeper born on a kibbutz. Her father came to the kibbutz as part of a military settler group and became a farmer. Around the time that Lee was born, her family left the kibbutz and moved to a nearby village. Lee's now-deceased maternal and paternal grandparents were Holocaust survivors. Her maternal grandparents were married before World War II and had two girls, both of whom were killed during the Holocaust. After the war they reunited and had Lee's mother—their only surviving daughter. Lee's father fought in some of the most brutal battles of the Yom Kippur War. She described him as a strong, handsome man who, while physically virile, is anxious and irritable. Although he was never diagnosed as suffering from posttraumatic stress disorder, he has recently been undergoing diagnostic processes that are now nearly complete. Lee stressed that when she was a child he would lash out at her violently when she opposed him; she described his severe fits of rage. She is angry at her mother for telling on her to her father when she did something wrong despite knowing that he would respond harshly. She said, "I will never forgive them for what they have done to me." Her father is proud of her and her military role. She says, "I connect to military heroism; it excites me, but actually, it has ruined our lives." Although the mother appears to be more accessible than Lee's father, she constantly needs to preserve her own strengths and thus abandons Lee. As a child, Lee found it difficult to fit in with her peers, frequently evoking resistance from them. Through Grades 4–6, her classmates ostracized her, and adult intervention proved futile. This memory, too, serves as a source of anger toward her parents: "They never know what to do," she said harshly and accusatively. During this period, Lee forged a suit of armor that became her identity—a conceited and critical stance toward others and a communicative withdrawal.

THE THERAPY

Lee has been in therapy for 2 years, an accepted duration in Israel for integrative psychotherapeutic process that focuses on awareness, acceptance, formulation, and change of maladaptive interpersonal and personal patterns. During the first period, we focused on her relationship with Udi, a charismatic and successful colonel in her unit. As Lee described him, he is the "perfect man"—well-built, good-looking, confidence-inducing, tough, and astute. The close affinities between Lee's description of her father and Udi are conspicuous. Both are well-built, closely associated with the military, barely speak, and are tough and hurtful—which is also what makes them attractive.

Lee has been engulfed by the relationship's pain and has gradually been more ready to see how her life has become a "waiting station" for Udi. We have discussed her sense of worthlessness and how she needs him in order to feel meaningful. We have united on a joint quest to enable her to feel herself. We have tried to discover what she feels and wants. The psychodynamic work of deepening her awareness by intensive working through of the interpretative narratives we co-create is accompanied by my profound emotional participation in the process. I also assimilate into the therapeutic process cognitive techniques—such as paraphrasing and challenging beliefs—and behavioral activation of a variety of actions she tends to avoid in her life (meeting friends, reading, and enjoying her time at home) in order to alleviate her cognitive, emotional, and physical depressive symptoms.

Lee invests hugely in the attempt to overcome the emptiness she feels in being with herself, her thoughts and feelings customarily being preoccupied with her yearning for Udi or her anger and accusations toward her peers, commanding officers, or parents. As time has passed, however, she has begun to evince a better sense of herself. Gradually reducing her feelings of dependency on Udi, she has begun to assert herself by refusing to automatically respond to his approaches.

We have addressed how her inner experience of weakness has led her to construct a suit of armor based on style, status, and appearance and how she attempts to create a sense of security and worthiness from this while simultaneously seeking similarly armored others in order to strengthen her own self. I have struggled to show her that she avoids seeking warmth, closeness, and softness out of fear of pain and humiliation. Following each confrontation, I am aware that she has responded not only to the contents—which hold a therapeutic message for her—but also to my style of presence and assertiveness. We have discussed the possibility that part of her involvement in the treatment is based on my adopting the role of the "armored other"—the type of relationship she seeks in order to gain a sense of herself.

The more I get to know Lee, the more I grasp the magnitude of the insult and terror she feels, but I can also understand why her father would lash out at her violently after repeated provocations. While I feel Lee's enormous pain, I also empathize with the mother, imagining the emotional pain she must feel as the only child of Holocaust survivors who lost both their other daughters.

Because, theoretically, I assume that development of subjectivity is inseparable from that of the ability to maintain vital, complex, and flexible intersubjective interaction, I endeavor to recognize and empathize with her pain and anger and help her formulate her experiences while simultaneously promoting her awareness of the narratives of the meaningful others in her life. This stance provides Lee with a feeling of relative relief and a greater sense of understanding of her parents and Udi, which mitigates the outrage that they have not been there for her. Her basic attitude nonetheless holds firm: "They should have behaved differently; they should apologize."

In my inner dialogue, I advise myself to stress my empathy with her pain, validate her suffering, and provide a forum for witnessing and articulating her anguish and thoughts. I am aware of the need to be very gentle when offering her the narratives and hurts of her parents' and Udi's wounds. "Stay empathic, don't confront her too often," I tell myself. At the same time, other intensive voices within me impulsively instruct me to confront her with an alternative narrative to the only one she appears to know. I understand these inner pressures as an enactment of the polarized dyads of "doer and done to" representing her relationship with her parents and Udi as well as polarized relational configurations in my world. This polarization repeats traumatic experiences while simultaneously preserving their dissociation in order to avoid experiencing the full intensity and complexity of the anxiety and pain that accompany the horror.

I share my experiences and insights with her openly. The more the process progresses, the more she is able to integrate her diverse feelings toward herself and her meaningful others.

Lee has a lesbian cousin to whom she relates in disgust, becoming very upset when her mother invites her, her partner, and their daughter to dinner. "I'll never be convinced that this is normal," she insisted. I lost my empathic ability upon hearing this and expressed my irritation. "I find that hard to hear. I have close friends who are gays and lesbians. It's difficult for me to hear them being defined as disgusting," I told her. Tension built between us, and I apologized for the aggressive manner in which I reacted, explaining that I find her ideology offensive. I expressed my willingness to try and accept her feelings and at the same time was aware of the modeling I was exemplifying via my apology and my inner search for mutual empathy when judgmental "guns" fired—hers toward lesbians and mine toward her.

I began to focus more and more on the issue of forgiveness. From a relational perspective, I find it important for the therapeutic process to allow movement in Lee's internal world, in me, and in our relationship between calling for forgiveness and remaining empathically connected with Lee's pain and anger; between a position that suggests she release her grasp on justice and one that acknowledges the many ways in which the trauma has prevented her from fully experiencing herself as a multiple subject who is deeply connected to other multiple subjects; and between yearning for intimidating closeness and remaining within the comforting yet restricting compounds of her protective armor.

As the therapy has proceeded, I have engaged more deeply with her angry accusations, and she has become better able to understand her parents' narratives. Her experience of their behavior as "inexcusable" and her perception of them as "wholly culpable" has softened; her depressive symptoms have decreased; her ability to regulate her emotions, organize her life, and feel ownership of her emotions has grown concomitantly; and her social life has introduced her to relational joys. At the same time, she still needs to feel pretty and successful and to engage with someone armored like Udi in order to feel good. Lee and I continue our therapeutic work toward the further enhancement of her personal development and growth as she increasingly accepts herself and creates more genuine and less armored relations with others.

DISCUSSION AND ANALYSIS

The therapeutic process as a whole was informed by the premise that the presence and effects of transgenerational and collective trauma create untouchable zones of experience (Faimberg, 2005), rigid intrapsychic patterns, and painful and compulsive interpersonal relationships (Benjamin, 2004). The therapy focused simultaneously on encouraging the formulation (Stern, 1983) and cointerpretation (Mitchell, 1993) of the client's experiences and narratives of herself and the meaningful others in her life. My readiness as the client's therapist to become emotionally and subjectively involved in these therapeutic processes while focusing on processing enactments in the therapeutic dyad fostered mutual recognition and halted the polarization of her experiences into dyadic victim–perpetrator patterns (Benjamin, 2004).

Behavioral activation (Dimidjian, Barrera, Martell, Muñoz, & Lewinsohn, 2011) was assimilated into the psychodynamic and cognitive therapeutic work in order to stimulate the client's physiological, social, intellectual, and emotional life. All these therapeutic channels contributed to a significant alleviation of her depressive symptoms and a rise in her self-esteem, self-awareness, and self-acceptance. They also fostered a comprehensive multiperspective understanding of herself and others, combined with an increasing ability to regulate her emotions, thoughts, and actions and a growing sense of ownership of herself.

As the therapy progressed, I began to focus more and more on the issue of forgiveness. Up until recent decades neither psychoanalysis nor psychotherapy has treated forgiveness as a psychological issue in its own right. In the domain of empirical research, the past two decades have witnessed a growing engagement with the concept and its potential contribution to therapeutic processes (e.g., Lundahl, Taylor, Stevenson, & Roberts, 2008).

Psychoanalytic theory has also paid increasing attention to forgiveness in recent decades. Akhtar (2002) suggested that forgiveness has three therapeutic aspects: revenge, reparation, and reconsideration. Revenge allows the victim to express his or her aggression, thus enabling the victim to move from a passive to an active stance while mitigating the split between self and other. This aspect addresses the need to make space in the therapeutic process for the anger and rage that Lee feels.

Reparation is vital for the healing process and involves the other's acknowledgment of his or her responsibility for the damage he or she has caused, which enables mourning and the transition to a more active position of forgiver or nonforgiver. In many cases—such as Lee's—the perpetrators (i.e., the parents/Udi) do not acknowledge their offense. In such situations, the therapist's acknowledgment that an offense has been committed serves as a type of a replacement for the actual perpetrators' acceptance of their responsibility—an acknowledgment that Lee seeks from me.

The third therapeutic aspect of forgiveness according to Akhtar (2002) is reconsideration. From a Winnicottian standpoint, reconsideration involves placing the perpetrator's deeds in a transitional space, thus facilitating examination of the traumatic events from different angles. The articulation of this aspect furthered my understanding of the urge I felt not only to make room for her anger and acknowledge her suffering in her parents' name but also to insist on showing her their narrative as well as her own.

From this standpoint, forgiveness promotes the liberation of dyads in Lee's life from their continual implosion into "doer and done to" patterns (Benjamin, 2004) and her intrapsychic world from the grasp of obstructing self-states (Bromberg, 1998). Thus, Lee can gradually release herself from the repetitive move between the positions of aggressor and helpless victim and can make space for experiencing other qualities and kinds of personal and relational configurations.

CONCLUSION

This case demonstrates the transgenerational effects of massive and collective trauma in the context of Israeli society. It illustrates how the mechanisms of dissociation are activated in order to avoid reexperiencing the traumatic horror. This dissociation, in turn, obstructs the processes of mourning, acceptance, and formulation; consequently, personal and collective past events and relations are reenacted through repetitive and painful polarized dyadic and social patterns. The capability to experience intimacy is paralyzed, and the consolidation of personal identity, self-esteem, and flexible gender roles is hindered. The inner and the interpersonal worlds are captured in armor, and polarized and rigid states are characterized by chronic reversals of roles between helpless victim and hostile perpetrator.

The psychotherapeutic process described demonstrates how the relational psychoanalytic approach—which views the therapeutic relationship as a major arena of change—can open up a mental space in which experiences and narratives can be formulated, facilitating a release from repetitive and polarized subjective and intersubjective states. The case study also illuminates how assimilating CBT interventions into the relational psychoanalytic process can augment cyclical therapeutic influence between behavior, experiences of the self, and relational exchanges. The case study presented herein thus reflects on and hopes to contribute to two of the primary challenges of the field of counseling and psychotherapy in Israel: coping with the painful, destructive, and frequently inaccessible impact of massive transgenerational traumas and promoting psychotherapy integration.

QUESTIONS

1. To what extent can we conceptualize the client's presenting issues as a consequence of the Israeli–Jewish historical, national, and social traumatic context in which she grew up, developed, and lives today?
2. What can be learned from the presented case regarding the complex interrelations between gender and national–social traumas?

3. What can be learned from the presented case and the described therapeutic process on the principles of treating transgenerational traumas and their effects on mental life and interpersonal–social patterns, with an emphasis on the contributions of the relational psychodynamic theory and Paul Wachtel's cyclical psychodynamics integrative model?

4. What are the interrelations between the influences of the therapeutic alliance and the active interventions that can be articulated when analyzing the presented case?

5. What can be concluded from the presented case on the role of forgiveness in the therapeutic process under different conditions, in different contexts, and from different theoretical points of view?

REFERENCES

Akhtar, S. (2002). Forgiveness: Origins, dynamics, psychopathology, and technical relevance. *Psychoanalytic Quarterly, 71*, 175–212.

Benjamin, J. (2004). Beyond doer and done to: An intersubjective view of thirdness. *Psychoanalytic Quarterly, 73*, 5–46.

Bromberg, P. M. (1998). *Standing in the spaces: Essays on clinical process, trauma, and dissociation*. Hillsdale, NJ: Analytic Press.

Dimidjian, S., Barrera, M., Jr., Martell, C., Muñoz, R. F., & Lewinsohn, P. M. (2011). The origins and current status of behavioral activation treatments for depression. *Annual Review of Clinical Psychology, 7*, 1–38.

Faimberg, H. (2005). *The telescoping of generations: Listening to the narcissistic links between generations*. London, England: Routledge.

Jacoby, R. (2013). Counseling and psychotherapy in Israel: Milestones, disputes and challenges. In R. Moodley, U. Gielen, & R. Wu (Eds.), *Handbook of counseling and psychotherapy in an international context* (pp. 371–382). New York, NY: Routledge.

Lundahl, B. W., Taylor, M. J., Stevenson, R., & Roberts, K. D. (2008). Process-based forgiveness interventions: A meta-analytic review. *Research on Social Work Practice, 18*, 465–478.

Mitchell, S. A. (1993). *Hope and dread in psychoanalysis*. New York, NY: Basic Books.

Stern, D. B. (1983). Unformulated experience: From familiar chaos to creative disorder. *Contemporary Psychoanalysis, 19*, 71–99.

Stricker, G., & Gold, J. (2005). Assimilative psychodynamic psychotherapy. In J. C. Norcross & M. R. Goldfried (Eds.), *Handbook of psychotherapy integration* (2nd ed., pp. 221–240). New York, NY: Oxford University Press.

Wachtel, P. L. (1997). *Psychoanalysis, behavior therapy, and the relational world*. Washington, DC: American Psychological Association.

Chapter 32

COUNSELING AND PSYCHOTHERAPY IN LEBANON: ZEINA'S STORY

Brigitte Khoury and Yasmine I. Fayad

INTRODUCTION

Lebanon is a Middle Eastern Arab country; although regional differences do exist, the country has been open to and significantly influenced by Western influence through education and the media. Over the years, and especially after several wars and security problems, mental health has been receiving increasing attention. Although professional mental health services were and still are considered a taboo for many Lebanese individuals, the need for mental health professionals has become much more pressing. As a result, the number of facilities for the treatment of mental disorders has increased in Lebanon; in addition, clinical psychology has been gradually introduced into universities as a degree on its own, with its own training requirements and with the aim that graduates will be able to fill society's needs for such services.

Many psychologists in Lebanon have been trained in France and adopt a psychoanalytic approach to therapy. However, in the last 15 years, with the return of many professionals from abroad, especially North America, all types of psychotherapy have been introduced in Lebanon, for example, cognitive behavior therapy (CBT), gestalt, psychodynamic, humanistic, and eye movement desensitization and reprocessing (Khoury & Tabbarah, 2013). More recently, the Department of Psychiatry at the American University of Beirut has offered a 2-year training program for clinical psychologists following a CBT approach, and it is expected that this approach will be available to service providers and service users.

Counselors and psychologists in Lebanon often have to exercise their own judgment to adapt their Western-based clinical knowledge and skills to the Lebanese cultural context in which they are practicing. Contextual factors such as family dynamics and religiosity as well cultural beliefs, values, and norms should be taken into account in case conceptualization and treatment planning (Dwairy, 2006).

In this chapter, we discuss the case of Zeina, who underwent counseling and psychotherapy through a CBT approach as well as other methods that are clinically useful with Arab clients, such as supportive counseling (Poulin, 2009) and family therapy (Rasheed, Rasheed, & Marley, 2011). Therapy also included indigenous and traditional healing methods, which have proven to be very effective for individuals whose identities are largely influenced by religion (Moodley, 2007). Family therapy techniques were also used to facilitate the confrontation between Zeina and her mother in a safe, therapeutic environment. Finally, religion was incorporated into the therapy to help Zeina achieve some level of peace and acceptance regarding her experience with her boyfriend, Samir.

THE CLIENT

Zeina is a 24-year-old Lebanese Arab heterosexual female; she is a Christian Catholic from a middle-class rural household and has no disability. Zeina is studying for her master's degree in business administration at a local university in Beirut and lives in a dorm while her family resides in their hometown 1 hour outside Beirut in the mountains. She has two younger siblings: one brother, who is 14 years old and still in school; and one sister, who is 20 years old and is studying for her bachelor's degree at a different university closer to their hometown.

PRESENTING ISSUES AND CHALLENGES

Zeina presented with impairing anxiety symptoms and fears about facing her parents with her desire to marry a man from a different religion. She was also very conflicted about having to convert to Islam. She had always been a believer and a practicing Christian, and, for her, conversion is a religious sin. She also could not imagine herself not celebrating Christmas with her husband and her children and was very worried that she would not be able to genuinely embrace Islam. Although her boyfriend tried to reassure her, telling her that she could still practice her religion even after she converted, she was nevertheless worried about the future of her children and their religious education. She also wondered whether or not she would end up resenting her husband in the long run if she were to convert and subsequently lose her family and the respect of society after marrying him. All this, of course, added pressure to her relationship with her boyfriend and made her resentful of him. Zeina was experiencing intense anxiety and fear of the possible consequences following her disclosure to her family. Her anxiety symptoms were expected given the conflict-ridden situation she was in and the difficult major decisions she had to make.

CASE HISTORY AND DEVELOPMENTAL BACKGROUND

Zeina sought counseling for anxiety symptoms that were distressing her and had been affecting her functioning for the past year. She had been in a relationship for the past 2 years with a young Muslim man from Beirut named Samir. They were serious about their relationship and wanted to get married in the future. The main problem was that that they were from different religions, and they feared Zeina's parents would be against their union. They had been dating in secret without her family knowing. She had already met his family, who were welcoming toward her. In Lebanon, the woman follows the man's faith; hence, she would need to convert to Islam if they were to marry. In some cases, the man's family displays less resistance to a multifaith marriage than the woman's family because the woman has to convert to the man's faith anyway. However, in general, many families oppose interfaith marriages.

Because their relationship had become serious and she anticipated telling her parents about it, Zeina had been feeling anxious and scared, dreading the prospect of facing her family. She feared they might force her to leave him and leave the university and her life in Beirut as a step to keep her away from him. Because she depended on them financially, her parents had the power to cut her off from money, which might force her to return home. Besides the financial stress, Zeina's main concern was that she would disappoint her parents by not marrying someone within their religion; she would be going against her community and society through an act seen as something close to treason. She would, most significantly, be turning her back on the religious teachings she grew up on and risk expulsion from the church.

No official census has been collected in Lebanon since 1932 because there is a delicate balance of political power between the presiding 18 recognized religious sects that would be potentially risky to disturb. According to the Central Intelligence Agency (2014) World Fact Book, Christians make up 40.5% of the population (21% of the total population is Maronite Catholic, 8% Greek Orthodox, 5% Greek Catholic, 6.5% other Christians), and they equally hold 64 seats, as do Muslims, in the Lebanese Parliament given that candidates for elections run for office posts on the basis of their sects. However, key positions in government are still held by Christians, such as the posts of president, chief of staff of the army, and the head of the treasury.

Zeina was raised in a middle-class rural Christian Arab household with a strict religious and traditional upbringing. Conforming to social and religious norms is part of her identity. Given that she is the first of her generation in the family to get a university education, she is a source of pride and hope for her parents. Thus, Zeina grew up highly influenced by her parents', society's, and family's expectations. For her, being successful entails conforming to these expectations and gaining the respect and admiration from her family and society. She derives great levels of gratification by pleasing her parents and being treated as an example for other people her age or younger. Her need to abide by social and religious norms is central to her survival given that she grew up in a rural traditional community where the importance of religion and society are particularly pronounced. Moreover, Zeina's educational background and upbringing always emphasized the importance of being an honorable and educated woman who marries a respectable man and successfully raises a family. She was meant to prepare herself for a good marriage that would honor her and her family. An interfaith marriage represented everything she thought she would never be involved in, and carrying through with it would entail giving up parts of her identity that she may never be able to recover.

THE THERAPY

I (Brigitte Khoury) saw Zeina for eight sessions. I used CBT as a main therapeutic approach because it—as well as other methods that are clinically useful, such as supportive counseling and family therapy—has been shown to be effective in the treatment of anxiety disorders, especially with Arab clients.

When Zeina first came in, we set the therapeutic goals. She wanted to tell her parents about her desire to marry Samir, face the consequences, and make a final decision about her future. She also wanted some relief from her anxiety symptoms, which were significantly impairing her functioning. In addition to empowering her and increasing her self-efficacy, I also had to understand how her experience of falling in love with a forbidden man and deviating from social, family, and religious norms was affecting her view of herself and shaking the diverse aspects of her identity. It was of paramount importance to acknowledge how this experience had affected who she is as a young Arab woman coming from a rural, traditional Christian family.

Therapy helped Zeina to feel less anxious and move gradually toward real action. The first few sessions were focused on practicing breathing and muscle relaxation techniques and learning about sleep hygiene. Then, we reviewed her fears and anxieties about her parents' reactions, established worst-case scenarios, and considered the options she had by reframing them, using successful examples from her past in similar anxiety-provoking situations, then having her explore the consequences of a different way of thinking and behaving. When Zeina was ready for action, facing the family was done gradually, starting with the sister because she was the closest and easiest to handle. Role-playing was used, allowing Zeina to practice how she would confront her sister, gently yet in an assertive way. Relaxation techniques were also used before and during the role-play to decrease Zeina's anxiety. Her irrational fears and anxieties were challenged to help her develop a more realistic outlook on the situation at hand. Zeina eventually told her sister, who was at first shocked but later on understood Zeina's position. Zeina's sister warned her that their parents would never accept such a union. However, she was ready to support Zeina. Informing her sister was a relief and achievement for Zeina. It increased her self-confidence that she could successfully manage another self-disclosure and encouraged her to face her mother. However, although she tried to face her mother, she could not directly tell her.

When her mother came to visit her, Zeina asked for a joint session to disclose to her mother. The mother did not take it well at all, and she did not accept it. She said harsh things to Zeina, which made her cry. The mother drew many negative scenarios about the father knowing, the shame Zeina would bring to the family, and the prospect that her sister might not find someone to marry her since Zeina brought shame to the family.

Because Zeina was a firm believer in Christianity and practiced her religion, she had many questions and inquiries about the conflict she was going through from a religious perspective. She told me that she was close to a young priest in her parish, so I advised her to discuss this issue with him, which she did. This discussion brought her some relief as well as answers to her questions related to her faith, her love of a man of different faith, and the problems she was having within her family.

As a result of these various interventions with CBT and supportive counseling, her anxiety symptoms were alleviated and her functioning was enhanced. She also learned to problem solve and finally got the courage to move to action and face her parents. The self-disclosure was very stressful. However, she was able to handle it, and finally she decided to leave her boyfriend and conform to her family's and society's expectations.

When I asked her how she felt, she did admit still feeling resentful and bitter about what happened to her, and she hoped one day she would be able to get over that resentment. As an attempt to console herself, she said, "I can't always be guided by how I feel if I want to live with and adapt to the constraints posed by my society, family, and religion. I have to learn to be more rational." When I asked her finally what would possibly reduce her resentment and bitterness, she mentioned praying and talking to a priest. Given that she was a believer, I encouraged her to do that more often to relieve some of the anger that resulted from this difficult experience. Using religion in the healing process can help her reach some level of acceptance and peace of mind.

Zeina terminated therapy free from anxiety symptoms, functioning well, and with effective coping methods to deal with the residual anger resulting from this difficult experience.

DISCUSSION AND ANALYSIS

The importance of the social context in the lives of Arab clients is pivotal. A closer look at the diverse sociocultural backgrounds of a client is essential to guide treatment and make it more individualized and person-centered (Lago, 2011; Moodley, 2007). As an Arab female, Zeina is expected to be much more submissive to the rules and expectations of her family and society than if she were male. A gender hierarchy exists within the patriarchal family, putting females in a subordinate position relative to males. In therapy it is critical to recognize the importance of the family in the lives of Arabs (Dwairy, 2006).

Coming from a rural middle-class household, Zeina might be experiencing more pressure to conform to her family and community's values, norms, and traditions, given that those communities in rural areas may be more collective than those in urban areas (Dwairy, 2006). Being a young Christian female, she is expected to marry someone from her own religious denomination. Her boyfriend, Samir, is a Sunni Muslim. Interfaith marriage is not accepted in the Arab world, including Lebanon. First, intermarriages require one of the members of the couple—usually the female—to convert, which is considered a religious sin and a dishonorable act by society. Second, Lebanon does not have civil laws for matters of personal status, and as such civil marriage is still not well accepted by religious authorities and society (Barakat, 1993).

In 2013, the Higher Committee for Consultations in the Ministry of Justice approved the first marriage of a young couple that requested to register their civil marriage in Lebanon after having figured out a loophole: A memo, "Karrar 60," issued in 1936 elaborates that individuals who do not belong to any of the recognized 18 sects can opt for civil marriage based on any foreign law of choice, provided that the statute is approved by Lebanon. Accordingly, a public notary can uphold the marriage of Lebanese citizens who either do not belong to any sect or have removed sectarian affiliations from their official documents (made possible in 2009 by the Ministry of Interior). The Lebanese constitution is committed to the Universal Declaration of Human Rights, making legislation for civil marriage supersede local legislation against it. However, notwithstanding the 2013 example, which was the closest to a civil marriage happening in Lebanon, civil marriages still are not considered a common procedure recognized by the government and accessible to all those who desire it. It is only performed under the condition of both parties (the couple) renouncing their religious affiliation, which is no small feat in a country divided along its sectarian lines.

In addition, one of the major concerns related to interfaith marriages is the religious upbringing of the children. With two parents of different religious backgrounds, the religious identity of their children may be at stake and become unstable. Teaching the children both religions and having them choose their religious membership later on may not be a realistic option. In addition, having the children grow up without being educated in any religion may not be an adaptive alternative in a culture where religion plays a pivotal role in the lives of its members. Finally, the ease with which a Muslim husband can divorce his wife by saying the statement "You are divorced thrice" and thereby delivering three divorces at once or by repeating the word divorce (*talaq*) three times may make an interfaith marriage with a Muslim man unappealing for some Christian families.

At 24 years old, Zeina is considered by society to be at marriageable age. Marriage is critical for the lives of Arab women because it provides them with what singlehood deprives them of. Arab women seek a marital union for various reasons other than love, such as sexual and emotional intimacy, freedom and independence, financial security, higher social status, and children (Dwairy, 2006). Throughout Zeina's therapy and self-disclosures with her family members, the therapist made sure that the process was empathic and supportive to help her process the strong negative emotions she was experiencing (e.g., anger, resentment, guilt, shame) and to help her when she felt her family was against her. At times Zeina was very conflicted, alternating between feelings of anger and guilt toward her parents. Although the conflict with the mother initially broke her, it did lead to new insights about who she was and what she wants with the help of the therapeutic process.

Despite a great deal of initial resentment, Zeina decided to give up Samir. By then, her relationship with him had become very strained because of the external pressures, and she had become very resentful of him. The price of keeping her boyfriend proved too high. Carrying through an interfaith marriage would have cost Zeina her family, her religion, and her education—all parts of herself that she might never be able to recover. For her, self-actualization involves achieving goals that are not directed against the family and religion and do not threaten her identity, which is largely based on her ties with significant others.

Most important, marrying a man from a different sect would have deeply threatened her identity and required her to relinquish parts of who she is. This prospect is significantly disturbing and would have considerably jeopardized her resilience, which might have led to the emergence of psychopathology manifesting in anxiety symptoms and feelings of weakness and vulnerability. Thus, resolving the conflict between her needs and the expectations of her society and family would reduce her symptoms and improve her mental health.

CONCLUSION

In the Arab world, one's family, society, and religion are considered to be central to the life of the individual. Those who deviate from the family's social and religious norms may experience rejection to the point of social ostracism. It is very difficult for Arab individuals to remain unaffected by these external pressures, especially if they were raised and socialized according to these norms. The counselor should be aware that with Arab clients, psychopathology may arise when an individual's needs and desires conflict with the norms and values set by the family, religion, and the wider social network. Hence, the therapist should consider the importance of these influences in the person's life and include key people in the therapy, such as families, spouses, relationships, and so forth; doing so may determine the success of the therapy and the positive outcome to the individual. Therefore, an integration of a particular therapeutic approach with family therapy and some indigenous treatments particular to the region can be the right combination when dealing with Arab clients and may lead to the most satisfactory results for the individual seeking our help.

QUESTIONS

1. If the client were a male and presenting with such a problem, do you think the treatment would have been different as well as the end result? In your opinion, would he have made different choices on the basis of his role as a man in such a conservative society where men have more freedom of action?
2. Do you think that the client actually suffered from a pathology, or was it purely contextual? Would this patient have sought help under different circumstances?
3. Having some knowledge about the Lebanese culture through this case, what do you think the patient could have done differently? What resources could she have used? In your opinion, was her choice based on positive coping or avoidance of conflict?
4. What are some other treatment approaches besides CBT that you think might have been helpful in this case, taking into account the culture and the family structure?
5. What do you think were some obstacles to the treatment, and how would you have done it differently? What were the limitations in your opinion to having a different result?

REFERENCES

Barakat, H. I. (1993). *The Arab world: Society, culture, and state*. Los Angeles: University of California Press.

Central Intelligence Agency (2014) *World Fact Book: Lebanon*. Retrieved from https://www.cia.gov/library/publications/the-world-factbook/geos/le.html

Dwairy, M. (2006). *Counseling and psychotherapy with Arabs and Muslims*. New York, NY: Teachers College.

Khoury, B., & Tabbarah, S. (2013). Counseling and psychotherapy in Lebanon: Past, present, and future. In R. Moodley, U. Gielen, & R. Wu (Eds.), *Handbook of counseling and psychotherapy in an international context* (pp. 383–392). New York, NY: Routledge.

Lago, C. (2011). Diversity, oppression, and society: Implications for person-centered therapists. *Person-Centered & Experiential Psychotherapies, 10*, 235–247.

Moodley, R. (2007). (Re)placing multiculturalism in counseling and psychotherapy. *British Journal of Guidance & Counseling, 35*, 1–22.

Poulin, J. (2009). *Strength-based generalist practice: A collaborative approach*. Belmont, CA: Marcus Boggs.

Rasheed, J. M., Rasheed, M. N., & Marley, J. (2011). *Family therapy: Models and techniques*. Thousand Oaks, CA: Sage.

Chapter 33

COUNSELING AND PSYCHOTHERAPY IN PALESTINE: SHADEN'S STORY

Shafiq Masalha and Rana G. Nashashibi

INTRODUCTION

Counseling and psychotherapy is a growing field in the Palestinian Occupied Territories, which are still under Israeli military control in spite of the fact that a Palestinian Authority (PA) is in place. According to Nashashibi, Srour, and Srour (2013), "the PA is very dependent on foreign aid. Consequently, the quality and availability of mental health services in Palestine are affected by the donor's policies" (p. 393). The Palestinian community of Jerusalem is made up of approximately 300,000 people. They reside primarily in the eastern part of the city, which was under Jordanian rule from 1948 until 1967, when it was occupied by Israel along with the rest of Jordan's West Bank.[1] Unlike the rest of the Palestinian population in the occupied territories, the Palestinians of East Jerusalem were given the status of *permanent residents*, which allows them to vote in the municipal elections in the city, collect social security, and access public health care. This status, however, is not equal to citizenship, and Palestinian Jerusalemites do not carry Israeli passports.

Ten years ago, following the eruption of the second intifada[2] and the failure of the Oslo Peace Accords, the Israeli government began constructing a wall around Jerusalem that divided Palestinians in the city from the rest of those in the West Bank (including neighboring cities such as Ramallah and Bethlehem). This wall only furthered the growing isolation of Palestinian Jerusalemites, who have also faced a widening gap between East and West Jerusalem throughout the last four decades. The impact of such segregation has been devastating. Recent reports from the Israel Bureau of Statistics indicate that 66.8% of the Palestinian families in Jerusalem live below the poverty line, compared with only 23.3% of Jewish families in the city. Statistics also show that more than 100,000 children in East Jerusalem live in poor circumstances[3] (Association for Civil Rights in Israel, 2010).

---

[1]In the 1967 war between Israel on the one side and Jordan, Syria, and Egypt on the other side, Israel ended up occupying the West Bank and east Jerusalem; the Golan Heights, which is part of Syria; and the Sinai peninsula, which is part of Egypt.

[2]*Intifada* refers to the Palestinian popular uprising against the Israeli occupation. There were two intifadas, one that erupted in 1987 and the other in 2000.

[3]Poor circumstances mean lack of adequate services in relation to health, education, and social welfare.

Upon first interviewing Shaden (the client in this case) and her parents, it became evident that two therapeutic paths ought to be taken to ensure her success: individual therapy with Shaden as well as therapy with her mother and father exclusively. These tracks each lasted for 3 years, with Shaden being seen twice per week for the first year and her parents once per week. The family was able to afford the intensive therapy program using the school insurance coverage. On certain occasions there was a third path, which was seeing the three of them together in one session.

THE CLIENT

Shaden is a 17-year-old woman from a traditional Muslim Palestinian community in Jerusalem. Shaden is the oldest of seven children, with three younger sisters and three younger brothers. Both she and her mother wear traditional Muslim dress and cover their hair. Like other Muslim teenagers in her area, Shaden began wearing the dress when she turned 13. She had a romantic relationship with another teenager her age. As an Arab girl living in a conservative family, this was a concept not accepted, and consequently, Shaden kept her relationship hidden from her parents. At some stage of the relationship she shared her secret with her mother, who kept it concealed from her father.

PRESENTING ISSUES AND CHALLENGES

Shaden was referred to psychotherapy by a court expert[4] following an accident a few months prior, where she fell from the roof of her school. Following the incident, she began to show signs of psychological trauma, including dysphoria, emotional outbursts, social withdrawal, and academic retreat. Prior to the referral, Shaden also attempted suicide. Both the psychiatrist and neurologist who examined her concluded that the symptoms Shaden displayed could be explained by psychological rather than organic factors.

As a result of the accident, Shaden suffered from a severe abdominal pain as well as bone fractures in her two legs. She was hospitalized for 40 days and went through two surgeries, one in the abdomen and the other in her two knees. After discharge from the hospital, she spent another month in a rehabilitation center, followed by getting physiotherapy on a weekly basis. The surgeries left Shaden with scars on her belly, which were covered by her traditional dress. She also had pain in her knees, which was exacerbated when she walked long distances.

CASE HISTORY AND DEVELOPMENTAL BACKGROUND

When Shaden became an adolescent her father's closeness to her became obvious, and in many ways she was like a "partner" to him, in times replacing her mother. Salem, the father, used to consult her on issues that were more fitted to consultations between the parents. He talked to her about problems concerning the other children in the family and asked her to mediate between him and other family members, including her mother.

---

[4]A court expert is a professional designated by the court to assess the damage physically and psychologically from an accident.

After Shaden's accident and injury, the tension between the parents grew. Salem felt that his wife became more distant, and he was unable to relate to her as a partner. After work he spent his time with friends and at times with his family in Ramallah. In a similar manner, Fatima, Shaden's mother, felt distant from her husband. She felt frustrated by his distant attitude, the lack of expressions of love from his side, and his authoritarian manner. She also felt that his attitude undermined her authority not only toward Shaden but toward all the children. In one incident, Salem came home late after Fatima had already gone to bed; he found no dinner prepared, got angry, and physically pulled Fatima out of bed while screaming and shouting. He felt that his wife ignored him and did not do her duty as a wife. When she resisted his pulling and screamed back at him, he slapped her on the face. She was physically and psychologically hurt. Fatima called the Israeli police, who came shortly after and arrested Salem. At the time Fatima was convinced that calling the police was the right move and she had no other choice. She recalled several incidents that had taken place within the past few months in which Salem had humiliated her and hit her. She felt that she had to act and stop his violence.

Salem was hurt that he had been jailed by his wife, who according to the culture is supposed to be obedient and submissive. Her family and leading figures in their community intervened and pressured her to withdraw her complaint. They convinced her to withdraw her complaint to the police and to declare to them that she accepted him back home.[5] This incident remained an open wound in the couple's relationship. Salem was unable to forgive, whereas Fatima felt protected, safe, and empowered. Shaden felt torn between the parents, unable to take sides and to stand with one against the other. Salem turned to his oldest son, trying to turn him against the females in the family.

Shaden kept suffering: On the one hand she was struggling with a physical and psychological injury, but on the other hand she felt abandoned by her family. No one was available to Shaden even when she was going through surgeries. Her academic functioning deteriorated, and she failed the high school exams. She began to manifest symptoms of depression. She suffered dysphoric mood, lack of energy, helplessness, and hopelessness. Her self-worth went down; she developed self-hatred and attempted suicide. At this point, she was referred to psychiatric care and was administered medications. She kept taking antidepressant pills while in psychotherapy. During that period the insurance company, which financially covered the treatment, agreed to double the therapeutic sessions. Shaden was seen twice a week, and her parents were seen once a week. The intensive therapy lasted for one more year. In the second and third years, Shaden was seen regularly once a week, whereas her parents were coming to sessions when it was warranted.

THE THERAPY

Therapy continued for 3 years with financial support from the insurance company. The therapy took two tracks: one track involving individual therapy with Shaden and the other involving family therapy with her parents. It was clear to the therapist (Shafiq Masalha) during the intake assessment period that Shaden needed help with the following: mourning the loss of her old self as well as some of her

---

[5]The family law of 2002 gives the woman the right to imprison or send away the perpetrator in cases of domestic violence.

functioning and relationships, restoring her self-esteem and confidence after they were crushed by the accident, and understanding and processing what had happened to her and how the trauma had affected her. She also needed help reorganizing her life, taking into consideration the trauma and working with her family to help her reintegrate.

To achieve these goals, the therapist worked to empower Shaden through pointing to her strengths and talent. She demonstrated high self-awareness and awareness to events that occurred in the family. On several occasions, Shaden was able to interpret the origins of their behavior and attitude. She said, for example, "Dad was never cared after as a child. He never experienced a father–child relationship, and that is the reason why he does not know how to treat us. He loves his children but has no way to reach to them." These qualities enabled her therapist to empathize with her.

Shaden brought up several topics throughout the therapy process. The details of the incident, the injury, and the hospitalizations were coming up often, especially in the first 2 years. She cried heavily when she recalled the surgeries. She was unable to stop the flow of tears when she remembered how her father never attended any of her surgeries and how he was always missing when she was on her way to the operating room and during her recuperation from surgery. Her mother's presence day and night at her bedside in the hospital was a major comfort for her. Hospitalization for a Palestinian person in an Israeli hospital is a difficult experience. The cultural gap and the problem of language between the Palestinian client and the Jewish health staff in the hospitals have been found to increase the stress of the Palestinian client (W. Masalha, 2001).

In therapy, Shaden mourned her abandonment by her boyfriend. He stopped responding to her phone calls. After her injury she saw him only twice. He explained to her that his parents and family resisted their marriage. It was clear to her that their attitude was influenced by the fact that she was injured and had undergone a surgery that left scars on her body.[6] Once Shaden mourned this separation in therapy, she worked on establishing a new relationship. She wondered how she would introduce herself to a new young man whom she met and liked. She was uncertain whether and at what stage she would share with this potential partner the details of her accident and the injury.

In the last year of therapy, Shaden was preoccupied with her future plans to fulfill her dreams on the academic and vocational levels. She was determined to pursue higher academic studies. With the help of her therapist, she solidified her belief that an academic degree would empower her ability to cope with cultural barriers. One major obstacle was the cultural judgment of her as a handicapped woman. She became convinced that academic studies would increase the chance for her to get married and have a job. Shaden developed a vision of her future: She visualized herself as a "paramedical" therapist running a multidisciplinary treatment center for children and adolescents who had suffered from trauma. She estimated that her studies would be completed in 3 years. Around the time she graduates she will receive a large amount of money in compensation from the insurance company. With that money she will start the project. The therapist expressed his admiration that her vision is feasible and possible to attain. It will be

---

[6]It is common among Arab families that there is a strict code of how a bride should look. Any damage or deformity, whether physical or psychological, might affect her chances of getting married.

the first private multidisciplinary treatment center in her community. She, however, anticipated one major obstacle that would hinder her plans. Her father will want to use the money for his own needs.

Shaden grew up not only under the influence of a "powerless" mother, but also under the influence of a self-centered father. At an advanced stage of therapy with Shaden, she clearly expressed this understanding of her parents' personalities and attitudes. The therapist not only made efforts to help her be aware of these negative influences but also develop skills to overcome them. Shaden used to describe events in which she experienced feelings of weakness. Those experiences were analyzed in therapy, and alternative ways of reacting to them were explored.

Six months prior to ending therapy, Shaden passed the final high school exams and was accepted to college. She was about to start her studies in one of the paramedical programs. She was convinced that after graduation she will fulfill her dreams of establishing a treatment center. The therapist was not certain how things would go on after therapy but felt that Shaden would be on a new track upon entering college. Being a student in college and living away from home will help her gain autonomy and find her way in life.

DISCUSSION AND ANALYSIS

Shaden came from a traditional Arab family. According to her social norms and culture, she had to obey her father's orders and demands. The family's cultural values would often disapprove of Shaden and her mother's behaviors. Shaden was expected to give her father the lead in determining her future and using her insurance money. The father's extended family or clan was supporting him against his wife and daughter. Haj-Yahia (2000) discussed the dynamics of the Arab families and their attitude toward domestic violence. Involving the Israeli police to arrest her husband put Fatima under severe pressure within her community. Within these circumstances, therapy took place. The therapist was trying to find the bridges between the cultural values represented by her father and the psychological health of Shaden. In a way this balancing act represents the conflict between individualism and collectivism. Clinical work and research have been confronting this dilemma in the last few decades. Several clinicians have called for accommodating Western therapy to non-Western cultures (Al-Krenawi & Graham, 2000; Dwairy, 1999), whereas other clinicians have warned against this accommodation and called for preserving the individual autonomy by following the universal approach in therapy (Coleman, 1995; S. Masalha, 1999). In his article on approaches in cross-cultural therapy, Coleman (1995) concluded that efficient therapy should focus on the individual in his or her cultural context. When therapy goes along this track, it takes into consideration three components: the culture, the individual, and the interaction between the two. In the case study discussed in this chapter, the therapist, himself, was trained as a Western psychotherapist and felt that Shaden ought to gain autonomy from her parents, though this may go beyond what her cultural values would permit.

Traditionally, much emphasis has been put on the intactness of women's bodies, especially when they become candidates for marriage. In many cases, brides have to endure body scrutinizing by women from the groom's family, which usually involves his mother and/or sisters. In Shaden's case, the scars on her body are a serious obstacle to getting married. The therapist believed that one way for Shaden to overcome this obstacle was to become an empowered woman and start an intimate relationship with a man who will develop unconditional love for her. Traditional marriage in her case may not work out because in such marriages families—not just the couple, themselves—play a major role in the process.

It is common for families to move to an extreme after a trauma; however, in Shaden's family, they never underwent a process of role reorganization. On the flexibility dimension, Shaden's family was in serious fluctuations between being rigid and chaotic. The rigid roles and manners that were passed to the family from previous generations were not able to withstand either the changes that occurred with the family life (the trauma) or the changes that were taking place in the "community in transition" from traditional to nontraditional.

The incident in which the police were called to intervene and Salem was arrested can be considered a turning point for this family. This incident created a new balance that introduced more boundaries and structure in the system. The incident resulted in the females gaining more power over the males in the family. The community, on the other hand, would not have allowed these women to go too far in gaining all the power. The women would pay a high price, like being ostracized not only by the extended family but also by the larger community. The case of Shaden and her family cannot be understood without using cultural as well as universal clinical terms.

CONCLUSION

A therapist in such cases has to be culturally sensitive without compromising the universal understanding of the human psyche. Attachment theory and the systemic approach to families were used in both case conceptualization and therapeutic intervention. A therapist working in non-Western contexts can be neither purely normative nor purely culturally based, as neither approach alone can be of real service to the clients' interests. Therapists must be talented and skilled to analyze and integrate the elements introduced in therapy and orchestrate the therapeutic process to the best interests of the client.

QUESTIONS

1. If Shaden were a male teenager, but all other qualities (age, injury, family, culture, etc.) remained the same, do you think that Shaden's life would have developed differently?
2. Imagine that Shaden, while keeping all qualities, was living in a Western culture; how would her life have developed?
3. The therapist in this case followed two approaches, individual and systemic. Would you recommend another way of treating the case?
4. In the family therapy, the therapist saw Shaden and her parents while excluding the rest of the family. How did this fact influence Shaden and her family? Would you, as a therapist, insist on seeing all family members, despite their relatively large number?
5. Shall the therapist in this case refer parents to another therapist and avoid being simultaneously the therapist for both Shaden and her parents?

REFERENCES

Al-Krenawi, A., & Graham, J. R. (2000). Culturally sensitive social work with Arab clients in mental health setting. *Health & Social Work, 25*, 9–12.

Association for Civil Rights in Israel. (2010). *A report and data of the association: A look in to East Jerusalem that is beyond titles.* Retrieved from http://www.acri.org.il/he/?p=2480

Coleman, H. (1995). Cultural factors and the counseling process: Implications for school counselors. *School Counselor, 42*, 180–185.

Dwairy, M. (1999). Toward psycho-cultural approach in Middle Eastern societies. *Clinical Psychology Review, 19*, 909–915.

Haj-Yahia, M. M. (2000). Wife abuse and battering in the sociocultural context of Arab society. *Family Process, 39*, 237–255.

Masalha, S. (1999). Psychodynamic psychotherapy as applied in an Arab village clinic. *Clinical Psychology Review, 19*, 987–997.

Masalha, W. (2001). *Hetmodedot Horeem Leyeladeem em Pgeaat Moah Hamora, Leahar Shehror Hayeled Memerkaz Hashekom* [Parental coping after discharge of their brain-injured children from the rehabilitation center] (Unpublished master's thesis). The Hebrew University of Jerusalem.

Nashashibi, R., Srour, A., & Srour, R. (2013). Counseling and psychotherapy in Palestine: Between occupation and cultural colonialism. In R. Moodley, U. Gielen, & R. Wu (Eds.), *Handbook of counseling and psychotherapy in an international context* (pp. 393–403). New York, NY: Routledge.

Chapter 34

COUNSELING AND PSYCHOTHERAPY IN TURKEY: CEREN'S STORY

Senel Poyrazli and Murat Balkis

INTRODUCTION

Psychotherapy in Turkey is practiced by a wide variety of mental health practitioners, such as counselors, psychologists, and psychiatrists (Poyrazli, Dogan, & Eskin, 2013). Because the pioneers of the mental health field were trained in the United States, primarily Western counseling and psychotherapy theories are practiced in Turkey (Dogan, 2000), such as the following: psychodynamic, person-centered, gestalt, behavior, and cognitive behavior (Dogan, 2000; Poyrazli & Eskin, 2013). In more recent years, an effort to incorporate indigenous and cultural information into psychotherapy and counseling training has been noticed (e.g., Bolak-Boratav, 2004). The purpose of this effort is to help mental health practitioners in Turkey provide more culturally appropriate treatment models.

In this chapter, we provide a case study to illustrate how counseling and treatment processes are carried out by mental health practitioners in Turkey and how cultural expectations could affect the type and severity of psychological problems experienced by Turkish individuals. The case we discuss is about Ceren, who self-referred to counseling at the counseling center of a university she attended. She was suffering from insomnia and recurring nightmares. The treatment that Ceren received was based on an eclectic approach that was drawn from psychodynamic, gestalt, person-centered, behavior, and cognitive behavior theories. While presenting her treatment, we also discuss how Ceren's ethnic cultural background, the gender-role socialization process she was subjected to growing up, and her religion contributed to her psychological symptoms. All of these diversity factors were taken into consideration during Ceren's treatment.

THE CLIENT

Ceren is a 22-year-old single heterosexual Caucasian female who is a Turkish college student in her sophomore year studying management. She lives with her father and mother in a condominium. Her only sibling, a 19-year-old sister, is a freshman college student attending school in a different city. Similar to her family, Ceren is a practicing Muslim. Both of Ceren's parents are close to their 50s. Her mother is retired, having taken advantage of the retirement laws that allow individuals to retire at a younger age in Turkey. Her father still continues to work as a small businessman. The family is considered middle class. Ceren's grandparents immigrated to Turkey from an Eastern European country.

PRESENTING ISSUES AND CHALLENGES

Ceren's initial presenting problem was insomnia that had been continuing for 3 years. She suffered from fatigue and lack of concentration caused by a lack of sleep. Some nights she could sleep for only 30–40 minutes. She indicated that she was currently sleep deprived, having slept only a few hours a day within the previous week. She wanted to be able to regulate her sleep. Besides insomnia, Ceren was also suffering from nightmares. She was afraid to fall asleep, being fearful that she would have a nightmare.

CASE HISTORY AND DEVELOPMENTAL BACKGROUND

Ceren's grandparents immigrated to Turkey in the 1950s from an Eastern European country after a change in its political regime. Both of Ceren's parents were very young at the time. The new government of this country severely discriminated against its Turkish inhabitants, resulting in a large group of Turks immigrating to Turkey to escape from ethnic discrimination (Cavusoglu, 2007). These immigrants settled in a particular neighborhood in a western Turkish city, where Ceren was brought up. Ceren stated in the sessions that this is a close-knit community. There is an emphasis on practicing their home culture, and grandparents play an important role in childrearing. Children are taught about their culture and are expected to marry individuals with similar cultural backgrounds. They are also monitored very closely and only allowed to visit the homes of family friends.

Ceren grew up in a family and neighborhood where she was subjected to traditional gender roles. Girls are strictly monitored by their own families as well as other families in the community. Courting or dating behaviors are not allowed. Preserving one's virginity and hymen until the marriage are crucial. According to her religion, having premarital sex is a sin. In the case of multiple daughters in the same family, the oldest one would be supervised much more closely and would be asked to set an example for the younger ones. Boys, conversely, would be given more freedom and independence. However, they would still be expected to inform their family about their activities and whereabouts at any given moment. For both genders, a strong tie to the parents and the extended family is expected even after the child becomes an adult and has his or her own nuclear family. There is a strong financial commitment to sons in this culture and a cultural expectation that a man should have at least a condominium apartment before he can get married. As a result, it is customary that parents buy a condominium for their son before his wedding.

Growing up in this culture, Ceren was expected not to date or have sexual relations until she was married. Strong messages about these expectations would be frequently stated to her by her father. Her father would also closely follow her activities, communicating a general mistrust in her ability to fulfill these expectations.

Ceren's personality development seemed to have been strongly affected by her culture and upbringing. She wanted to be always in control over her life and had a perfectionist tendency. She wanted to meet the expectations of her father, but at the same time she was afraid of making mistakes. She also seemed to have low self-confidence.

The Therapy

Following Ceren's wishes and a discussion between her and the counselor, it was decided that the initial treatment goal would be the treatment of insomnia. An eclectic approach that included psychodynamic theories, gestalt theory, behavior theory, and cognitive behavior approaches was used in Ceren's treatment. Socratic questioning and systematic desensitization (Beck, 2011; Corey, 2012) were among the techniques used. Ceren's treatment consisted of 55-minute weekly sessions for close to a year. Toward the end of the treatment, the sessions were held every other week. In total, she attended approximately 40 sessions. Health care services in Turkey are predominantly offered by the government and include extensive psychological treatment services. College campuses are mandated by the government to provide medical and mental health services to the students. Ceren was able to take advantage of these services, free of charge, because she was a college student.

While her insomnia was being treated, Ceren shared that she also suffered from nightmares. These nightmares were three different recurring dreams. In one, she would see her father getting out of his portrait picture that was hung in her bedroom, getting bigger, and coming toward her. In the second one, she would see snakes crawling up her legs. In the third one, she would see stray dogs chasing her on the street. She would wake up from these nightmares frightened and unable to go back to sleep. She did not feel safe at night and was anxious that she would have these nightmares again. To help herself go to sleep and to lower her anxiety, she would sleep with the lights and the TV on. She had visited a psychiatrist for the treatment of insomnia a few years earlier; however, she did not want to use the medication that she was prescribed. Considering these symptoms and nightmares, in the intake session the counselor explored any type of trauma Ceren might have experienced. She denied any history of trauma and/or sexual abuse by her father.

To eliminate the stimuli in her room that may have been contributing to her insomnia and nightmares, the counselor asked that Ceren move her father's portrait picture to another room. Ceren reported immediate improvement in her length of sleep and also a reduction in the frequency of her nightmares. The counselor also made the observation that Ceren was more trusting of his skills and more open toward him when the first assignment he gave (i.e., removing the father's picture from the bedroom) resulted in positive outcome.

In the sessions, when they discussed the relationship dynamics between Ceren and her father, the counselor would often make the observation that Ceren's voice sounded angry and resentful. Ceren would frequently cry in the sessions. The counselor asked her to "give a voice" to her tears and let them state what they tried to say. Through this exercise, Ceren developed awareness that she felt powerless and hopeless, especially toward her father and what the future was to bring for her. When Ceren and the counselor discussed cultural expectations and how those expectations may have been related to her father's treatment of her, Ceren did develop some awareness that the unfair treatment she received from her father was based on her culture and that this type of treatment is commonly practiced in her community. She stated that similar to her, other girls and young women in her community would be subjected to restrictions because of their gender. Developing this awareness helped Ceren lower her anger toward her father. However, she was still upset that he treated her and her sister differently. She could not understand the permissive style he had toward her sister.

The counselor used dream analysis and interpretation based on psychodynamic theories and gestalt theory to help Ceren analyze how her dreams may be related to her fears and anxiety. Ceren was continuously being told to avoid men and to protect her hymen. The primary person who communicated these messages was her father. She was also told that men should not be trusted and that they might take sexual advantage of her. Furthermore, given the cultural expectation of protecting one's hymen, she developed an awareness in the sessions that she was afraid of male sexual organs and had generalized her strong dislike of her father toward other men. In relation to her dream where the snakes would crawl up her legs, she came to the conclusion that perhaps she was identifying snakes with male sexual organs. When the snakes crawled up her legs, she would fear that her own sexual organs would be violated.

While her therapy sessions were continuing, the pressure Ceren felt exerted by her father was alleviated somewhat when a development related to her sister took place. Ceren's sister secretly married her boyfriend and became pregnant shortly thereafter. When her parents learned about this and the fact that she had dropped out of college, they were very upset. Ceren, however, was glad to see that her sister had done the things her father feared Ceren, herself, would do. While feeling bad for her sister, Ceren also felt empowered toward her father. When her father was being overly restrictive of Ceren and somewhat permissive of her sister, Ceren would bring this up frequently with her father and criticize his preferential treatment. In these arguments, she would also warn her father that his permissive style might result in her sister doing things that would not be culturally appropriate. Therefore, when the news about her sister's marriage was revealed, Ceren felt empowered toward her father and believed that she deserved more acknowledgment and trust from him for acting in culturally appropriate ways. She shared in the sessions that her father's attitude did change somewhat toward her. He started to listen to her more and was more likely to say yes to her requests. He also became more trusting of her and would not question her whereabouts. She stated that she could see that deep down he knew that he had treated Ceren too harshly and was regretful.

During the sessions, the counselor worked through Ceren's transference where she would often treat the counselor as if he were her father. She would argue strongly and raise her voice. Through the counselor's patience, empathic understanding, and unconditional acceptance, Ceren was able to trust him and move away from her generalization that "all men are not to be trusted, and all men are disgusting" to "some men can be trusted, and not all men are disgusting." As the treatment progressed, she was also able to develop an attraction and trust toward a man she met at her internship site. Initially, she was confused about her feelings of attraction; however, with the help of the counselor, she came to accept the fact that these were normal feelings and that it was acceptable to like somebody.

Within the treatment process, the counselor also uncovered some of Ceren's maladaptive thoughts. She believed that everyone must like her and that she should please everyone. Through Socratic questioning, Ceren was able to gain awareness that this belief was related to her cultural upbringing and her father's expectations of her. She wanted to gain approval and praise, especially from her parents. She also felt that she should protect herself against any type of cultural criticism by behaving well and following the gender roles that were assigned to her. With the help of the counselor, she then was able to determine the consequences of not pleasing everyone and not having everyone like her. When she received criticism from one of her parents or from another adult in the community, she felt worthless and unimportant. One consequence of not pleasing everyone would be that she would experience these emotions. Another consequence was related to her socioeconomic status. She was from a middle-class family, and she herself did not have economic freedom. She thought that she could only exist within her family, not by herself. Therefore, she believed that not pleasing the adults around her might lead to them not financially supporting her. On the other hand, she became aware of the fact that she still experienced certain negative emotions even when she pleased everyone, such as anger toward the age- and gender-related cultural restrictions she was subjected to and feeling that this was unfair.

Ceren decided to terminate the counseling process when she no longer suffered from nightmares or insomnia. The therapist agreed with her wish to terminate and invited her to come back to see him if her symptoms were to return or if she needed help for other psychological reasons. In the termination session, Ceren acknowledged several factors that helped her get better. The awareness she gained about her culture, the positive close relationship she achieved with two men (the counselor and the man she met at her internship site), and her father's trusting attitude toward her after her sister secretly married her boyfriend were among the top reasons that helped Ceren reach psychological well-being.

DISCUSSION AND ANALYSIS

The counselor in this case was a Caucasian male from an ethnic minority group in Turkey. He was brought up in a Muslim culture; however, he was not a practicing Muslim. The client was aware of the counselor's minority status. These background characteristics came into play in different ways during the treatment process.

Similar to Ceren, the counselor, too, was brought up in a culture where the relationships between men and women were strictly defined and premarital romantic relationships were discouraged. Communication between both genders (especially among nonrelatives) either did not exist or was kept to a minimum. He thought that these types of gender relations were too restrictive. When he went away to attend college, he realized that he, himself, had some difficulty communicating and building close relationships with women because this was not something he did growing up. Initially, he felt uncomfortable around women and could not easily open up to them. He used this background to understand Ceren's experiences and empathize with her. He knew that it would be difficult for Ceren to share her emotional experiences and thoughts about intimacy with him because of his gender.

Establishing trust and building a relationship were two of the initial therapeutic process goals the counselor had. However, on the basis of the intake session, he knew that it was not going to be easy to gain Ceren's trust. She was taught not to trust men. In addition, it seemed like she was generalizing the anger she had for her father onto other men. The counselor knew that his gender was putting him at a disadvantage when it came to building initial trust. As a result, the counselor paid particular attention to being empathic, nonjudgmental, and patient (Rogers, 1995) with Ceren so that she would not put him in the category of men not to be trusted or liked. He also wanted Ceren to see that not all men are the same and that she could trust and feel close to some of them.

Helping Ceren become aware of her culture and the gender-role socialization she was subjected to seemed to help her empathize with her father and see the cultural expectations he was subjected to for his role as a father. When she became more aware of the fact that the majority of the other girls and women were also subjected to the same cultural expectations and restrictions, she understood that she was not being singled out. Moreover, through self-disclosure (Corey, 2012), the counselor shared some information about his upbringing and the restrictive gender roles that he grew up with in his community. A comparison of his upbringing and Ceren's upbringing helped Ceren realize that there were other communities in Turkey that practiced more restrictive gender roles than her community did.

An additional factor that strengthened Ceren's trust toward her counselor was the fact that he, too, was from an ethnic minority group. Although this ethnic group was different than Ceren's, she knew that because of his minority status, the counselor was likely to understand and support her strong ties to her own culture and pride in her cultural heritage.

Conclusion

This case shows how cultural expectations in Turkey, particularly related to gender roles, can affect an individual's psychological well-being. The treatment plan in this case illustrated different theories and techniques that are being used in Turkey. In this particular case, we see that the treatment approach was drawn from psychodynamic, gestalt, Rogerian, behavior, and cognitive behavior theories. The case also illustrates how multicultural background characteristics both on the therapist and client sides could play an important role in the therapeutic process and that consideration of these characteristics is crucial to the success of the treatment process.

Questions

1. How do you think Ceren's religious background, gender, and ethnic minority status contributed to her psychological symptoms?
2. Identify reasons that caused Ceren to develop mistrust toward men. In this regard, was it helpful or not to have a male counselor?
3. Ceren was living in a neighborhood that was predominantly dominated by immigrants who had moved from an Eastern European country to Turkey. How might this community have given power to Ceren's father to be more influential on her?
4. Ceren's counselor used an eclectic approach to treat her. What type of theories or approaches would you have used if Ceren were your client?

5. Some of the techniques the counselor used were Socratic questioning and systematic desensitization. Considering your own training, what other techniques would you have used with Ceren?

REFERENCES

Beck, J. S. (2011). *Cognitive therapy: Basics and beyond*. New York, NY: Guilford Press.

Bolak-Boratav, H. (2004). Psychology at the cross-roads: The view from Turkey. In M. J. Stevens & J. Wedding (Eds.), *Handbook of international psychology* (pp. 311–330). New York, NY: Taylor & Francis.

Cavusoglu, H. (2007). "Yugoslavya-Makedonya" topraklarından Türkiye'ye göçler ve nedenleri [Immigration from Yugoslavia–Macedonia to Turkey and its reasons]. *Bilig Dergisi, 41*, 123–154.

Corey, G. (2012). *Theory and practice of counseling and psychotherapy*. Belmont, CA: Brooks/Cole.

Dogan, S. (2000). The historical development of counseling in Turkey. *International Journal for the Advancement of Counseling, 22*, 57–67.

Poyrazli, S., Dogan, S., & Eskin, M. (2013). Counseling and psychotherapy in Turkey: Influence of Western theories, unique challenges, and the need to develop culturally-inclusive methods. In R. Moodley, U. Gielen, & R. Wu (Eds.), *Handbook of counseling and psychotherapy in an international context* (pp. 404–414). New York, NY: Routledge.

Poyrazli, S., & Eskin, M. (2013). Bisexual identity in a traditional culture: A case study from Turkey. In S. Poyrazli & C. E. Thompson (Eds.), *International case studies in mental health* (pp. 69–83). Thousand Oaks, CA: Sage.

Rogers, C. (1995). *On becoming a person: A therapist's view of psychotherapy*. New York, NY: Mariner Books.

CONCLUSION

Chapter 35

THERAPY WITHOUT BORDERS: BRIDGING COUNSELING AND PSYCHOTHERAPY ACROSS CULTURES

Roy Moodley and Bhisham Kinha

INTRODUCTION

Wherever it is practiced in the world, all counseling and psychotherapy has a cultural component as it is "embedded in distinctive socio-cultural milieus" (Draguns, 2008, p. 21). The infusion of counseling into the myriad of complex cultures around the world has been made possible through globalization and internationalization of Western health and mental health care practices; in addition, it has been made easier by the economic enterprises of neocolonial practices that still exist in the former colonies of the Western countries. Currently, it is the scholarly endeavors of some researchers, psychiatrists, and psychologists supported by large multinational pharmaceutical companies that are at the forefronts of dispensing the message of global mental health. The traditional knowledge and healing practices of low- and middle-income countries that were underground during the colonial period and that made a feeble attempt at resurrecting themselves since independence were quickly laid to rest by the domination of Western mental health practices. There are, of course, some exceptions; for example, Mao Tse-Tung and the Cultural Revolution prioritized traditional Chinese medicine (TCM) and politically resisted this kind of repression, thus making it possible for TCM to flourish—resulting in its worldwide practice.

In our analysis of the cases, we were struck by the dominance of the Western Eurocentric models across all chapters, with the exception of the Nigeria case (see Chapter 4; reflecting on traditional healers and healing as the source of therapy) and, to a lesser extent, the West Africa case (see Chapter 3). Although cognitive behavior therapy appears to be popular, it is not the dominant approach as anecdotal evidence seems to suggest; humanistic approaches also have a strong foothold in clinical practice in the world (see Table 35.1 for an analysis of the various presenting issues and the particular approaches used in each country).

The growth of multicultural or intercultural counseling in Canada, the United States, and Europe has also helped counseling to become transcultural, or transnational. This proliferation of counseling and psychotherapy across the diaspora cultures and the globe have been supported by scholars, researchers, and practitioners, many of whom were trained in the West and who, in turn, teach and train

TABLE 35.1
THERAPY ACROSS BORDERS:
PRESENTING ISSUES AND COUNSELING APPROACHES

Country	Presenting Issue	Counseling Approach
Egypt	Frustration, hopelessness, financial strain, cultural identity	Eclectic (psychoeducational, behavioral) and traditional
West Africa	Anxiety, decreased concentration, headaches, sleep disturbance	Traditional healing, person-centered
Nigeria	Low mood, confusion, worthlessness, fatigue, headache, sleep disturbance.	Traditional healing
Morocco	Borderline personality disorder, suicidal depression	CBT
South Africa	Impaired motor functioning, decreased memory, mood fluctuation, insecurity, sadness	Integrative
Sub-Saharan Africa	PTSD, grief	Trauma-focused CBT
Australia	Anxiety (GAD symptoms), depression, sleep disturbance	CBT
China	PTSD, depression, grief, loss of identity	Interpersonal psychotherapy
India	Infertility, difficulty in marital relationship, infertility-based familial discord	CBT (modified with relevant cultural practices)
Japan	Issues with child's misbehavior and aggression, societal shame	Humanistic integrative, play therapy (for child)
Malaysia	Moderate to severe autism (hyperactivity, acting out, destructive and obsessive behaviors)	Behavioral (computer-based multimedia cognitive aid)
Pakistan	Depression, marital difficulties	Emotion-focused therapy
The Philippines	Depression, life dissatisfaction, hopelessness	Solution-focused story sharing (culturally modified)
South Korea	Somatization disorder (neck pain, blurred vision), anxiety	Focusing-oriented approach
Argentina	Stress, anxiety, depression	Psychoanalysis
Brazil	Anxiety (existential)	Psychodynamic
Canada	Anxiety, decreased concentration, headaches, sleep disturbance	Solution-focused
Trinidad and Tobago	Suicidality, major depressive disorder, anxiety	Rational emotive behavior therapy
Mexico	Anxiety, stress, depression	Brief
United States	Existential guilt, suicidal ideation	Existentialism (modified to include spiritualism)
Denmark	Borderline personality disorder, self-harm behaviors, eating disorder not otherwise specified	Dialectical behavioral therapy
France	Depression, concerns over future	Vocational counseling

(Continued)

TABLE 35.1 *(Continued)*
THERAPY ACROSS BORDERS:
PRESENTING ISSUES AND COUNSELING APPROACHES

Country	Presenting Issue	Counseling Approach
Germany	Traumatic brain injury (increased aggressive behavior and impulsivity, decreased cognitive functioning), decreased self-evaluation	Clinical child neuropsychology, CBT
Italy	Anger, anxiety, fear of opposite sex	Nondirective intervention (based on person-centered)
The Netherlands	Depressive mood, fatigue, increased anger, alcohol abuse, withdrawal	Stepped treatment (problem-orientation, CBT, group mentalization-based treatment)
Spain	Major depressive disorder, anxiety, loss, parenting issues	Psychobiological, transactional analysis
Russia	OCD, dependent personality disorder, depressive symptoms, decreased impulse control	Integrative (CBT, family systems, social psychoanalysis)
United Kingdom	Selective mutism, racism, abuse from childhood peers	Talking pictures therapy
Iran	Nasal deviation, anxiety, depression, decreased impulse control, increased anger	Psychoeducation, CBT (modified for culture and language needs)
Israel	Relationship issues, depressive moods, increased emotionality, avoidance behaviors	Relational-oriented psychoanalytic psychotherapy, CBT
Lebanon	Anxiety symptoms, relationship concerns	CBT, supportive counseling, family therapy
Palestine	Psychological trauma (dysphoria, increased emotional reactivity, withdrawal), suicide attempt, intrafamilial conflict	Attachment theory, systemic approach
Turkey	Insomnia, nightmares	Eclectic (psychodynamic, gestalt, person-centered, behavioral, CBT)

Note. CBT = cognitive behavior therapy; PTSD = posttraumatic stress disorder; GAD = generalized anxiety disorder; OCD = obsessive-compulsive disorder.

counselors across the world. As a result, non-Western countries tend to produce their own experts in this field to undertake research and practice in local contexts. When these practitioners disavow the traditional knowledge and healing practices of the countries they live and work in, they further marginalize indigenous healing practices (see Moodley, Gielen, & Wu, 2012, for a discussion on counseling and psychotherapy in an international context). Although this marginalization may be happening in many non-Western cultures, mental health practices in the West have taken an ironic twist. After years of colonial oppression and suppression of the cultural and traditional healing practices of non-Western cultures, there appears to be a growing interest in research, theory, and practice of indigenous knowledge. Many of these healing ideas and methods are now becoming a part of the mainstream curriculum in counselor training. For example, Buddhist mindfulness and meditation courses, although not called Eastern methods of health and mental health, are now a norm in counseling and psychotherapy training and practice. Credit needs to be given to the work of scholars who engage with indigenous or aboriginal healers and healing practices who started the profession on this journey of discovery of alternative and complementary healing practices. Some examples include Salish Indian rituals (Jilek, 2004), sweat lodges (Smith, 2005), medicine wheel (McCormick, 2005), and storytelling (Poonwassie & Charter, 2005). This openness to alternative therapy has opened the way for other cultural practices, such as Caribbean healing traditions (Sutherland, Moodley, & Chevannes, 2014).

Although the cases in this book do not reflect the infusion and integration of each country's cultural and ethnic healing traditions in substantive ways, it is critical to remember that the cases themselves reflect Western counseling and psychotherapy as it is practiced in specific sociocultural and geopolitical contexts. It is these multivaried transnational contexts and the specific stories that are told to particular counselors and psychotherapists that make therapy without borders possible. Both as individual cases and as collective stories, they project a larger human dimension of the pain and suffering of the human condition and ways in which healing can take place both individually and collectively.

Although we do not claim to offer a detailed analysis of the cases, as we are not in a position to undertake this kind of exploration—which required each author's consent of such a process before they agreed to contribute to this volume—we intend to offer a broad and cursory overview of some of the main themes and ideas that emerge in the chapters. First, we discuss how culture, gender, and social class issues interact in a multicultural and diversity context. This reflection leads to a discussion of the therapeutic integration and the collective self, followed by an exploration of the divided subject—body, mind, and spirit—that featured prominently in many cases. Finally, we look at the question of case study evaluations and its value in forming generalizations across borders.

CULTURAL, GENDER, AND SOCIAL CLASS CONSIDERATIONS

Many chapters commented on demographic information, particularly the intersectionality of the Group of Seven identities—such as race, gender, class, sexual orientation, disability, age, and religion (Moodley, 2011)—and its relationship with the presenting issues (see Table 35.2). Some of these identities were discussed and incorporated into the clinical work (see Chapters 10 and 13), whereas in others it did not feature in any significant way into the clinical treatment or outcomes of the cases. Certainly, tethering particular cultural or multicultural meanings to an individual client increases the risk of stereotyping and generalizing. Clients are varied, complex, and contradictory in the way they represent and present their psychological distress to the counselor. Because each client inhabits a particular clinical niche with the therapist, the Group of Seven identities become the background that informs the evolution of the narrative and its interpretation of it. Within a dynamic spatial, temporal, and relational context, the clients' identities play out or enact their potentialities. In other words, the Group of Seven identities provide the basis for both psychopathology and for resilience in clinical work. Although these identities are not all active, experienced, and expressed at the same time in therapy, counselors may need to be cognizant of the lived experience of clients. For example, a client's identity as a lesbian will feature and be felt differently when she is home alone reading, on a date in a public space, or performing religious rites with family. We might find that forms of identity are dynamic in that they are activated in unique permutations depending on the context and that certain identities and the performance of these identities emerge to provide us with forms of access and power. In Kamalpreet's case (see Chapter 18), we see a negotiation between various identities. A 22-year-old woman of South Asian descent living in Canada, the client presented that the intersecting gender and ethnocultural expectations of marriage prevented her pursuit of professional fulfillment. With psychotherapeutic intervention, Kamalpreet, who did not have a strong affiliation to her religious community, came to inhabit religious spaces to access mentorship from her aunt and to generate a positive presence in the community that would alleviate the scrutiny from her deferral of marriage. In a sense, the client leveraged religious membership for its relational benefits as a means of countering the challenges of being a young Punjabi woman to her personal goals.

Similar consideration can be undertaken in relation to social class membership or socioeconomic status (SES). We observe that several chapters reflected on how this identity influences treatments and outcomes. Twenty-seven of the 34 cases implicitly or explicitly describe clients as either middle- or upper-middle class. Of the remaining six clients arguably reflecting aspects of working-class or low-SES backgrounds (in Brazil, Trinidad and Tobago, China, Malaysia, the Philippines, and Iran), their cases include medical/diagnostic intervention at some point in the treatment history.

Indeed, individuals with low-SES membership are at an increased risk of psychopathology (Chen, Matthews, & Boyce, 2002; Lorant et al., 2003; Wohlfarth, 1997). In their work on the psychological implications of low-SES, Pope and Arthur (2009) suggested that the related toll of daily life negatively affects the individual's physical and emotional state, and they noted that access to psychological service is often restricted to those who can afford private treatment or who have insurance coverage through their place of employment. As result, mental health treatment for clients of low-SES standing can be limited to medical domains, and those clients are more likely to be given a psychiatric diagnosis (Leeder, 1996). It is important to note that our analysis of the cases and the cases themselves are located within a Western paradigm, particularly when this book intends to use a broader international scope.

There are important factors to note as we investigate trends in the interplay between SES and access to psychological services. Although the authors throughout this text do not use a consistent methodology for defining and measuring SES, they nevertheless make explicit and implicit reference to SES. It is clear that there are variations between regions and countries in the health care services provided and to whom they are made available, which have serious mental health consequences for clients. For example, 17-year-old Javad (see Chapter 30), in the absence of his father, has taken on a provider role within the family; this role has undermined his ability to further his education and to access the surgical treatment he desires.

TABLE 35.2
THERAPY ACROSS BORDERS: GROUP OF SEVEN IDENTITIES

Country	Gender	Age	Ethnicity/Race	Religion/Spirituality	Sexual Orientation	SES	Disability
Egypt	Male	36	Arab	Muslim	Heterosexual	Middle	Unknown
West Africa	Male	27	Togolese	Christian	Heterosexual	Middle	Unknown
Nigeria	Male	44	Yoruba	Unknown	Heterosexual	Middle	Unknown
Morocco	Male	25	Arab	Muslim	Heterosexual	Middle	Unknown
South Africa	Male	30s	Unknown	Christian	Heterosexual	Middle	Unknown
Sub-Saharan Africa	Female	26	Unknown	Christian	Unknown	Middle	Unknown
Australia	Female	61	Caucasian	Jewish	Heterosexual	Middle	Unknown
China	Female	41	Chinese	Unknown	Heterosexual	Working	Unknown
India	Female	32	Indian	Hindu	Heterosexual	Middle	Unknown
Japan	Female	39	Japanese	Unknown	Heterosexual	Middle	Unknown
Malaysia	Male	5	Chinese	Unknown	Unknown	Working	Autism
Pakistan	Female	43	Pakistani	Muslim	Heterosexual	UM	Unknown
The Philippines	Male	54	Filipino	Unknown	Bisexual	Working	Unknown
South Korea	Female	50	Korean	Christian	Heterosexual	Middle	Unknown
Argentina	Male	66	Anglo-Saxon	Catholic	Gay	Middle	Unknown
Brazil	Male	83	Unknown	Catholic	Heterosexual	Working	Unknown
Canada	Female	22	Punjabi	Sikh	Heterosexual	Middle	Unknown
Trinidad and Tobago	Female	28	African/Indian	Catholic	Heterosexual	Working	Unknown
Mexico	Female	32	Mixed	Catholic	Heterosexual	Middle	Unknown
United States	Male	22	Unknown	Catholic	Heterosexual	Middle	Unknown
Denmark	Female	24	Caucasian	Agnostic ("spiritual")	Heterosexual	Middle	Unknown
France	Female	25	Caucasian	Unknown	Unknown	Middle	Unknown
Germany	Male	17	Caucasian	Christian	Unknown	Middle	TBI
Italy	Female	37	Italian	Catholic	Heterosexual	Middle	Unknown
The Netherlands	Male	40s	Caucasian	Unknown	Heterosexual	Middle	Unknown
Spain	Male	45	Caucasian	Catholic	Heterosexual	Middle	Unknown
Russia	Male	52	Russian	Unknown	Heterosexual	Middle	Unknown
United Kingdom	Male	13	African	Unknown	Unknown	Middle	Mutism

(Continued)

TABLE 35.2 (*Continued*)
THERAPY ACROSS BORDERS: GROUP OF SEVEN IDENTITIES

Country	Gender	Age	Ethnicity/Race	Religion/Spirituality	Sexual Orientation	SES	Disability
Iran	Male	17	Persian	Muslim	Unknown	Working	Unknown
Israel	Female	31	Caucasian	Unknown	Heterosexual	Middle	Unknown
Lebanon	Female	24	Arab	Catholic	Heterosexual	Middle	Unknown
Palestine	Female	17	Arab	Muslim	Heterosexual	Unknown	PS
Turkey	Female	22	Caucasian	Muslim	Heterosexual	Middle	Unknown

Note. SES = socioeconomic status; UM = upper-middle; TBI = traumatic brain injury; PS = physical scarring.

283

As discussed earlier in this section, an individual's experience is often shaped by the intersection of multiple identities. In Javad's case, being the first-born male and living in Iran shapes his worldview and behaviors. In other words, his gender, culture, and social class determinants are variables in which Javad is constituted as a subject. SES might become a centralizing agent in maintaining gender and ethnocultural identity if for these reasons he is positioned as the family provider in the absence of his father.

In the case of Zohra (see Chapter 13), a 43-year-old woman living in Pakistan, we find a different expression of how SES affects a client's experience. In this case, the client is unlikely to carry the sense of financial insecurity and resource scarcity as Javad given the prominent SES of her and her family. Yet, given the gender and subcultural norms of the social sphere she inhabits, Zohra's roles inside the domestic realm are as carved out for her as they are for the young man made to go out to work. Inhabiting spheres of social and economic standing also comes with a degree of social scrutiny that works in tandem with "unforgiving and punitive" religious prescriptions inhibiting Zohra's autonomy and sense of security. To explore SES as a larger category of identity in these cases is also an exercise in the inherent subjectivity within such groupings.

Although attachment to forms of identity can have negative implications, particularly when identity–classification deviates from a majority or what has been broadly defined as the "normative" body, it can be valuable to recognize that we might have other connections and communities that influence our experiences. In doing so, we might come to create the movement needed to promote health and well-being.

THERAPEUTIC INTEGRATION AND THE COLLECTIVE SELF

In the majority of the cases, we noticed the concept of *integration*, considered broadly in this context as the (re)introduction or (re)aligning of an aspect of the client's experience into a larger whole. In other words, how does counseling help the client to integrate and assimilate the new meanings and metaphors that become available in counseling and psychotherapy? This notion might come to evoke the psychoanalytic practices of uncovering unconscious, repressed, or disavowed parts of the self that negatively influence the client's engagement and ability to engage with the present. In so doing, this process brings to consciousness the unconscious aspects of the self. For example, Olivia, a 28-year-old woman residing in Trinidad and Tobago (see Chapter 19), explored the unprocessed trauma caused by significant figures in her past (i.e., abandonment by her father, forms of abuse from her stepfather, lack of protection from her mother). Such historical ruptures affected her ability to find safety in current relationships or to access and activate intrinsic mechanisms of self-validation. It also seemed that her initial sense of helplessness as having her experiences as an adult distilled through the perspective of her younger, wounded self produced her current state of psychological distress. This aspect of self-identity was ill-equipped to function adaptively in Olivia's adult present, creating a cycle of distress whereby the young self is consistently called on to extinguish suffering without the resources to do so. Regularly failing at this task ultimately maintained her helplessness.

Moving beyond the realm of intrapsychic disturbance, we might consider that the issue of integration is represented in cases where there is discrepancy between a client's intrinsic and extrinsic spheres. In the case of Jojo (see Chapter 14), a 54-year-old man in the Philippines, we find that forms of suffering (shame, isolation, and hopelessness) could be found in his difficulty disclosing his HIV status to family and close friends. Because of the very real threat of social stigmatization and rejection, the client was unable to align his self-knowledge as a person who has HIV with his self-expression. This discrepancy compounded Jojo's sense of disconnection and despair.

Through some of the case studies, we can begin to see that issues of integration into the collective self can echo experiences of disconnection and loss of agency and that discontinuity both consciously and unconsciously can be limiting and restricting in the client's self-actualizing process.

The collectivist presence in the cases expresses the theme of integration into a collective self. In some instances, the "self" is framed within a collective that emphasizes the values, wants, and needs of the ethnic or cultural group before those of the individual. In the story of Mazabalo (see Chapter 3), a 27-year-old man from Togo, we find traces of a collective structure, or what we might think of as a *collective-self*, as a relevant aspect of the client's identity and experience. The client's presenting anxiety, onset of headaches, and disrupted concentration and sleep were explored in the therapy by Mazabalo and members of his maternal lineage and came to be understood as one facet of a larger affliction affecting the *djed-jewiye*, or clan. Although religious or spiritual ideology was seen as the cause of the separation between the client and members of the group, it was the inclusion of the group that provided the relevant background information and resources of support to inject the therapeutic encounter. Without the group's engagement, Mazabalo's disconnection from the already fractured and fragile collective may have been compounded, particularly if the approach to treatment focused solely on his Christian beliefs. Instead, calling on the insight of the collective and uncovering ways in which multiple processes of healing (Christian and African indigenous healing) could be performed offered restorative experiences of connection and healing for Mazabalo and the group. Integration is not only reflected in having the client recognize that his own religious values can operate alongside the African ontological beliefs but it can be found in renewing community intimacy through the acknowledgment of the ancestors (the past) and the recognition of the desire and hopes of the group (the future). *Re*integration into the collective comes to be the site of resilience where the individual member can rely on the group for needed psychological comfort, and the group is sustained by the involvement of the individual in the maintenance of culture, language, and society.

MIND, BODY, AND SPIRITS IN "TALKING THERAPIES"

Western Eurocentric tradition has historically considered the mind as the fertile ground for counseling and psychotherapeutic inquiry. Through the "talking therapies" (talking heads), the client's traumas, memories, associations, appraisals, and assumptions have been explored, deciphered, analyzed, and laid bare. For many multicultural clients, this process can be much more invasive and challenging than a surgeon's scalpel. This fact is one of the reasons that in the diaspora with particular ethnic communities, such as South Asians, we see a lack of interest in engaging in counseling and psychotherapy. Asian traditional healing therapies, themselves, are much more focused on body-oriented therapies, for example, TCM, acupuncture, meditation, reike, ayurveda, astrology, and Unani (see Moodley & West, 2005).

Emerging as a theme in the case studies is the role of the body in mental health treatment, specifically emphasizing that pertinent relationships exist between the body and features of a client's presentation. Western psychotherapies have historically focused on intrapsychic processes, transference in the therapeutic dyad, and ego-defense (Corey, 2012), providing limited engagement with the physical dimensions of a client's experience. Codes of ethics put in place by psychological associations warn practitioners against engaging in inappropriate physical relationships with clients (American Psychological Association, 2010; Canadian Psychological Association, 2000). In the context of the therapeutic dyad, the body may not always be acknowledged and attended to in counseling and psychotherapy.

Reviewing this text offers us access to a range of communities, clients, and identities, and along with these we can come to see that the body is another arena tied to individual experience and experiencing. Arguably the most apparent connection between the client's mental (emotional, relational) and physical health occurs when expressions of distress are coupled with emergent physical symptoms. Somatization, or an expression of one's mental state through physical symptoms, can be found in a number of the cases, for example, the case of Misun (see Chapter 15). A woman of Korean background, Misun presented with neck pain, vision issues, and anxiety-related sensation in the chest area in addition to the distress caused by intrafamilial discord. What is particularly poignant is that cultural influences bring the mental and physical together rather formally within a culture sensitive framework. *Hwa-byung*, a Korean somatization disorder recognized in the *Diagnostic and Statistical Manual of Mental Disorders* (4th ed.; American Psychiatric Association, 1994), has been connected to sustained repression of anger on the basis of certain cultural codes.

Chapter 6 tells the story of Mr. Dlamini, a South African client who was eventually referred to psychological treatment after a series of inconclusive neurological tests. This case provides us with another example of how the body becomes a site of psychological and emotional expression. In this case, issues related to motor control and decline in memory and concentration function emerged as the surrounding circumstances that triggered psychic and emotional distress. The death of Mr. Dlamini's father and the assumption of greater responsibility for and within the community activated forms of suffering that needed release. In Mr. Dlamini's case, the body may have been the most appropriate platform to represent his experiencing. "Being physically, rather than mentally, 'ill' appeared to have been a safer option as the latter is in direct conflict with the social expectation of high personal integrity that Mr. Dlamini aspired to fulfill as a traditional leader in his community" (see Chapter 6, p. 52). The physical plane comes to be the holding environment for an individual's internal states that may not otherwise be accessed and accommodated.

This theme of the body is also expressed in cases where a client's presentation included chronic illness and disability status. Experiences and appraisals of the body in some of these instances became the source of affliction explored through psychotherapeutic intervention. Michael's story (see Chapter 16) is one shaped at least in part by chronic illness and the implications of living with multiple health challenges. Hand in hand with having fought cancer, being HIV positive, and now having cirrhosis are the client's narratives of these experiences. We find that these are not exclusively medicalized ones. Michael's descriptions of his physical conditions connected to stories of relationality, that is, what it has meant and will mean to inhabit a body that does not "function" sexually and how it prevents him from building forms of intimacy with other men. The author waxes poetically that the body and the language of the body came to facilitate dialogues of desire, love, and romantic history: "In a sense, we had stopped talking about his liver and started talking about his heart" (see Chapter 16, p. 129).

In the case of Radha, a married woman of Indian background presenting with issues relating to infertility, we continue to witness the relevance of the body to mental health treatment (see Chapter 10). The concept of relationality continues because it was in the context of relationships—to her husband and mother-in-law—that the client's disability status was first identified and emphasized. Then the body became an entry point for the critical exploration of identity, identity performance, and cultural influences. It became poignant that childbearing may not be possible for the client when we recognized that being gendered and connected to a particular ethnocultural context is tethered to forms of performance. Furthermore, that value is attached to how well an individual performs his or her "identity." To be a married Indian woman in Radha's intrinsic and extrinsic worlds initially means that motherhood is a "blessed" state and that being unable to access it caused her distress on various fronts. If the body comes to be a reflection of an individual's mental state and the site of one's relational access, it might also be the carrier of various codes of identity and environment that are relevant to what one thinks, feels, and experiences. The same can be said for spirituality.

Central to exploring the intricacies of the client's subjective self-experience in terms of religion and spirituality, or any of the Group of Seven identities, is an attempt to "put the pieces of the story together as a means of seeing the client from his or her own frame of reference" (Ridley & Udipi, 2002, p. 320). As religious affiliation might evoke preexisting ideology, figures, and practice that may or may not reflect the client's or counselor's own experience in the cases, our analysis of this issue tended to focus on spirituality rather than religion, which is no less critical in counseling.

The story of Dayo (see Chapter 4) is arguably the most reflective of bringing spiritual practice into the therapeutic setting. A 44-year-old married father of Yoruba descent and living in Nigeria, Dayo presented with low mood, confusion, and various physical symptoms (headaches, fatigue, and sleep disturbances). After seeking Western-oriented service, the client found that traditional healing practices led by a *Babalawo* or *Ifa* priest were more appropriate forms of treatment in his situation. In this form, the client underwent forms of initial assessment, cleansing, immunity building, and reconnecting to his community. Although we recognize that traditional healing may not be appropriate for all clients and certainly should not be saddled to all ethnocultural, minoritized, or racialized clients, this case reflects its potential in attuning to aspects of the client's subjective inner world so that one works appropriately with the person's own systems of belief and understandings of illness and distress. Such an approach echoes with person-centered values that position the client at the heart of psychotherapeutic exchange.

As noted at the beginning of this chapter, Western models of counseling and psychotherapy dominate the landscape of cases presented in this text. This approach highlights the mind as the prime site for exploration in relation to subjective distress and suffering. The mind is a concept—albeit a Western one and one that is relatively new (since the time of the Enlightenment)—that counselors ought to be critical of as the sole arena of providing information about the person. Several cases in this text have shown that the body and spirit are also significant therapeutic spaces for healing and transformation.

EVALUATIONS AND GENERALIZATIONS FROM CASE STUDIES

For several decades, the evaluation of a single client case study has been criticized for its contribution to theory and practice of counseling; that is, there was doubt about its ability to extend and expand on theory or even construct new theories. There were also questions about the utility of case-study analysis in providing generalizations concerning treatment. Indeed, "Studies of individual cases allow the evaluator to learn the intricate details of how a treatment is working, rather than averaging the effect across a number of cases" (Kennedy, 1979, p. 663). Carl Rogers (2002) emphasized this point when he said a "meticulous analysis of the single case" is necessary in the development of counseling as "a source of emerging knowledge and generative hypothesis" (p. 12). Kennedy (1979) suggested that the functional relationships between the treatment and the subject are invariably looked at, allowing for "a *relationship* between treatment, context, and recipient . . . because the treatment may be recast in its more fundamental form, the conclusion may be applicable to a wider range of contexts or cases" (p. 670). Furthermore, Kennedy argued that when generalizations are necessary then they are to be "done by the user of the case data rather than by the person who originated the case data. And generalization is not from a case to a population but rather from a case to another case" (p. 676). Even if this was possible, generalizing from one case to another case would also require careful consideration as to the contexts and differences that each case offers.

Case study advocates, however, contend strenuously that generalizations are not the purpose of their craft. As Dooley (2002) noted, "Case study research generally does not lend itself well to generalization or prediction" (p. 336), but he argued that "Case study research has the ability to embrace multiple cases, to embrace quantitative and qualitative data, and to embrace multiple research paradigms" (p. 336). Although these objectives in themselves are not strictly about theory building, they do, however, offer the possibility for practitioners to understand the various ways in which therapists attend to clinical matters. As Dooley contended,

> New theory does not emerge quickly but will be developed over time as the research is extended from one case to the next and more and more data are collected and analyzed. This form of reiteration and continuous refinement, more commonly referred to as the multiple case study, occurs over an extended period of time. (p. 336)

In exploring one case to the next, we found that whereas counselors and psychotherapists did not rigidly adhere to single therapeutic approaches, they nevertheless maintained a strong reference to the Western Eurocentric models of working (with one exception: Chapter 4, the Nigeria context). It is clear that therapy without borders offer practitioners an opportunity to use a multimodal, integrated, and eclectic approach with the possibility of using dual interventions that accommodate the insight, input, and experience of the individuals they are working with. Indeed, although neither theory building nor predictions and generalizations about theory and practice are the prime objective of the case analysis, it nevertheless will indirectly contribute to ideas about how theory can be changed or elaborated on. An integrated approach in transnational settings, as most of these cases show, eventually adds to and changes theory in a way that is beneficial to both practitioners and clients alike. For example, the idea of dual interventions has moved beyond a research observation and is effective in several different practices (see Moodley & Sutherland, 2010). Although the Nigeria chapter may have presented a single case of traditional healing, and the other cases in this text are not a representative sample of cases in their respective countries, it is not difficult to find—other than the literature on aboriginal healing practices cited earlier—that the psychology, counseling, and mental health literature purport the advantages of integrating traditional healing practices in counseling and psychotherapy. These advantages are often illustrated through detailed case study examples that highlight the work of traditional healers (see Moodley & West, 2005). Although these practices are not immediately available to Western scientific enquiry, they nevertheless have been around for a much longer period than conventional psychology, counseling, and psychotherapy and have stood the test of time (evaluation, reliability, validity, variability) within their own cultural setting. Given that religion and spirituality as discourses of psychopathology and resilience are presently available in counseling and psychotherapy, it seems that the inclusion and the acceptance of traditional healing practices will not be limited to just racialized patients or clients.

Any discussion of alternative or complementary approaches in therapeutic practice will both critique current counseling and psychotherapy theory and practice for its limitation in multicultural contexts and, at the same time, promote ways of healing that may not be consistent with mainstream dominant worldviews. For example, the focus on the body (as discussed earlier), which several cases have highlighted in an integrated way across borders and continents, may challenge the normative traditions of the talking cure. Because the body emerged as a carrier of distress and a barometer for various cultural codes in so many of the cases, it leaves us without any doubt that the Cartesian divide that informs and enforces so much in Western thinking needs to be bridged. Even the "talking-therapy" counselors may need to be open to the potentiality of the body in counseling and psychotherapy. This kind of analysis is not to make gross generalizations about the body but to engage the body either metaphorically, spiritually, or even concretely to bring about transformation and healing.

The single-case design (and psychological analysis) may be a form that is consistent with a Euro-American counseling and psychotherapy approach and its emphasis on the singular narrative and psychopathology. Nevertheless, it is ideally suited to explore the psychopathology, resilience, and cultural forces that inhabit and affect the client. Therapy without borders is not without any boundaries and borderlines as its name suggests. The cases in this book demonstrate that the Euro-American approach is a structure that produces a certain kind of psychopathology and frames a particular kind of resilience in clients. However, it is flexible and malleable enough to transform its theory, practice, and research in different transnational places and cases.

REFERENCES

American Psychiatric Association. (1994). *Diagnostic and statistical manual of mental disorders* (4th ed.). Washington, DC: Author.

American Psychological Association. (2010). *Ethical principles of psychologists and code of conduct*. Washington, DC: Author.

Canadian Psychological Association. (2000). *Canadian code of ethics for psychologists* (3rd ed.). Ottawa, Ontario, Canada: Canadian Psychological Association.

Chen, E., Matthews, K. A., & Boyce, W. T. (2002). Socioeconomic differences in children's health: How and why do these relationships change with age? *Psychological Bulletin, 128*, 295–329.

Corey, G. (2012). *Theory and practice of counseling and psychotherapy* (9th ed.). Belmont, CA: Brooks/Cole.

Dooley, L. M. (2002). Case study research and theory building. *Advances in Developing Human Resources, 4*, 335–354. doi:10.1177/1523422302043007

Draguns, J. (2008). Universal and cultural threads in counselling individuals. In P. Pedersen, J. Draguns, W. Lonner, & J. Trimble (Eds.), *Counseling across cultures* (pp. 3–21). Thousand Oaks, CA: Sage.

Jilek, W. G. (2004). The therapeutic aspects of Salish spirit dance ceremonials. In U. P. Gielen, J. Fish, & J. G. Draguns (Eds.), *Handbook of culture, psychotherapy, and healing* (pp. 151–159). Mahwah, NJ: Erlbaum.

Kennedy, M. M. (1979). Generalizing from single case studies. *Evaluation Quarterly, 3*, 661–678.

Leeder, E. (1996). Speaking rich people's words: Implications of a feminist class analysis and psychotherapy. In M. Hill & E. Rothblum (Eds.), *Classism and feminist therapy: Counting costs* (pp. 45–57). New York, NY: Haworth.

Lorant, V., Deliege, D., Eaton, W., Robert, A., Philippot, P., & Ansseau, M. (2003). Socioeconomic inequalities in depression: A meta-analysis. *American Journal of Epidemiology, 157*, 98–112.

McCormick, R. (2005). The healing path: What can counselors learn from Aboriginal people about how to heal? In R. Moodley & W. West (Eds.), *Integrating traditional healing practices into counseling and psychotherapy* (pp. 293–304). Thousand Oaks, CA: Sage.

Moodley, R. (2011). *Outside the sentence: Readings in critical multicultural counseling and psychotherapy*. Toronto, Ontario, Canada: Centre for Diversity in Counseling and Psychotherapy.

Moodley, R., Gielen, U., & Wu, R. (Eds.). (2012). *Handbook of counseling and psychotherapy in an international context*. New York, NY: Routledge.

Moodley, R., & Sutherland, P. (2010). Psychic retreats in other places: Clients who seek healing with traditional healers and psychotherapists. *Counselling Psychology Quarterly, 23*, 267–282.

Moodley, R., & West, W. (Eds.). (2005). *Integrating traditional healing practices in counseling and psychotherapy*. Thousand Oaks, CA: Sage.

Poonwassie, A., & Charter, A. (2005). Aboriginal worldview of healing: Inclusion, blending, and bridging. In R. Moodley & W. West (Eds.), *Integrating traditional healing practices into counseling and psychotherapy* (pp. 15–25). Thousand Oaks, CA: Sage.

Pope, J. F., & Arthur, N. (2009). Socioeconomic status and class: A challenge for the practice of psychology in Canada. *Canadian Psychology, 50,* 55–65.

Ridley, C. R., & Udipi, S. (2002). Putting cultural empathy into practice. In P. Pedersen, J. Draguns, W. J. Lonner, & J. Trimble (Eds.), *Counseling across cultures* (pp. 317–333). Thousand Oaks, CA: Sage.

Rogers, C. (2002). Carl Rogers on the development of the person-centered approach. In D. Cain (Ed.), *Classics in the person-centred approach* (pp. 11–12). Ross-on-Wye, United Kingdom: PCCS Books.

Smith, D. P. (2005). The sweat lodge as psychotherapy: Congruence between traditional and modern healing. In R. Moodley & W. West (Eds.), *Integrating traditional healing practices into counseling and psychotherapy* (pp. 196–209). Thousand Oaks, CA: Sage.

Sutherland, P., Moodley, R., & Chevannes, B. (Eds.). (2014). *Caribbean healing traditions*. New York, NY: Routledge.

Wohlfarth, T. (1997). Socioeconomic inequality and psychopathology: Are socioeconomic status and social class interchangeable? *Social Science & Medicine, 45,* 399–410.

Index

Tables are indicated by "t" following page numbers.

A

Abandonment
  of children after divorce, 90
  by community, 33
  by family members, 151, 184, 261
  protection against, 207
  by spouse, 80, 112
Abuse
  child, 150–151
  from childhood peers, 228–229
  spousal, 211–217, 261
  substance. *See* Substance abuse
Academic difficulties, 141–146
Acculturation model, 144
Activity theory, 219
Adekson, M. O., 31–32
Adultery, 104–108
Affective spectrum disorders, 219–225
Africa, counseling and psychotherapy in, 15–38
  Egypt, 15–21
  Morocco, 39–45
  Nigeria, 31–37
  South Africa, 47–53
  Sub-Saharan Africa, 55–61
  West Africa, 23–38
Age, issues resulting from, 70, 133–138
Age of therapists, 43
Aggressive behaviors of children, 88, 90, 189–193
Akhtar, S., 247–248
Alcoholism, 66, 205, 220
Alexithymia, 224
Alternative therapies, 280–281
Amer, Mona M., 15
American Psychiatric Association, 40

Ancestors, influence of, 23
Anger, 118, 196–200, 286
Anger management, 237–241
Animal sacrifice rituals, 26, 28, 34, 36
Anorexia nervosa, 176
Anxiety
  CBT for, 40, 65–70, 237–241, 252–257
  existentialism and, 165
  integrative psychotherapy for, 48–51
  nondirective intervention (NDI) for, 196–200
  psychoanalysis for, 125–130
  psychobiological and transactional analysis for, 212–217
  psychodynamic therapies for, 134–138
  rational emotive behavior therapy for, 150–154
  single-session and brief counseling for, 158–162
  solution-focused therapies for, 141–146
  traditional healing for, 24–28, 32
Appetite loss, 57
Approval-seeking behaviors, 82
Arden, J. B., 115
Argentina, counseling and psychotherapy in, 125–131, 278t, 282t, 286–287
Argentine School of Psychoanalysis, 125
Arthur, N., 281
Asia, counseling and psychotherapy in, 73–121
  China, 73–78
  India, 79–86
  Japan, 87–94
  Malaysia, 95–101
  Pakistan, 103–109
  Philippines, 111–116
  South Korea, 117–121
Assertiveness training, 152–153

Asthma, 158–162, 238–241
Attachment theory, 259–265
Australia, counseling and psychotherapy in, 65–71, 278*t*, 282*t*
Authoritarian clients, 197–200
Autism, 95–100
Autonomy, promoting in clients, 205, 223–224, 263
Avoidance symptoms, 57, 90, 114

B

Badinter, Elisabeth, 199
Balkis, Murat, 267
Baudouin, Nicole, 183
Beck Anxiety Inventory, 49–50, 159
Beck Depression Inventory, 49, 159, 179
Bedi, Robinder P., 141
Behavioral activation, 247
Behavior issues of children, 18, 88, 90, 189–193
Beiman, Sharon Ziv, 243
Belghazi, Dounia, 39
Bendor, S. J., 70
Berry, J. W., 144
Birashk, Behrooz, 237
Bisexual clients, 112–116
Blier, S. P., 23
Body, acknowledging in therapy, 286
Body image, 127, 240–241, 262–264, 262*n*6
Body-oriented therapies, 117–121, 285–286, 289
Bojuwoye, Olaniyi, 31
Bonfanti, Thierry, 195
Borderline personality disorder (BPD), 175–180
Brazil, counseling and psychotherapy in, 133–139, 278*t*, 282*t*
Breathing techniques, 68
Brief counseling, 158–162, 227
Brizendine, L., 212, 216
Buddhism, 65, 95
Bullying, 92, 228–229

C

Canada, counseling and psychotherapy in, 141–147, 278*t*, 281, 282*t*
Cancer, 126–128, 286–287
Cárdenas, Samuel Jurado, 157
Career counseling, 183–188
Carey, V., 161
Caribbean, counseling and psychotherapy in, 149–155, 284
Case selection, 4
Case study based practice and training, 3–10, 288–289
Catastrophizing cognitive distortions, 67
Catholic clients, 24, 196–200, 215–216, 252
CBT. *See* Cognitive behavior therapy
Chain of evidence, 5

Chang, Doris F., 73
Child abuse, 150–151
Child–parent relationships. *See also* Families; Family counseling
    child caring for parents, 206–207, 238–241, 284
    children of survivors (COS), 66, 70
    child unifying parents, 127–128
    mother–child parallel therapy, 87–93
    parental expectations of child, 16, 18, 50–51
    repairing, 152–153
    restrictions placed on child, 268–272
    transgenerational trauma and, 244–245
Children
    with autism, 95–100
    behavioral issues of, 18. *See also* Aggressive behaviors of children
    care of, anxiety of caregivers and, 196–200
    death of, treating parents after, 73–78
    divorce, effect of, 215
    gender roles of, 76
    illness of, stress of caregivers and, 158–162
    play therapy for, 88–94
    psychological development of, 223–224
    religious upbringing of, 255–256
    selective mutism of, 228–232
    with traumatic brain injury (TBI), 189–193
Children of survivors (COS), 66, 70
China, counseling and psychotherapy in, 73–78, 277, 278*t*, 282*t*
Christianity
    anger with God and, 56
    Australia, 65
    Catholic clients, 24, 196–200, 215–216, 252
    father's role and, 215–216
    Germany, 190
    interfaith marriage and, 252–257
    Lebanon, 253
    Malaysia, 95
    prayer and, 58
    self-determination and, 120
    South Africa, 48
    South Korea, 118, 120
    Sub-Saharan Africa, 55–56, 58–59
    Togo, 23–24
    traditional healing and, 26–27
Circular causality, 19–20
Class differences, 15–16
Client-centered psychotherapeutic model, 31–32, 103
Client feedback, 6
Clinical child neuropsychology, 189–193
Clinical knowledge, 3
Clinicians
    age and nationality of, 43
    case databases of, 10
    counselors vs. psychologist, 65, 196, 199–200

credibility of, 43–44
gender of, 84, 231
Group of Seven identities and, 52
internalized culture of, 10
learning position of, 8–9
licensure and certification, 111, 185
professional vs. nonprofessional, 157
self-disclosure and, 20, 272
transference and, 129, 134, 270
verbal and nonverbal communication of, 44
Coexperiencing psychotherapy, 219
Cognitive aid for autistic children, 97–100
Cognitive behavior therapy (CBT)
Australia, 65–70
defined, 203
Egypt, 20
Germany, 189–193
India, 80–84
Iran, 237–241
Israel, 243–248
Japan, 87
Lebanon, 251–257
Mexico, 157
Morocco, 39–44
Russia, 220–225
Sub-Saharan Africa, 55–60
United Kingdom, 227
Cognitive distortions, 67–69
Cognitive restructuring, 57, 59
Cohen, S., 161
Coleman, H., 263
Collection points of clinical information, 4
Collective-self, 285
Collective trauma, 243–248
Collectivism
India, 79, 84
Japan, 87, 91
Lebanon, 255
Palestine, 263
Philippines, 115
South Korea, 117
West African, 23, 31, 36
Colonization
Caribbean and, 150
Egypt and, 15
neocolonial practices and, 277
Pakistan and, 103
Communication styles of clinicians, 44
Computer-based multimedia cognitive aid,
97–100
Concentration issues, 24–28, 48–52, 141–146
Conflict resolution skills, 129
Confucian culture, 76
Coping strategies, 50, 81, 222
Cross-cultural counseling, 16, 141–146, 165–170,
263
Cultural–historical concept, 219, 223–224

Cultural identity, 145
Culture. *See also* Cross-cultural counseling
behavior understood through, 36
case study based practice and training and,
8–10
consideration of, 263
effectiveness of psychotherapy and, 34
gap in hospital setting, 262
indigenous cultural rituals. *See* Traditional
healing
internalized, 9–10
mental illness, meaning of, 26–27
overdiagnosis of, 47–48
Culture-centered therapy, 36, 237
Curses, 167–170

D

Damianova, Maria, 47
Davidson, J., 241
Death, anxiety and, 133–138
Debt, stress and, 178
Decision-making, 68
Denmark, counseling and psychotherapy in,
175–181, 278*t*, 282*t*
Dependent personality disorder, 220–225
Depression
attachment theory and systemic approach
for, 261
CBT for, 40–44, 65–70, 220–225, 237–241,
244–248
emotion-focused therapy (EFT) for, 104–108
existential counseling for, 165–170
humanistic and psychoanalytic approaches
for, 184–188
psychoanalysis for, 125–130
psychobiological and transactional analysis
for, 212–217
rational emotive behavior therapy for, 150–154
single-session and brief counseling for,
158–162
solution-focused story sharing for, 112–116
stepped-care model for, 204–208
talking pictures therapy for, 228–232
traditional healing for, 32–36
Despair, 103–108
Developmental experiences, 149–154
*Diagnostic and Statistical Manual of Mental
Disorders* (4th ed.; APA), 40, 286
*Diagnostic and Statistical Manual of Mental
Disorders* (5th ed.; APA), 73, 118, 206
Dialectical behavioral therapy (DBT), 175–180
Disabilities, persons with, 189–193, 228–232
Diversity. *See also* Multicultural clients
of identities. *See* Group of Seven identities
intersectionalities of, 8–9, 280–284, 282–283*t*
socioeconomic, 125

Divorce
    Catholicism and, 199
    family relationship after, 89–91
    Islam and, 104, 256
    spousal abuse and, 211–217
Dixon, Andrea L., 175
Domene, José F., 11, 141
Domestic violence, 211–217, 261
Domingues, Vânia Maria, 133
Dominican culture, 165–170
Dooley, L. M., 288
Drawing therapy for autistic children, 97–99
Dream analysis and interpretation, 270
Drug abuse. *See* Substance abuse
Dryden, W., 35
Dual interventions, 288–289
Dynamic sizing, 7
Dysphoria, 259–264
Dysregulation, 177–178
Dysthymic disorder, 66–70

E

Eating Disorder Examination–12th Edition
    (EDE-12), 179
Eating disorders, 175–180
Eclectic therapy
    Argentina, 125
    Egypt, 15–21
    Turkey, 267–272
Economic oppression of women, 198–199
Edwards, S. D., 48
Ego, symbolic sacrifice of, 28
Egypt, counseling and psychotherapy in, 15–21,
    278t, 282t
Elders, consulting, 103
E-mail, counseling and, 152, 154
Emotion-focused therapy (EFT), 103–108
Employment, 184–188
Empowering clients, 69, 161, 262, 264
Empty-chair dialogue, 106
Enns, Carol Zerbe, 87
Environment's importance in nondirective
    intervention, 195
Euro-American Western dominance, 7, 277, 280
Europe, counseling and psychotherapy in,
    175–232
    Denmark, 175–181
    France, 183–188
    Germany, 189–194
    Italy, 195–201
    Netherlands, 203–209
    Russia, 219–228
    Spain, 211–218
    United Kingdom, 227–232
Evil eye, 56

Existentialism, 165–170, 227–228
Experiential avoidance, 114

F

Fallow time, 186–187
False self, 206–207
Families
    collectivism and. *See* Collectivism
    conforming to values of, 254–257
    disapproval of therapy, 143
    hierarchical dysfunctions of, 220–222
    importance of in Italian culture, 199
    in-laws, issues with, 79–84, 158–162
    interventions of, 20
    involving in counseling sessions, 20, 25–28,
        57–58. *See also* Family counseling
    male responsibility for, 50–52
    pediatric asthma control and, 161
    postdivorce relationships of, 90
    in post-war Russia, 220
    reputations of, 16–17, 25
    roles within, 214–216. *See also* Gender roles
    support for recovery of client, 83–84, 168,
        192–193, 240–241
    systemic approach to, 259–264
Family counseling, 223–225, 254, 256–257, 260–262
Family systems psychotherapy, 219, 220–225
Fathers, role of, 215–216
Fatigue, 32–36
Fayad, Yasmine, 251
Financial problems, strain of, 16–20
Fishman, D. B., 10
Fkih healers, 40–42
Focusing-oriented therapy, 117–121
Forgiveness, 247–248
Fortune Telling cognitive distortion, 67
France, counseling and psychotherapy in,
    183–188, 278t, 282t
Fregoso-Vera, María, 157
Freudian concepts, 133–134
Friendships. *See* Social networks
Frustration, 16–20
Fuku (Dominican curse), 167–170
Furth, G. M., 99

G

Gardner, Richard A., 215
Gender diversity, 196–200
Gender roles
    Caribbean, 153, 166, 169
    China, 74, 76
    Egypt, 16–19
    India, 82–83, 287
    Indo-Canadian, 145

Italy, 196–200
Japan, 90–92
Lebanon, 252–253, 255
Mexico, 158–162
Morocco, 42–43
Nigeria, 33
Pakistan, 104–105, 284
Palestine, 261
Russia, 220
South Africa, 52
Spain, 213, 215–216
Turkey, 268–272
Generalizations of case studies, 288–289
George, Tony Sam, 79
Germany, counseling and psychotherapy in, 189–194, 279t, 282t
Gillberg, C., 96
Globalization, 79
Gobodo, P., 47–48
Gold, D., 161
Gomes, William B., 133
Gordon, Thomas, 197
Grief process, 50–52, 55–60, 73–78
Group of Seven identities
    clinician sharing with client, 43–44, 52
    in France, 183
    intersectionality of, 8–10, 280–284, 282–283t, 287
    tailoring therapy to, 146
    in United Kingdom, 228, 231
Group therapy. *See also* Family counseling
    for behavior modifications, 191–192
    for HIV diagnosed clients, 112–113
    for marital problems, 223–225
Guilt, 104–108, 165–166
Gurman, A. S., 165

H

Habrias, Nicole, 200
Haj-Yahia, M. M., 263
Hakoniwa, 89–90, 92–93
Han-bang approach, 120
Hansen, Nanja H., 175
Hayes, S. C., 114
Headaches, 24–28, 141–146
Health issues. *See* Physical health issues
Heimann, M., 96
Helplessness, 150–154, 214, 238, 261, 284
Help-seeking behaviors, 36, 44
Hillman, J., 28
Hinduism, 80–81, 83, 95
HIV diagnosed clients, 112–116, 125–130, 284–285, 286–287
Ho, D. Y. F., 9
Holocaust survivors, children of, 66, 70

Home remedies, 161
Homework, 58–59, 67, 152, 160, 240
Homosexual clients, 125–130, 286–287
Hopelessness, 16–20, 112–116, 152
Hormones, mood disorders and, 212, 216
Hospital settings, 32, 134–135, 262
Humanistic therapies
    France, 184–188
    Japan, 87–93
    Mexico, 157
    Pakistan, 103–108
    Russia, 219
Hutchinson, Gerard, 149
Hutschemaekers, Giel, 203
Hwa-byung (Korean somatization disorder), 117–121, 286
Hyperarousal, 57
Hypnosis, 68–69

I

Identity, 228, 231–232, 256. *See also* Group of Seven identities
Ikemi, A., 120
Illness. *See* Physical health issues
Imagery, 68
Immigrants, 168–169, 228–232, 267–272
Impulse control, 189–193, 237–241
India, counseling and psychotherapy in, 79–86, 278t, 282t, 287
Indigenous cultural rituals, 58–59
Indigenous knowledge, 280–281
Individualism vs. collectivism, 263
Indo-Canadian culture, 141–146, 281
Infertility, 79–84, 287
Information-oriented sampling, 4
In-laws, issues with, 79–84, 158–162
Insomnia, 267–272
Integrative approach, 204
Integrative psychotherapy
    Russia, 219–225
    South Africa, 47–52
    Sub-Saharan Africa, 59–60
    United Kingdom, 227–232
Internalized culture, 9–10
Internalized marginalization, 168–169
International Classification of Diseases–10th Edition (ICD–10) diagnostic system, 177
Interpersonal psychotherapy (IPT), 73–78
Interpreting clinical information, 5–6
Intersectionality of diversities, 8–10, 280–284, 282–283t, 287
Intervention procedures, 5, 169–170, 195
Intifadas, 259, 259n2
Intimacies, exploring, 20
Involuntary body movements, 48–52

Iran, counseling and psychotherapy in, 237–242, 279*t*, 281, 283*t*, 284
Islam
    divorce and, 104
    Egypt, 15–16
    gender roles for, 18, 104–105
    healing techniques of, 103
    interfaith marriage and, 252, 255–256
    Lebanon, 253
    Malaysia, 95
    Morocco, 39–40
    oppression of, 107–108
    Pakistan, 103–108
    Palestine, 260–264
    suicide and, 42
    Togo, 23
    Turkey, 267, 271
Israel, counseling and psychotherapy in, 243–249, 279*t*, 283*t*
Italy, counseling and psychotherapy in, 195–201, 279*t*, 282*t*
Iwakabe, Shigeru, 87

J

James, Naomi, 55
Japan, counseling and psychotherapy in, 87–94, 278*t*, 282*t*
Javier, Roberto E., 111
Jejeebhoy, S. J., 83
Jerusalem, 259–260, 259*nn*1–3. *See also* Palestinian Occupied Territories
Jews, 66, 70, 262
Jin, 40–41
Joo, Eunsun, 117
Journaling about emotions, 167–168, 178, 215

K

Kadri, Nadia, 39
Kamtou, 25–26
Karma, 80–81, 83
Kennedy, M. M., 288
Khan, Masud, 187
Khina, Bhisham, 277
Kholmogorova, Alla, 219
Khoury, Brigitte, 251
Khyal attacks, 118
Kirschner, E., 120
Kpanake, Lonzozou, 23
Krause, Karen, 189
Kuwentuhan (story sharing), 113

L

Lantz, J., 169
Lebanon, counseling and psychotherapy in, 251–257, 279*t*, 283*t*

Lee, Eunjung, 3
Licensure and certification of clinicians, 111, 185
Lindford, L., 115
Lobrot, Michel, 195, 200
Loewenthal, Del, 227
Loneliness, 90, 114, 151, 199, 206–207
Loyo, Diego Benegas, 125
Luck, 41

M

Maladaptive behaviors and emotions, 65–66, 104, 114, 271
Malaysia, counseling and psychotherapy in, 95–101, 278*t*, 282*t*
Marín-Martín, Carolina, 211
Maristans, 39
Marital problems
    adultery, 104–108
    divorce, 89–91, 104, 199, 211–217, 256
    family counseling for, 223
    infertility and, 79–84, 287
    lack of love, 198
    parenting stress, 16–18
    somatizations and, 119
    spousal abuse, 211–217, 261
Marriage. *See also* Marital problems
    Canada, 143–144, 281
    Lebanon, 252–257
    Palestine, 262–264, 262*n*6
Masalah, Shafiq, 259
Maternal instinct, 199
May, R., 168
Mayo, J., 168
Medication for depression and OCD, 214, 221, 223, 261
Melgar, Maria Isabel E., 111
Memory issues, 48–52, 74
Men. *See also* Gender roles
    admitting to psychological distress, 19
    disciplinary role of, 158
    dominant role of, 42–43, 52, 76
    emotions of, acceptable, 42, 44
    Japanese, expectations of, 92
    mental illness manifestations in, 44
    passive role of in families, 215–216
    relationship with women, 198, 271–272
    sexual role of, 166, 169
Mental filtering, 68
Mentalization-based treatment, 207
Messer, S. B., 165
Mexico, counseling and psychotherapy in, 157–163, 278*t*, 282*t*
Mey, See Ching, 95
Middle class values, 91
Middle East, 237–273
    Iran, 237–242

Israel, 243–249
  Lebanon, 251–257
  Palestine, 259–265
  Turkey, 267–273
Mind–body integration therapies, 117–121
Mood disorders, 212–217
Moodley, Roy, 277
Morocco, counseling and psychotherapy in,
  39–45, 278t, 282t
Mother–child parallel therapy, 87–93
Motherhood, role of
  India, 82–83, 287
  Italy, 197
  Japan, 92
  Mexico, 158, 161
Mothers of the quake-hit area (China), 73–78
Multicultural clients, 16, 141–146, 165–170, 263
Multimedia presentation for autistic children,
  97–100
Muslim clients. *See* Islam
Mute clients, 228–232
Mutuality of feelings, 137
Mwiti, Gladys K., 55

N

Narrative psychotherapy, 59–60, 77, 82–83, 113–114
Nasal deviation, 237–241
Nashashibi, Rana G., 259
Nationality of clinicians, 43
Negative filtering, 68
Negative self-talk, 67, 69, 113
Negligent fathers, 216
Nelson, K. E., 96
NEO Personality Inventory–Revised, 49
Nervios, 158–162
Netherlands, counseling and psychotherapy in,
  203–209, 279t, 282t
Neurological/neuropsychological complaints,
  48–52
Neuropsychological assessments, 189–193
Nicholas, Lionel J., 47
Nigeria, counseling and psychotherapy in,
  31–37, 278t, 282t, 284, 287
Nightmares, 267–272
Nondirective intervention (NDI), 195–200
North America, counseling and psychotherapy in
  Canada, 141–147
  United States, 157–172
Ntantiso, M., 47

O

Oasis Africa's Transformational Psychology
  model, 55, 59
Obesity, 165–170, 175–180

Obsessive-compulsive disorder (OCD), 220–225
Obsessive traits, 136
Old age, issues regarding, 70, 133–138
On Personal Power (Rogers), 197
Ontology, West African, 27–28, 285
Oppression
  of minorities, 167–169
  religious, 18, 107–108
  of women in patriarchal societies, 107,
    118–119, 198–199
Overspending, 178

P

Pakikipagkapwa, 115
Pakistan, counseling and psychotherapy in,
  103–109, 278t, 282t, 284
Palestinian Occupied Territories, counseling
  and psychotherapy in, 259–265, 279t, 283t
Parental alienation syndrome (PAS), 215
Parents. *See also* Families; Family counseling
  attachment issues with child, 76
  care of child, anxiety resulting from,
    196–200
  child abuse and, 150–151
  children, transgenerational trauma and,
    244–245
  children caring for, 206–207
  conflicts between, 18, 261. *See also* Marital
    problems
  death of child, treatment after, 73–78
  divorce of. *See* Divorce
  failure at role of, 114
  illness of child, stress resulting from,
    158–162
  mental health issues, effect on child, 179
  mother–child parallel therapy, 87–93
  relationships with children. *See* Child–parent
    relationships
  therapy of child and, 191, 240–241, 259
Patriarchal societies
  female therapists in, 43
  gender hierarchy in, 255
  infertility issues and, 79–80, 82–83
  oppression of women in, 18, 107, 118–119
Pelling, Nadine, 65
People with disabilities, 189–193, 228–232
Perfectionism, 222, 269
Personality disorders
  CBT for, 40–44, 220–225
  stepped-care model for, 206–208
Person-centered approaches, 79–84, 195,
  203–208
Persons, J. B., 241
Phenomenology, 227
Philippines, counseling and psychotherapy in,
  111–116, 278t, 282t, 284–285

Photographs used in brief therapy, 227–228
Physical health issues
    body, acknowledging in therapy, 286–287
    as externally caused, 35
    HIV diagnosis, 112–116, 125–130, 284–285
    low socioeconomic status and, 281
    somatizations, 24, 44, 48, 117–121, 286
    sorcery causing, 25
    stigma of, 112–113, 133–138, 262–264, 262*n*6,
        284–285
    surgery, 126–127, 133–138, 237–241, 260–264
    witchcraft causing, 51
Physical-oriented therapies, 285–286, 289
Pieta, Maria Adélia Minghelli, 133
Pignatiello, Vincent, 165
Pillay, A. L., 34
Ping, Yu, 73
Play therapy, 87–93
Pope, J. F., 281
Positive feedback loops, 19–20
Positive thinking, 215
Posttraumatic stress disorder (PTSD), 55–60, 73–78
Pothan, Priya, 79
Pouyaud, Jacques, 183
Poverty in Jerusalem, 259
Poyrazli, Senel, 267
Prayer, 58, 80–81
Prieto, José M., 211
Problem-oriented psychotherapy, 203–208
Progressive muscle relaxation (PMR), 57–58, 68
Prozac, 214
Psychoanalytic therapies, 125–130, 133–138,
    184–188, 243, 284–288
Psychobiological analysis, 212–217
Psychodynamic-interpersonal skills model, 57,
    60
Psychodynamic therapies, 87, 134–138, 157
Psychoeducation, 57–59, 87, 159, 237–241
Punjabi culture, 141–146, 281

Q

Qijia, Shi, 73

R

Racism, 227–232
Rational emotive behavior therapy, 149–154
Rational interventions, 128–129
Reconsideration, forgiveness and, 247–248
Reconstruction, 113–115, 219
Referrals, 52, 57, 184
Reframing experiences, 70
Regulation of psychotherapy, 196, 199–200, 203
Relational-oriented psychoanalytic
    psychotherapeutic process, 243–248

Relationships
    as cause of illness, 35–36
    child–parent. *See* Child–parent relationships
    counselor–client, dependence and, 177
    friendships. *See* Social networks
    marriage. *See* Marital problems; Marriage
    rebuilding, ritual for, 34
    romantic. *See* Romantic relationships
Relationship theory, 219
Relaxation techniques
    Australia, 68
    Caribbean, 152
    India, 82
    Iran, 240
    Lebanon, 254
    Sub-Saharan Africa, 57–58
Religious supports, 20, 168, 254–255. *See also*
    specific religions
Reparation, forgiveness and, 247
Reputations of families, 16–17
Revenge, forgiveness and, 247
Rituals for healing, 26, 28
Robertson, B, 47
Rogers, Carl, 31–32, 183, 195, 197, 199, 288
Role-plays, 43, 77, 152
Romantic relationships
    Argentina, 126–130, 286–287
    Canada, 143–144, 281
    Caribbean, 151, 153
    Israel, 244–248
    Lebanon, 252–257
    Palestine, 260, 262–264
    Philippines, 112–116
Rosas, Angélica Riveros, 157
Roysircar, Gargi, 165, 169
Ruminative thoughts, 67–68, 142
Russia, counseling and psychotherapy in,
    219–228, 279*t*, 282*t*

S

Sacrifice, 199
Saving face, 92, 145
Schneider, Silvia, 189
Scholte, Wubbo, 203
School guidance counseling, 95
Self-awareness, 169
Self-confidence, 238–241, 269
Self-determinism, 168–169
Self-disclosure, 20, 272
Self-discovery, 36
Self-esteem, 169, 192
Self-harming behaviors, 175–180
Self-worth, 151–152, 245, 261
Senf, Wolfgang, 73
Seroquel, 223
Sexual dysfunction, 127

Sexual orientation, 112–116, 125–130, 286–287
Shame, 89, 92, 104–108, 212–213
Sheikhs, consulting, 18
Sikh culture, 141–146
Single-session counseling, 158–162
6 Cs in therapy, 69
Sleep issues
    CBT for, 65–70
    eclectic therapy for, 267–272
    interpersonal psychotherapy (IPT) for, 74
    solution-focused therapies for, 141–146
    traditional healing for, 24–28, 32–36
    trauma focused CBT for, 56–58
Social networks
    China, 76–77
    Iran, 238–240
    Nigeria, 35–36
    Russia, 222
    Spain, 215
    United States, 168
Social psychoanalysis, 219
Social ranks, 91
Social status of clinicians, 43
Social values, 76
Social withdrawal, 206
Sociocultural identities, 107, 146
Socioeconomic status, 178–179, 281
Socratic questioning, 270–271
Solution-focused counseling (SFC), 141–146, 203–204
Somatization disorder, 117–121
Somatizations, 24, 44, 48, 286
Sorcery, 25
Sources of clinical information, 4–5
South Africa, counseling and psychotherapy in, 47–53, 278t, 282t, 286
South America, counseling and psychotherapy in, 125–139
South Korea, counseling and psychotherapy in, 117–121, 278t, 282t, 286
Spain, counseling and psychotherapy in, 211–218, 279t, 282t
Spiritual causes of illness, 34–35
Spiritual ethnic groups, 23–27, 35, 287
Spiritualism. *See also* Religious supports
    honoring in counseling, 168
    vs. obligation, 105
Spousal abuse, 211–217
Srour, A., 259
Srour, R., 259
Stepped-care model, 204–208
Stereotypes, focusing-oriented approach and, 120
Stigma
    of mental illness, 40, 44, 52, 167
    of physical illness or deformity, 112–113, 133–138, 262–264, 262n6, 284–285
Stogdill, R. M., 215

Story sharing, 113
Stress
    cultural gaps and, 262
    from debt, 178
    management of, 18, 158–162, 220, 239. *See also* Relaxation techniques
    from work, 33, 55–56, 152
Strosahl, K. D., 114
Subjective units of distress (SUDS), 57–58
Sub-Saharan Africa, counseling and psychotherapy in, 55–61, 278t, 282t
Substance abuse, 65, 178–179, 220, 239. *See also* Alcoholism
Success Books, 191
Sue, D., 43
Sue, D. W., 43
Sue, S., 7
Suffering, client's role in, 128
Suicide
    attachment theory and systemic approach for, 261
    CBT for, 40–44
    dialectical behavioral therapy (DBT) for, 175–180
    existential counseling for, 165–170
    psychoanalysis for, 126–127
    rational emotive behavior therapy for, 150–154
    solution-focused story sharing for, 112–116
Surgery, 126–127, 133–138, 237–241, 260–264
Survivor syndrome, 70
Symptom Checklist 90 (SCL-90), 179
Symptom-oriented approaches, 203–208
Systemic approach to families, 259–265

T

Talking pictures therapy, 227–228
Technology use in counseling, 95–100, 152, 154
Territorial dominance, 212, 216
Thairu, K., 55
Theoretical sampling, 4
Theory of the client, developing, 7
Theory testing, case studies for, 6–7
Therapeutic alliances, 137
Third culture, 16
Third-wave approaches, 227
Time orientation, 19
Tjus, T., 96
Togo, counseling and psychotherapy in, 23–29, 278t, 282t, 285
Traditional Chinese medicine (TCM), 277, 285–286
Traditional community leaders, 51–52
Traditional healing
    Asia, 277, 285–286
    dual interventions and, 289

(Continued)

Traditional healing *(Continued)*
India, 82
Mexico, 161
Morocco, 40–42
Pakistan, 103
South Africa, 47–48
South Korea, 120
West Africa, 25–28, 33–36, 285, 287
Western Eurocentric models vs., 277, 280
Traditional values, 20, 50–52, 87, 103, 254–255
Transactional analysis, 212–217
Transference, 129, 134, 270
Transgenerational trauma, 243–248
Transnational community, 16
Trauma, 55–60, 243–248
Trauma focused CBT, 55–60
Trauma severity assessment, 57–58
Traumatic brain injury (TBI), 189–193
Trinidad and Tobago, counseling and
psychotherapy in, 149–155, 278*t*, 282*t*, 284
Trust, 271–272
Tuberculosis, 133–138
Turkey, counseling and psychotherapy in,
267–273, 279*t*, 283*t*
Two-chair dialogue, 106

U

Uncertainty avoidance, 90
Unipolar depressive episodes, 206
United Kingdom, counseling and psychotherapy
in, 227–232, 279*t*, 282*t*
United States, counseling and psychotherapy
in, 165–172, 278*t*, 282*t*
Universal Declaration of Human Rights, 255

V

Values
Confucian, 76
of families, conforming to, 254–257
middle class, 91
social, 76
traditional, 20, 50–52, 87, 103, 254–255
women, social value of in China, 76
Violence
aggressive behaviors of children, 88, 90,
189–193
child abuse, 150–151
domestic violence, 211–217, 261
Vissers, Wiede, 203
Vocational counseling, 183–188
Volikova, Svetlana, 219

Vontress, C. E., 165
Vossen, Caroline, 203

W

Wahabi movement, 103
Walsh, J., 169
Wassennaar, D., 34
Weiss, S., 161
West Africa, counseling and psychotherapy in,
23–38, 278*t*, 282*t*, 285
Western-oriented practice
adapting, 251
dissatisfaction with, 33–34
globalization and, 277, 280
indigenous knowledge vs., 280–281
negative influence of, 55
traditional healing and, 34–35, 87, 103
Wilson, K. G., 114
Witchcraft, 51
Women. *See also* Gender roles
body image, 240–241, 262–264, 262*n*6
China, social value in, 76
conflicting roles of, 153
divorce of, 216. *See also* Divorce
economic oppression of, 198–199
marital problems of. *See* Marital problems
marriage and, 143–144, 252–257, 262–264,
262*n*6, 281
mental illness manifestations in, 44
as mothers. *See* Motherhood, role of
oppression of in patriarchal societies, 18,
107, 118–119, 198–199, 264
as parents. *See* Parents
relational self of, 79
relationship with children. *See* Child–parent
relationships
relationship with men, 198, 271–272
Work stress, 33, 55–56, 152
Worthlessness, 32–36, 245
Wright, R., 161
Writing about emotions, 167–168, 178, 215

Y

Yalom, I. D., 165, 168
Yoruba culture, 33–36, 287
Yusuf, Humair, 103

Z

Zola, E., 198
Zoloft, 223